When the GREAT SPIRIT Died

The
Destruction of the California Indians
1850–1860

by

William B. Secrest

Word
Dancer
Press

Sanger, California

Printed in the United States of America.

Published by
Quill Driver Books/Word Dancer Press, Inc.,
1831 Industrial Way • Sanger, California 93657
559-876-2170 / 800-497-4909
QuillDriverBooks.com

Word Dancer Press books may be purchased in quantity for educational, fund-raising, business or promotional use. Please contact Special Markets, Quill Driver Books/Word Dancer Press, Inc. at the above address or phone numbers.

ISBN 1-884995-40-3

**To order a copy of this book, please call
1-800-497-4909.**

Second Printing March 2003

Also by William B. Secrest
I Buried Hickok (College Station, Texas, 1980)
Lawmen & Desperadoes (Spokane, Washington, 1994)
Dangerous Trails (Stillwater, Oklahoma, 1995)
California Desperadoes (Word Dancer Press, California, 2000)
Perilous Trails, Dangerous Men (Word Dancer Press, California 2001)

Quill Driver Books/Word Dancer Press Project Cadre:
Doris Hall, John David Marion, Stephen Blake Mettee,
Joshua Blake Mettee, Brigitte Phillips
Cover and interior design by William B. Secrest

Library of Congress Cataloging-in-Publication Data

Secrest, William B., 1930-
  When the great spirit died : the destruction of the California
Indians, 1850-1860 / by William B. Secrest.
    p. cm.
Includes bibliographical references.
  ISBN 1-884995-40-3
  1. Indians of North America—California—History—19th century. 2.
Indians, Treatment of—California. 3. California—Gold discoveries. I. Title.
  E78.C15 .S43 2002
    979.4004'97—dc21
                    2002012149

"My people do not want anything from the 'Great Father' you tell me about. The Great Spirit is our father, and he has always supplied us with all we need. We do not want anything from white men. Our women are able to do our work. Go, then; let us remain in the mountains where we were born; where the ashes of our fathers have been given to the winds. I have said enough.*

— Chief Tenaya, of the Yosemites,
to Major James D. Savage, 1851.

■ Tolowa Indian, photograph taken at Crescent City prior to 1874. *Smithsonian Institution.*

CONTENTS

ACKNOWLEDGMENTS

Any writer of history owes a great debt to a great many people. Although the long, tedious hours of reading and research, writing, revising, and arranging can assume awesome proportions, gradually the author becomes more and more involved with people. It's people who take the time to pass on information that might be helpful. It's people who provide clues, who point out directions and who encourage and help in a hundred ways. Friends and strangers, laymen and scholars, all helped and are in a large measure responsible for this work. I want to share with all of them any virtues of this work, while accepting any faults as mine alone.

My first thanks must go to people like Alfred Kroeber, Sherburne F. Cook, Frank Latta, Robert Heizer, Lowell Bean, Hubert H. Bancroft, and hosts of other ethnographers, anthropologists, and historians who set the stage for any study of California Indians. Through interviews and digs, patient years of study and diligent detective work, they have given us the substance of primitive life and life in another age.

Professor Cook and Robert Heizer were perhaps among the first to delve deeply into the underlying violence and tragedy of the California Indians. Cook's monumental study *The Conflict Between the California Indian and White Civilization* gave us an early, startling look at the causes and results of the meeting between two vastly different cultures. Heizer's many published collections of primary source materials are an invaluable aid to any study of California Indian troubles, while his original published work has made important contributions in the anthropological field. Valuable insights into California Indian history can be found in the published works of George Harwood Phillips and James J. Rawls.

An overwhelming debt is owed Dr. Lowell Bean and Sylvia Brakke Vane by anyone researching California Indian history. Their Primary Resources reference volume on native Californian source materials will be a standard and invaluable work for many years.

My brother, Dr. James Secrest, was of inestimable help in the early years of my research, as together we combed the California newspapers of the 1850s for Indian material. My son, Bill, Jr., also spent many long hours going through both microfilmed newspapers and the ten years of Indian superintendency records which we carefully researched. At the California State Library, the Bancroft Library, the California Historical Society and the State Archives, Bill spent many wearying hours searching, typing, making notes and discovering much of the raw material that is here made public. To my brother and my son, a grateful thanks.

Ron Mahoney, former curator of the special collections department at the California State University Fresno library, has been most helpful over the years in securing theses and other little-known material for me. Ron has called my attention to many items I might otherwise have overlooked, as well as giving me access to his Californiana collections. His help and friendship are greatly appreciated.

The late Estle Beard of Round Valley was more than generous with his vast research materials and knowledge of Northern California history. His illuminating letters (some of them manuscripts in themselves) always carefully detailed the information I had requested, not with monosyllabic answers, but often with copies of original source material. Through Estle, important data and early photos were obtained from the generous and helpful Peter Shearer, a descendant of Indian trader Simmon P. Storms. Estle's friendship, generosity, and seemingly unlimited knowledge of his area have been a cornerstone of this work.

All California history writers owe a special debt to the many fine institutions and organizations that preserve the raw material of our past. My grateful thanks to Laverne Mau Dicker, Jay Berry and the staff of the California Historical Society, Deborah L. Ginsberg of the Society of California Pioneers, W. N. Davis and David Snyder of the California State Archives, and Allan Ottley, Thomas M. Fante, Richard H. Nicholes and Madeleine Ann Darcy of the California State Library. William M. Roberts provided much help and information over the years, as did his fellow staff members at the Bancroft Library, frequently pulling me from the quagmires of my investigations.

Mrs. Valerie Franco and Edwin Carpenter provided assistance at the Huntington Library, as did Mrs. Ruth M. Christenson and Kathleen Whitaker at the Southwest Museum. Mary S. Pratt of the history department of the Los Angeles Public Library was most helpful. My thanks to Sandra Yeffa at the Redding Public Library, Nicholas Lapkass of the Ukiah Public Library, Mrs. Patricia Felthouse of the Tehama Public Library and Anne Caiger of the University of California at Los Angeles Library. Valuable source materials were supplied by Erich F. Schimps, associate librarian for special collections at the Humboldt State University Library, Arcata, California.

Mrs. Elsa Thompson and Robert J. Lee of the Mendocino County Historical Society were especially helpful in my research in that area of California. My thanks also to Christine Sellman and Eleanor Brown of the Siskiyou County Historical Society.

Mrs. Ruth Marra of the Lake County Historical Society supplied some important material for which I am most grateful. Particular thanks go to the late Pat Jones, of Chicago Park, a wonderful friend who unselfishly shared her own work on Simmon Storms. Thanks also to George Hunter of the Ukiah *Daily Journal* and Viola Richardson, also of Ukiah. Henry Mauldin of Clear Lake was kind enough to share his information on the early history of that area with my brother, Dr. James Secrest.

Peter Palmquist of Arcata supplied many rare photographs for this work. The author of many published articles and books on early California photography, Peter is as fine a photographer as he is an historian and writer and has done invaluable work in identifying and researching the early pictorial recorders of California history.

Others who have assisted me in great and small ways are the late Bertha Schroeder of Mariposa, Terry Ommen of Visalia, Carlo M. De Ferrari and Mary Etta Segerstrom of Sonora, Keith Arnold of Yreka, and Richard Dillon, former head librarian of the Sutro Library at San Francisco. Jeff Edwards of Porterville supplied many early Yokuts photographs and much encouragement over the years. My thanks also to Raymond E. Westberg of the California Department of Parks and Recreation.

Out-of-state aid was supplied by Jeff Gunderson of the Indiana Historical Society Library, who provided valuable information on Thomas J. Henley. Ann C. Altemose of the Indiana State Library was most helpful also, as were Jim Davis of the Idaho State Historical Society; Deanna Cecotti of the Portland (Oregon) Public Library; Allan E. Mushin of the Oregon Historical Society, and Carol Harbison-Samuelson of the Southern Oregon

Historical Society, Medford. Lloyd A. Biscamp of Houston, Texas, a descendant of Martin B. Lewis, helped me with a particularly knotty problem.

At the National Archives, Michael P. Musick, Elaine Everly, Robert W. Krauskopk and others were most helpful in searching out old army records, reports and photographs. Paula Fleming of the Smithsonian Institution provided much data and early photographs pertaining to the California Indians.

Closer to home, the late Dr. Sam Suhler and the staff of the reference department of the Fresno County Free Library have provided much valuable aid over the years in securing microfilmed records, newspapers, rare books, and theses through interlibrary loans. Their knowledge and courteous service is much appreciated. The staff of the Fresno County Historical Society has also been helpful over the years. Mrs. June English of Fresno and Annie Mitchell of Visalia, two stalwarts of local history who are now deceased, helped immeasurably by supplying material, advice, and encouragement in the course of this work.

I owe a special debt those who read the manuscript with and without criticism: Vern Crow, the late June English and Estle Beard, Lowell Bean, Thomas Blackburn, Ron Mahoney, and Dick Johnson. George Harwood Phillips was very helpful in reading the manuscript and offering valuable suggestions. My grateful thanks to you all.

My wife, Shirley, deserves a special thank you, not only for her help in research over the years, but for allowing our vacations to include visits to musty museums, libraries, and archives, besides the more conventional recreational places. She has done much more than her share to allow me the time to explore the past and to her I owe a debt I can never repay.

Steve Mettee and his wonderful staff at Word Dancer Press have done their usual fine job of editing and publishing. Thanks, guys, let's do it again.

To you all and to anyone I may have overlooked, thank you. Without your help, the story of *When the Great Spirit Died* might never have been told.

INTRODUCTION

At first glance, there appears to be little justification for telling the story of California's early Indian wars. Aside from the brief Modoc conflict of 1873, and possibly the Mariposa war of 1851, few people are aware that California had any Indian troubles during the Gold Rush days of the 1850s. Certainly the Far West never had a Custer's Last Stand or a grand retreat such as that made by Chief Joseph of the Nez Perce. There were no Sitting Bull or Geronimo; no spectacular uprisings, like Adobe Walls or Beecher's Islands. On the contrary, many California tribes were generally peaceful by nature, few having even a war club or a tomahawk as part of their culture.

Yet in California, the bloodiest drama in the settlement of the West took place, a brutal disruption and destruction so devastating that by the 1870s many native groups were extinct.

The term "Indian Wars" does not apply to this book. The conflicts described here were not truly "wars." They were merely the ongoing disputes between the native inhabitants and the miners and settlers who swarmed over their lands. The historian Bancroft said it well: "The California valley cannot grace her annals with a single Indian war bordering on respectability. It can boast, however, a hundred or two of as brutal butcherings on the part of our honest miners and brave pioneers, as any area of equal extent in our republic."

"Root Diggers" was the epithet used by the early pioneers to describe the California Indians, and they were, in truth, a simple people living close to the earth. They did not build spectacular dwellings as did the Hopi, nor did they have the elaborate traditions and ceremonies of the Plains and

Eastern tribes. "Saw some Indians at a distance," wrote David Cosad in his 1849, diary, "...Root diggers, a thieving, filthy race." Yet those few who knew well the California Indians and their traditions came to appreciate their honesty, their culture, and their reverence for the land. "In the loss of the Indians," wrote early pioneer William Meek, "we have lost the best foresters we had."

There were roughly 100,000 Indians in California at the advent of the Gold Rush in 1848. By 1870, this figure had been cut in half—primarily by disease and violent means. These are conservative figures; some casualty estimates run even higher.

In assessing this particular period of our history, it must be remembered that the generation rushing for California's gold had been brought up on Indian tales. Fighting "savages" was a way of life and had been since the Pilgrims landed. Indians were barbarians who killed, scalped, and tortured their victims. Indians were "bad." Ergo, to kill an Indian was a civilized act and there are many accounts of Easterners crossing the plains who actually shot the first Indian they came across. This type of thinking was deeply inculcated in large segments of American society.

Manifest Destiny also played a part in the proceedings. The United States was a young nation in the 1850s, restless, eager, and flushed with the recent victory over Mexico. It was American destiny to have acquired the vast, new lands of the great Southwest. The title to the West was ordained and no "inferior races" could halt the inexorable American march.

Also, this was the era of slavery. Even Northerners, for the most part, accepted this "peculiar institution" within the culture. Southerners, in the forefront of the Gold Rush immigrants, helped to assure that the California natives would become a new class of slaves in the new state through the economic necessity of a laboring class. Indenture laws and other "civilized" means legitimized the new society.

There are two basic methods by which man can feed his ego and make himself seem important. One is by genuine accomplishment. The other is by making a second party appear inferior so as to make himself superior by comparison. This is the root cause of bigotry and can occur in the most learned of men, when circumstances are such that ethics can be conveniently shunted aside. Politics, tradition, loneliness, or idleness can create these circumstances. It is a trait that has been with us since the dawn of time. Bigotry is a cross we will probably have to bear forever.

Hordes of men in Gold Rush California found themselves not only thousands of miles from home, but in a rough, frontier country with little law, few of the restraints of civilized society, and generally without even the gentle, guiding hand of a woman to help smooth out the rough spots.

It's well to remember, however, that not all of our early pioneers were bloody-handed Indian killers. On the contrary, such people were in the minority. Many who fought against the Indians felt genuinely compelled to do so out of motives of self defense or loyalty to their race and community. Even considering those who acted upon these motives, there would still be only a very small number who actually fought and killed Indians.

But the cold, hard fact remains that the Indians were ruthlessly destroyed in California. This was accomplished, not only directly by the most brutal class of settler, but through the acquiescence all the "decent" people who did not care enough to be outraged about what was taking place. And, most did know full well what was happening.

"Properly conditioned," the late historian Mari Sandoz once noted, "any people will produce a good percent of men (including women) who look upon the extermination of those who differ from them (and have something they want) as the proper destruction of a predatory animal. It is not only the Nazis that do these things, or the wool hat boys of the South. We can all be led down this path if the approach is insidious enough."

Californians of the 1850s *had* been conditioned. Conditioned by governors who spoke of inevitable wars of extermination; conditioned by officials who referred to degraded and filthy red men; conditioned by a press making sly and constant remarks about the degraded "Digger" and "Por Lo."

Strangely enough, the army tried desperately to avoid conflict with the Indians in frontier California. With no political ax to grind and a minimum of social pressures to shape their thinking, army officers often had the perspective to see clearly what was happening to the Indians. It seemed obvious the Indians had historically always occupied the best land—land the whites coveted for their mines, farms, and towns. The army was in no position to benefit from the land-hungry yearnings of the settlers, and California became one of the few areas in the West where the military protected the Indians from the settlers, instead of the other way around.

The disgust of the more humane pioneers towards the Indian killers was summed up by an army officer during the summer of 1859. When

Walter Jarboe, leader of a group of Mendocino County rangers, asked for help in attacking an Indian village, his messenger was refused by Brevet Major Edward Johnson. The officer was well aware of Jarboe's Indian-killing activities.

"Mr. Jarboe," growled the major, "is not worthy of notice and I hope the Indians kill him."

Sometimes the killers themselves recognized the tragedy in which they were taking part. William Perkins, an intelligent merchant, felt compelled to join a volunteer group seeking some marauding natives near Sonora, in Tuolumne County. After the group attacked and burned a village, Perkins had second thoughts about his actions: "To say the truth, I was not entirely satisfied with myself.... We invade a land that is not our own, we arrogate a right through pretense of superior intelligence and the wants of civilization, and if the aborigines dispute our title, we destroy them!"

But, the most persistent enemy of the native Californians was the firmly rooted white philosophy which preached that, one way or another, the Indian was doomed. Beyond the callous references to "Diggers" and "Poor Lo," the single most important catchword of the period was "extermination." It was used early and often and picked up by the newspapers and repeated in the army reports, letters, government documents, and journals of the time. It was a word that set the stage for slaughter:

"It is now that the cry of extermination is raised...men, women and children...of the Indian race...shot down." Sacramento *Placer Times*, April 1849.

"There will be safety then, only in a war of extermination." San Francisco *Daily Alta California*, May 1850.

"That a war of extermination will continue to be waged...Until the Indian becomes extinct, must be expected...." Governor Peter Burnett to the State Legislature, 1851.

"The blame [for some robberies] as usual [was] laid at the door of the Indians...And a war of extermination...determined on." Indian Agent Redick McKee to the governor, 1852.

"A party of men went out, discovered the rancheria...and killed 140 Indians.... Their destiny is to be exterminated." A Weaverville merchant writing home, 1852.

"The northern settlers [will visit] their savage enemies with a thorough and merciless war of extermination." *Marysville Herald*, October 1855.

"This will, of course, continue until the force of the whites is sufficient to overwhelm the Indians and exterminate them...." Superintendent Thomas J. Henley to James W. Denver, October 1857.

Extermination! Not "annihilate" or "destroy," but exterminate. The term suggests the killing of rodents or vermin rather than people, and further emphasizes the prevalent white contempt for the California natives. Extermination! The word was repeated endlessly to a public that easily accepted its premise. It was a predestined notion and inevitable—a great tragedy, but hopeless to try to avert. Charles Darwin and others of the time fostered this concept of doomed, aboriginal peoples who had lived out their allotted time in history. "Extermination" suddenly assumed the stature of some monstrous, natural law. The term "vanishing American" became a self-fulfilling prophecy.

At this late date, we can hardly comprehend the climate, conditions, and mentality that countenanced the terrible conditions in frontier California. An interview between an army officer and a former Northern California Indian fighter will serve, perhaps, as a chilling reminder of another time, long ago:

> One of these very Indian fighters is now sitting before me.... He is dignified as well as good-hearted—in fact, there is nothing in his appearance and manner [different] from those of any other well-meaning citizen. And yet, he has just been telling me, with a slight, satisfied smile playing over his lips as he spoke, how he once hanged an Indian and again how he cut the throat of another.... Am I disgusted when he tells me how he once cut a steak with his bowie knife out of an old Indian? Yes, but there he stands before me....

The endless attacks and retaliations between the two races escalated to a point where the theft of a horse could, and frequently did, result in the destruction of a whole village of Indians. The clash of cultures in nineteenth century California was so disastrous as to result in a 90 percent decimation of the native peoples.

Other factors muddied the waters of California Indian policy. This was a time of lackluster presidents, a Knownothing political party, and a viciously divided Democratic Party. Having literally voted itself into the Union, California was in need of vast amounts of federal aid to establish the machinery of state. This federal money, plus a boom town mining economy, brought hordes of political hacks, land speculators, criminals, and opportunists of every description who all wanted their share of the loot. In the resulting power and property struggle, the native Indians never had a chance.

This story of our California Indian troubles is, I believe, an important and neglected aspect of our Gold Rush history. Not being an Indian historian or anthropologist, I have tried to let the pioneers tell their own stories where possible and have quoted liberally from their diaries, letters, and memoirs, and from government reports of the period. In recording tragedy of such magnitude, the unvarnished impact of their actual words seemed important. Although a balance of native viewpoints is lacking, the words of the white man tell us all we need to know about the terrible fate of the California Indian.

California

Areas of Principal Indian Groups

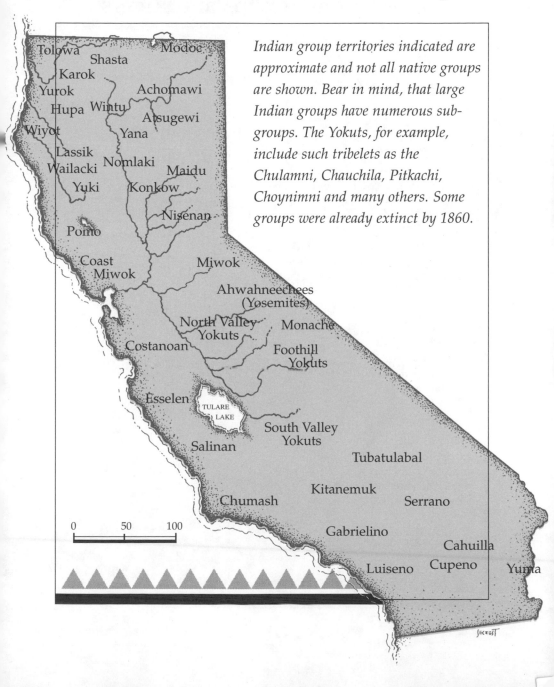

Indian group territories indicated are approximate and not all native groups are shown. Bear in mind, that large Indian groups have numerous sub-groups. The Yokuts, for example, include such tribelets as the Chulamni, Chauchila, Pitkachi, Choynimni and many others. Some groups were already extinct by 1860.

Tolowa
Shasta
Modoc
Karok
Yurok
Achomawi
Hupa Wintu
Atsugewi
Wiyot
Yana
Lassik
Wailacki Nomlaki
Maidu
Yuki Konkow
Nisenan
Pomo
Coast
Miwok
Miwok
Ahwahneechees
(Yosemites)
North Valley
Yokuts
Monache
Costanoan
Foothill
Yokuts
Esselen
TULARE
LAKE
South Valley
Yokuts
Salinan
Tubatulabal
Kitanemuk
Chumash
Serrano
Gabrielino
Cahuilla
Luiseno Cupeno
Yuma

0   50   100

California

Location of Principal Indian Reservations, Towns and Rivers

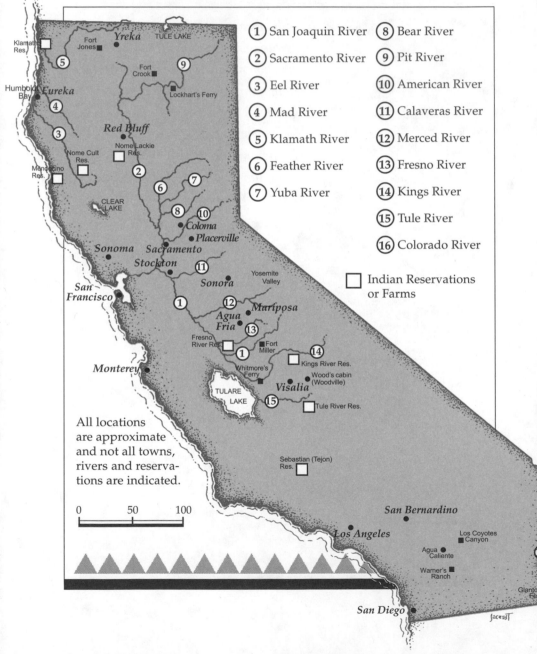

(1) San Joaquin River   (8) Bear River

(2) Sacramento River   (9) Pit River

(3) Eel River   (10) American River

(4) Mad River   (11) Calaveras River

(5) Klamath River   (12) Merced River

(6) Feather River   (13) Fresno River

(7) Yuba River   (14) Kings River

   (15) Tule River

   (16) Colorado River

☐ Indian Reservations or Farms

All locations are approximate and not all towns, rivers and reservations are indicated.

0   50   100

Map labels

Klamath Res., Fort Jones, Yreka, TULE LAKE, Fort Crook, Lockhart's Ferry, Humboldt Bay, Eureka, Red Bluff, Nome Lackie Res., Nome Cult Res., Mendocino Res., CLEAR LAKE, Coloma, Placerville, Sonoma, Sacramento, Stockton, Sonora, Yosemite Valley, San Francisco, Agua Fria, Mariposa, Fresno River Res., Fort Miller, Monterey, Whitmore's Ferry, Kings River Res., Wood's cabin (Woodville), TULARE LAKE, Visalia, Tule River Res., Sebastian (Tejon) Res., San Bernardino, Los Angeles, Los Coyotes Canyon, Agua Caliente, Warner's Ranch, Glanton's Ferry, San Diego

Chapter 1

PRECEDING 1850

Origins of the California Indians are shrouded in the mists of history. The theory that the ancient ancestors of the native Americans transversed a land bridge across the Bering Strait from Asia is generally accepted and man's emergence in the New World has been established as sometime around 13,000 years ago. Archeological site dating begins within the past 7,000 years for most of California, with the northern coast being occupied at a somewhat later date.

As the primitive Ice Age hunters followed the foraging animal herds across the now-vanished land bridge from Asia, they gradually fanned out over thousands of years to occupy a pristine, new world. They ranged from Alaska to Canada and down onto the Great Plains from where they gradually pressed to the east and west. Others hugged the coast and drifted down into the farthest reaches of South America.

Wandering farther and farther over the centuries, following either game or the climate, straggler groups constantly splintered off to settle in the new lands they found. In what is now California, these peoples grouped and evolved in a manner distinct from other native groups on the continent. Here the climate ranged from the wet and cold northern mountains to the temperate inland valleys and the grim deserts of the Colorado River country. Here was a land rich in natural foods and game—a land where they need not worry about the gnawing pain and lingering death of starvation. Here, sequestered in landlocked valleys, the great herds of elk and antelope could not wander off into a distant horizon. And, even if they did, other foods were abundant—small game, birds and lizards, grasshoppers, larvae, seeds, grasses, and nuts, bulbs, and acorns. Rather than base their existence on a particular animal or crop, the California natives evolved into highly omnivorous inhabitants. When one food source was not available, another generally was, although the conditions fluctuated, particularly in desert country.

Predominant among the staple foods was the acorn. There is abundant oak tree growth stretching from the Umqua Divide in Oregon down through the desert foothills of Southern California. Although not native to every area of California, oak trees are found in most locales. Acorns gathered in the fall could be stored throughout the winter. After they were pounded into a flour, it was a simple matter to leach out the offending tannic acid, leaving a nourishing and tasty staple food dish.

Derided and scorned as "root diggers" by the early Anglo visitors to their lands, the California natives nonetheless had a rich and varied culture. Living close to the earth as did most primitive peoples, they developed a proximity and awareness to nature which pervaded every aspect of their lives. They had a mystical reverence for their surroundings—for the game they killed or worshipped, for the seeds they ate, and for the rich land in which they lived.

Religion was integral to their way of life. It encompassed morality and entertainment and was expressed through the initiation rites and the cults and shamanism on which they depended for healing. They lived in a shadow world of friendly and evil spirits who were pacified by ritualistic ceremonies and dances.

Indian mythology was deeply rooted in nature and the animal life with which it abounded. Although differing widely, all California Indian groups had creation myths which related directly to the area in which a particular group lived. The creator took many shapes. To the Wiyot of the

■ Ohlone Indians, poling their tule canoe on San Francisco Bay. A lithograph by the Russian artist Ludovic Choris, who visited California in 1815-16.
From his book Voyage Pittoresque autor du Monde, *published in 1822.*

northern coasts he was Gudatrigakwitl, "above old man," who existed before the earth and made all things. The Maidu had their earth names, or Kodoyanpe, while the Wintun had Olelbis, referred to as "he who sits in the above." The Juaneno and Luiseno, in the south, call their deity Chinigchinich, "the creator."

Other native groups tied this Great Spirit, or Creator, to more vague concepts or more closely to the animals of their world. To the Yokuts of the great Central Valley, the eagle is not so much the creator as the chief of the assembly of animals who participated in the creation. Supernatural beings, powers, or the human spirit are called tipni, a word denoting "above," "sky" or "up." With the Yokuts, as with many native peoples, the coyote is closely linked with the prevailing deity and all other birds and animals are tied to their myths, folklore and worship.

Among the California Indians, true tribal units were nearly nonexistent. Tribal groupings of over five hundred people occurred only among the Yokuts of the San Joaquin Valley, the Chumash, and the Yuma and Mohave Indians of the Colorado River country. Of these, the Yokuts were closest to having true tribal status. The Yokut group name did not refer to a particular locality; the Yokut language, although frequently similar to neighboring dialects, was distinctive; and the Yokut territory was larger than that of most other native groups. Members of a Yokut tribe might number anywhere from one hundred fifty to five hundred.

Although differences might vary widely the farther one moved from a particular Indian group, the closest neighbors might still be quite similar in culture. Thus, while the central Maidu might bear traces of both Miwok and Atsugewi culture, the Miwok and Atsugewi themselves might have little in common. This was not always true, of course, but the similarities within the seven main language families in California are particularly indicative of this overlapping feature of the native culture.

Dress among the native Californians was quite standardized. For the women, it consisted of a short skirt of bark or grass, while the men wore nothing or various kinds of breechclout. Rabbit skin capes were utilized in winter, as well as blankets of otter, deer, and elk hide.

Variations in dress consisted mainly in head and footwear. In the north and along the coast, women traditionally wore basket caps, as did many of the southern groups. This was partly custom and partly utility since most packs were carried by means of a head strap. Men sometimes wore the cap, but infrequently. The central native groups wore headdresses only on ceremonial occasions.

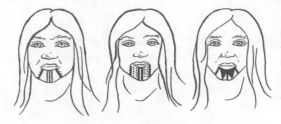
■ Many Indian women tatooed their faces in various ways after marriage. Men sometimes did so also, as well as painting the face and body for ceremonies or war. Illustrated are Luiseno women's tatooed chins. *Author's collection.*

In camp, most native groups went barefoot, but for travel various types of moccasins or sandals were used. Again, footwear varied with the territory. In the south, sandals predominated, while moccasins of various degrees of complexity existed elsewhere. Usually, the ankle piece was not worn turned down as with Eastern tribes. Skin leggins were used sparingly—usually for snow travel.

Several types of calendars were utilized among certain native groups such as the Maidu and Yurok, but generally the Indians did not record long intervals of time or think in larger units than ten. The word for "year" was not generally used; instead, "world," "summer," or "winter" was employed. Aside from the fact that foods must be gathered at certain times of the year, time itself was relatively unimportant.

Warfare among the California Indians was indulged in primarily for revenge and seldom for plunder or distinction. Feuding could be caused by territorial disputes or the belief that witchcraft had caused a death, theft, or family problems between villages. In some areas, there appears to have been constant strife, while other sections seemed to be more placid. This, of course, shifted and varied over periods of time. Larger groups, such as the Yokuts, seem to have been the most peaceful.

Pablo Tac, a Luiseno mission Indian of the 1830s, recalled that his people were constantly at war with the Digueno Indians before the Spanish missionaries arrived. "The life of that time," he recalled, "was very miserable because there was always strife." This intertribal fighting existed right up to the Gold Rush, as noted in a letter of Charles Bush, a miner on the Feather River in 1850:

> The Indians are very numerous here—some days 15 will visit our camp....They are very friendly towards the whites, but at war with other tribes continually; a short time ago they had a great battle a few miles from my camp. They fight with bows and arrows. The arrows pass through the air so swift that a white man cannot see them, yet the practised eye of the Indian discovers them in time to dodge them. Often times they would bound in the air six or seven feet while the arrow would pass under them, then again they would spring off to one side with the rapidity of lightning and from the fact that there was only five or six killed and wounded on a side during a two hour fight amply proves their dexterity....

4

Scalps were taken by some native groups, with the exception of such interior peoples as the Yokuts, Valley Maidu and the Pomo. When taken, scalps were likely to encompass more area of the head than those taken by Eastern tribes—and sometimes the whole head was removed. The Colorado River tribes seem to have developed more ritual connected with scalp-taking than other California groups.

The atlatl, or spear-throwing stick, was perhaps the principal advance in California Indian weaponry until the introduction of the bow and arrow. Although clubs were utilized by various native groups, war clubs, or tomahawks, were not known and the bow and arrow remained their primary weapon through contact with the Spaniards—and indeed including much of the Gold Rush period. Some tribes made better bows than others and such articles were frequently traded. There was much bartering and some exchange of information among the native Californians, certain groups of whom traveled extensively.

Structures varied from large ceremonial and communal houses to smaller family dwellings measuring ten to twenty feet across. Earth-covered dwellings were built by the Modoc, Achomawi and Yuki in the north, as well as the Sierra Miwok and Yokuts. Bark and slab-type teepee structures were utilized primarily by mountain tribes. Thatched houses and shelters were used in the south, while tule structures were developed in the lake and slough areas.

The Yokuts had five types of houses, their principal structure being erected within a circle that had been dug out about a foot deep. Poles were then placed around the sides about six inches apart and tied at the top to a willow hoop which would form the smoke hole. Tule mats or brush were then placed around the outside and the whole covered with earth several inches deep. When grass and brush grew over the earth, it became a snug and warm home in winter.

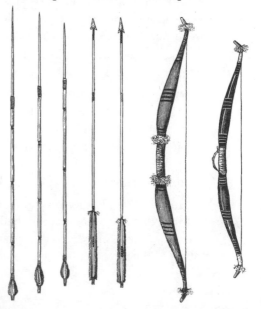

■ Bows and arrows of the California Indians were skillfully made but were often traded between tribes because of the degree of craftsmanship or access to particular types of wood. *From Stephen Powers' Tribes of California.*

In summer, brush huts were popular, as were shade tule mats erected on four poles.

Houses were primarily for sleeping and shelter since cooking and most activities were done in the open whenever possible. Some native groups had communal homes, while in others the men slept separately so as not to be surprised in their sleep by an enemy.

Chieftanship of a group might be hereditary, or it might depend on ability or wealth. The chief's authority varied, but ordinarily his was a civil office and he led in battle only if he were an outstanding warrior as well.

In their pristine state, the California Indians lived in a virtual Eden of vast, rolling plains, sparkling, tree-lined rivers and streams, oak groves, deserts and awe-inspiring mountains. A white boy living with the Choinumni Yokuts during the 1850s recalled his stay as the happiest days of his life. His Indian friends were decent, happy, honorable, and clean, and they actually helped the white intruders who were to disrupt their world in such a devastating manner. But their doom had been sealed many years before.

The Spanish incursions and development of the Americas is well known and need not be treated here. The Spanish presence in Mexico and explorations in the Southeast made it inevitable that Alta California would eventually fall under their sphere of influence. The Portuguese pilot Juan Cabrillo was the first visitor to the wild shores of California. He discovered San Diego Bay in September 1542 and continued up the coast, making various stops between San Miguel Island and probably Monterey Bay. At several points, the Indians told him of other white men to the east, presumedly the Coronado expedition.

The freebooting of Sir Francis Drake and his brief visit to Alta California in 1579 disturbed the Spanish. The later coastal explorations by Gali, Unamuno, and Vizcaino were for the purpose of establishing an early-warning system against such incursions. When the explorations of Father Kino established that Baja California was a peninsula and not an island, it was just a matter of time before a colony was established along the coast. Spain felt compelled to act when the Russians and English showed an interest in the late 1700s.

In July 1769, Father Junipero Serra founded the first mission in California at San Diego. Nine more had been established by 1784 and by 1824 twenty-one missions lined the coast along El Camino Real, and the colonization of the new territory was well under way.

Bringing "civilization" to California was a task which cost the Spanish dearly—an undertaking they could hardly afford. Lacking enough of their own people with which to establish their new land, they were determined to Christianize and utilize the 300,000 native inhabitants. They

■ Mission San Francisco Solano at Sonoma was quite humble compared to Mission Santa Barbara. For a time, the string of missions stabilized the California frontier.
From Engelhardt, Missions and Missionaries of California.

would train, intermarry and assimilate the Indians to create a Spanish-influenced population and so build a Spanish new world. As in Mexico, the missions were to be the nucleus of this new society. The soldiers and padres set about to bring to the missions as many natives as possible inorder to convert them and to train them for their new life and role in the Spanish scheme of things.

Despite the dubiously laudable intentions of the Spanish conquerors, their methods left much to be desired. Ranging in ever-widening circles, the Spanish began rounding up Indians, converting them and indoctrinating them in the ways of the Spanish culture. Overawed by the padres and soldiers at first, the Indian neophytes quickly learned to resent the disruption to their lives, the forced lessons in a foreign way of life, and the whippings for rule infractions. The resentment soon led to uprisings and runaways from the missions.

When the natives did not willingly come into the missions, Spanish soldiers raided villages and brought Indians in at gunpoint. Often natives were killed and families disrupted in these Spanish raids, but making "Christians" of the heathen was considered the all-important goal, as hypocritical as it was in reality. By 1790, all the native Indian groups along the coast range, on the west side of the San Joaquin Valley, had been removed, their villages and land never to be reoccupied.

In 1772, Captain Pedro Fages led an expedition into the then unknown great interior valley. He had been preceded only by several deserting Spanish soldiers who had been killed by the Indians for mistreating their women. Fages found the Indians friendly and numerous, living in a country of vast plains, "…a labyrinth of lakes and tulares [tules]." In his diary, he describes the Indians in their aboriginal state as a colorful and graceful people who dressed with "neatness and decency."

Other Spanish expeditions followed. Some were seeking mission sites in the great valley, while others sought converts for the coastal settlements. Always, these expeditions were escorted by tough, brutal units of Spanish cavalry—made up of convicts and misfits who needed civilizing much more than the natives. As early as 1804, the valley tribes were widely infected with El Mal Gallico—syphilis. This and other diseases took up where the bloody Spanish raids left off, giving future generations of Indians a legacy which would haunt them for generations.

Even at the missions themselves, disease wreaked havoc among the neophytes. Between 1813 and 1815, church authorities in Spain required a questionnaire to be filled out by the mission fathers. The questions dealt with various phases of mission life and were to be used as a gauge of the faraway venture. The answers varied widely, with one exception. All agreed that deaths outnumbered births, primarily because of the prevalence of venereal disease among the natives. A sampling from these reports is horrifying:

■ Sketch of a mission Indian woman made in 1849 by James W. Audobon. *Huntington Library.*

Mission San Diego "During the last year, 1814, deaths numbered 118 and baptisms 75."

Mission San Gabriel "The number of deaths is double the number of births."

Mission San Buenaventura "Their most dominant diseases are the gallico (syphilis), consumption and dysentery.…For every two that are born, three die."

Mission San Juan Bautista "…Deaths over births is all out of proportion."

Mission San Francisco "The dominant disease among them is syphilis…The number of births does not equal the deaths."

The tragedy was summed up quite succinctly by the padre at Mission

San Gabriel, near Los Angeles: "Unchastity…has permeated them to the very marrow with venereal diseases to such an extent that many of their children at birth give evidence immediately of the only heritage their parents give them…."

In contrast to these grim reports, nearly every Spanish explorer noted in his reports that Indians encountered in the wild were always healthy. After 1800, however, both Spanish explorers and fleeing Indians from the missions were spreading venereal diseases among the natives of the interior. Other maladies—typhus, smallpox, and cholera—made their appearance also, resulting in the disastrous epidemics of 1816, 1833 and later.

The mission system was clearly on its way to failure by the time Mexico won its independence from Spain in 1821. No longer did the padres and soldiers gather up converts in the valley. By this time, the Spanish were engaged in a constant series of raids to capture runaways or chase renegade bands of Indian raiders who regularly kept the settlements on the alert.

When the missions were finally secularized, beginning in 1833, it was hoped the Indians would adapt to the loss of their overseers and accept the new ways. It never happened, however. The Indians were not equipped to cope with their freedom. Some worked as vaqueros, as workers in the fields and vineyards, and as tradesmen, making adobes, tiles, and furniture. Many simply fled from the settled areas and again took up the old life of their forefathers. Others became derelicts about the settlements.

Non-Spanish visitors had been making their presence felt in Alta California since trapper Jedediah Smith crossed the Sierra in 1826. Besides the Russian post at Fort Ross, trading ships from Boston began appearing on regular schedules, as well as those from other countries.

Captain John A. Sutter had come to California in 1839 and wrangled citizenship, grants of land, and other favors from the Mexican authorities. Assembling a group of whites, Indians, and Hawaiians, the Swiss captain built an adobe fort in the Sacramento Valley, far from the coastal settlements. Here he hoped to establish himself as some sort of ruler over an area he called New Helvetia. Operating on credit and Indian labor, Sutter became prosperous and influential. From his small kingdom on the present site of Sacramento, Sutter lived on good terms with the Mexican authorities at Monterey, the Russians at Fort Ross, and the few American ranchers and merchants scattered about the country. The Mexicans, however, began looking on these grasping foreigners with an increasingly suspicious eye.

Northeast of Sutter's Fort was the northernmost outpost of Mexican California, the presidio at Sonoma. In 1835, young Mariano G. Vallejo, a lieutenant in the Mexican Army, was given command of this post, along with the title of Military Commander and Director of Colonization of the Northern Frontier. It was an important responsibility for the twenty-eight-year-old officer, his main task being to arrest the progress of the Russian settlements at Bodega and Fort Ross. This would be done primarily by colonizing the area and utilizing Vallejo's great power and authority to grant large parcels of land.

Although brutal in his earlier dealings with Indians, Vallejo secured a treaty with the Suisun Indians and their chief, Solano. The tribe members became subsidiaries to his detachment of Mexican troops and aided in maintaining peace with other native groups, as well as in rounding up Indian workers for the settlers.

In the spring of 1843, Salvadore Vallejo, brother of the commandante, led an expedition to Clear Lake where he owned a land grant. Besides a small group of soldiers, a large force of Suisun Indians was included in the group. The purpose was to acquire laborers for the ranchos of Sonoma Valley.

Seeking new trading grounds in the 1820s and '30s, free-lance American trappers and Hudson Bay employees moved down from the Northwest. Pierre Navarre (above), a French-Canadian, was looking for opportunity in California, also. *Monroe County Historical Museum, Monroe, Michigan.*

Arriving at the lake after a five-day march, Vallejo tried to get the local Pomo Indians to return with him, but all his inducements proved futile. After arguing most of the day, Vallejo tricked a large party of Pomos into entering a hut for a conference. Blocking the doorway, Vallejo's men now set fire to the hut and killed everyone who tried to flee the flames. Some forty or fifty natives were slaughtered by nightfall when it was decided that safety dictated a retreat from the gathering hordes of Indians.

During his flight from Clear Lake, Vallejo attacked another Indian village and obtained some three hundred captives. These were taken to Sonoma and were soon at work harvesting the local crops.

Although the manner of acquiring workers was sometimes brutal, to say the least, there are indications that once acquired, the Indians were reasonably well treated. Competent labor and loyalty were not to be gained by forcing servants to work. Besides, expeditions to find runaways were expensive. Indeed, the relationship quickly assumed all the feudal aspects of the antebellum South. Salvadore Vallejo himself once commented on this association:

> Many of the rich men of the country had from 20 to 60 Indian ser-
> vants whom they dressed and fed.... Our friendly Indians tilled our soil,
> pastured our cattle, sheared our sheep, cut our lumber, built our houses,
> paddled our boats, made tiles for our homes...and made our unburnt
> bricks; while the Indian women made excellent servants, took good care
> of our children, made every one of our meals.... These people we consid-
> ered as members of our families. We loved them and they loved us.

A Southern plantation owner could not have expressed himself more clearly!

■ A beacon for Gold Rushers flooding into California was Sutter's Fort at New Helvetia (later Sacramento) in 1849. *From J. W. Revere,* A Tour of Duty in California.

In Southern California, Indians had been utilized as a work force since the founding of the Los Angeles colony in 1781. Some of these southern natives allied themselves to powerful California families, as other tribes had with Vallejo and Sutter in the north. The southern Cahuilla Indians became the wards of the Lugo family in the San Bernardino area. As such, they not only worked for the Lugos, but provided a buffer against the more warlike natives who might be tempted to acquire a taste for Lugo horse flesh. The Cahuillas, and others who ranged far beyond the settlements, were to fare somewhat better than those tribes situated in closer proximity to "civilization."

Although Sutter's treaties and alliances with the local Indians gave him a feeling of safety, an incident occurred in the fall of 1844 which threatened to ignite an Indian war of serious proportions.

A party of some forty Oregon Walla Walla, Nez Perce and Cayuse Indians were on a trading expedition, exchanging furs and horses for cattle. They ranged down through the Sacramento Valley led by one Leicer, a son of the Walla Walla chief, Peupeumoxmox. Educated as a Christian, Leicer was also known by his white man's given name of Elijah Hedding. After some horse trading with local Indians, the party set up camp at Sutter's Fort where they obtained permission to hunt and trade in the area.

Grove Cook, a lanky Kentuckian who had come overland with the Bartleson-Bidwell party of 1841, was running the distillery for Sutter at that time. Cook was a rough sort, characterized as being a notorious killer of Indians. The Walla Wallas had been trading with various bands of interior Indians and had apparently picked up some stolen horses in the process. When Cook recognized one of his missing mules among the Indian ponies, he voiced his complaint to Leicer. Leicer, knowing only that he had acquired the mule in good faith, refused to return the animal to Cook.

Sutter, in recounting the affair, described Leicer as "saucy and haughty" and accused him of killing one of his own people while camped near the fort. When Cook became belligerent, Leicer pointed his rifle at him and told him to take the mule when he felt brave enough.

During the squabble, Sutter tried to settle the matter by telling Leicer that he would have to give up any stolen property he had acquired, but that he would be compensated for it. The Indian refused any inducements, however. As Sutter continued his efforts at mediation, he was called out of the room by the Russian agent who was visiting at the time. About a half hour later, as he was still conversing with the Rus-

■ While professing a benevolent attitude toward his Indian workers, Salvadore Vallejo was ruthless in securing these laborers for his own and others' use. *Bancroft Library.*

sian, Sutter heard a shot. Rushing to where the men had been quarreling, he discovered that Cook had shot and killed Leicer.

Sutter was horrified. He regarded Leicer as a troublemaker and was not concerned with his death, but his isolated position on the frontier made him quite vulnerable to attack. Located a week's travel time from his nearest neighbors, Sutter was in an extremely exposed situation should the natives become hostile. He kept the local Indians in check mainly through stern discipline and swift and ruthless retaliation at the first hint of trouble. These Cayuse and Walla Wallas, however, had a warlike reputation and might very well stir up their more docile California neighbors.

Still, Sutter had a domain and a reputation he must uphold. Riding out to the Indian camp to inform them of the tragedy, he found the news had preceded him and the Indians had left. Wishing to maintain control of the situation, Sutter dispatched a group of men to pursue the fleeing Indians, but the posse returned in a few days, empty-handed.

■ The German-born John Augustus Sutter was Swiss by parentage and was one of the first Indian agents in California. *California State Library.*

The Oregon Indians were indeed cause for concern to the Californians. Arriving home, the Walla Walla party vowed vengeance and immediately began talking of a raid to the south. When they tried to buy guns from the Hudson Bay Company, however, Dr. John McLoughlin refused their requests and instead convinced them of the futility of such a move.

In California, there was considerable apprehension about a raid from the north. The American consul at Monterey, Thomas Larkin, noted that "...[S]hould they come to California to redress themselves they would injure a people who not one in a hundred know anything about the affair and cause trouble to themselves and this government.... It would end in miseries to hundreds of both parties, and no satisfaction be obtained." Larkin's views were shared by many, and rumors spread between villages and isolated ranches throughout 1845 and the following year.

In September of 1846, a large party of Walla Wallas was reported as having entered the upper Sacramento Valley and the long-awaited Indian war was feared to be at hand. California was already embroiled in a war between Mexico and the United States, although the northern portion of

California had been secured by the Americans. At the time, Lieutenant Joseph Revere of the U.S. Navy had just returned from a tour of the Clear Lake area with a force of some fifty volunteer settlers. The trip had been uneventful and when they heard of the approaching Walla Wallas, the men were jubilant at the prospects of a fight.

Captain John B. Montgomery had occupied Yerba Buena (San Francisco) and had no men to spare for an Indian war. When he received word of the invasion, he appealed to the Vallejos at Sonoma to meet the emergency. Salvadore Vallejo promptly mustered a cavalry squadron to meet the supposed attack. The defenses at Sutter's Fort were also beefed up and the men put on the alert.

When the invading Indians showed up at Sutter's Fort, they proved to be a small band of about forty men, women, and children on a peaceful trading expedition. After paying their respects to Leicer's grave, they called on Sutter and requested justice in the case. Meanwhile, Revere's men were spoiling for a fight and were only prevented from an assault after visiting the inoffensive Indian camp. The great Oregon Indian-war scare seemed to be over at last. In later years, however, it was said that the Leicer killing was a contributing cause to the Whitman massacre and the bloody Indian wars of the Northwest.

Lieutenant John C. Fremont and his exploring party had occupied Sutter's Fort during the early stages of the Mexican War. He had put together the California Battalion for service against the Californios and was anxious to add to his ragtag army. Some Walla Walla warriors joined his force, along with various San Joaquin Valley Indians. Among the latter was a Tachi Yokuts named Gregorio. The name indicates he was a mission Indian, but when he enlisted with Fremont as a "servant," his age was not given. Gregorio subsequently accompanied Fremont when he traveled east for a court martial, then returned as a member of the explorer's disastrous fourth expedition.

The same month the Walla Wallas had entered the Sacramento Valley, Captain Montgomery had issued one of the first American proclamations regarding the Indians. In his capacity as commander of the military district of San Francisco, Montgomery ordered that "all persons holding Indians against their will without a contract and without regard to their rights as free men, shall immediately release them unless a valid contract can be made." "The Indian population," he declared, "must not be regarded in the light of slaves, but it is deemed necessary that the Indians within the settlements shall have employment, with the right of choosing their own master and employer...."

14

Having freed the natives, Montgomery proceeded to enslave them again in his next paragraph. "All Indians must be required to obtain service, and not be permitted to wander about the country in idle and dissolute manner; if found doing so, they will be liable to arrest and punishment by labor on the Public Works at the direction of the Magistrate."

The Americans were adopting the general methods of the Spaniards and Mexicans in their policy towards the Indians, but had no official plan to follow. Although the Spaniards and Mexicans made earnest efforts to

■ Sutter's farm on Feather River was worked by Miwok Indians, also known as the Ochejamnes. This is their village near the farm, a collection of earth-covered lodges sketched by someone named Wilkersheim about 1850. *Bancroft Library.*

educate and assimilate the natives, the Americans merely tried to maintain the status quo for the time being. The new military governor of the territory, General Stephen W. Kearny, made this reasonably clear in his letter appointing Captain Sutter as Indian agent for the Sacramento Valley area:

> I wish to explain to the Indians the change in the administration of public affairs in this Territory; that they must now look to the President of the United States as their great father; that he takes good care of his good children; that the officers now here are acting under his orders and instructions; that the Americans and Californians are now one people, and any offenses which they may commit against the latter will be punished in the same way as if committed against the former...

Sutter's appointment was perhaps the best that could be made at the time considering his experience with the natives. Still, the appointment was unfortunate in other respects. Early travelers reported that Sutter kept his work Indians at the fort under something less than ideal conditions. James Clyman, recalling a visit in July 1845, wrote:

> The Capt. keeps 600 or 800 Indians in a complete state of slavery and as I had the mortification of seeing them dine, I may give a short description. Ten or fifteen troughs three or four feet long were brought out of the cook room and seated in the broiling sun. All the labourers grate and small ran to the troughs, like so many pigs and feed themselves with their hands as long as the troughs contained even moisture."

Other early visitors made similar observations.

At this time, Sutter was no longer in control of his fort. Fremont had placed Lieutenant Edward M. Kern in command since Sutter was a Mexican citizen and the Americans were now in possession of the territory. There was an immediate need for the establishment of military posts to hold the new country, and Sutter's Fort was in an extremely strategic location.

There was a good deal of horse stealing being indulged in by the Indians during this period. It had been going on since the Spanish days, perfected during the Mexican pastoral period, and there was no reason to believe it would stop now. Horses were for traveling, hunting, and trading, and rather than capture and train wild animals, it was much easier to steal the already tamed horses of the rancheros. After all, had not these invaders stolen the Indians' whole country? There was occasionally more serious trouble with the natives, but mostly it was a time of fear and rumors in a vast and sparsely settled territory.

In April 1847, various articles in the *California Star*, being published at Monterey, mentioned "serious Indian depredations" in the Sacramento and San Joaquin valleys. One article chronicles Lieutenant Kern's expedition with a twenty-man force to chastise some troublesome Indians in the upper Sacramento Valley. Kern's men were made up of Sutter's Indian troops and they fought at least one battle near Snowy Buttes.

On April 10 the *Star* reported an attack on a white settlement on the San Joaquin River during which all the inhabitants were slain. "Cannot the authorities do something," wailed the newspaper, "for the protection of the frontier?" At this time, there were no white settlements on the San Joaquin River, or in the whole valley for that matter. A correspondent of the *Star*, traveling through the valley at the time wrote:

> You have…given credit to a rumor for you publish the massacre of some settlers on the San Joaquin River by the Indians. Probably you allude to the settlement forming on the "Stanislaus" called New Hope [a Mormon village]; and who knows, but it may be my little party to which you have reference. At any rate, you may assure your readers that such is not

■ Captain John B. Montgomery, a naval officer, was military commander of the District of San Francisco.
California State Library.

■ A Maidu girl, photographed in the 1870s. The native California Indians quickly adapted to the invaders' clothing, but for special events would utilize their tribal ornaments. *Smithsonian Institution.*

the case; that the Indians, though indulging in their natural propensity to thieve on all occasion, have made no attempt (and I am correctly informed) to either kill the settlers, or destroy the settlements....

But despite all the rumors, speculation, and actual Indian raids, the seeds of serious trouble were constantly being sowed. In November 1847, the old Indian village on the outskirts of Los Angeles was destroyed on the orders of the city council. Too many natives, complained residents, were loitering in town. Employers of Indian servants were now held responsible for their shelter and care, and natives were required to stay off the streets at night. Unemployed Indians were to be assigned to public work projects, or go to jail.

In the north, continuous trouble was being fomented, as reported by Sutter in a letter to General Kearny: "Even some of the frontier residents," complained the agent, "with little or no cause shoot them, steal away their women and children, and even go so far as to attack whole villages, killing without distinction of age or sex, hundreds of defenseless Indians." Later Sutter would report a more specific incident which came to be known as the "Growling" Smith affair.

In July 1847, Sam Smith, a settler in the upper Sacramento Valley, called on Sutter. Smith was representing himself and several other settlers who were complaining to the agent about the actions of three residents of the Sonoma District. Some two weeks previously, three men named Antonio Armijo, "Growling" Smith, and John Eggar had visited an Indian rancheria in the Feather River country—probably a southern Maidu village. An account of the incident was published in the *Star* on July 24:

> On going into the village these Indians manifested the most friendly feelings, offering acorn bread and other food. The Spaniards, after having partaken of their hospitality, commenced making prisoners of men, woman and children, and in securing them, some ten or twelve were killed—shot by the Spaniards in attempting to escape. Thirty were secured, principally women and children, tied together, and driven to the settlements. Young children who were unable to proceed, were murdered on the road. In one

instance, an infant was taken from its mother and killed in her presence, and that too in the most brutal manner.

After sending Sam Smith off with a report to the alcalde (mayor) at Sonoma, Sutter wrote to the new governor, Colonel Richard Mason at Monterey, and asked just what he should do in such cases. Responding quickly to Sutter's report, Mason noted that prompt action must be taken in matters of this kind:

> I very much regret to hear that such great outrages have been committed upon the Indians as those reported in your above mentioned letter. I beg that you will use every exertion to cause the guilty persons to be arrested, for which purpose you will call on the military officer nearest you for all the assistance in his power to afford. The good citizens of the country, as they value its peace and safety, should also render what assistance they can to arrest those men and bring them to condign punishment. When arrested, I will organize a tribunal for their trial; and if sentence of death is passed upon them, will have it executed. The safety of the frontier shall not be put at hazard by a few lawless ruffians.

> The Indians that have been captured you must at once seize by any means in your power, and restore them to their people; tell them that these atrocious acts have been committed by lawless scoundrels, and are entirely condemned by the authorities and all good men of the country, and that the perpetrators of the outrages shall be made a public example of.

Mason also immediately wrote to Lieutenant Charles Anderson of the 7th New York Regiment stationed at Monterey. Anderson was advised to render all assistance possible to Sutter in arresting the criminals and returning the Indians to their village. By August, the culprits had been arrested and Sutter and General Vallejo, also an Indian agent, were appointed special judges to try the case. Although the men were not convicted, Governor Mason praised Sutter for his conduct, again reminding him of his obligation to protect the Indians and counsel them as to the government's good intentions.

■ The plaza at Sonoma in the 1850s. *California Department of Parks and Recreation.*

The pastoral Mexican period in the new land drew to a close with the Treaty of Guadalupe Hidalgo in February 1848, and the end of the Mexican War. A new era was dawning. The trickle of fur trappers and sea captains who began arriving on the coast beginning in the 1820s and '30s, had continued with the arrival of the Bartleson-Bidwell party in 1841 and later arrivals. The Californians treated all these newcomers with a guarded cordiality. They hired them, sold them property, and even watched as some married their women. The new arrivals were advised that the local Indians were the country's labor source and could be utilized at little cost.

The Hispanic experience was not a happy one for California's Indians. During the Mission Period alone, the native population between San Diego and San Francisco had fallen from 72,000 to 18,000, a 75 percent decline. The Indians would learn soon enough that their situation was not going to get any better.

CHAPTER 1 / SOURCES

UNPUBLISHED MATERIAL

U.S. Congress, 31st Congress, 1st Session; House of Representatives, Executive Document 17:

Brigadier General Stephen W. Kearny to Captain John A. Sutter, April 7, 1847.

Colonel Richard B. Mason to Brigadier General R. Jones, June 18, 1847.

John A. Sutter to Colonel Richard B. Mason, July 12, 1847.

Colonel Richard B. Mason to Lieutenant Charles Anderson, July 21, 1847.

H. W. Halleck to John A. Sutter, August 16, 1847.

Colonel Richard B. Mason to Captain J. D. Hunter, December 1, 1847.

Proclamation; Richard B. Mason, Colonel, 1st Dragoons and Governor of California.

Colonel J. D. Stevenson to Colonel Richard B. Mason, August 20, 1848.

Bush, Charles, letter to parents, August 23, 1850, unpublished letter in Bancroft Library, Berkeley, California.

Knoap, Anna Marie, "The Federal Indian Policy in the Sacramento Valley, 1856-1860," unpublished thesis, 1941, in Bancroft Library, Berkeley, California.

Unbound documents, Archives of California, manuscript in Bancroft Library.

NEWSPAPERS

The *California Star*, February 20, March 20, April 10, 17, May 1, July 24, August 21, September 18, December 11, 1847; April 1, 1848.

PRINCIPAL PUBLISHED WORKS

Brandon, William. *The Men and the Mountain*. New York: William Morrow, 1955.

Caughey, John W. *California*. New York: Prentice-Hall, Inc., 1940.

Cook, Sherburne F. *The Conflict Between the California Indian and White Civilization*. Berkeley: University of California Press, 1976.

_____. *Expeditions to the Interior of California's Central Valley, 1820-1840*. Berkeley: *Anthropological Records*, Vol. 20, No. 5, 1962.

Clyman, James (Charles L. Camp, editor). *James Clyman, Frontiersman*. Portland: Champoeg Press, 1960.

Egan, Ferol. *Fremont, Explorer for a Restless Nation*. Garden City, NJ: Doubleday & Company, Inc., 1977.

Forbes, Jack D. *Native Americans of California and Nevada*. Healdsburg, CA: Naturegraph Publishers, 1969.

Geiger, Maynard, O.F.M. *As the Padres Saw Them*. Santa Barbara: The Santa Barbara Mission Archive Library, 1976.

Heizer, Robert F., editor. *Collected Documents of the Causes and Events in the Bloody Island Massacre of 1850*. Berkeley: Department of Anthropology, 1973.

_____ and Whipple, M.A. *The California Indians*. Berkeley: University of California Press, 1973.

Hodge, Frederick W., editor. *Handbook of American Indians*. Washington, DC: Bureau of American Ethnology, 1907.

Jackson, Robert H. and Castillo, Edward. *Indians, Franciscans, and Spanish Colonization*. Albuquerque: University of New Mexico Press, 1995.

Kroeber, Alfred L. *Handbook of the Indians of California*. New York: Dover Publications, Inc., 1976.

Latta, Frank F. *Handbook of Yokuts Indians*. Santa Cruz, CA: Bear State Books, 1977.

Lewis, Oscar, *Sutter's Fort*. Englewood Cliffs, NJ: Prentice-Hall, Inc., 1966.

Lyman, George D. *John Marsh, Pioneer*. New York: Scribner, 1930.

McKittrick, Myrtle M. *Vallejo, Son of California*. Portland: Binfords and Mort, Publishers, 1944.

Nevins, Allan. *Fremont, Pathmarker of the West*. New York: Longmans, Green and Company, 1955.

Phillips, George Harwood. *Chiefs and Challengers*. Berkeley: University of California Press, 1975.

_____. *Indians and Intruders*. Norman, OK: University of Oklahoma Press, 1993.

Rawls, James J. *Indians of California: The Changing Image*. Norman, OK: University of Oklahoma Press, 1984.

Tac, Pablo. *Indian Life and Customs at Mission San Luis Rey*. San Luis Rey, CA: Old Mission, 1958.

OTHER SOURCES

Arbuckle, Clyde C. "Grove C. Cook of San Jose." *Westways*, December 1951.

Heizer, Robert F. "Walla Walla Indian Expeditions to the Sacramento Valley, 1844-47." *California Historical Society Quarterly*, March 1942.

Hurtado, Albert L. "Controlling California's Indian Labor Force: Federal Administration of California Indian Affairs During the Mexican War." *Southern California Quarterly*, Fall 1979.

Hussley, John A. and Ames, George Walcott, Jr., "California Preparations to Meet the Walla Walla Invasion, 1846." *California Historical Society Quarterly*, March 1942.

Roster of Fremont's California Battalion, Mexican War, 1846. Pierson B. Reading Papers, California State Library, Sacramento.

Sadovszky, Otto J. von. "Sierra's Frozen Mummy & The Genesis of California Indian Culture." *The Californians*, November/December 1985.

Chapter 2

CLEAR LAKE

The Kelseys were an ubiquitous lot. They had arrived in California during the fall of 1841 with the Bartleson-Bidwell party—the first wagon train of American settlers to come overland to California. There were four Kelsey brothers, all tough frontiersmen from Missouri and anxious to make their mark or fortune in the new land. Samuel and Isaiah had gone to Oregon when the wagon train had split up, while Ben and Andrew Kelsey found work at Sutter's Fort.

Always on the move, Ben and Andy soon left Sutter and began hunting and trapping north of San Francisco Bay. Eventually they were able to buy a herd of cattle which they drove to Oregon, but by 1844, they were back living at Sonoma where Ben worked for General Vallejo. Acquiring tracts of land from Vallejo, the Kelseys should have gone on to a long and peaceful life of farming in the beautiful Napa Valley. But there was a violence in the Kelsey men, and a restlessness, which was to give them no peace throughout their lives.

In the spring of 1846, rumors were rampant that further American immigration to California was to be forbidden, and even present settlers would perhaps be driven from their homes. Indian war scares were being circulated also, and a general uprising in the Sacramento Valley was feared. Although the United States had declared war on Mexico in May, the Sonoma settlers were primarily conscious only of the invisible tug-of-war that had long existed between the British, Mexicans, Americans, and Russians over California.

Driven by these fears and anxious that if any overt acts were to be committed it would be by them, a group of American settlers led by one Ezekial Merritt stormed into the Sonoma plaza early on the morning of June 14, 1846. Capturing the Vallejo brothers and their principal lieutenants, the Americans, including the Kelsey brothers, hastily proclaimed the California Republic and named William B. Ide as their commander-in-chief. Ben Kelsey's wife, Nancy, is credited by some as making the flag for the new republic—the celebrated Bear Flag—at the suggestion of a young rancher named Henry L. Ford. The organization was supplanted less than a month later, however, when the stars and stripes took the place of the bear flag in the plaza. Later, the Kelseys are thought to have served with Fremont, although they are not listed on the California Battalion muster rolls.

In the fall of 1847, Andy and Ben Kelsey, together with Charles Stone and E. D. Shirland, bought Salvadore Vallejo's interests in Clear Lake Valley. Stone and Andy Kelsey took possession of the property and stock which included horses and cattle. The cows were of the Texas longhorn variety and a set of horns found some years later measured four feet four inches from tip to tip.

■ Even today, Clear Lake is a beautiful spot with little indication of the horrors that took place there in Stone and Kelsey's time. *Photo by Jim Secrest, ca. 1970.*

Both Kelsey and Stone were fearless and apparently gave little thought to their precarious position in the midst of hundreds of Indians. After checking on the vaqueros who were herding their stock, the new owners cast about for a suitable site on which to build a house.

Just how many Indians lived in the area is hard to determine. A newspaper report in 1859 stated that some 10,000 natives made the Clear Lake area their home in 1840, while Indian Agent Redick McKee reported a population of 1,000 in 1851. Living at the three villages on the lake were Pomo Indians—more particularly the Kuhla-napo, the Habe-napo, the Lile'ek and other native groups. No doubt many local Indians had moved to more remote areas to avoid the roundup of native workers for the large Mexican ranchos in the surrounding country. These were peaceful Indians and Vallejo's men had lived among them for years without any trouble—even after Salvadore Vallejo's 1843 massacre.

Utilizing Indian labor, Stone and Andy Kelsey began work on their home. Adobe bricks were manufactured and a commodius building forty feet long and thirteen feet wide was erected some three or four miles from the lake. It was a one-story structure, divided into two rooms, with a fireplace at one end and a loft. The roof was of poles, covered and thatched with tule from the lake. An outbuilding, or granery, was constructed next and a corral was put up close by the nearby creek. Hogs were brought in and a garden planted. With some eighteen vaqueros herding stock, the ranch was taking on impressive proportions and the two white men must have been pleased at the results of their labors.

Pomo informants maintained that Stone and Kelsey began abusing their Indian wards almost immediately. For the several hundred workers

■ A Pomo village near Clear Lake, ca. 1870s. *The Bancroft Library.*

engaged in constructing the ranch, only one beef per day was provided to feed them. In working for the Californians over the years, the Indians were used to some kind of token pay—certainly they were fed while on the job. When the ranch buildings were completed, the Indians must have retreated sullenly to their villages, wondering just who were these strange and unfriendly white men.

Relations between the two ranchers and the Pomo rapidly went from bad to worse. Stone and Kelsey were tough, hard-bitten frontiersmen who saw no reason to treat the Indians any better than animals. They insisted that Indians were ignorant savages who deserved even less consideration than slaves and who were destined for extinction, anyway. Like the blacks of their native South, the Indians were suited only to serve their masters.

In early 1848, Ben Kelsey tried his luck at mining during those first months of the great Gold Rush. He found "color" in the area near Culloma and founded a mining camp known as

■ A brutal and tough frontiersman, Ben Kelsey regarded the native population as slaves to be used any way he saw fit. *The Bancroft Library.*

"Kelsey's Diggings." Returning to Sonoma, Ben enlisted his brother Sam and various other settlers in another venture into the goldfields. This time they secured some fifty Clear Lake Indians to be used as packers and laborers in the venture.

Once again in the goldfields, Ben reportedly found it more profitable to sell the company's supplies than to pan gold. Soon the group disbanded and made its way back to Sonoma. The Indians, poorly cared for as usual, were abandoned and left to fend for themselves. Many died in the mines or in making their way back to their Clear Lake homes. Only a handful ever saw their families again. This mining venture caused great bitterness towards the Kelseys and Stone, but the worst was still to come.

Despite their cruelties, the two ranchers achieved a remarkable degree of control over the Clear Lake Indians. Reportedly, they starved the natives, but one inevitably wonders why the Indians did not flee or hunt and fish for food. Early accounts state that the Indians' weapons were confiscated and they were controlled in this way. This seems to be the case, since even Indian informants mention the starvation and control manifested by the two white men. Also, stockades had been built around the native villages, enabling the ranchers to keep closer tabs on their wards.

Firmly in control, Stone and Kelsey began taking Indian women as concubines. For a time, Kelsey forced the fifteen-year-old wife of Chief Augustine to live with him. Parents or husbands dared not object since they had seen friends shot down for less. The cruelty of the whites can only be explained in terms of men drunk with power and with all the restraints of civilization removed.

Pomos who broke rules laid down by Stone and Kelsey were tied to a tree limb and whipped mercilessly. Others were hung from the rafter of a building for days with their toes barely touching the ground. Reportedly, the two ranchers would whip or shoot at an Indian merely to amuse a visiting friend. When raccoons ruined some ripening watermelons one night, the Indian gardener was killed for his lack of attention.

Sometime in 1848, the natives became so terrorized they determined to kill their tormentors. When they beseiged the ranch house, the whites somehow managed to send one of their Oregon Indians to Sonoma for help, and soon Ben Kelsey was riding for Clear Lake with an eight-man posse. It was a long, hard ride, and the grim-faced men knew they were in a desperate race against time.

Arriving at the lake late at night, they discovered the ranch house beseiged by a howling mob of Pomos. Only the fact that Stone and Andy Kelsey had confiscated the Indians' weapons had saved their lives, but they couldn't have held out much longer.

There was no lack of nerve among the rescuers, and the men charged into the Indians, making as much noise as possible to give the effect of being a small army. As the natives scattered in panic, Stone and Kelsey unbarred their doors and rushed out to meet their friends.

Far from learning a lesson, the ranchers quickly resumed their cruel behavior. The whippings and starvation continued, and Andy Kelsey is reported to have taken Pomos from the lake and sold them in the surrounding country like livestock.

During the summer of 1849, a large group of Clear Lake Indians were put to work in Sonoma building a home for Salvadore Vallejo. They were badly mistreated as usual. When a young Indian was accused of threatening Nancy Kelsey, he was sentenced to 100 lashes by the alcalde. Learning of the incident, Ben Kelsey quickly found the young Indian and shot him through the head. Many of the workers then fled back to the lake where, if caught, they were cruelly punished.

Late that year, the Pomos decided they had had enough. There are various versions of subsequent events, one account stating that Chief Augustine's wife poured water down the barrels of the ranchers' rifles in preparation for the Indian attack. Other stories said that the men's guns were hidden by their Indian servants. Whatever happened, it seems clear the whites were unarmed when the attack came.

On a crisp December morning, Charles Stone came out of his cabin carrying a large iron pot with which to cook wheat for some of his herders. As he prepared the fire, one of a group of natives present fitted an arrow into his bow and shot him in the stomach.

With a look of shock and horror on his face, Stone pulled out the arrow and, swinging the kettle in an arc to keep the Pomos at bay, fought his way back into the house. Receiving several more wounds during the struggle, Stone managed to climb up to the loft where the Indians were afraid to follow him.

When Andy Kelsey came out to see what all the ruckus was about, he suddenly found himself fighting for his life. He received several stab wounds before managing to break away and run for the creek. Just before jumping into the water, he took an arrow in the back. He managed to swim across the stream, but as he pulled himself out on the other side he was speared to death by several waiting Pomos. His body was left where it fell.

Back at the house, the Indians had cautiously made their way up to the loft where Stone's body was discovered. The hated rancher was thrown from a window and all the Indians were invited to come in and help themselves to the stock of supplies. With both their tormentors dead, there must have been a grand celebration and feast that night. But it was to be a hollow victory. As they gorged themselves on wheat and beef in celebration, the Pomos could not have known of the terrible price that they would pay for their actions.

Since June, Sonoma had been headquarters of the Pacific Division of the U.S. Army under the command of Brigadier General Persifer F. Smith. The general and his staff occupied the Jacob Leese adobe while officers of the First Dragoons were quartered at the Ray adobe on Spain Street. On Christmas day, Ben Kelsey burst into the

■ Nancy Kelsey was the only woman with the Bartleson-Bidwell party when it left Missouri in 1841. Only eighteen years of age and with a young baby, she was the first white woman to cross the Sierra into California. *The Bancroft Library.*

dragoon headquarters and informed Lieutenant John W. Davidson that his brother and Stone had been killed at Clear Lake. Kelsey was already in the process of rounding up a posse and was no doubt vowing to kill every Indian in California. Kelsey and his fifteen-man volunteer force galloped out of town a short time later, but it was the following day before Davidson and a detachment of troops could begin the trip. Kelsey's threats had prompted Davidson to report that he was "anxious to reach the farm as early as Mr. Kelsey."

Taking along Moses Carson, Kit's brother, as a guide, Lieutenant Davidson reached Clear Lake about noon of the third day. Kelsey and his men were already on the scene, and together the parties prowled about the premises. Stone's mangled body was discovered under a pile of hides. As he was being buried, a group of Indians was brought in by some soldiers and it was with difficulty Kelsey and his men were restrained from killing them. These Indians blamed the crime on another Pomo group located on an island, so Davidson sent several of them to bring in the hostile chiefs, keeping the balance as hostages. When the hostages broke and ran, three were shot and killed by the soldiers and Kelsey's men. The lake Indians ignored the request for a parley, and not being able to attack the island without boats, the whites gave up any immediate plans of retaliation.

Andrew Kelsey's body was found and buried next to Stone, then the soldiers and volunteers all helped round up what cattle could be found. The abandoned ranch houses and Indian village were a ghostly sight as the men began the long ride back to Sonoma. The weather was bad, and any punitive action would have to be postponed.

In a report dated January 6, 1850, Lieutenant Davidson gave the details of the expedition and proposed another campaign. This time it was suggested that two boats be transported to the southern end of the lake from where an attack could be launched on the island. Other troops on the shores of the lake at the north end would cut off any escape. The plan seemed quite feasible, but would require that the trails be in good enough condition to haul the boats. It seemed clear the Indians must be punished, but a second expedition would have to be put off until spring.

■ A Pomo village on Clear Lake. Although taken around 1900, the lake still looked much as it must have at the time of the Bloody Island massacre. *Robert J. Lee Collection.*

When Ben Kelsey heard of the army's delayed plans, he was furious. A member of his family had been murdered by treacherous savages, and he did not intend to stand idly by while the army did nothing. It was not difficult to assemble another group of volunteers, particularly when he told them they were going to the scene of the Clear Lake murders. Kelsey had other ideas, however, and the results of his rabble-rousing were first chronicled by a letter dated March 2 at Sonoma:

> "Our little town has since yesterday been the scene of a tremendous excitement, but I trust the worst is over. Ever since the murder of Andrew Kelsey at the Clear Lake by the Indians, a party of men have caused much excitement among the peaceful inhabitants of this place and Napa. On the 31st ultimo, a meeting was got up in Napa for the purpose of driving all the Indians from the country. A party of 24 armed horsemen, mostly from the Red Woods, proceeded to Mr. Yount's rancho, set fire to the rancherie [Indian camp], and chased near 100 Indians to the mountains; thence proceeded on to Fowler's ranch, and there shot down 15 innocent Indians. After this, they passed on to Santa Rosa, chased the Indians from thence and came on to Jesse Beasley's ranch in Sonoma, and there killed two of his household, Indian servants, a third was fired at but escaped. That same evening another meeting was got up in Sonoma for the same purpose...."

According to newspaper accounts, Sam and Ben Kelsey had organized two bands of raiders—one to work the upper, the other to move into the lower portion of the Napa Valley. First indications of trouble came when settlers noticed the sky lit up from burning Indian huts across the valley. The route of the raiders could literally be traced by the bodies of dead

Indians, ten corpses being found above Harbin's Mills and buried there by a settler named Nash.

George Yount recalled that the posse passed itself off as an official organization sanctioned by General Smith for the purpose of driving all the Indians from the valley. Ranchers were told they could keep several of their favorite Indians, but all others were killed or driven off. Several of the ranchers armed themselves and told the raiders to keep moving, but this just made it worse on the next band of Indians that was encountered.

When a group of raiders rode through Sonoma threatening to kill every male or female Indian found in the county, the decent settlers rallied, deciding they had had enough. A warrant for the arrest of the killers was issued by the alcalde, while an armed band of Napa citizens dispersed the raiders as they prepared to attack the Indian village on Don Cayatano's ranch. However, after nearly a week of burning and murder, the Kelseys were satiated. They had had their revenge.

Eight of the raiders were arrested and lodged in jail, while Ben Kelsey and six others were granted bail as being only accessories. Others remained at large. Nine of the men were arraigned before Judge Cooper of the Sonoma district court. Seven of the group were bound over to stand trial for murder, but the following day their attorney appeared before the new California Supreme Court in San Francisco. It was a strange and unique situation.

California was still a territory, with statehood yet several months away. A State Supreme Court, however, had been established by the recent Constitutional Convention at Monterey. The Sonoma raiders' case was the first heard by the new tribunal, which was composed of Chief Justice Serranus C. Hastings and two associate justices. The court acknowledged the murder charge, but because of doubts concerning precedent, legal definition, and the scope of their authority, they simply remanded the men to bail in the sum of $10,000. And because of the unsettled times and the lack of jurisdiction of the district courts, the raiders were apparently never tried for their crimes.

As the weather cleared, the second army expedition was organized under the direction of Major Washington Seawell. When Seawell was ordered to Oregon, Captain Nathaniel Lyon took charge and the command rode out from Benicia on May 6. A company of dragoons under Lieutenant Davidson, an infantry troop, and a mountain howitzer made up the expedition, along with two whale boats mounted on the running gears of wagons. By the 11th, the troops had reached the southern end of Clear Lake and prepared for action.

The dragoons and infantry quickly secured the shores of the lake by attacking a rancheria and killing four Pomos. Setting up a command post on the western shore, Lyon detailed Davidson's dragoons to line the shore and prevent any escape. Two boatloads of troops were then dispatched toward the island, where the hostiles were camped in seeming security. The Pomos reportedly jeered at the troops on shore until they saw the boats approaching. When the trap became obvious, the natives set up a dreadful wail. Wrote Lyon in his official report:

> "The landing on the island, was effected under a strong opposition from the Indians, who, perceiving us once upon their island, took flight directly, plunging into the water, among the heavy growth of tula which surrounds the islands, and which on the eastern and northern sides extends to the shores. Having rapidly cleared the island, I saw no alternative but to pursue them into the tula, and accordingly orders were given that the ammunition be slung around the necks of the men, and they proceed into the tula to pursue and destroy as far as possible. The tula was thus thoroughly searched with severe and protracted efforts, and with most gratifying results. The number killed I confidently report at not less than sixty, and doubt little that it extended to a hundred and upwards. The Indians were supposed to number about 400. Their fire upon us was not effective, and no injury to the command occurred. The rancheria extending about half way around the island, was burnt, together with a large amount of stores...."

The battle at Bloody Island, as the Clear Lake fight came to be known, was little more than the slaughter of a people who wished merely to be left alone. The fact that the troops could kill between sixty and a hundred Indians with no injury to themselves indicates what really happened. Indian informants described an indiscriminate slaughter of men, women, and children, with babies pilloried on bayonets and thrown into the water. It was a terrible lesson to the demoralized natives of Clear Lake.

The San Francisco *Daily Alta California* of May 28 noted that "We have just received particulars of the recent slaughter of a large body of Clear Lake Indians, by an expedition sent against them from the U.S. garrisons at Sonoma and Benicia... it was the order of extermination fearfully obeyed...."

The article caused a furor among the military, and General Smith himself pronounced the story false and questioned the newspaper's motives. No order for extermination was ever given, Smith blustered, and on June 1, the *Alta* back-pedaled and gave another account of the fight which was more favorable to the military. During the exchange, the *Alta* had grumblingly demanded the official reports of the expedition, but apparently never received them. But by now, it was old news and no one really cared that much about what happened to some distant Indians, anyway.

In the late summer of 1850, the Kelseys decided to move on. Nancy Kelsey blamed her husband's health on their frequent moves, but they were a wandering family and could not stay in one place very long. Oregon was a fine country. Packing their belongings, the families crossed the mountains towards Humboldt Bay, but

■ Charles Stone and Andy Kelsey are buried beneath this monument near Clear Lake.
Photo by Jim Secrest.

were quickly attacked by the Indians who had suffered so much at their hands. The *Alta* noted:

> On their way across the mountains which separate the valley of the Sacramento from the coast waters, they were attacked by a party of Indians, and quite a severe battle ensued. Some gentlemen who arrived in Sonoma on Monday last brought intelligence of the skirmish, from which the Kelseys emerged unhurt. These gentlemen are from Trinity, and report having been robbed of everything on the route, by the Indians, who are much infuriated against the whites, particularly against the Kelsey brothers.

The Kelseys lived for a time in Oregon but were soon back in California. In 1856 they were living in Visalia, reportedly quite poor and applying for compensation to the government for cattle they had lost at Clear Lake. Traveling south and east, the family spent time in both Texas and Mexico.

Returning to the coast, Ben Kelsey died in Los Angeles in 1888. His wife, Nancy, remembered as the first American woman to enter California by the overland route, died near Bakersfield a few years later. She lies next to a daughter, also named Nancy, who had married one J. Wesley Clanton during the family wanderings in Texas. Several of the younger Nancy's brothers-in-law moved to Arizona, where they took up cattle ranching near the mining town of Tombstone. It was here that Ike and Billy Clanton were to gain everlasting notoriety when they collided with the Earp brothers and Doc Holliday in the gunfight at the O.K. Corral.

CHAPTER 2 / SOURCES

NEWSPAPERS

San Francisco *Daily Alta California,* March 11, 16, 19, May 28, June 1, 3, 27, 1850; September 3, 1859.

The Fresno Bee, January 19, 1966.

The Sonoma Democrat, July, 4, 1885.

The Oakland Tribune, September 23, 1956.

PRINCIPAL PUBLISHED WORKS

Bancroft, H. H. *History of California*, Vol. IV. San Francisco: The History Company, Publishers, 1887.

California Pioneer Register and Index 1542-1848. Baltimore: Regional Pub. Co., 1964.

Bruff, J. Goldsborough. *Gold Rush: The Journals, Drawings & Other Papers of*, edited by Georgia Willis Read and Ruth Gaines. New York: Columbia University Press, 1949.

Camp, William Martin. *San Francisco: Port of Gold*. Garden City, NJ: Doubleday, 1948.

Gregory, Tom. *History of Yolo County.* Los Angeles: Historic Record Co., 1913.

Heizer, Robert F., editor. *Collected Documents of the Causes and Events in the Bloody Island Massacre of 1850*. Berkeley: University of California Press, 1973.

_____, editor. *The Destruction of California Indians*. Santa Barbara, Salt Lake: Peregrine Smith, Inc., 1974.

Ide, Simeon. *The Conquest of California by the Bear Flag Part and A Biographical Sketch of the Life of William B. Ide*. Glorieta: The Rio Grande Press, Inc., 1967.

Kroeber, A. L. *Handbook of the Indians of California*. New York: Dover Publications, Inc., 1976.

McKittrick, Myrtle M., *Vallejo, Son of California*, Portland: Binfords & Mort, Publishers, 1944.

Palmer, Lyman L. *History of Napa and Lake Counties.* San Francisco: Slocum, Bowen & Co., 1881.

Smilie, Robert S. *The Sonoma Mission.* Fresno: Valley Publishers, 1975.

Woodward, Ashbel. *Life of General Nathaniel Lyon*. Hartford, 1862.

OTHER SOURCES

Benson, William R. and Radin, Max. "Stone and Kelsey Massacre on the Shores of Clear Lake in 1849—the Indian Viewpoint," *California Historical Society Quarterly*, Vol. 11, 1932.

Le Baron, Gaye, "The First Case Ever Heard by the California Supreme Court," *Pomo Bulletin*, Lake County Historical Society, February and May, 1978.

Mauldin, Henry, Lake County historian, private collection. Kelseyville, California.

Sherman, Edwin. "Sherman was There," *California Historical Society Quarterly*, Vol. 24, 1945.

Chapter 3

NISENAN

When gold was discovered in California in January 1848, the area around the discovery site quickly filled up with hordes of prospectors hoping to strike it rich. These first miners were for the most part native Californians from San Francisco, Monterey, Los Angeles, or Sonoma. Others were Mexicans from the Mexican state of Sonora who had swiftly received news of the discovery. The Kelseys and other Americans also flocked to the area, as did U.S. Army troops and sailors who were deserting in record numbers. Oregon pioneers were early arrivals also, while San Francisco Bay was becoming clogged with empty ships whose crews had fled inland to search for gold.

As the discovery site, Sutter's new sawmill on the American River was naturally the magnet that attracted these erstwhile miners. Soon tents were scattered everywhere and Sutter was fruitlessly advertising in the newspapers for the squatters to keep off his land. The few shacks of the workers at the sawmill quickly mushroomed into the village of Culloma, nestled in a beautiful mountain valley. Besides the troubles with squatters, Sutter and James Marshall, who had discovered gold while building Sutter's sawmill at Culloma, soon found themselves embroiled in Indian problems over which they had no control.

Even the earliest arrivals in California quickly observed the callous treatment accorded the native Indians. While conceding that the Indians were a "puny, cowardly, and perhaps treacherous race," a correspondent of the San Francisco *Alta California* noted that he did not believe the Indians wished to take American lives:

> We have often witnessed, on the part of many white men, a disposition to wantonly maltreat and abuse the Indians whenever it was in their power. This has become so much a matter of fact with some, that they regard an Indian's life as little better than the life of a dog...it will probably be found that in nine cases out of ten it is to the wantonness of the whites, more than to the criminality of the Indians, that difficulties and outbreaks are owing.

These comments, penned in January of 1849, clearly portend the ominous early trends of California Indian-white relations. When Marshall and Sutter tried to mediate differences between Indians and whites, they were accused of siding with savages against their own kind. One of the incidents that touched off the troubles around Culloma was noted in this same issue of the *Alta*:

> Yesterday an old Indian, well known in this neighborhood, and who had a good character, came to a camp of Oregonians and one of them claimed one of his horses. The Indian said he had bought the horse from a white man, and did not like to give him up—showed the fresh 'vent,' etc. The white man persisted that it was his horse, and took him away from him. The Indian was enraged and rode off making use of expressions which were not agreeable to the Oregonian and he took up his rifle and shot him. The Indian's horse went home, his saddle covered with blood, but without his rider. Today, some time, armed Indians came to the camp of, or met some Oregonians, and the latter knowing the occurrence of yesterday, presumed they had come to take revenge and gave them battle, and were whipped. One of them came in to the Fort [Sutter's] and told his story, and the whole garrison turned out to their rescue; but when they returned, having heard other stories, they were pretty generally sorry the Indians had not whipped them worse.

The natives of the area, between Bear River and the Cosumnes, were Nisenan, or Southern Maidu. Their language varied greatly from north to south, but in other ways they were quite similar to neighboring Indian groups. The Pushuni camped at the mouth of the American River, while the Kolo-ma gave their name to the town growing up around the discovery site. That the Indians sometimes stole clothes, blankets, and utensils from the miners is undoubtedly true. But they were generally friendly and often quite helpful. In early May of 1850, the *Placer Times* reported a miner on Bear Creek "...who, assisted by several Indians, turns out about forty dollars per day. At the Dry Diggings...a considerable number are employed."

However, according to one pioneer, Indians were, one way or another, a principal cause of trouble in the area. William Case noted that some of the Oregon men around Culloma found it easier to sell shirts to Indians for gold than to mine themselves. Some of the old trappers and mountain men who had first arrived on the scene had begun selling shirts for the gold dust weight of three silver dollars, or forty-eight dollars. The Oregonians then began charging thirty-two dollars for a shirt, and when the trappers undercut this, the Oregonians reduced the cost to the weight of a fifty-cent piece. Shortly after this, five competitive Oregonians were killed, the implication of Case being that it was mercenary white men, not Indians, who originated the trouble.

John Ross and a party of Oregon men had been in California for several months when they took up prospecting some thirteen miles from Culloma, along the middle fork of the American River. Most of the men were veterans of the Cayuse Indian War in Oregon and were inveterate Indian haters. Shortly before April 11, 1849, Ross and one of his men left five companions on the river while they rode over to Culloma for supplies. Returning a few days later, they found their camp torn up and belongings scattered about the stream bank. Footprints, splotches of blood, and arrows lying about indicated Indians had killed their friends and thrown the bodies into the river. The names of the missing men were James Johnson, Robert Alexander, Benjamin Wood, Henry English, and a man named Thompson.

Riding into Culloma, Ross and his surviving companion organized a posse to try to locate the bodies of their partners. Living in town at the time was the noted mountain man and guide, Caleb Greenwood, and two

of his sons. John and Britton Greenwood were half-bloods who jumped at this chance for excitement. A party of some twenty young men was organized by the Greenwoods and led back to the plundered camp by Ross. They failed to find the bodies, but some gold dust was recovered that had been buried on the site. Moving upstream, the posse came to an Indian village and immediately opened fire. John Greenwood reportedly killed three Indians, while a fourth was killed as he attempted to dive into the river. Before the rancheria was burned, supplies and personal effects of the missing men were discovered, but still the bodies were not found. After scalping the four dead natives, the posse returned triumphantly to Culloma. Sam Osgood, a correspondent for the *New York Tribune*,

■ John E. Ross, whom the historian Bancroft referred to as "that Indian butcher."
Bancroft Library.

was horrified when one of the group threw a scalp in his lap as a souvenir of the affair.

That night, Indian fires lit up the surrounding hilltops around Culloma. Most of the miners felt only John Greenwood and his men were in any danger, however. Greenwood himself was not worried at all. "He says," reported Osgood, "he is sorry for them as he shall be obliged to kill them all; that he shall call the boys…together, and go out and if they do not lay down their arrows, he will shoot them all."

When two other miners were reported killed, Greenwood organized

 Sutter's sawmill, where the great gold discovery was made by builder James Marshall.
California State Library.

another group of some forty volunteers and again went out looking for Indians. Marshall and others tried to object to the stern tactics of the Indian hunters, but they were told to shut up or get out. "Many of these men are so violent," wrote one resident, "that they denounce every one who advances any reason why a wholesale slaughter should not be made, and charge him with taking the part of the Indians...." It was not healthy to stand up to veteran frontiersmen such as John Greenwood or the Oregonians. In their minds, only blood could atone for blood.

While decrying the fact that seven "worthy and inoffensive citizens have been...treacherously and brutally murdered...by a degraded, ignorant and depraved tribe," the *Placer Times* still knew where the fault lay:

> It is not long since an Indian rancheria near Bear Creek was pounced upon by a small party of whites and twenty-five of the unsuspecting inmates, of both sexes, taken and cruelly murdered. Why was this? It was because numerous thefts had been committed by the Indians in that vicinity, and it was necessary to make an 'example.' But traced to causes more remote, a murder had been committed last fall by Indians in that neighborhood (though still anterior to this, a fact scarcely worth mentioning, however, several Indians had been killed by whites coming through from Oregon).... Three Indians were shortly afterwards hung, in justification of which act we are sorry to say we know nothing.
>
> From these instances...it may be readily believed the Indians have wreaked vengeance for deeds of blood, the bloody and cruel murders recently committed on the American River.

Back at Culloma, a petition had been sent to Sutter asking him to come mediate the troubles. The petition was no sooner on its way than the Greenwood posse returned with some forty Indian prisoners. Placing a guard over the captives, Greenwood and his men again sallied forth, heading for Weber Creek where more Indians had been reported. John Ross later reported that two natives from this first captured group had promised to

lead them to the rancheria of the murderers, and the posse now galloped confidently towards the Indian camp.

Theodore Johnson described Greenwood's gang as they rode out of town as being "well-mounted, and equipped with the enormous jingling California spurs…each man carried besides his inseparable rifle, a long, Spanish knife, usually mounted with silver and stuck in the folds of his deer-skin leggins; and many were also provided with a brace of pistols or bowie knife, worn in the red Mexican sash around the waist." They were a colorful and deadly group, against whom the natives stood little chance.

The Indian guides led the posse straight to the rancheria on Weber Creek where they quickly surrounded the village. While some of the whites rounded up the inhabitants, others looked about and reportedly found some papers and clothes of the murdered men. While the Indians were being questioned and threatened (some reports insist several of the guilty Indians confessed), they became surly and realized the danger of their situation. Details of what happened next are sketchy, Ross reporting that they had surprised the Indians in the midst of a victory feast. Taking the whole village as prisoners, the group joined forces with a posse of "Spaniards" on their way to Culloma. The cavalcade was described by a witness:

Following closely this motley group (the "Spaniards"), came on foot a body of about sixty California Indians. Warriors and boys, squaws with papooses tied on boards and slung at the back, all were prisoners. Clustered together like sheep driven to the slaughter, they hastened through the gorge with uncertain steps, the perspiration rolling off their faces now pale with fright….

In flank and rear rode the war-party, which had left the Culloma Valley two days previous. Every man's rifle lay across the pommel of his saddle, and dangling at both sides hung several reeking scalps.

On April 18, the posse herded their captives into Culloma and paraded them from one end of the village to the other. While the prisoners were being secured, Ross rode over to Hastings' store. A lawyer from Ohio who had traversed the continent several times, Lansford Hastings had written a highly unreliable book on the emigrant routes to California. The "Hastings Cut-off," which he recommended, had resulted in much grief and suffering to wagon trains headed west. At this time, Hastings was in partnership with Sutter in a mining supplies store at Culloma. Like many Sutter ventures, the store failed.

Ross had somehow become convinced that a "pass" he had taken from a dead Indian had been used to gain the confidence of the white men so the Indians could surprise and kill them. Confronting Hastings with the pass, Ross asked if he had indeed given it to the Indian. When the shopkeeper said that he had, Ross told him he had countermanded the pass and would countermand *him* if he ever issued another.

In Culloma, a public meeting was held to decide what to do with all the Indian captives. Some were for turning them loose since it seemed impossible to determine the guilty parties. Carter, a miner who had escaped when the last two men had been killed, was reported in the *Alta* to have recognized seven of the natives who had attacked his party. These seven were detained while the other terrified natives were released. Word had been received from Sutter that he would not intercede in the matter, since he had been threatened by both Indians and whites.

The committee could not decide whether to kill all seven of the Indians, or just the chiefs and alcaldes. Most of Greenwood's men were roaring drunk by now, along with a mob of miners and assorted troublemakers. They demanded the committee take some action and it was finally decided to put the prisoners on trial.

Mrs. Peter Wimmer, one of the few white women in town, was particularly sympathetic to the natives and even tried to hide one in her home. Osgood, the *Tribune* correspondent, noted the following in a dispatch to New York:

> I went over to the room where the prisoners were confined to see them. They appeared dejected. The faces of most of them were covered with their blankets, as they sat in two rows with their hands resting upon

■ Chief Tom, a Nisenan leader, wearing a headdress of yellow hammer's feathers and his rabbit skin robe. *Smithsonian Institution.*

their knees. From the room I went with them, to the place which was said to have been their judgement-seat, but which proved to be their place of execution.

It was about six o'clock in the evening when the seven Indians were led down to the river for their trial. The mob was loud and drunk and there was little restraint or order of any kind. When Marshall attempted to defend the Indians, a man named Everhard tried to shoot him, Ross claiming to have knocked the man's weapon aside. Osgood, who witnessed the whole ugly scene, continued:

> The poor wretches then followed the chiefs out to a triangular space, bounded on one side by the hills, on another by the village, and on the other by the rapid current of the swollen river. When within five paces of the pine tree which that night had been laid low by one of the peaceful inhabitants to build him a shelter for the coming winter—they broke and run, some towards the hills, and others towards the river; the word was given to fire, and two immediately fell, one upon the log on which he was to have been tried, the other 6 or 7 paces

■ Britton Greenwood (above) and his brother John were leaders of the Indian-killing gang in the Culloma

> beyond, and the others who had fled to the hills were overtaken, and stabbed with bowie knives. Of the two who plunged into the almost freezing waters of the American Fork, one was shot, but yet swam till halfway across the river, when some white men were seen running down to the opposite bank to head him off. He immediately turned and swam back to the shore from which he had first plunged, and when he reached the brush which grew along the bank, one of the Oregon men drew one of the Colt's revolvers and put a ball through his brain, he never moved afterward, and when I passed again a few minutes after he was entangled in the bushes...The other swam to the opposite shore, but was prevented from landing by two mounted men, who threw stones at him, until one of the numerous stones from this side struck his head, and he sunk to rise no more. When the chase was over and the party returned to where the first shots were fired, the two Indians were still alive; one was lying on his face, with his bed blanket spread over him. One of the captors perceiving that he still breathed, drew a knife and plunged it into his side, while another beat his brains out with a large stone. The other miserable victim who fell over the log, and whom I saw making an effort to rise ...another ball had extinguished the little life that the first had left...Farther to the left, on the side of the hill, I saw another of the party bending over his victim, busily engaged in removing the scalp."

Members of the mob proposed burning the dead Indians, but for some reason Greenwood insisted on burying the bodies and this was done. Many of the local Indians ran to Mrs. Wimmer and begged her to save them. "That evening," continued Osgood, "they were gathered around their fires crying like so many children."

When a miner named Jack Doyle was found murdered on the road near Culloma, the "war-party" again took up arms. "His body," noted the *Placer Times* on May 5, "was found secreted by the wayside shockingly disfigured…. The prevailing impression among the miners of Culloma appeared to be that this murder had been committed by white men, and every item of evidence seemed to justify this conclusion."

Nevertheless, Greenwood and his men again took the field.

William Daylor, who formerly worked for Sutter, was one of the discoverers of the Old Dry Diggings, later known as Placerville. At this time he was a ranch and mine owner who employed some of the local Indians in his mining operations. About the 26th of April, Greenwood's party approached Daylor's mine where a number of natives were working. Taken completely by surprise, one Indian was shot to death as he worked. Another was wounded as he tried to run and his brains were beat out with rocks. Daylor later reported what happened next to the *Alta*:

> "The company of whites now followed on the trail of the Indians and about ten miles from my house overtook a party traveling to their home and surrounded them without difficulty; in a few moments commenced separating the men from the women and children. When apprehending danger, the men broke and attempted to escape…. Three were allowed to get off, the rest, fourteen in number were slaughtered on the spot…. The white [Greenwood's] men report having killed 27 before coming to the house. Twenty-two men and thirty-four women and children are yet missing from the rancheria."

The *Placer Times* noted that most of the slain Indians worked for Daylor and had fled the river in fear of the Greenwood posse. The avenging whites again approached Daylor's house as he and his wife and several Indians were burying a deceased member of the family. After killing several of the Indians, Greenwood had the nerve to ask Daylor to kill a cow to feed his men, but the rancher angrily refused.

■ William Daylor could do nothing to stop the drunken killers in Greenwood's gang. *California State Library.*

As the sated Oregonians returned to work, James Marshall, the man who had discovered gold in California, fled in fear for his life. He took with him a petition signed by some sixty-six settlers of the area and addressed to General Persifer F. Smith. The document recorded the events of the past few weeks and asked that an army post be established in the vicinity to maintain order.

A small military force was sent to the area in May under the command of Major J. J. Kingsbury. Cantonment (or Camp) Far West, as the post was called, was established for the purpose of "putting an end to outrages that were being committed by the whites upon the Indians." The endeavor was anything but a signal success, however. By the end of the year, a captain, twenty-seven enlisted men and all the teamsters had deserted and headed for the gold fields.

James W. Marshall opposed the rampant Indian killing and was forced to leave the area. *California State Library.*

On the middle fork of the American River, the spot where the first five miners were killed became known as "Murderer's Bar."

A correspondent of the *Alta* described meeting a New Yorker in the village of Culloma, which was now being referred to as Coloma. The newcomer was still dressed in his city duds; "sack coat, flashy vest, pantaloons with straps on," carrying flour, tools and a box of cigars, one of which he offered the writer in exchange for some advice. When these newcomers asked how the beautiful name of Coloma originated, they were told it was taken from a nearby Maidu native village and tribe.

Huddled in their villages or seeking refuge in the mountains, the Indians knew that their beautiful valley had been bloodied and scarred and changed forever.

CHAPTER 3 / SOURCES

UNPUBLISHED MATERIAL

Reed, William. "Journal," manuscript in the Bancroft Library, University of California, Berkeley.

Ross, John E. "Narrative of an Indian Fighter," manuscript in the Bancroft Library, University of California, Berkeley.

NEWSPAPERS

San Francisco *Alta California*, January 18, April 14, 22, May 10, 17, 31, 1849.

New York *Daily Tribune*, June 22, August 15, 16, 1849.

The Mountain Democrat, January 2, 1969.

The Placer Times, April 28, May 5, 12, July 9, December 15, 1849.

PRIMARY PUBLISHED WORKS

Bancroft, H. H. *History of California*, Vol. XXVI. San Francisco: The History Company, Publishers, 1887.

Gay, Theressa. *James W. Marshall: A Biography*. Georgetown, CA: The Talisman Press, 1967.

Gudde, Erwin. *California Gold Camps*. Berkeley: University of California Press, 1975.

Hart, Herbert M. *Old Forts of the Far West*. Seattle: Superior Publishing Company, 1965.

Kelly, Charles and Morgan, Dale L. *Old Greenwood*. Georgetown, CA: The Talisman Press, 1965.

Kroeber, A.L. *Handbook of the Indians of California*. New York: Dover Publications, Inc., 1976.

Lewis, Oscar. *Sutter's Fort*. Englewood Cliffs, NJ: Prentice-Hall, Inc., 1966.

Powers, Stephen, *Tribes of California*, Berkeley: University of California Press, 1976.

Ryan, William R. *Personal Adventures in Upper and Lower California in 1848-49*. London: William Shoberl, Publisher, 1851.

OTHER SOURCES

Bekeart, Philip Baldwin. "James Wilson Marshall," *Quarterly of the Society of California Pioneers*, Vol. 1, No. III.

DeGroot, Henry. "Six Months in '49," *Overland Monthly*, April 1875.

Chapter 4

THE GILA EXPEDITION

John Glanton was a hired gun. Reportedly born in Tennessee and reared in Texas, he had served in the Mexican War as a lieutenant in a Texas Ranger company. In late 1848, the *Corpus Christi Star* reported Glanton had been acquitted of killing a soldier on the grounds of self-defense. He married a lovely belle of old San Antonio after threatening to kill his future father-in-law if he refused consent to the union. A roaming adventurer by nature and inclination, Glanton remained home only long enough to get his bride pregnant, then was off on an expedition with a group of cronies.

The state of Chihuahua, Mexico, was being plagued by a series of bloody Apache raids in 1849. Troops seemed ineffectual against them, and the governor finally offered a standing reward of two ounces of gold for each Apache scalp taken. When Glanton's men rode into Chihuahua City and learned of the offer, they eagerly took to the field and brought back a bumper crop of Indian hair. They were hailed as great heroes by the locals and were wined and dined as befitted their new-found celebrity status.

After a hiatus in town, the scalp hunters again sallied forth and were soon back exchanging more hirsute souvenirs for *el oro*. While they were being feted as before, a keen-eyed official noticed that many of the scalps seemed to be of Mexican, rather than Apache, origin. Glanton and his followers barely kept their own hair now, as they reportedly galloped out of town with an avenging mob howling at their heels.

After some further adventures in Sonora and Arizona, Glanton led his fifteen-man party west on the southern Gila Trail. He probably was heading for the California gold fields, but when he reached the Colorado River, another opportunity presented itself. At this southeastern tip of California, where Mexico, Arizona, and the Golden State come together, a ferry was in operation, and the Glanton group set up camp near the adobe home of A. L. Lincoln, the owner.

The lower Colorado was Quechan, or Yuma Indian country. It was a steaming desert land of cactus, rocks, and mesquite, complemented only by the river and the cottonwood bottom lands. The Yuma were farmers and gatherers and usually subsisted on a variety of foods. They accepted the early Spanish explorers who prowled their lands, and by 1780 two missions and a settlement had been established along the river. Father Francisco Garces labored hard to bring Christianity and civilization among the Yuma. Any type of endeavor was an uphill battle in that blistering country, however, and everything seemed to go wrong from the start.

The Spanish promised too much, and the Indians were quickly disillusioned. Although the padres tried to be kind and patient with their wards, the settlers and soldiers treated the Yuma harshly. Large tracts of Indian land were being taken by settlers, and native food supplies were used to feed the Spanish first and the natives second. When a force of Spanish settlers and soldiers arrived and confiscated some Yuma horses, as well as whipping some objecting owners, the bitterness boiled over.

Striking swiftly and with overwhelming numbers, the Yuma killed all the male inhabitants of the Mission San Pedro y San Pablo. Turning their fury upon the newly arrived Captain Moncada and his men, the Indians next wiped out his eighty troops, but again spared the women and children. Father Garces was shut up along with another priest in the Mission Conception while the Yuma chief, Palma, tried to save their lives. His words could not calm the maddened natives, however, and the following day a group of young braves burst through the mission doors and clubbed the two priests to death as they knelt in prayer. The following year, 1782, a relief force from Mexico City rescued the Spanish women and children, but the Yuma had effectively expressed their hatred of the white man.

◼ A ferry on the Colorado, such as Dr. Lincoln and John Glanton operated. The ferries were usually boats like the ones shown below. Animals were tied together and swam across .
Williamson Railroad Survey Report, 1853.

Dr. A. L. Lincoln, a relative of the future president and also a native of Illinois, came to California from Mexico in 1849. He spent some time in the mines, but being unsuccessful and seeing a need for a safe method of crossing at the junction of the Gila and Colorado rivers, he established a ferry there in January of 1850. The venture made money from the start.

Earlier, a Mexican boundary party had established a ferry near this point and had grossly overcharged emigrants utilizing its service. When a party headed by one General Anderson built its own boat in defiance of the ferry, the Yuma helped them in various ways. After his group had been ferried across, Anderson gave the boat to the Indians with a certificate of ownership. The one stipulation was that they must ferry all Americans across the river for only a dollar, or the boat would be forfeited. This Indian ferry was located about six miles downstream from the Lincoln crossing.

When Glanton and his men were offered jobs by Dr. Lincoln, nine of the party went to work at the ferry. From all accounts, Glanton was a tough and overbearing desperado, and Lincoln soon came to regret hiring him. Many Mexicans and Americans were crossing the river at this point and a good deal of money was to be made. Indications are that Glanton quickly made himself a partner in the venture and proceeded to become even more overbearing. Not content with the profits of the Lincoln ferry, Glanton was soon casting greedy eyes downstream toward the Indian crossing.

A deposition given by Jeremiah Hill before Los Angeles Alcalde Able Stearns seems to be the most authentic account of the origin of trouble between Glanton and the Yuma. Hill was an emigrant who had camped a short distance from the Lincoln ferry. One night he received some Indian callers who complained bitterly of the actions of Glanton and his men:

> Since the departure of Gen. Anderson, many Mexicans had come to cross at the Indian ferry, which had made Glanton mad, and that he (a Yuma chief) knew of no other offense the Indians had given said Glanton; that one day Glanton sent his men down, and had the Indian boat destroyed, and took an American whom they had with them, engaged in working their boat, up to his camp, with all said American's money, and that Glanton had shot said American and thrown him into the river. The chief said that he then went up to see Glanton, and made an offer that Glanton should cross the animals of the emigrants, and thus they would get along quietly. Whereupon, Glanton kicked him out of the house, and beat him over the head with a stick: the chief said he would have hit him back, but was afraid as the Americans could shoot too straight....

After telling the Yuma he would kill an Indian for every Mexican they ferried across the river, Glanton left for San Diego with Dave Brown and several others to deposit some money and pick up needed supplies. While in the coastal town, Glanton and his men got into a saloon brawl and killed a soldier. Brown was captured and thrown into jail, but Glanton and the others managed to avoid arrest. After bribing the jailer and obtaining his confederate's release, Glanton returned post haste to the ferry on the Colorado.

During Glanton's absence, the Yuma had determined to kill all the Americans at the ferry. About noon on April 23, 1850, the Yuma chief looked in the door of Lincoln's adobe where the ferrymen lived. He was surprised to be invited in for a drink. Glanton and four others were guzzling their lunch, and before long all were dozing in their bunks and makeshift chairs. Carefully checking to be sure all the whites were asleep, the chief quickly ran to a nearby hill and gave a signal. Then he ran back into the house.

The scalp hunter never knew what hit him, as the Yuma chief swiftly beat Glanton to death while he slept. Dr. Lincoln and the several others in the hut were all dead in a few moments. The Yuma vengeance was swift and merciless. Indians were now swarming along the river searching out the remaining whites.

A short distance up river, three of Glanton's men were engaged in cutting poles for some construction work. When a group of Yuma approached and acted suspiciously, the men pulled their pistols and chased them away. Suspecting something was

A Yuma warrior, photographed some years after the Glanton troubles on the Colorado River.
Los Angeles Public Library.

wrong, the men stepped from the willow thickets and headed for the houses, but were immediately shot at by the waiting Indians. In a shower of arrows and rifle balls, the men ran first for the houses and then for the river. Bill Carr was hit in the foot with an arrow, but Marcus Webster and Joe Anderson were able to chase some Yuma away from a boat, and the three men quickly pushed out into the current.

While Carr and his companions were making for the river, they saw five of their men just landing on the opposite shore to ferry some Mexican stock. Indian helpers were usually employed to jump into boats and assist in landings. This time, however, the natives rushed into the boat and clubbed and stabbed to death the surprised whites before they knew what was happening. John Jackson, a black man, was clubbed and thrown into the river to drown. The other murdered men were Tom Harlin, a Texan, Henderson Smith and Tom Watson from Philadelphia, and John Gunn from Missouri. Quickly changing into the dead men's clothes, the Indians headed back across the river and almost succeeded in pouncing on Carr and his friends before they were discovered.

■ A Yuma woman and her child. *California State Library.*

Heading their boat downstream, Carr, Webster, and Anderson kept busy dodging the missiles of the Yuma who raced along the river bank. When the white men cut loose with a pistol volley and killed several of the pursuers, the Indians gave up the chase. The three made their escape and were able to land their boat several miles downstream. They hid out in the underbrush until nightfall.

After several other brushes with the Yuma, the three made their way back to the ferry, arriving at daylight of the 25th. The tired trio were fed by some of the Mexican inhabitants and told what had happened to Glanton and his men. All of the dead white men were burned in their houses, and the Yuma declared that they were now at war with the Americans.

Carr, Webster, and Anderson made their way to Los Angeles where they spread the alarm and gave an account of the massacre to Alcalde Able Stearns on May 9. This deposition and Jeremiah Hill's deposition are the first and most accurate accounts of the Glanton troubles.

When Governor Peter Burnett heard of the massacre late that month, he ordered the state militia general Joshua Bean to organize an expedition against the Yuma. Bean was instructed to have the sheriffs of Los Angeles and San Diego raise a force of sixty men, with elected officers to be in charge. The expedition was to rendezvous at Los Angeles on June 22, armed and ready to go. A few days later, Burnett wrote and suggested that one hundred men be raised instead of sixty.

The rendezvous date at Los Angeles came and went, and in early July Bean ordered militia general J. C. Morehead to head the expedition and begin buying supplies. Dave Brown, who had fled to Los Angeles from San Diego, was hired as a guide, and the campaign finally got underway.

Apparently, Morehead had second thoughts about the size of his force and began recruiting men from among wagon trains encountered along the way. By the time he arrived at the ferry, he had some one hundred twenty-five men in his command. There was some skirmishing, and a dozen or so Indians were killed, but for the most part the Yuma just fled upstream. After destroying the native food supplies and foraging their stock in the Yuma crops, the troops set up camp and did little but eat up their supplies for the next few weeks. When the governor ordered Bean to disband his force in September, the campaign came to an end.

The "Gila Expedition," as the Morehead expedition came to be known, was the first of the California Indian war debts that were to later plague the state, its cost amounting to $125,000. Everyone got into the act, from the merchants who overcharged for supplies, to the good samaritans who

■ Los Angeles in 1850 was a sleepy village of mostly one-story adobes.
California Historical Society.

nursed Bill Carr's wounded heel. The doctor who dressed Carr's foot charged $500 for his services; his landlord submitted a bill for $120; another man who boarded him charged $45, and a kindly Angeleno who changed his bandages wanted $30 for his efforts. The Los Angeles Court of Sessions charged all these bills to the state, and it was fortunate that Carr was the only casualty of the affair.

Considering himself to be an experienced military leader now, Morehead promptly absconded with state funds and supplies and led an ill-fated filibustering expedition into Mexico. He was even less successful in Mazatlan than he was along the Colorado.

After escaping jail in San Diego, Dave Brown had fled to Los Angeles where he joined Morehead's expedition. Later he returned to the city and the Los Angeles census of 1850 lists him as being twenty-five years old, from Texas, and having no occupation. While Brown was working as a cowboy during the summer of 1854, he stabbed a friend to death and was lynched by a mob led by Los Angeles Mayor Stephen C. Foster.

CHAPTER 4 / SOURCES

UNPUBLISHED MATERIAL

Office of the Secretary of State, California State Archives, Indian War Files, Sacramento:

Governor Peter Burnett to J. H. Bean, San Jose, June 1, 4, 1850.

Major General J. H. Bean to General J. C. Morehead, (n.d.) July, July 9, 1850.

NEWSPAPERS

Corpus Christi Star, November 11, 14; December 23, 1848.

Yuma Sun, October 27, 28, 1954.

PRINCIPAL PUBLISHED WORKS

Harris, Benjamin B. *The Gila Trail*. Norman, OK: University of Oklahoma Press, 1960.

Newmark, Maurice H. and Newmark, Marco R., editors. *Census of the City and County of Los Angeles, California for the Year 1850*. Los Angeles: The Times-Mirror Press, 1929.

Woodward, Arthur. *Feud on the Colorado*. Los Angeles: Westernlore Press, 1955.

OTHER SOURCES

Guinn, J. M. "Yuma Indian Depredations and the Glanton War," *Annual Publication of the Historical Society of Southern California*, Los Angeles, 1903.

Secrest, William B. "The Mayor of Old Los Angeles," *Old West*, Spring 1966.

Veeder, Charles H. "Yuma Indian Depredation on the Colorado in 1850," *Annual Publication of the Historical Society of Southern California*, Los Angeles, 1907-1908.

Chapter 5

KAWEAH

While the Colorado River incidents could be considered a stalemate, other troubles were being fomented by the steadily encroaching emigrants. To the northwest, the great Tulare—or San Joaquin—Valley stretched south from Sutter's Fort for nearly 300 miles. Much of it was a part of the vast, newly formed Mariposa County, which reached almost to Los Angeles. Varying between 150 and 200 miles in width, it was a wild country of semiarid plains, vast rolling grasslands studded with oak groves and tule swamps which housed an abundance of wildlife. An early Spanish explorer described it as being rich in "…grain, deer, bears, geese, ducks, cranes, indeed every kind of animal, terrestrial and aerial." Elk and antelope were plentiful also, as were wide-ranging bands of wild horses. And there were Indians.

One of the few California native groups to be divided into true tribes, the valley Yokuts extended from the present cities of Stockton in the north to Bakersfield in the south. The term Yokuts meant "people," and at one time there were over sixty tribes gathered in villages along the marshes, rivers and foothills of the area. They were generally peaceful, although the Chauchila and Nutunutu were known as fighters.

The Wowol and Tachi lived along the shores of Tulare Lake. To the north was the territory of the Apiachi and Wimilchi tribes. The Pitkachi and Dumna ranged along the San Joaquin River with their neighbors the Hoyumne, bitter enemies of the Chauchila. The Choinumni and various other tribes occupied the land along the Kings River. To the east, in the mountains of the Sierra, the Miwok and Monache, distinct from the Yokuts, roamed and lived in the days before the Gold Rush.

Along the eastern edge of the great valley, in the south central area, lived the Gawia Indians. They occupied what was known in the early days as the Four Creeks country, a drainage area of lush grassland and oak groves between the foothills and Tulare Lake. The Gawia had a reputation for being mischievous and quarrelsome, but seem to have gotten along

■ A log cabin in Mooney Grove, at Visalia, is probably smaller than the Woods cabin, but shows 1850s construction.
Author's collection.

well enough with their neighbors. They took their names from the Yokuts word "Gaw," meaning raven, that often noisy and troublesome bird.

Traveling through the valley with a small topographical party in May of 1850, Lieutenant George Derby found the Gawia anything but troublesome:

> At this time each of the creeks was at its height...and we should have found it difficult to cross had it not been for the kind assistance of the neighboring Indians who flocked to meet us, and eagerly went to work carrying instruments and other property...without the slightest accident occurring. These poor people accompanied us from creek to creek, assisting us cheerfully at each crossing....
>
> Nothing could exceed the kindness and hospitality with which they treated us, and I gave the captain certificates to that effect... The second rancheria is the Cowees (Gawia); their captain, Francisco, is an old mission Indian from San Luis Obispo...

Derby treated the Indians kindly, gave them what provisions and clothes he could spare, and proceeded on his way. The lieutenant's report is in interesting contrast to the tragedy which was to take place just a few months later.

After traveling overland in early 1850, the John Hudgins wagon train disbanded in Los Angeles. Hudgins and sixteen men were hired by the Los Angeles Merchants Association to improve the road into the San Joaquin Valley—probably to encourage trade with the northern settlements and the mines. The men worked on the road and bridged various valley rivers, then in March continued on into the mining country. One of the Hudgins party, John Woods, was back in the valley that fall with fourteen men. Their purpose was never definitely established, but they brought in cattle and cleared land for a farming operation. The men built a sturdy log cabin on the south bank of the Kaweah River, near the bridge they had previously constructed. Speculation is that Dr. Thomas Payne and other interested parties who had financed the valley road had employed Woods and his men to establish an area that came to be called Woodsville. It was an isolated and unknown region, located just south of the present city of Visalia.

Woods and his men seem to have had trouble with the Indians very soon after their arrival. Isolated as they were, they could still talk to travelers heading north, and from time to time notices appeared in the press. Details vary as to the origin of the conflict, but most accounts agree that Francisco, the chief of the Gawia, gave the white men just ten days to pack up and leave the country. One early newspaper notice stated that Woods and his men insisted on corraling their cattle under a huge and sacred oak tree beneath which generations of chiefs had been buried. Other accounts insist the white men had tormented the Indians in some fashion — probably by taking Indian women. Whatever prompted the trouble, Woods and his men ignored or delayed acting on the warning and suddenly the day of the deadline arrived.

During the afternoon of December 13, most of Woods' men were out gathering their horses. All were unarmed, having left their weapons at the cabin. Suddenly, Indians appeared to be everywhere. The Gawia apparently had been watching the whites closely and did not intend to take any chances. Unarmed and caught in the open, the herders were quickly killed by the swarming natives who then rushed towards the cabin.

Woods was close by the cabin when he heard the war cries. He had been talking to sixteen-year-old Frank Boden, a traveler, who had stopped by the lonely cabin for a visit. Suddenly, the Indians were running towards them, and the air was full of arrows. Boden received several shafts in his arm before he managed to return fire. Both men then ran towards

A Yokuts Indian warrior of the San Joaquin plains.
Williamson Railroad survey Report, 1853.

the cabin, but Boden was able to grab a horse and gallop away, holding his bloody arm.

Woods ducked into his cabin where there was a supply of pistols and rifles. After barricading the door, he began firing at the screaming Indians, but was careful never to allow all his weapons to become empty at the same time. For several hours he held off the circling Gawia, while flaming arrows and torches failed to ignite the tough, damp logs of the cabin. There were a dozen or so dead Indians scattered around the cabin when Woods began running low on ammunition. Suddenly, Gawias dropped through a hole in the roof. It was just about dusk when the white man was dragged from his fortress into a howling mob of Indians. The Sacramento *Daily Transcript*, February 21, 1851, reported:

> About four weeks since, it appears the Indians attacked a party of whites and carried off the person of a Mr. J. L. Woods, of Jackson County, Missouri, a young man who has been living for a year or two in California. He had been literally skinned alive as his body presented that appearance. He had no other marks upon his body when found, save blue lines round the neck and ankles showing that he had been bound to a tree while he was skinned alive...

Most early accounts mention the skinning and only differ in extent. Some say all the skin was removed, while others maintain that a patch was removed from his back and attached to a tree as a warning. Various early Indian informants insist that after his skin was removed, the ghastly, whitened and bloody John Woods had staggered to his feet and actually walked six rods before falling face down on the river bank. He soon bled to death from his wounds.

After destroying the bridge, the Indians drove off the cattle and left the desolate scene of the Woodsville massacre.

Young Frank Boden was not the only survivor of Woods' ill-fated party, however. At least two others had slipped into the river at the time of the attack, swam downstream, and then headed south when safely distanced from the Gawias. Boden joined these survivors, and the three met a wagon train at the Kern River several days later.

After tending Boden and his companions, the wagon train people continued their journey north, into the valley. Boden elected to stay with the train and a doctor, while his comrades headed south towards Los Angeles. They wanted no part of having to enter the Four Creeks country again. The wagon train people were uneasy, also. They had strength in numbers, but were poorly armed. As they passed through Gawia territory, the men carried sticks and boards on their shoulders, to appear to be well equipped with weapons. They saw no Indians, but were elated to reach the first settlement at Cassity's Crossing on the San Joaquin River. They had experienced a terrifying welcome to California.

There were enough miners lining the river banks by Cassity's to offer security to the wagon train, but even here signs of disgruntled Indians had caused Cassity and his partner, Major Lane, to strengthen the log fortifications around their trading post. Wiley Cassity was a native of Washington, D.C., and his settlement was frequently referred to as Fort Washington.

Dr. Lewis Leach, a twenty-seven-year-old surgeon from Saint Louis, had come in with the wagon train and had looked after young Boden. He was dis-

Dr. Lewis Leach had just arrived in California when he had to amputate young Boden's arm at Cassity's Ferry. Author's collection.

appointed in this new country, and the Indian scare had unnerved him to the extent that he planned to return home with the first eastbound wagon train. At Cassity's, Leach had turned his patient over to another doctor and kept his belongings packed, ready to move at the first opportunity.

It was several days later that Major Lane became concerned about Boden and asked Leach to look at the boy's arm. One glance and the young doctor knew the swollen and discolored member must come off. Having lost his medical kit on the trip across the plains, Leach took out his pocket knife and asked Lane for a wood saw. A bottle of whiskey served as both antiseptic and anesthesia.

In the Four Creeks country, the rolling grasslands and oak groves were temporarily peaceful again. Dr. Thomas Payne, owner of the destroyed bridge over the Kaweah River, visited the scene of tragedy early in February of 1851. He reported thirteen dead bodies and all the livestock driven off by the Indians. Payne was not bothered by the Indians, nor was a nearby settler named Loomis St. Johns. There seemed little doubt that Woods and his men had been the cause of their own deaths along the banks of the placid Kaweah.

CHAPTER 5 / SOURCES

UNPUBLISHED MATERIAL

U.S. Congress, 32nd Congress, lst Session, Document 110:
    A Report on the Tulare Valley by Lt. George H. Derby, 1850.

Barton, Orlando. "Early History of Tulare County," scrapbook in Bancroft Library, Berkeley, California.

Leonard, Charles Berdan. "The Federal Indian Policy in the San Joaquin Valley, Its Application and Results," unpublished Ph.D. thesis, University of California, 1928.

Annie R. Mitchell to the author, December 30, 1976.

NEWSPAPERS

San Francisco *Daily Alta California*, January 8, 20, 1851.

San Francisco *California Courier*, February 19, 1851.

Mariposa Gazette, August 12, 1859.

Stockton *San Joaquin Republican*, February 15, 1851.

Stockton Times, June 29, 1850.

Visalia Times Delta, June 25, 1959.

PRINCIPAL PUBLISHED WORKS

Bolton, Herbert E. (ed.). *Font's Complete Diary*. Berkeley: University of California Press, 1933.

Brown, Robert R. *History of Kings County*. Hanford, CA: A. H. Cawston, 1940.

Bell, Horace. *Reminiscences of a Ranger*. Santa Barbara: Wallace Hebberd, 1927.

Carson, James H. *Recollections of the California Mines*. Oakland: Biobooks, 1950.

Caughey, John W. *California*. New York: Prentice-Hall, Inc., 1940.

Chamberlain, Samuel E. *My Confession*. New York: Harper & Brothers, Publishers, 1956.

Egan, Ferol. *The El Dorado Trail*. New York: McGraw-Hill, 1970.

History of Fresno County. San Francisco: Elliott and Co., 1882.

Latta, Frank F. *Handbook of Yokuts Indians*. Santa Cruz, CA: Bear State Books, 1978.

Mitchell, Annie R. *The Way It Was*. Fresno, CA: Valley Publishers, 1976.

Vandor, Paul E. *History of Fresno County*. Los Angeles: Historic Record Co., 1919.

OTHER SOURCES

"Dr. Leach, Pioneer Doctor," *Fresno Past & Present,* publication of the Fresno City and County Historical Society, December, 1971, March, 1972.

Journals of the House and Assembly and Senate of California, Second Session, Sacramento, 1851.

Chapter 6

EL DORADO

A continent away, in Washington D.C., the government had been made aware of California's Indian troubles. Many of the eastern Indian tribes had been removed to the Indian Territory in what is now Oklahoma, but by the late 1840s removal was no longer practical. The federal commissioner of Indian Affairs, William Medill, proposed isolating the California Indians on land guaranteed to them by the United States government. More precisely, in his annual report, Secretary of the Interior A. H. Stuart ruminated that the Indians must be either civilized or exterminated, although he was convinced the former objective could be achieved.

In April 1849, Adam Johnston was appointed subagent for the California Indians residing along the San Joaquin and Sacramento rivers. Little was known of the Indians at this time, and Johnston's duties consisted mainly of gathering information that would aid in making treaties with the tribes. In September 1850, the House and Senate passed a bill authorizing the President to appoint three agents, or commissioners, for the California Indians. Twenty-five thousand dollars were included for expenses in the bill. On October 10, George W. Barbour, Oliver M. Wozencraft, and Redick McKee were notified of their appointments and the new commissioners promptly prepared to sail for the West Coast.

During the fall of 1849, gold was found some thirty-five miles north of Culloma on Deer Creek. Miners were soon streaming into the area, and tents were blossoming in the brush-choked gullies and ravines. Soon a village was taking shape. Miner John Pricket visited the area and under the date of May 19, 1850, made the following entry in his diary:

> ...[V]isited the town of Nevada which is a village of tents and canvas houses, almost entirely, which has sprung up in the gold diggings on Deer Creek within the last 5 or 6 weeks....The drinking shops and gamblers have found their way here and are doing a pretty fair business...."

Other merchants and sawmills were in operation at an early date, and nearby mining camps such as Boston Ravine, Rough and Ready, and Jones Bar were soon in existence. Miners' tents and huts were spread up and down the Yuba and Bear rivers and the many creeks of the area. Not surprisingly, the local Nisenan Indians looked with increasing alarm at this invasion of their home lands and hunting lands.

The native inhabitants of the area were Southern Maidu, a peaceful and simple people. Evidence suggests they were quite numerous at one time, one early ethnographer enumerating some eighteen villages along Bear River from Sacramento into the foothills. Approximately fourteen villages were located within a two-mile radius of the Deer Creek Diggings — which was soon called Nevada City. The Indian villagers closest to the new town called themselves Ustumas, a Nisenan word for town.

A young Maidu woman named Betsy was in her early thirties then. To her and her tribe, the whole world existed in the rolling hills, creeks, and ravines between the Yuba and Bear rivers. Food was easy to obtain and was everywhere. The Ustumas lived in simple brush huts, in rancherias that were frequently moved to avoid vermin or contamination. Their weapons were the bow and arrow and slingshot, the preferred missile for the latter being stones of gold-bearing quartz which were quite heavy.

Betsy saw the first four white men arrive in an ox-drawn wagon. Later, other wagons arrived and then they became a steady stream. Her people were driven from their home on Deer Creek and again and again found themselves forced to move by the arriving pioneers.

The white invaders scared off or destroyed most of the Indians' food supply in a very short time. Once, a white man's ox strayed from his corral and was seized by an Indian near Jones Bar. Killing the ox, the Indian invited several neighboring villages to a feast, compliments of the white invaders. While en route to the banquet, Betsy and her family inadvertently were present when the ox's owner located his animal. The

■ Nevada City in 1852, several years after the Indian troubles. *California State Library.*

Indians all fled into the brush when the white man shot and killed the alleged thief.

In later years, Betsy recalled how the Indian children would hide and peek around trees at the white people who always seemed to be frantically scurrying about. When they visited town, the children would blacken their faces to discourage the newcomers from stealing them. The Ustuma world was changing rapidly.

Commenting on how little Indian interference had occurred to inconvenience the hordes of miners overrunning the state, the San Francisco *Alta California* noted that Indians were still being murdered and driven from their lands:

> This, as we stated a day or two since, was one of the fruits of intercourse with an inhuman, unprincipled, ignorant and grasping class of miners who outraged the Indians in their early teachings of civilization, and were afterward made the special objects of Indian hatred and revenge. And the work of blood has not ended. The innocent are again the sufferers. Vengeance has been heavily visited upon those whose crime is but their color, and by men who we blush to believe are Americans....

As in the Culloma troubles, much mischief was initiated by Oregonians who had fought Indians previously in the north. As early as 1848, Pierson B. Reading had been driven from a mining claim by Oregonians who objected to his use of Indian labor.

"I have more than once," wrote Stephen Powers, an early ethnologist, "when sitting at the fireside in winter evenings, listened to old Oregonians telling with laughter how when out hunting deer they had shot down a 'buck' or a 'squaw' at sight and merely for amusement, although the tribe to which they belonged were profoundly at peace with the Americans."

In November of 1849, George and Samuel Holt set up a sawmill several miles below the later site of Grass Valley. James Walsh and Zenas Wheeler built another sawmill on a hill overlooking the Holt brothers' operation, but there was plenty of business for both. The Holts were apparently friendly with the Indians and employed them when possible.

On May 3, 1850, the two brothers were busy in their mill when Indians suddenly burst into the room and attacked them. Samuel Holt fell dying, his body pierced by a dozen arrows. George fled the building, fighting his way through crowds of Indians with no other weapons than a pocket knife and rocks. Running up the hill to the other sawmill, he fell into the arms of one of the men there, bleeding from thirteen arrow wounds.

■ An early day mountain sawmill. *Fresno County Public Library Collection.*

During the night, the Holt mill and other property were burned, and the Indians threatened the Walsh mill where local miners and some friendly Indians had taken cover. The next day, old Chief Weima of the Wemea-Maidu tribe brought in the blackened body of Samuel Holt. George Holt was sent to the Deer Creek Diggings, where it was determined he was dangerously, but not fatally, wounded. A messenger was sent to Cantonment Far West for some soldiers, and soon miners from Deer Creek began arriving at the scene.

A hastily assembled group of volunteers pursued the Indians in an effort to recover the Holt cattle and a Negro slave. The posse, containing some seventy-five men, caught up with the fleeing natives about sundown. A brief and bloody fight took place, resulting in a reported eleven whites being killed. These casualties were likely exaggerated, and after taking some Indian prisoners, the volunteers limped back to Deer Creek.

Rumors were rampant. Several teamsters had reportedly been shot by Indians from positions of ambush. A certain Captain Ford was reported as being overdue from a prospecting trip, and a Mr. McKinley was reported as having shot an Indian during a brief skirmish.

Letters to newspapers and pleas to the state for aid brought Thomas J. Green to the mining camp of Oro on May 16. Green, a robust Texan, was a member of the legislature from Sacramento County and author of the notorious foreign miners' tax law which had gone into effect this same month. Called "the most objectionable piece of legislation that has ever appeared in the Statute B Books of California," this law forced foreigners working in the mines to pay a license fee of twenty dollars per month. Besides being grossly unfair, the law was unworkable and was repealed in March of 1851.

Green was also a major general of the state militia, and upon his arrival he found a volunteer group preparing to pursue the Indians once again. The men were commanded by Captain Nicholaus Allgeier, a German immigrant who operated a ferry and trading post at the junction of the Feather and Bear rivers. Additional companies also were being formed.

After looking over the situation, General Green sent Governor Peter Burnett a brief report of the situation:

> "It has been reported that an engagement took place on Deer Creek a few days since in which eight whites and fifteen Indians were killed. Much excitement prevails in this quarter upon this subject. I have, therefore, thought it my duty, in the absence of orders from your excellency, to take the field as well to protect our citizens as to prevent excesses on their part, hoping very soon to receive your orders."

On the 17th, Green took charge of the Indian pursuit at the head of Allgeier's company. Lieutenant Bell and ten men were sent ahead to scout and quickly ran into a war party. After a brief engagement, the patrol reported killing five natives and returned with six prisoners.

Green and his men scouted the Deer Creek area where a number of depredations had been reported. Local Indian villages were deserted and the posse moved south in the direction of Bear River and Grass Valley. Upon arrival at Colonel Holt's burned mill, they found the mining camp at Grass Valley deserted and the local Indian rancherias also abandoned. Again, they followed the Indian trail south.

On May 20, the company crossed Bear River and entered a native village on the south bank. They prowled through the deserted encampment, then followed tracks that crossed the river, heading north. Green's troops had no sooner recrossed the river than word was received that a large body of Indians had taken positions on top of a hill some two miles away. Galloping to the scene, the whites found several hundred natives gathered to do battle. Green described the resulting fight in another report to the governor, written May 25:

> After examining their position, I ordered Captain Hoyt with twenty men to take station upon the foot of the hill upon the left, and with Capt. Allgeier, Lieut. Bell, and the balance of the men, in all 30, I charged up the most accessible side of the hill upon the right into camp, and drove the Indians upon Captain Hoyt's position, where a smart skirmish ensued. We pursued them for several miles in the hills and ravines, killing and wounding a number, and took eight prisoners; their chiefs report eleven of their men killed, besides wounded. We had none killed—wounded Capt. Hoyt, Lieut. Lewis, and Mr. Russell. My aid, Major Frederick Emory, was accidentally shot through the thigh by the discharge of a rifle—all doing well.

After caring for the wounded and reorganizing his men, Green sent a note to the Indian chiefs asking for peace. He told them they must stop killing white people and destroying property. When this happens, he told them, the white people will stop killing Indian men and taking their women and children. "If you wish peace," the note concluded, "come down to Johnson's old rancho on Bear River, and report yourselves to Captain Charles Hoyt, who will protect you until your Great Father shall speak." The note was sent after the retreating Indians by way of an old Indian woman who had been captured.

On the 25th, Chiefs Weima, Buckler, Poolal, and several others did meet with Green near Oro and signed a peace treaty. Both Green and many of the miners who knew the Indians, were convinced that they wanted peace and the chiefs were sent to the north fork of the American River to bring in other hostiles.

Green received a letter from Governor Burnett in response to his report of the 25th in which the executive fully approved of his actions. Green then left for the East, leaving General Thomas Eastland, also of the militia, to await the arrival of the chiefs. Camped on Bear River, some sixty miles north of Sacramento, Eastland waited, and waited, and waited.

On June 15, Eastland wrote to inform the governor of the failure to contact the hostiles. "This failure is to be regretted," concluded Eastland, "believing as I do that had the chiefs come in, and we had counselled together, the terms of a truce might have been agreed upon, which, if not faithfully carried out to the letter, would have prevented, in some degree, a continuation of the disturbances occurring so frequently, causing the indiscriminate and wholesale murder of both white men and Indians..."

Just a few days previously, Eastland had examined the nude and butchered bodies of two miners whose corpses had been discovered in the river. In his diary, miner John Pricket identified the bodies as two men he had been traveling with. He assumed they had been killed by the Indians, but made no direct charge of this. Eastland's report noted:

> While no one will attempt to justify the Indians in such barbarous deeds, it may well be asked if they may not frequently be perpetrated in retaliation for similar ones committed (mostly, no doubt, by lawless white men) upon their people? It is a well-known fact that among our white population there are men who boast of the number of Indians they have killed and that not one shall escape them. If they have been wronged by certain individuals, and thus gratify their revengeful feelings, they do it at the cost of many of the lives of their own countrymen, and make sorrow and mourning for the widow and orphan. Far better would it be that the

guilty should escape, than that such consequences should result from indiscriminate revenge.

In any case, General Green's treaty had resolved nothing. The cause of the tragic series of events that had cost so many lives was elucidated in a report by Captain Hannibal Day, commanding officer at Camp Far West. Writing to the state adjutant general on May 16, Day told of the murder of Dr. Holt and of sending a detachment of troops to investigate:

> From the same reliable source, I am informed of the probable cause of this otherwise unaccountable affair, as Messrs. Holt have been all winter on the most friendly terms with the Indians, and even more, have treated them kindly and hospitably. It seems that on or about the 6th inst. some ten white men made an attack on this Indian camp and killed two (if not three) Indians, under the impression that said Indians or some others had stolen and killed some of their cattle which were then missing. But behold, the very next day, after having boasted of their feat, the lost cattle were found. It may readily be supposed that in revenge, the natives fell upon the Holts as the most available victims and considering that after such outrages, all white men were equally at fault...."

Captain Day concluded his report by noting that "If there be any agent of the Indian Department for this valley, I would respectfully suggest that he be advised to make an excursion among the natives with an interpreter to notify them, at least, of what will be their probable fate unless they discontinue their thieving and submit with better grace to being shot down."

■ The native Maidu Indians discovered early that they could not co-exist with the burgeoning white population. *Author's collection.*

Although the officer was being facetious, Adam Johnston called on Captain Day at his small post on June 7. Johnston, the new subagent for the Indians living on the San Joaquin and Sacramento rivers, had arrived in California in November 1849. He had heard of the troubles and knowing that Captain Sutter had refused his reappointment as agent, traveled north to see if he could be of any service.

■ Hannibal Day as he appeared while a general officer during the Civil War. *National Archives.*

After examining Green's treaty, the agent pronounced it worthless and stated as much in a report to his Washington superior. One of the stipulations of the treaty was that the Indians be paid a semiannual annuity of $1,000. Johnston noted that paying money to "the most degraded…beings on the continent would not only be unnecessarily expensive to the government, but wholly useless to the Indians. They have not the least conception of the value of money, and the consequence would be it would fall into the hands of a few avaricious whites without benefitting the Indians."

Johnston was just beginning to learn the ways of the Indian, but he well knew the ways of the white man.

Betsy, the Maidu woman, died in 1923. Although over one hundred years of age, she never forgot the cruelties of the whites. When she died it was the end of her race. She was the last of the Ustumas.

The avengers of the Holt's mill episode had barely gone back to work when gun smoke from another quarter drifted their way. Along the emigrant trail over the Sierra, just south of Grass Valley, the mining camp called "Hangtown" mustered forces for its own war following a series of troublesome incidents.

Old Dry Diggings had been founded in June of 1848, but the village was subsequently called Hangtown after a lynching that occurred during the winter of 1849. Actually, Hangtown was never more than a nickname. Old mining records dating back to late 1849 mostly refer to the town as Placerville. This is true also of newspaper references, although the press also used the name Hangtown over the years for local color. Pioneers, writing back to the states, were often more likely to use the picturesque name of Hangtown in lieu of the more prosaic Placerville, and the informal cognomen has persisted to the present.

There were various reports of Indian troubles in the Placerville area during the summer of 1850. An article in the San Francisco *Alta* in June reported a prospector coming upon a group of Maidu Indians who were panning for gold. The natives wounded the prospector with an arrow, after which he fled to Hangtown, where a posse was promptly organized. A nearby rancheria was raided, the inhabitants were chased away, and one Indian was wounded.

Later that summer, four miners were crossing the mountains between Placerville and a neighboring camp when they encountered a Nisenan warrior and his wife. When one of the men attempted to rape the woman, she was defended by her husband, who was shot and killed by the miners. The story goes that the local Indians tried to obtain redress for this murder, but were ignored by the whites, so they took matters into their own hands. In any case, they attacked a party of miners, killing two of them.

There were other Indian troubles at the time, including attacks along the emigrant trail. When a volunteer group was organized around the middle of October, the El Dorado County sheriff, William H. Rogers, assumed command. John Carr, who had known Rogers in Illinois, later wrote that Rogers was a former Mississippi gambler who had been driven out of Natchez.

Even at this early date it was realized that to receive compensation for their efforts, any volunteer group would have to obtain some kind of official status. A letter from Rogers to the governor brought a reply by October 28, authorizing Rogers to muster two hundred men and report regularly to General A. M. Winn of the state militia.

■ Originally christened "Hangtown" for obvious reasons, the more gentle name of Placerville was adopted as soon as a more stable population established itself. *Author's collection.*

Two companies of volunteers were mustered — one in Mud Springs and the other in Placerville. Sheriff Rogers marched his men up the emigrant road to William "Cock-eyed Jack" Johnson's ranch, where camp was officially established. Johnson had a store and saloon at his place and did a rousing business with the troops. At an election of officers, Johnson was elected adjutant, L. H. McKennie lieutenant colonel, and John Brown, Stewart Munson, and a man named Reed were selected as captains.

Rogers called his post Camp Hall, and although he had no prior military experience, he quickly took the initiative. As early as October 29, he wrote to General Winn and reported the movements of his troops:

> Pursuant to the necessity of our situation in accordance with the order of the governor, I have collected two hundred men armed and equipped and provisioned for five days at this point, I have rendezvoused & sent scouting parties in various directions to wit; Capt. Stewart [Munson] proceeded to the South Fork of the American River near the emigrant trail, who returned into camp last night reported no Indians found in that direction. Captain Johnson was ordered on the emigrant trail to branch off at will, a part of which company came into camp and reported no hostile Indians discovered. A residue of said last mentioned company are still out or likely had an engagement. Captain Reed was sent with his company to the forks of the Cosumnes from whom we have had no report and no doubt had a severe engagement. At the same time Lt. Colonel McKennie was sent out with 16 men under his command who met with a party of from 150 to 200 Indians on the banks of a deep canyon on the north branch of the Cosumnes who immediately fired upon him, a report of which engagement is enclosed.

When McKennie's command found the remains of a large group of emigrant cattle that had been slain, they pressed on after the Indians. A short time later, they suddenly came upon the natives in rough, mountain territory. McKennie's figure of 150 to 200 Indians is probably exaggerated, but the surprised natives fired on the whites and the fight was on.

"A severe engagement ensued," wrote McKennie, "in which three Indians were killed and many wounded. The very difficult situation of the canyon prevented us from following as our own men, as well as the Indians, were stumbling and falling down the steep declivities, making it entirely impossible for us to secure captives."

On November 3, Rogers had his first fight with the enemy and reported that the engagement lasted some five hours, during which fifteen Indians were killed. Two volunteers were listed as killed, Hugh Dixsen and Calvin Everts. Another man was dangerously wounded. Rogers reported 150 Indians in the fight, but just how many volunteers were engaged is not known. In concluding his report, Rogers noted that "we are satisfied that there are white men amidst them. There was one killed in the party that attacked us yesterday."

On November 4, McKennie's sixteen-man mounted company was still on the river when they had another encounter with the Indians. Still in very rough terrain, the cavalrymen came upon an Indian whom they surmised was the rear guard of a larger force. E. W. Boone's report of the skirmish gave no details, but other accounts agreed that Lieutenant Colonel McKennie chased the fleeing Indian. As the gap between the white men and the Indian closed, McKennie's troops heard gunfire and saw their officer fall from his horse. An account in a county history book notes that as McKennie caught up with his quarry, the Indian "...finding himself at bay, turned and fitted an arrow to his bow — then, as the major, bending forward, discharged the contents of his gun into the Indian's body, the dying man sent his arrow up to the feather in the breast of his cowardly assailant, killing him almost instantly. Major McKennie's friends, instead of hanging him in effigy for his part in this disgraceful affair, honored him with a costly and imposing funeral."

No one, of course, knows just who shot first, the Indian or the white man. An old-timer who had no sympathy for this particular "war" wrote just the opposite: "...the Indian shot McKennie first, then when mortally wounded, the officer 'dispatched his murderer.'" The writer remembered McKennie as a veteran of the Mexican War and a brave man who was highly regarded by all who knew him. Whatever happened, McKennie died shortly after being shot. A private was also reported as being slightly wounded in the action, but no details were reported.

Returning to Johnson's ranch, Lieutenant Boone was elected to fill McKennie's staff position, and the company rested after its recent hard marches. Rogers, meanwhile, headed for Sacramento to report in person on the progress of the war.

In Sacramento, Rogers called on General Winn, who was disturbed by the sheriff's lack of military knowledge.

Rogers had no sooner left his presence than the general wrote to Governor Burnett and complained of the burgeoning fiasco:

> It does seem to me that it would be better to disband the present troops and, if necessary, reorganize according to law, as there are certainly too many officers for the number of men. The expense now accruing will be immense. Men expect to get $8 per day and officers at least $16 per day. They have now 250 men at $8 per day and would be $2000 per day. For officers additional, say at least $1000, then say $2 per day to each man for supplies, including everything amounts to $500 per day, the whole making $3500 per day, or $22,500 per week. Such debt cannot be paid by the state when we know that she cannot borrow more than $300,000 which will do no more than pay her officers and civil incidental expenses....

◾ General A. M. Winn of the California State Militia.
California State Library.

General Winn also dispatched Major J. H. Kelly of his staff to Rogers' camp to keep an eye on the campaign. Kelly was impressed by the "soldierly bearing" of the men, but thought it expedient that one of the four companies be dismissed, which was done. With the rains setting in and his scouting parties having made little contact with the hostiles, Rogers disbanded his men on November 28, 1850. The following day he received a letter from the governor ordering him to reduce his force to one hundred men. Rogers' final report to General Winn, on December 10, signified the end of the first El Dorado County war.

There seems to have been little real reason for the Rogers campaign, and various newspapers made no attempt to hide their distaste for the recent expedition. The *Alta* summed up the campaign quite well:

> From all that we have seen and known of the Indians of this country, we fully believe there has been no necessity for warfare with them. And the position taken by the *Placer Times*, which avers that the recent ridiculous attempt to get up an Indian War in El Dorado County had its origin in a desire on the part of a few provision dealers to supply the troops with their "grub" is to our mind a fair indication of the patriotism of the plotters in the whole matter.

Lucius Fairchild, a miner in the area during October of 1850, visited Placerville frequently, yet in his letters home he makes no reference to Indians or an Indian war. John Hume, a local lawyer, was more impressed with the proceedings:

We have for several weeks been in the midst of an Indian war and troops are marched almost daily through our streets, to and from the seat of war. Several skirmishes have already been had and several have fallen on each side. The Indians are living on every side of us and we frequently hear of their attacking mining parties within three or four miles of town. We enlisted in this place some 200 men for the army and since they have been gone, I have seen, on a sudden alarm, at least 400 men turn out at an hour's notice, armed to the teeth. No place in the States could equal this, for here the population is composed of men fit to bear arms and all have arms at hand.

As insignificant as the "war" was, it had cost the state over $25,000 for its one month of duration. Five years later ex-members of Rogers' command were still trying to collect what they considered was due them for their efforts.

War or not, Indians and whites had died and nothing had really been resolved. Rogers' scouting parties had driven the natives deeper into the mountains where they waited to renew hostilities.

William Graham had captained a mounted squad of Rogers' men. After disbanding, he had begun to build a ranch some five miles east of Johnson's place, in Pleasant Valley. Early in January about fifty Maidu suddenly attacked Graham and six of his men as they were at work. The Marysville *Herald* reported some nine Indians killed in the fight which followed, while one white man was wounded in the leg.

A letter to Sheriff Rogers from J. H. Phillips at Johnson's ranch reported further depredations in the area. "Several dead bodies" were mentioned as being found on the south fork, while various attacks on mining companies were noted. Both Johnson's and Taylor's ranches were attacked, the former place reporting a fight 300 yards from the house. A Mr. G. C. Smith was noted as being badly wounded. Phillips closed by asking that Rogers "make use of all honorable means in your power to get the executive to render us some assistance."

Writing from Coloma on February 22, Rogers again sounded the alarm to General Winn:

> Some firm and decisive step must be taken at once against them as I learn that they are concentrating all their forces near south Fork. A strong indication of warfare is manifested by the Indians in this immediate neighborhood. But a few days since several came in to town with their bows and quivers and their faces tattooed and painted red which is a certain sign that mischief is intended....

Because of the widespread criticism in the press, the authorities were hesitant to respond to any new call and it was spring before new rumors rekindled the fires of war.

About the first of May, Rogers received further reports of Indian depredations, "...started," noted the historian Hubert H. Bancroft, "by interested traders and their shiftless customers whose appetite had been whetted by the state's money." Despite Bancroft's assertion, the Sacramento *Daily Union* of May 13 noted that two miners had been killed and volunteers were being raised to give the natives "a little more grape." Mustering a force of 150 men, Rogers again set up camp at Johnson's ranch and petitioned the governor for official status. On May 13, blessings were received from the state executive and the second El Dorado County campaign was on.

Not feeling he had enough men for the job at hand, Rogers set out to enlist more volunteers while instructing his two companies in the field to locate the Indians. A veteran of the previous company, Captain Graham of A Company, was left in charge with orders to keep scouts on the lookout for the hostiles. Captain John C. Tracy was ordered to direct B Company to make contact with the Indians and on or about May 20 he did just that. In correspondence between Captain Tracy and Captain Graham, the two officers planned a pincers movement whereby they would both cross the river at separate points and attack the Indian camp from different locations.

Heading east up the south fork of the American River, Captain Graham proceeded with his part of the plan. Tracy set up camp at a lower section of the river, but when he attempted to cross, his command was fired on by the Indians. Keeping up a steady fire, the natives drove the whites back to their camp, but early the next morning the volunteers successfully made a crossing. Dividing his men into two groups, Tracy swept through the Maidu village, chasing the natives before him. After burning the village, the whites pursued the fleeing Indians, fully expecting to chase them into the fire of Graham's men.

Graham had meanwhile made his crossing some twenty miles above Johnson's ranch, and he proceeded toward the native village. After a slight skirmish during which two Indians were killed and a rancheria destroyed, the men pressed on, not knowing that Tracy had not yet effected his crossing. When he couldn't locate Tracy, Graham recrossed the river, having a man drowned in the process.

Tracy continued chasing the Indians, and when the men in the lead saw several horses tied in a steep canyon, they ran to secure them. Suddenly, a flight of arrows and a rifle volley killed Edwin Jenks and wounded three others. Quickly posting his men, Tracy exchanged shots for several hours, but was unable to rout the Indians or retrieve Jenks' body.

"At the commencement of the action," Tracy reported, "I sent an express to Capt. Graham for all the men he could spare. At last, thinking that the express had been cut off, I withdrew my men with the wounded, but could not get at the dead body, he being too near the enemy. I then returned to camp."

Graham received Tracy's message, but by the time he reached the ambush site, Tracy had retreated. He sent two of his Delaware Indian scouts to retrieve the tied horses, and though fired on, they were successful. Graham then detailed four others to retrieve Jenks' body, which was accomplished. By this time, one of his men had been wounded by an arrow and Graham too retreated, joining Tracy's men at the river.

"It is impossible for me to say how many Indians were killed," noted Graham's report. "Many were killed by the men. I can account for two, one killed by a Delaware, and another by one of the command."

On May 25, Major Rogers rejoined his volunteers at Johnson's ranch. Accompanying him was Major G. D. Hall, representing General Winn, along with another company of sixty volunteers. After all the reports were completed, Rogers again prepared to move against the hostiles who had so effectively routed his men.

Rogers tracked the Indians to the south, but was unable to make contact. Finally, on the Mokelumne River, he was able to capture several Indians, one of whom claimed to be a chief named Santiago. Returning to Johnson's ranch with Santiago and the other hostages, Rogers waited for the announced arrival of Oliver Wozencraft, one of the recently appointed California Indian commissioners. For a change, it seemed as though the Indians had come out on top — or had at least held the skirmish at a draw. When Wozencraft arrived on June 11, Pegleg Smith, an old, drunken mountain man, was engaged as an interpreter for the treaty talks. The war again seemed to be at an end.

Writing from Los Angeles, Redick McKee, another of the three Indian commissioners, noted that "…Dr. Wozencraft has gone to El Dorado County….. The late war in that section was, I am told, a greater piece of tomfoolery & humbug than even the former was on the Frezno and San Joaquin…." In his own account of the situation, Wozencraft had little praise for the conduct of the whites:

> …[T]he state having sent out troops against the Indians, after having several engagements they finally left them in the same position they found them…. They then went into a rancheria occupied by those who had been known to be friendly to the whites, and captured several as prisoners [Santiago and the others]. Soon after, the troops were disbanded and the war…terminated.

I have been informed that on former occasions those Indians who had been at peace with the whites have been cruelly persecuted by those who either killed or abused their men without assigning a cause therefor…making it difficult for me to have an interview with or conciliate them. When I am favored with a talk, they have but little confidence in my promises when they witness so many acts proving the reverse of my statements….

I have, however, made preliminary arrangements by which I expect to consummate a treaty with them. This will take time, as it can only be done after inspiring them with confidence. In order to effect this, I have licensed traders who have sufficient influence with them to conduct their trade and disseminate the friendly talk; have sent men among them who speak their language, and are influential, and placed beef cattle under the care of the traders, in order to supply their pressing necessities for food, and induce them to come down from out of their mountain fastnesses; all of which will have the desired effect of causing them to come in and conclude a treaty….

■ William Byrnes was one of Captain Tracy's men who guarded Mormon Station. *Author's collection.*

Wozencraft had done all he could for the present. At one point in his report the agent summed up his whole, discouraging assignment: "As previously stated, they have learned to distrust the white man, and it would appear that the difficulty of treating with them is in due ratio to the comparative length of time that the whites have been among them."

Rogers was in the process of disbanding his troops in July 1851 when a message arrived stating that the emigrant trail was again being harassed by the Indians. Rogers dispatched a picked group of men under Captain Tracy to Mormon Station, in the Carson Valley. The men had no sooner arrived than word was received that the volunteers had again been dismissed by the governor.

General Winn and an entourage rode up from Sacramento to attend Rogers' dismissal of the troops. By this time, Lieutenant George Stoneman and a body of U.S. soldiers were camped near the vol-

DISBURSING OFFICE.
Coloma, May 12th, 1851.
GENERAL: Enclosed herewith, you will find a letter directed to the Governor, informing him of the outbreak amongst the Indians, and that I have commenced raising a force of from 50 to 75 men to go out at once and meet them. I feel confident that both yourself and the Governor will approve of the course I have taken. Major Graham has just arrived from Placerville, confirming the reports I received yesterday.
You will see the necessity of having the letter forwarded at once to the Governor.
I remain,
very respectfully,
your, ob't. serv't.,
W. ROGERS, Maj. Com'g.
1st Bat. Cal. Vol.
To Brig. Gen. WINN.
The above letter was handed us by Gen. Winn, who received it from Mr. Wm. L. Ferguson, the Special Messenger despatched by Major Rodgers. The messenger met the Governor on his way to this city, but as he had sealed orders to Gen. Winn, they were not delivered. Gen. Winn immediately on receipt of the letter, sent it back to the Governor at Coloma.

■ Sacramento *Daily Union*, May 14, 1851.

unteers, along with Ben McCulloch and a variety of politicians who considered the county a Whig stronghold. The closing scenes of the "war" now took on the holiday air of a Sunday outing. The Sacramento *Daily Union* reported:

> Johnson's Ranch, where the camp is located, is a beautiful spot, finely covered with pine trees of immense size, and in a most beautiful valley, with fine grass and limpid springs of good water. The barley and garden vegetation looks well, while several hundred head of sheep and cattle...brings back to us the thoughts of other days....

■ Mountain man Thomas L. "Pegleg" Smith interpreted at the peace talks. *Hutchings' California Magazine.*

When the volunteers were in formation, parades, speeches and all the military protocol that could be mustered in a frontier setting was indulged in. General Winn addressed each company as it was dismissed, hailing their bravery and military bearing in the rigorous, late campaign. When the oratory was finished, a long line of troopers shouldered their rifles for a musket salute to the general.

With muskets aimed skyward, the troops all fired at the word, but were surprised at the snap and popping of a multitude of caps as all the weapons missed fire. Upon examination it was discovered that a barrel of black sand had been sold to the quartermaster as gunpowder, along with sundry other bogus supplies. Although the incident was not noted in contemporary newspapers, a Union correspondent some years later wrote that "the name of the man who sold black sand for powder and pickled sausages for corned beef, can be given.

Although there was continued trouble that summer, the second El Dorado County war had ended in a draw. That seemed to be the best the Indians could ever hope for in any case.

There were few newspapers in 1850 California, but these few were widely read. Letters, word-of-mouth, and rumors picked up where the press left off. The Culloma war, Glanton's death, the Clear Lake, Woodsville, and El Dorado County troubles all were discussed and forgotten in the busy quest for gold. The decent miners, the ones who would help, feed, and employ Indians in their vicinity, looked around at these inoffensive people and wondered how they could originate any such troubles. Then, busy with their own problems, they went back to work.

CHAPTER 6 / SOURCES

UNPUBLISHED MATERIAL

National Archives, records of the office of Indian Affairs, California Superintendency, Record Group 75, M234:

> O. M. Wozencraft to Luke Lea, July 12, 1851.
>
> Redick McKee to George Barbour, June 10, 1851.

Office of the Secretary of State, California State Archives, Indian War Files, Sacramento:

> Governor Peter Burnett to William Rogers, October 25; November 15, 1850.
>
> William Rogers to Brigadier General A. M. Winn, October 26, 29; November 4, 1850.
>
> L. H. McKennie to William Rogers, October 25, 1850.
>
> L. G. Johnson to Brigadier General A. M. Winn, November 3, 1850.
>
> E. W. Noon to William Rogers, November 4, 1850.
>
> William Graham to Brigadier General A. M. Winn, November 7, 1850.
>
> L. G. Johnson to William Rogers, November 8, 1850.
>
> William Graham to William Rogers, November 8, 1850.
>
> Brigadier General A. M. Winn to Governor Peter Burnett, November 11, 1850.
>
> Major J. H. Kelly to Brigadier General A. M. Winn, November 25, 1850.
>
> Brigadier General A. M. Winn to William Rogers, November 25, 1850.
>
> H. Phillips to William Rogers, January 28, 1851.
>
> Brigadier General A. M. Winn to Governor John H. McDougal, July 21, 1851.

Pricket, John, microfilmed diary in the Bancroft Library, University of California, Berkeley.

NEWSPAPERS

San Francisco Daily *Alta California*, March 13, May 20, June 5, November 4, 29, December 15, 1850; June 1, 13, 14, 1851.

Sacramento *Daily Union*, April 9, May 13, 17, 24, 27, 28, 30, June 2, 3, 6, 12, 23, July 14, September 23, December 30, 1851.

Sacramento *Daily Record-Union*, March 27, 1875.

Marysville *Herald,* November 5, 1850; January 10, 1851.

Placer Times, May 29, October 25, 1850.

Sandusky (Ohio) *Clarion*, July 22, November 4, 1850.

PRINCIPAL PUBLISHED WORKS

Bancroft, Hubert H. *History of California*, Vol. XXIV. San Francisco: The History Company, Publishers, 1887.

Carr, John. *Pioneer Days in California*. Eureka, CA: Times Publishing Company, 1891.

Dillon, Richard. *Wells Fargo Detective*. New York: Coward-McCann, Inc. 1969.

Gudde, Irwin G. *California Gold Camps*. Berkeley: University of California Press, 1975.

Heizer, Robert F., editor. *The Destruction of California Indians*. Santa Barbara: Peregrine Smith, Inc., 1974.

Kephart, Horace, editor. *The Gold Hunters*. New York: Outing Publishing Co., 1917.

Kroeber, A. L. *Handbook of the Indians of California*. New York: Dover Publications, Inc., 1976.

Sioli, Paoli. *Historical Souvenir of El Dorado County*. Oakland: Author, 1883.

Powers, Stephen. *Tribes of California*. Berkeley: University of California Press, 1976.

Schafer, Joseph. *California Letters of Lucius Fairchild*. Madison, WI: State Historical Society of Wisconsin, 1931.

Steed, Jack and Steed, Richard. *The Donner Party Rescue Site: Johnson's Ranch on Bear River*. Sacramento: Pioneer Publishing Co., 1988.

Upton, Charles Elmer. *Pioneers of El Dorado*. Placerville, CA: Author, 1906.

Wells, Harry Laurenz. *History of Nevada County, California*. Oakland: Thompson & West, 1880.

OTHER SOURCES

Appendix to the Journal of the Senate of California, 2nd Session, Sacramento, 1851.

Journal of the House of Assembly of California, 2nd session, Sacramento, 1851, 1852.

Douglas, Belle. "The Last of the Oustomahs [Ustumas]," Nevada County Historical Society Publication, March, 1960.

Foley, Doris. "The Indians of Nevada County," Nevada County Historical Society, May, 1953.

Chapter 7

YOSEMITE

"This is our country: why do the Americans come here? They are good and brave, but they come upon the lands of my people. What do they intend to do? I want to know, and must know RIGHT NOW! ...Heretofore my people did not permit any stranger to pass over our country or stop in it, except Mr. Savage—he made us many presents. If you will make us presents too, you may remain in our country awhile."

So spoke a Chauchila chieftain to Adam Johnston in the spring of 1850. The government had early recognized the need for a policy in dealing with the numerous Indians in California. In his message to congress on December 5, 1848, President James Polk recommended a suitable number of Indian agents for the new territory. Accordingly, John S. Wilson and Adam Johnston were appointed in April of the following year. That same month, Thomas Butler King was dispatched to California to gather information and make recommendations on the natives of the Far West. Little of King's information was reliable, but he did recommend that the Indians could be taught civilized arts if they were brought together in some way. This was one of the earliest references to a reservation system in America.

Appointed subagent for the Sacramento and San Joaquin valleys, Adam Johnston arrived in California via the overland route in October of 1849. The winter of 1849-50 was a severe one, and the agent was forced to stay around the settlements and pick up what Indian information was available. As soon as possible in the spring, he began traveling among the natives of the northern portion of the San Joaquin Valley. He issued a trading license to George Belt, who had a store on the Merced River, and made Belt's tent his headquarters as he traveled throughout the area.

In his early reports, Johnston noted the low state of development of the natives and how, even at this early date, they were noticeably declining in numbers. He also reported that the influx of miners was rapidly crowding the Indians off their lands and depriving them of much of their food supply. Like King, Johnston recommended that depots be established where supplies could be distributed to the Indians — another early reference to the reservation concept.

In the 1840s there were a number of large Spanish land grants in the San Joaquin Valley owned by both Mexicans and Americans. Few were inhabited, however. Along the barren west side, beside El Camino Viejo, there were a few villages such as Poso Chane, Las Juntas, and Los Banos, occupied by Californio and mestizo ranchers.

When Johnston arrived, the first signs of settlement by Americans was beginning in the great central valley. Lieutenant Derby had reported a man named Shumway traveling south in the valley in May of 1850 to establish a ferry on the Kern River. One B. Oscar Field claimed to have mined and established a ferry on the Kings River as early as February of 1850, but when the Indians robbed him in May, he left the area. In June, two men named Jones and Rider and a man named Hampton had ferries on the Kings River, also, but seemed to have left by the time William J. Campbell and John Pool set up a trading post and ferry the following spring. In March, a road-building party, headed by John Hudgins, was also in the valley.

At the edge of the Sierra foothills, Wiley Cassity and C. D. Gibbes established a ferry on the San Joaquin River in the spring of 1850. One Major Lane and several of his sons went into partnership with the ferry owners and the men established a mining claim about eight miles upstream at Cassity's Bar.

■ Ferries were the precursors of civilization and there was usually a store and saloon in conjunction with the operation. *Author's collection.*

At the ferry itself, the shacks and tents became known as Cassity's Crossing. There was some trade with the Indians of the area, but Cassity treated them cruelly, a fact that may or may not have been noticed when Johnston visited there. When another trader, headquartered farther north, asked for a license to trade on the Fresno River, Johnston readily agreed. If there were to be any kind of peace and harmony between the races, there must be understanding, a common ground to meet on. Trading posts could well be such a common ground. Besides, Cassity was a swaggering bully, and competition would do him some good.

James D. Savage, the new trader on the Fresno River, was rather small of stature, but big on reputation. Johnston had heard of him as soon as he had entered this wild country and although he could not give Jim Savage a formal license to trade, he did give him oral permission to locate his post.

Savage had come overland to California in 1846 from Illinois. A young man in his early twenties at the time, Savage had lost a bride and child to the hardships of the overland trail. In California he joined Fremont's Battalion during the Mexican War and afterwards worked for a time at Sutter's Fort.

Having heard of the Indians in the great Tulare (San Joaquin) Valley from some of Fremont's native troops, Savage went to live among them in the fall of 1847. When gold was discovered early the following year, Savage mined for a time, then traveled to San Francisco to buy stock for a trading post he planned to establish.

In the Bay city, Savage visited the makeshift shop of Charles L. Ross. Arriving on the barque *Whiton* in April 1847, Ross carried a large cargo of goods from the East, but he had sold most of his stock by the time Savage wandered into his store. All he had left were some tall crowned hats, a case of military uniforms and a case of hardware—hinges, door knobs, keys, and the like. Ross later recalled the visit:

> A man by the name of Savage, who was mining on the Merced among the Indians, came in one morning and said, "I will give you this bag of gold dust for everything you have in the store." The remnants of stock were worth about $125.00. The bag contained about nine hundred dollars worth of dust. I accepted the offer. As Savage could not read or write, he asked me to mark on the outside of each package a sum several times what he had paid for it, as representing the cost to him as a guide in selling, and when I made out the invoice at those rates, it amounted to about nine thousand dollars....

Later, a visitor to the trading post related how Savage had traded heavy brass hinges and door knobs to the Indians for equal weights of gold.

Savage became quite prominent in the Mariposa area. He took several Indian wives from among the more important tribes and chiefs and in this way established a power base. Next, he determined to outdo the Indian

■ Several photographs of Jim Savage were taken, but none have survived. He probably had many of the characteristics of his father, Peter (above).
Author's collection.

■ San Francisco was growing explosively in 1850, almost as fast as the legend of Jim Savage. *Author's collection.*

medicine men with clever tricks and devices. Crafty and a good judge of character, in a short time Savage became a powerful figure among the natives, known far and wide as the "King of the Tulares."

By trading insignificant articles to the Indians in exchange for gold and by charging exorbitant prices to the miners for their supplies, Savage became wealthy. When Adam Johnston met him for the first time in the foothills of the Sierra, he had already heard fabulous tales of the man. It was said that he had over thirty Indian wives, a flour barrel full of gold, and that he ruled with an iron hand over the Indians in the valley. After all the wild stories, Johnston found Savage to be unimpressive in size, but very muscular and active. His face was deeply tanned and he wore his hair long to his shoulders. A red shirt and corduroy trousers tucked into high boots made up his costume. He knew a great deal about the natives and told the Indian agent much about his new territory and its inhabitants.

Located at the headwaters of the Merced River, Savage's trading post was some fifteen miles below the mysterious canyon home of the Yosemites, an assortment of Indians from both sides of the Sierra. Ethnologically, the majority of these natives belonged to the Mariposa dialect group of the southern Sierra Miwok. They called themselves Ahwahneechees, an Indian term meaning "grizzly bear," but the whites soon corrupted the name to Yosemite. Although they traded at Savage's post, the Indians were alarmed at the hordes of white men flowing into their country.

Whether it was covetousness of Savage's well-stocked shelves or a warning to the encroaching whites, the Yosemites attacked the trading post early in 1850. Savage and his Indian miners drove the hostiles off, but the

86

trader took a second look at the exposed position in which he found himself. He decided it would be safer to move down closer to the settlements in the foothills, and it was at this time that he asked Johnston for another trading license for the Merced and Fresno rivers.

Savage did a thriving business at both his trading posts, but his prosperity was to be short lived. In the fall of 1850 several of his wives warned Savage that the Yosemites were again planning to make war. Finding it necessary to make a trip to San Francisco, Savage conceived the idea of taking along some of the local tribesmen to impress them with the power of the whites and the futility of war. He invited Chief Jose Juarez of the Chauchilas to go along since he knew the Yosemites were trying to form an alliance with that tribe.

■ An Indian camp on the Merced River. Photograph by Eadweard Muybridge, about 1872. *The Bancroft Library.*

In San Francisco, things did not go the way Savage had hoped. Although impressed with the teeming life in the big city, the Indians were even more intrigued by the free liquor offered to them at every turn. The natives were drunk during most of their stay, Jose Juarez becoming so obnoxious that Savage was forced to knock him down at one point. The trip did little to change white-Indian relations in the foothills of Mariposa County and Savage returned to his trading posts in a grim frame of mind.

At home Savage found rumors of war everywhere. The Indians seemed quiet, but were no longer trading. Anxious to discuss matters, he called various Indians to a council in front of his Fresno River post. He told them he knew they were upset with the influx of the white men, but that war was out of the question. "It is no use trying to fight the Americans," he counseled, "they are as numerous as the wasps and ants. If war is made, every Indian engaged in the war will be killed before the whites will be satisfied."

Savage then asked Jose Juarez to tell his brothers of the vast multitudes of white men in the cities who would come to destroy them if fighting erupted. Rising to his feet, the Chauchila chief agreed with much of what Savage had said. Although the white man was many, the Indian continued, he was of many different tribes that would not come to help the miners in the hills. Savage watched helplessly as the chief harangued and incited his brothers to war. Furious and worried, Savage dismissed the council and headed for his Mariposa store.

At Agua Fria, Savage found Indian Agent Johnston, who had also heard the rumors of trouble. The trader brought Johnston up to date on events, then tried to alert the local miners. When no one would believe him, Savage sought to warn the miners at Horseshoe Bend in the Merced Canyon, but again his warnings fell on deaf ears.

At another scheduled meeting with the Indians, no one showed up, and Savage began to worry in earnest. On the evening of December 17, 1850, he noticed that even his own Indians had disappeared from camp. Gathering some men together, the trader set out to try to at least keep his own natives from joining the hostiles. He caught up with the fleeing Indians late that night and engaged in a shouting match across a small canyon. To his horror, Savage now learned that his Fresno River store had been raided and his clerks killed. Although shaken by the news, Savage still pleaded with his Indians to come back with him and forget the war. They replied that digging for gold was too hard a way to make a living and they were determined to drive the white man from their lands. Wearily, the trader headed back toward Agua Fria.

Earlier, at the Fresno River trading post, there had been a noticeable surliness among the local Indians. Four of Savage's clerks and hired hands were at the store — Greely, James Kennedy, John Stiffner, and Anthony "Long-haired" Brown. While the others saw nothing unusual and went about their work, Brown was wary of the Indians' behavior. There was not much business that day and all of the men worked outdoors, except for Brown, who remained in the store.

Savage's post was a crude affair. It consisted of poles erected vertically in the ground with canvas stretched over the top to serve as a roof.

Agua Fria was the first county seat of Mariposa County and was the seat of operations for the Indian commissioners during the Indian wars. *Author's collection.*

Outside, corrals housed work oxen along with horses and mules, while a herd of beef cattle were tended nearby. A few stools, a plank counter, and a profusion of shelves and packing crates filled with trading goods filled the interior of the store. A safe stood in one corner, while barrels and boxes took up much of the floor space. The men lived in several nearby tents.

James Kennedy had recently lost his mule, and when an Indian reported seeing it in a nearby canyon, the white man left to look for it. He was no sooner out of sight than he was hit by a flight of arrows. As he dropped to the ground, a crowd of Indians quickly clubbed and stoned him to death.

Stiffner and Greely heard Kennedy's death cry and were caught in another shower of arrows as they scrambled for the safety of the store. On hearing the whoops of the attacking natives, Brown practically slammed the door in the men's faces, but quickly admitted them at the sound of their cries and pounding. The two men tumbled into the room amidst another flight of arrows, both of them looking like pincushions. As Brown closed the door, his arm was broken by a club-wielding Indian outside. Somehow he managed to bar the door as the Indians circled the place in a screaming mass.

Inside, there was just time for one terrified glance at his dying friends before Brown caught sight of the burning canvas roof. He had no sooner sloshed it out when it was again ignited and again he doused it with a bucket of water. As his arm began to pain him greatly, the terrified Brown tried desperately to think clearly.

There are various accounts of Brown's actions at this time, including the deposition he later gave to Adam Johnston. A correspondent of the San Francisco *Daily Pacific New*s gave what was purported to be a detailed account of Brown's adventure in the January 26, 1851, issue. After barring the door and fighting off several attempts to fire the roof, Brown devised a desperate plan of escape. His scheme reads like a paragraph from a Street and Smith dime novel:

> Brown now stripped off his clothing, tied his trousers around his neck, belted on his six shooter, and through a crack in the door called to a chief. When he came near, Brown opened the door, seized the chief with one hand and held the pistol to his head with the other, and pushed his way through the amazed Indians til he was half way across the Fresno. Releasing the chief and backing the rest of the way over, he took to his heels, the Indians meanwhile being more intent on robbing the store than in knocking him in the head. He ran toward the Mariposa camp, but soon found that five Indians were in pursuit. Several of these he shot, and then continued on his thirty-five mile run to safety.

A party of men headed by Savage and Adam Johnston arrived at the Fresno store at dawn, December 21, 1850. Kennedy was found where he had fallen. Wild animals had reduced the body to almost a skeleton. Stiffner and Greely were sprawled near the store, both shot full of arrows and stoned to death. After burying the dead, Savage led his men back toward Agua Fria and Mariposa where Johnston immediately dispatched a report of the situation to the governor. There would be no difficulty now convincing the miners that an Indian war was at hand.

Back in town, Savage and Johnston quickly formed a company of volunteers. Rumors were flying everywhere, and friendly Indians insisted that the hostiles were gathering to attack the settlements at Mariposa and Agua Fria. Several other miners were reported killed and a man named Owen was reported to have narrowly escaped death in an ambush.

On January 7, James Burney, sheriff of Mariposa County, was elected captain of the volunteer group. One J. W. Riley was elected first lieutenant, and an Austrian with some prior military experience, Skeane S. Skeens, was elected second lieutenant. Savage was appointed guide for the expedition.

Leaving Agua Fria, the volunteers soon struck the trail of a large herd of horses that the Indians had stolen from rancher William J. Howard. The volunteers were joined at this point by Howard and several of his men, and the command pushed on after the Indians. Early on the morning of January 11, Savage located the hostile camp on top of a mountain. From close observation, it was determined that the camp contained a mixture of several tribes, including the fierce Chauchilas. Burney posted sentries and planned an attack on the Indian village at dawn.

At first light, the volunteers scaled the slopes of the Indian retreat.

When they were spotted by a native sentinel, Burney gave the order to charge and led his men whooping into the rancheria. The official report of the action noted that about four hundred Indians were engaged in the fight which lasted about three and a half hours. Some twenty-six natives were reported killed in the village and many others in the brush and surrounding forest. After burning the rancheria and its food supply, the volunteers moved back down the mountain with their wounded as the natives fired at them from surrounding ridges.

Burney and his men traveled about four miles down the mountain slopes, finally reaching a level area at the present site of Ahwahnee. Here, the six wounded men were taken from their litters and cared for. Lieutenant Skeens soon died from his wounds. Burney's report says nothing of the manner of his lieutenant's death, but Howard, who was present, states that in the excitement of the battle, the inexperienced troops shot several of their own men. Skeens, a bachelor, was buried next to a hastily thrown up rock and log fort. The other wounded were left with a force strong

■ Mariposa Sheriff James Burney, leader of the volunteer Indian fighters. *Courtesy Pelk Richards.*

enough to protect them, while Burney, Savage, and the balance of the volunteers headed for Agua Fria for supplies and reinforcements.

In the mining camps, rumors were rampant. The *Stockton Times* reported on January 11 that some 150 Indians had attacked ten whites at Alsbury's ferry on the upper San Joaquin River, killing one and wounding three. Another newspaper reported that the Four Creeks Indians had camped 120 miles from Mariposa, stealing all the animals they could get their hands on and killing three Americans and two Mexicans.

In a report to the governor dated January 13, Burney repeated a highly exaggerated rumor that "72 men were killed on Rattlesnake Creek." Actually, no one had any accurate knowledge of the extent of the war, but the slaughter at Savage's post and Skeens' death gave credibility to the wildest of reports.

Burney's report to the governor was a recital of recent events, but it was also an appeal for what he intended as his next course of action. Primarily, he was concerned with being officially commissioned to form a militia unit that would be paid and equipped by the government.

The governor acted faster than Burney could have hoped. In a letter dated January 13, Governor McDougal authorized the forming of a troop of one hundred volunteers to punish the Indians. The men were to be organized into not more than four companies; they were to supply their own mounts and elect their own officers. With the wheels of war now turning, the governor set out to convince the legislature of the need for action.

When Peter Burnett, California's first governor, resigned from office early in January of 1851, Lieutenant Governor John McDougal found himself thrust into both the governor's chair and the midst of an Indian war. Adam Johnston's letter of the 2nd convinced McDougal of the seriousness of the situation, and when General Persifer F. Smith, commander of federal troops on the coast, refused aid because of a supposed lack of authority, the new governor acted at once. In an address to the legislature, McDougal presented the letters from Johnston and Burney, plus other pe-

■ Lt. Skeens was first buried beneath the tree in this Ahwahnee meadow, near present day Oakhurst.
Author's collection.

titions from Mariposa. He convinced the lawmakers that the federal government would eventually pick up the tab anyway, and by January 24 he was able to inform the embattled miners that they had been authorized to raise an additional one hundred men.

Meanwhile, Savage and Burney gathered more volunteers and prepared to relieve their comrades in the mountains. These men, far from

huddling in their makeshift fort, had kept close tabs on the Indians and had even recaptured some stolen horses. Captain John Boling, commanding about a hundred men with Savage as scout, headed into the mountains while Burney headed south with another party to reconnoiter the Four Creeks country.

About January 18, Boling and Savage rejoined the men in the mountains and were shown another Indian village. This camp reportedly contained Chauchilas, Gawias, Yosemites, and members of three or four other tribes, nearly five hundred in number. The volunteers mounted another early morning assault and managed to kill some twenty warriors. Jose Rey, an important chief, was mortally wounded. With the hostiles scattered and discouraged, the volunteers headed for home.

After returning to Agua Fria with Boling and his men, Savage headed south to warn the outlying mining camps and do some recruiting. He rode into Cassity's Bar late in January and informed Wiley Cassity of the massacre on the Fresno and the subsequent battles near Ahwahnee. Cassity probably suspected Savage of trying to scare him out of his competitive, and lucrative, trading post business. In any case, Cassity had already built some minimal fortifications at his down-river ferry, consisting of earthworks surrounding about one acre. Cassity did not believe there was going to be any serious trouble, but he invited Savage to accompany him down to his ferry and trading post where he could warn the others.

■ Mariposa rancher William J. Howard was out chasing Indian horse thieves when he joined Burney's volunteers. *California State Library.*

The two men arrived at Cassity's Crossing the next day and at that time first learned of the Woods party massacre in the Four Creeks country. Savage was even more alarmed at this evidence of Indian complicity. Frank Boden, the only survivor of the Woods massacre, was pale and still in great pain from his amputated arm, but seemed to be recovering nicely. Dr. Lewis Leach, who had been caring for Boden, related further particulars of the Woods tragedy, but Cassity still insisted there would be no serious trouble.

That night Cassity refused to take his turn at guard. He was so unconcerned about the safety of his property that no one else took a turn either. Savage slept in a wagon, evidently unaware that no one was on watch.

In the morning Indian "signs" were everywhere. An arrow was stuck in the roof of a tent, and many of the animals within the corral had been wounded. Scouting about the premises, the men found Indian footprints in abundance, some within the fort itself.

Savage was more convinced than ever that a general war with the Indians was at hand, and he left for Agua Fria that morning. Dr. Leach went with him, determined to join any Indian fighting group that was to be formed. At Agua Fria, they found volunteers assembling at Whittier's Hotel, and they quickly signed themselves up. Savage was being talked about as commander of the force; Leach was content to enlist as a private. About February 3, Burney and his men returned from the Four Creeks area, where they had buried the bodies of Woods and his men.

Although Burney had seemed to be the most logical choice to command the volunteers, indications are that he willingly stepped aside in favor of Savage. As sheriff of the largest county in the world at that time, Burney could certainly claim that he was too busy to assume any additional duties. Mariposa County, one of the original California counties established in February of 1850, comprised nearly one-fifth of the state, extending nearly to Los Angeles. Also, the supervisors' minutes of the time indicate that Burney's job was quite lucrative. He probably had no intention of chasing Indians for a paltry sum when he could chase lawbreakers at a better rate.

Savage's familiarity with the area and his knowledge of the Indians made him the logical choice to command any volunteer force. Although exaggerated, the following letter written by volunteer T. G. Palmer gives some indication of the aura of glamour that surrounded Savage:

> From his long acquaintance with the Indians, Mr. Savage had learned their ways so thoroughly that they cannot deceive him. He has been one of their great chiefs and speaks their language as well as they can themselves. No dog can follow a trail like he can. No horse can endure as much. He sleeps but little, can go days without food and can run 100 miles in a

day and a night over the mountains, and then set and laugh for hours over a campfire as fresh and lively as if he had just been taking a little walk for exercise. He pointed out their fires, could hear them sing and could smell them, but his eyes were the only ones that could see, his ears alone could hear and his nose smell anything unusual.

The Mariposa Battalion was mustered into official service at noon, February 12, 1851. Robert Eccleston, a member of the group, recorded that James Savage was elected major without one dissenting voice. Officers were then selected with John Kuykendall elected captain of A Company, John Boling elected captain of B Company, and William Dill captain of C Company. Lieutenants and noncommissioned officers were then voted on, and the command adjourned to Dutch Frank's saloon for refreshments. "Dutch Frank," Francis Laumiester, who had donated some supplies to the group, was elected quartermaster. Camp was set up in a meadow near Agua Fria, and the officers began planning their campaign.

John G. Marvin had been born in northern Pennsylvania in 1815. He was a brilliant student and obtained a good, liberal arts education. At an early age, he became principal of an academy and later was able to tour Europe. He graduated from Harvard Law School in 1844 and after editing some distinguished literary work, published a prestigious legal bibliography in 1847. A bachelor by temperament, Marvin had longed for some sort of legal appointment in one of the western territories. When gold was discovered in California, it seemed like the answer to his prayers and he arrived in San Francisco aboard the *Europe* in early February 1850.

After practicing law for a brief time in the Bay city, Marvin headed for the frontier country of the San Joaquin Valley. He promoted a town on the Tuolumne River, as well as establishing a ranch and ferry. Later he became a justice of the peace in Sonora where he established that town's first newspaper in July of 1850. Late that year, Marvin was elected the new state's first superintendent of public instruction. Clearly, Marvin was a young man going places.

Having known James Kennedy, who had been killed at Savage's post, Marvin now took a strong stand within the government for the punishment of the Indians in Mariposa County. When Governor McDougal sent an emissary to Mariposa with authorization to form a battalion, the new superintendent heard the siren call to adventure and went along.

Marvin stopped over in Stockton, where he expected to recruit a force of men for the war. While in town, he heard that an aide to the governor named J. Neely Johnson had just arrived with the three United States Indian commissioners who had long been expected from the east. Commissioners Redick McKee of Virginia, George W. Barbour of Kentucky, and Oliver M. Wozencraft of Louisiana, had arrived with a $25,000 appropriation with which to make treaties with the various native tribes. They had reported to Governor John McDougal, who instructed them to go directly to Agua Fria, suspend operations of the volunteers and see if further bloodshed could be averted. The commissioners and Johnson hastened to leave for Agua Fria. Marvin was in-

■ Robert Eccleston, who served in Captain Dill's C Company, kept a diary of the campaign. *Author's collection.*

vited to join the group and together they headed for the mines. Captain Erasmus D. Keyes was in charge of a two hundred-man U.S. Army escort, and the troops, along with their wagon train and herd of beef cattle, made up a formidable party.

The expedition arrived at Agua Fria on the evening of February 13. They found the volunteers busily stockpiling supplies, pressing animals into service, and drilling. Now, suddenly, war preparations were coming to a screeching halt.

Captain Keyes was traveling under secret orders instructing him to obey the orders of the commissioners so long as there was hope for a peaceful settlement of the troubles. In the event of a breakdown in negotiations, however, Keyes was to assume control and make war. It was good duty for the soldiers, the officers at least, and Keyes was later to write, "Our wagons carried an abundant supply of wines, hams, buffalo tongues and condiments, and a herd of fat steers supplied us with plenty of fresh beef. Our hunters brought in venison, antelope and birds, and everything conspired with youth and health to make me happier than I have ever felt in the haunts of fashion and envy."

On February 15, J. Neely Johnson addressed the volunteers. He made it clear they were only to make war against Indians who could not otherwise be dealt with and that they were now under the orders of the commissioners.

"While I do not hesitate to denounce the Indians for the murders and robberies committed by them," stated Johnson, "we should not forget that there may perhaps be circumstances which...might, to some extent, excuse their hostility to the whites." Johnson was choosing his words carefully now, for he was talking to bitter men who had lost friends and property. "They probably feel," he continued, "that they themselves are the aggrieved party, looking upon us as trespassers upon their territory, invaders of their country."

Johnson closed by noting that he hoped "in the performance of your duties, you will in all cases observe mercy where severity is not justly demanded." The governor's aide was given a polite round of applause, but that's all it was. Only blood could pay for the death and destruction that had been wrought by the Indians.

Marvin, as an elected official of the state, was introduced to Major Savage and the other officers of the battalion. Quickly noting the complexities of supplying the volunteers, Johnson must have looked down his nose at

■ Redick McKee, one of the Indian Commissioners, quickly discovered that good intentions and poor funding were a bad combination. *Carnegie Library, Pittsburgh.*

"Dutch Frank," the saloon-keeper who had been selected quartermaster of the troops. He made a field appointment, and Marvin found himself the new quartermaster with Dutch Frank demoted to his assistant. The new officer quickly set out to arm and equip his men as best he could.

The commissioners immediately began treaty negotiations as Savage brought the various native bands into camp. Through promises, threats and presents, Savage assembled group after group, acting as interpreter and otherwise making himself useful. Adam Johnston, who had worked with Savage to recruit the company of Mariposa volunteers, did what he could also, but must have felt pushed into the background by the new-comers.

Early in March, word was received from Fine Gold Gulch that a dead man had been seen in the road alongside a deserted train of wagons. When further dispatches indicated Cassity and his men had been driven from their claims, Captain Kuykendall and part of A Company were detailed to investigate. Lewis Leach was part of the thirty-man group that marched south towards the San Joaquin River. The young doctor must have been concerned about the friends he had left working for Cassity at the crossing.

A dispatch rider soon brought word that four teamsters had been killed at Fine Gold Gulch. And Cassity was dead. Savage wrote to a friend:

> His tongue was cut out, laid on his side, and an arrow shot through it into his heart—his right leg was cut off and taken away. There were two arrows in his person. It would appear from the signs that they came in personal collision with him before they succeeded in killing him....

Many of the volunteers with Kuykendall had not been able to secure mounts yet, and some of his men were still afoot. When some mustangs and cattle were captured near Cassity's, the walking troops were elated and began selecting their new mounts.

Part of the troops were sailors who had jumped ship and headed for the gold country. Most of them did not know a horse from a whale boat. When the men tried to mount up, the untamed animals began rearing, bucking, and plunging off in every direction. In a moment, surprised sailors were scattered all over the ground while their erstwhile steeds galloped off towards the plains and freedom.

From Cassity's, Kuykendall was ordered to the headwaters of the San Joaquin to bring in Tomquit and his band of Dumnas, Pitkachis and others. He and his men encountered the natives in the mountains, where there was a fight and thirteen Indians were reported killed, with some wounded. Soon after, old Tomquit brought his band in.

Early in May, Captain Kuykendall apparently objected to the way local Indians were being treated and he was ordered to be court-martialed for insubordination. The trial was held in June, but the former captain had already left the scene, along with some of his men.

By March 19, the commissioners had completed treaties with six of the local Indian tribes, but the Yosemites had failed to come in. The troublesome Yosemites were reportedly in their rancheria, deep in the recesses of

■ An early view of an Indian village in Mariposa County, photographed by Carleton Watkins in 1859. *The Bancroft Library.*

a great, hidden valley. That same day, Major Savage, in command of companies B and C, was ordered to bring in Chief Tenaya and his people, as well as a group of recalcitrant Nutunutus. The Indians considered themselves safe in their hidden valley, behind the winter barrier of deep snow and mountains, but Savage and his men confidently headed east towards the headwaters of the Merced.

After a hard march through bitter cold rain and hail, Savage and his men set up camp on the south fork of the Merced on March 24. The men were weary, but after their recent inactivity were anxious for a scrap with the Indians.

■ Captain Erasmus D. Keyes.
National Archives.

By daylight of the following morning, the volunteers headed downstream towards the camp of the Nutunutus. Sighting the village, the men formed a skirmish line and advanced across open ground upon the Indians. Taken completely by surprise, the natives surrendered and their chief, Ponwatchee, came forward to talk with Savage. The chief was told that he would have to take his people to the valley to live and that they must sign a treaty with the white commissioners. The chief agreed, and knowing the soldiers would destroy the village in any case, set fire to the place himself to show good faith. If they were allowed to keep any captured women, the chief even offered to help fight the Yosemites.

Moving the Nutunutus across the river to a nearby plateau, the battalion now set up a new base camp. Savage had meanwhile sent an Indian messenger ahead to inform the Yosemites of his intentions to either fight them or bring them in to the valley. Surprisingly, the next day old Chief Tenaya walked into camp.

The Yosemite chief was sullen and uncooperative. He did not want to take his people to the valley and he wanted nothing from the "Great Father" in Washington. "Our women are able to do our work," he grumbled. "Go...let us remain in the mountains where we were born; where the ashes of our fathers have been given to the winds."

Savage told the old chief in no uncertain words that he must either bring all his people down to the valley, or they would be killed. Reluctantly, Tenaya finally agreed to bring in his tribe, then left and returned to his hidden valley.

When several days passed and the Yosemites still had not made an appearance, Savage prepared to go after them. Asking for volunteers, the whole command responded, so foot races were held to determine who should go. With Indian guides and Savage in the lead, fifty-seven volunteers headed into the rugged mountains toward the Yosemite stronghold.

As they struggled through the deep snow, the volunteers suddenly came upon a group of some seventy Yosemites. The Indians said they were coming in, but had been held up by the weather. Savage, however, did not believe this was the whole tribe and after detailing several men to stay with the Indians, again resumed his march. The date was March 27, 1851.

Climbing over the crest of a rocky mountain, the volunteers suddenly came upon a wide, deep valley rimmed with gigantic walls of vertical granite. At last, the mysterious Indian stronghold had been discovered.

"The rancheria of the Yosemites," wrote Judge Marvin in the first newspaper account of the discovery, "is described as being in a valley of surpassing beauty, about 10 miles in length and one mile broad. Upon each side are high, perpendicular rocks, and at each end through which the Middle Fork runs, deep canyons, the only accessible entrances to the valley...." Yosemite Valley, one of the great wonders of the world, had been officially discovered, although trappers may have viewed it earlier.

Descending into the great valley, Savage and his men came upon the Yosemite village, but found it empty. They destroyed the village and acorn stores and searched the area thoroughly for Indians. An ancient man and  woman, the parents of Tenaya, were discovered in a cave at the base of a cliff, where they had been left behind to die of exposure and starvation. Tenaya later told Savage that they were too old to take care of themselves any more and he had thrown them away. Savage had several men deposit a load of firewood in the cave, along with a supply of acorns.

That night, around a campfire beneath a towering waterfall, the volunteers discussed naming this wonderful valley. However, most members of the command paid little attention to the beautiful setting. They were too cold and hun-

Andrew D. Firebaugh served in Captain Boling's B Company in the Mariposa Battalion. *Bess Anderson.*

gry — too frustrated at not finding any Indians to fight. Young Lafayette Bunnell, a private in B Company, was deeply impressed with the unmatched beauty that surrounded him. Bunnell suggested they name the valley after the Indians who lived there, and a vote made it unanimous. It was a lovely name, a name that would quickly take the place of the ancient Indian name for the location — Ahwahnee, meaning deep, grassy valley.

On March 29, Savage and his men were back at the base camp preparing to leave. Forage for the animals had been as scarce as the rapidly diminishing rations for the men, and the troops were quite anxious to return to Agua Fria. Soon the long column of whites and Indians were winding down through the snow and trees towards the foothills and home.

The Indian captives, because of the large number of old people and children, traveled very slowly. A member of Boling's command, Edward W. Haughton, described the trek some years afterwards:

We brought out about 300 of them [Indians], of these at least half were women and children. All of us had a pretty rough time on this trip, but unavoidably the poor Indians suffered the most. They were, towards the last, actually starving, although all the able bodied squaws were heavily laden with acorns, and as a last resource they ate up every one of their dogs. An Indian village invariably swarms with these animals.

It was often pitiful to see the suffering of the papoose. Little children as naked as when born would crowd about our campfires and fight like dogs over scraps of bacon and bread thrown to them.

Pokotucket was said to be the Indian who led Boling's company into Yosemite, although a native named "Bob" is usually credited as the guide. Pokotucket may have been "Bob's" Indian name, however.
Society of California Pioneers.

With food supplies nearly depleted, it was decided to leave Captain Boling and eighteen men to escort the Indians, while the rest of the command made a forced march for home. Haughton reported:

> Things at last became desperate, and we concluded to leave all our little store of food with a few good men who were to keep and guard the Indians if possible, while the rest of us made a bee-line, and as good time as our starving horses would permit, for headquarters on the Fresno River, which we reached in a perfectly ravenous condition after a two days fast. In a few days we were not surprised to hear that the Indians had all broken back for the mountains the same night we left.

After all the hardships of the campaign, there had been no Indian fights and now not even any prisoners. Except for Lafayette Bunnell, no one had even paid much attention to the discovery of Yosemite.

For the next few weeks, the volunteers rested from the rigors of the first Yosemite campaign. Captain Boling was embarrassed to have to report the escape of his prisoners, but a friendly tribe had gone after the runaways and brought most of them in. Tenaya and some followers had not come back, however, and had returned to their hidden valley. The commissioners had fed and clothed the returning Yosemite Indians, but had refused to treat with them until the Chauchilas also arrived. When the Chauchilas repeatedly ignored messages demanding that they come in, the volunteers again readied themselves for the field.

On April 11, Savage issued his orders for 170 men selected from all three companies to prepare to seek out the Chauchilas. Moving again into the mountains, scouting parties scoured the area for signs of the Chauchilas, and although Indians were frequently seen watching them, no contact was made. Finally on April 25, the Chauchila village was sighted and the men prepared for a fight.

The rancheria was located on top of a hill, but by the time the battalion had crossed the river and climbed to the village site, the rancheria was deserted. Another camp was located nearby, and soon both villages were in flames, along with a quantity of stored acorns. At the second village a funeral pyre disclosed a collection of bones which were determined by the Indian guides to be those of Jose Rey, the Chauchila chief fatally wounded in the battle on February 18. His death was confirmed in letters of the commissioners which stated that the reason the Chauchilas had not come in was that a chief had been wounded and they were waiting for him to die.

About this time, Savage was ordered to the San Joaquin River to aid the commissioners. Leaving Boling in charge, Savage arrived at the com-

■ This 1866 Carleton Watkins' view shows Yosemite Valley much as it appeared to the volunteers. The breathtaking beauty was lost on the tired and hungry men of Boling's company. Only Lafayette Bunnell appreciated the wonderful discovery. *Yosemite Museum.*

missioners' camp about April 21, accompanied by an Indian retinue of some fifteen warriors. Riding down out of the low hills, he saw the camp from across the river and was probably struck by the contrast between the orderly tents of the soldiers and the scattered Indian camps. All were clustered among the oak trees which dotted the area.

The commissioners and their military escort had arrived and set up camp on April 14. After concluding a series of treaties at Camp Fremont on Mariposa Creek, they had traveled south to the San Joaquin where they named their selected meeting place Camp Barbour. Messengers had preceded them, and they were met by delegations of Indians representing the Chukchansi, Nutunutus, Chauchilas, Pitkachis and many other bands from the surrounding mountains.

A few weeks previously, Savage had called an Indian council to announce the imminent arrival of the commissioners. Taking along a four-man army escort, the trader had visited the ancient Dumna village on the banks of the San Joaquin River. After greeting Tomquit, the chief, Savage told him that representatives of the "Great White Father" would soon arrive to treat with the Indians. When told that he must send runners to all the other valley tribes to have them come to meet the commissioners, old Tomquit demurred. It was a long way to visit all the tribes and with summer coming on, it was just too hot to travel.

Savage did not intend to argue the matter: "I'm a big medicine man for the big father in Washington, You have to do as I say. I can hurt you and make all your people die. I can make all the fish leave the river and the antelope and the elk go away."

He told the Indians that he could kill them, but that they could not kill him. Attaching a white handkerchief to an oak tree, the trader cocked his pistol and fired six shots into the improvised target. Reloading as the natives watched, Savage palmed the lead bullets instead of stuffing them into the cylinder. The Indians supposed the pistol had been reloaded. The cap and ball pistol would fire, but was now firing blanks.

Handing the weapon to the nearest Indian, Savage told him to shoot him. The Indians were aghast at the request, and it was some time before the trader could get an Indian to do as he asked. Finally a native took the pistol, aimed it directly at Savage and fired six times. At each shot Savage lunged and appeared to be snatching the bullets in midair. After the last shot, he walked over to Tomquit and the shooter and showed them the six bullets in his hand.

The Indians were astounded. There was no more arguing about sending runners to bring in the other tribes.

Once again, Savage was kept busy explaining the benefits of the proposed treaties to the 1,200 assembled Indians. They were to give up all title to their lands and settle on a piece of land designated by the treaty. The Great Father in Washington was to take care of the Indians now—feed, clothe, and help them adapt to the white man's ways.

By April 29, everything was in order. After several speeches, all the Indian chiefs and head men were ready to sign. The peace pipe was passed around and the natives all affixed their marks to the treaty, technically bringing an end to the Mariposa war.

Still, Savage was troubled. He had yet to reckon with the Yosemites and he blamed them for much of the loss he had suffered at the outset of the trouble. When Boling and a portion of B Company rode into camp, he

■ Dr. Lafayette Bunnell. *Author's collection.*

made plans to return with them to battalion headquarters on the Fresno. Before leaving, however, he sought and obtained permission to proceed against the Yosemites in the high Sierra. Now he would settle with old Tenaya.

Back at camp, Savage called Adjutant Martin Lewis to his tent and dictated several written orders pertaining to the coming campaign in the mountains. The trader could neither read nor write, but in a time when much of the population was illiterate, no one thought less of him for it. A man was judged by his abilities and his word. Besides, a rich man could always employ someone to write his letters and read to him.

Savage's battle plan was to send Captain Boling and B Company into Yosemite Valley to either attack the Indians or bring them out to treat with the commissioners. Savage was to lead the balance of the command and cut the Yosemites off from any escape routes. A small token force would be left behind to guard the camp.

■ An Indian strikes a pose for photographer J. J. Reilly in Yosemite in the early 1870s. The natives had lost their secret hideaway forever.
Society of California Pioneers.

Several Indian men and women accompanied the command as guides when it rode out of camp on the afternoon of May 4. The weather was cloudy and cold, and although the men under Savage saw many Indians, they could never get close enough to engage them. After some hard traveling, during which provisions ran out, Major Savage led his men back to the Fresno, where they arrived on May 17. Robert Eccleston, of Dill's command, noted in his diary that on this day "We heard that Capt. Bolen [sic] had captured Yohemite, [sic] Chief, and five other Indians and that two of them in trying to make their escape were shot down by the guard."

Boling and his men had reached the great valley on the 9th and sent out scouts to locate the Indian rancheria. The volunteers must have looked about in wonder now as they saw Yosemite Valley in all the glories of early summer—deep grassy meadows crisscrossed by a river and creeks with magnificent waterfalls cascading down massive, towering, granite walls.

The following day, five Indians were captured as the men headed up the valley. One of the captives proved to be a son of Tenaya, who offered to bring in his father and the tribe if they would turn him and a companion loose. Boling fed the two youths and, after telling them that the tribe must come down to the valley and treat with the commissioners, turned them loose with a message for Tenaya. The other three natives were kept in custody. In a report dated May 15, Boling wrote:

■ Edward W. Haughton, a private in Boling's company.
Jeff Edwards Collection.

> We watched the others close, intending to hold them as hostages until the dispatch bearers returned. They appeared well satisfied and we were not suspicious of them, in consequence of which one of them escaped. We commenced searching for him, which alarmed the other two still in custody, and they attempted to make their escape. The boys took after them and finding they could not catch them, fired and killed them both. This circumstance, connected with the fact of the two whom we had sent out not returning, satisfied me that they had no intention of coming in.

Lafayette Bunnell gave a different version of the hostages' death which was corroborated by another of Boling's men, Edward Haughton:

> Some of the boys cornered five Indians among a lot of big boulders on the day of our arrival in the valley. Three of these escaped the next morning by outwitting the guard who had released them from their bonds in order to see their skill in shooting arrows at pine cones. Their proficiency in this was quite astonishing; they seldom missed the mark. At each shot they cunningly increased the distance and finally forgot to return (from retrieving their arrows).
>
> The fourth man was shot while trying to escape. He had been tied with his hands behind him to a sapling, and one of the crowd, a mere boy in years, noticed him trying to untie himself. Without saying a word to anyone, he sauntered carelessly to a tree against which some guns were leaning, and quietly awaited results. When at last the Indian had released himself, he of course, made a break for freedom, but before he had run forty yards a bullet between the shoulders stayed his course forever. The force of his speed was so great, I remember distinctly, that his face plowed quite a deep rut several feet long in the sand where he fell. This deliberate

murder, for it was nothing else, was as unnecessary as it was unexpected, and injured our cause with the Indians irreparably, the more so as he proved to be a chief's son. The fifth and last (Indian) our captain sent out to tell his countrymen that we were friends and had come with peaceful intent, but in view of the fact that we had destroyed their winter's store of food, burned their village and shot down one of their chief men it cannot create surprise that the Indians refused to accept the olive branch of peace presented under such suspicious circumstances. .

The Indian had undoubtedly been murdered by Joel Brooks, a corporal in Boling's company and a worthless character who killed Indians at every opportunity. While guiding Gwinn H. Heap across the San Joaquin Valley in 1853, Brooks boasted that he "had killed more Indians than any other man in California, not only in open fights, but also, and most frequently, after they were captured and made prisoners." Unfortunately, it was no idle boast.

The dead Indian was dragged aside and covered with brush, since no tools were available for burial. In the evening, Haughton was detailed for sentry duty and found himself thinking about how good an Indian scalp would look tied to his shot pouch. He sharpened his knife and late that night strolled to where the dead Indian had been left:

> After passing and repassing that pile of brush under which the body lay a number of times, I finally succeeded in getting up a sufficient resolution to pull off the brush covering, but the horrible glaring look of the dead man's face distorted and disfigured by the agonies of death, gave me, as the women say, 'a turn.' I did manage, however, to catch his hand in order to pull him in to a more convenient position, but the icy touch of that dead flesh and the knowledge that I was about to commit an abominable desecration of the dead man, was more than I could endure. I dropped the hand as if it had been a red hot iron, and left the spot in a hurry...and was very glad when my relief came along and gave me a chance to leave the hateful place.

The next day when no Indians made an appearance, Boling and his men started up the valley again, seeking the Yosemites. The rancheria was discovered in a small valley with signs indicating the inhabitants had left only moments before. Pursuing the Indians up a rocky cliff, the volunteers were suddenly assaulted by a shower of large rocks and boulders from above. Climbing and firing alternately, the men were able to scramble to the top and kill one Indian and wound several others. Here, among the other warriors, Tenaya was captured.

Boling and his men stayed in the valley for over a week, sending out scouting parties to try to locate the Indians. Finally, on May 22, the Yosemites were discovered camped on the shores of a lake on the eastern side of the valley. Caught completely by surprise, the harried natives surrendered without a struggle. Herding their captives out of the valley, the volunteers arrived back at the Fresno River headquarters on the 29th.

"During the afternoon," Eccleston noted in his diary, "the remainder of the boys were arriving, and all got in before night…. Capt. Bolen [sic] was made a present of a young Indian boy about 5 years old who has lost his parents. He is handsome and smart…."

Just how many Yosemites had been captured is not clear, but they were placed on the Fresno River reservation created by the commissioners and the "war" was declared officially over. On July 1, 1851, the Mariposa Battalion was mustered out and the men went back to their mining pursuits. The Yosemite Indians were sullen and grumbling, but an uneasy peace had been secured in the Mariposa mountains, foothills, and plains.

To the north, however, beyond the headwaters of the Sacramento in the Klamath River and Modoc country, the terrible work of slaughter went on.

CHAPTER 7 / SOURCES

The standard authority for the Mariposa Indian war is the published diaries of Robert Eccleston, excellently edited and annotated by C. Gregory Crampton. L. H. Bunnell's book is important also, as is the work of the late Annie Mitchell of Visalia. The author was fortunate in locating the reminiscence by Edward Haughton which he had written for a friend. Jeff Edwards brought this item to my attention after it was published in the Porterville *Farm Tribune* in 1970. Haughton's account is garbled, but quite interesting.

UNPUBLISHED MATERIAL

U.S. Congress, Senate, 31 Congress, 2nd Session, Doc. 1:

Report of the Secretary of the Interior, 1851.

U.S. Congress, 33rd Congress, Special Session, Doc. 4:

Journal and reports of the three Indian Commissioners in California, 1851.

National Archives, Records of the Office of Indian Affairs, California Superintendency, Record Group 75, M234:

Adam Johnston to Orlando Browne, January 31, March 1, 7, July 6, September 6, 1850.

National Archives, Records of the Office of Indian Affairs, California Superintendency, Record Group 75, Special Files, M574:

These files contain a great many "detailed explanations" of the claim vouchers submitted by Adam Johnston during his tenure as Indian agent.

Leonard, Charles Berdan. "The Federal Indian Policy in the San Joaquin Valley, Its Application and Results," unpublished Ph.D. thesis, University of California, Berkeley, 1928.

John G. Marvin Scrapbook, McHenry Museum, Modesto, California.

Journals of the House and Senate of California, various sessions, Sacramento, 1851-1852.

Ross, Charles L. Statement, Bancroft Library, University of California, Berkeley.

Wright, George W. "History, Life and Indian Affairs of the San Joaquin Valley in the early 50's in Depositions of Actors Therein," bound manuscript in collections of the California Historical Society, San Francisco.

NEWSPAPERS

San Francisco *Daily Alta California*, January 3, 14, 15, 16, 21, 26, 29, February 7, 12, 14, March 8, 11, April 23, October 6, 1851.

San Francisco *Daily Pacific News*, January 26, 1851.

Sacramento *Daily Union*, March 19, 25, May 12, 1851.

The Farm Tribune, November 5, 1970.

The Fresno Bee, October 23, 1935, March 11, 12, 1970.

The Daily Herald, January 6, 22, 25, 28, February 14, 1851.

The Stockton Journal, December 28, 1850, January 18, 29, February 15, 1871.

The Stockton Times, January 1, 2, 3, 4, 11, February 19, March 5, 8, 12, 15, 1851.

PRINCIPAL PUBLISHED WORKS

Bingaman, John W. *The Ahwahneechees: A Story of the Yosemite Indians*. Lodi, California: End-Klan Publishing Company, 1966.

Bunnell, Lafayette H. *Discovery of Yosemite and the Indian War of 1851 which led to that Event*. Golden, Colorado: Outbooks, 1980.

Cossley-Batt, Jill L. *The Last of the California Rangers*. New York: Funk & Wagnalls Company, 1928.

Crampton, Gregory C., editor. *The Mariposa Indian War, 1850-1851, Diaries of Robert Eccleston*. Salt Lake City: University of Utah Press, 1957.

No author given. *History of Fresno County*. San Francisco: Elliot and Company, 1882.

Ferris, Daniel F. *Judge Marvin and the Founding of the California School System*. Berkeley: University of California Press, 1962.

Keyes, E. D. *Fifty Years Observation of Men and Events*. New York: Charles Scribner's Sons, 1884.

Latta, Frank F. *Handbook of Yokuts Indians*. Santa Cruz, CA: Bear State Books, 1978.

Mitchell, Annie R. *Jim Savage and the Tulareno Indians*. Los Angeles: Westernlore Press, 1959.

Phillips, George Harwood. *Indians and Indian Agents*. Norman, OK: University of Oklahoma Press, 1997.

Russell, Carl P. *One Hundred Years in Yosemite*. Yosemite: Yosemite Natural History Association, 1968.

Smith, Wallace. *Garden of the Sun*. Los Angeles: Lymanhouse, 1939.

Vandor, Paul E. *History of Fresno County*. Los Angeles: Historic Record Company, 1919.

Wood, Raymund F. *California's Aqua Fria*. Fresno: Academy Library Guild, 1954.

OTHER SOURCES

Winchell, L. A. "Ft. Washington: A History," *Fresno Past & Present*, Journal of the Fresno County Historical Society, September-December, 1971.

Chapter 8

MODOC

In the north, Indian troubles developed as the pioneers gradually became aware of this vast, near-pristine country. The early trapping parties of the 1820s and '30s, the exploring party of Dr. Josiah Gregg, and the 1850 voyage of the schooner *Laura Virginia* all contributed to a knowledge of, and gradual settlement of, the area. The discovery of Trinidad and Humboldt bays quickly brought shiploads of settlers and promoters, and soon the pounding of tent stakes gave way to incessant sawing and hammering as more permanent structures were built. Conscious of their exposed condition, the whites at first maintained good relations with the local natives. As more and more miners ranged the creeks and rivers looking for gold, however, the Indians became apprehensive.

The Yurok Indians of Trinidad Bay are described by an 1851 visitor as "the finest looking and most intelligent of all the Indians of California." There were many fine-looking inhabitants in these northern mountains and plains—from the Wailaki and Yuki of the Eel River country to the Shastas in the north and over to the Modocs in the rugged northeast corner of the state. To the east, across the wild Sacramento Valley, the Yana and Maidu ranged, while along the upper reaches of the Sacramento River the Achomawi lived in freedom and sanctity from all but the enemy Modoc.

The bloodshed had begun early—the first small fissures in the dam of isolation that had lasted as long as even the Great Spirit could remember. Two American trappers had killed a Shasta Indian in 1837, and later Fremont's command had been attacked by Klamaths in 1846 and three whites had been killed. In retaliation, Fremont assaulted a local Indian camp and killed some fourteen warriors, after which he fired the village and destroyed quantities of stored food. Later, an emigrant was reported killed. Word of these troubles spread from the redwood forests of the Eel River to the blighted lava beds of the far northeast. And the Indians, with their own feelings of pride and territorial rights, looked with more and more uneasiness at the chopping, digging white intruders who camped on the graves of their fathers.

In the late summer of 1849, Captain William H. Warner of the U.S. Topographical Engineers was leading a twelve-man group in search of overland routes and passes through the Sierra Nevada. On September 26, they were ambushed in a northern California pass, near the Nevada border—probably by a wide-ranging group of Paiutes. Warner and a guide were killed, while several others of the party were wounded. The captain was a popular young officer and earlier had helped survey and lay out the city of Sacramento. It was not until the following spring that Captain Lyon and his avenging troops from the Clear Lake campaign located the spot where Warner died, but no body or bones were ever found.

Visiting the Trinity River mines in May of 1850, Alexander Andres, a Frenchman, described the surliness and growing suspicion of the mountain tribes:

■ An Indian fishing on a northern stream. Mining often disrupted this Indian food supply and was just one more source of constant trouble. *Peter Palmquist.*

A group of Indians took advantage of the fact that there were only three men left at the camp to invade it. First, they approached timidly; soon, boldness arriving with reinforcements, a few crossed the barriers. Our sentries ordered them, through signs, to leave the camp area. At that, one of the Indians, a venerable old man, with a few white whiskers, straightened his head indignantly. He addressed us a few brisk words, and pointing at the mountains, the forests, the prairies, and the river around us he seemed to say: "All that is mine." At the same time, grabbing our belongings and blankets, he threw them aside disdainfully, as if to say "Get out, you are not the masters here." In the same moment, all the Indians, obeying the wise man, disappeared. A Roman senator could not have shown a more imposing majesty than this Indian, and, indeed, he was quite right when he said he was the master, but poor devil, despite his undeniable right to the land, he will nevertheless be chased away from it by the damned Americans who kill Indians with as little concern as though they were shooting deer or rabbits.

Andre's account is an early reference to what came to be the peculiar diversion of a certain class of California pioneers: killing Indians. When a miner was found dead on the trail, it was automatically blamed on Indians. When cattle were stolen, strayed or lost, it was blamed on the Indians. And when business was slow or life seemed too monotonous in a mining community, an Indian scare was a sure way to stimulate prices and get up a little excitement.

■ Ki-we-lat-tah, a Wiyot Indian of the Humboldt Bay region, painted from life in 1852 by Stephen Shaw. It depicts a Northern California native just as he appeared to the encroaching Gold Rushers. *Humboldt County Historical Society.*

On his trip into the mines, Andre and some French companions had discovered a dead man on the trail. They were convinced he had been killed by a suspicious Spaniard they had met earlier and upon returning to the coast were further convinced of the man's guilt:

The sheriff at LaTrinite, hearing of the murder of Mr. Malapere, had us come to his office when we arrived. There were no ships in the port, and none had come since our departure....

If the Spaniard...had been in La Trinite, he had...not been able to leave town. We went to see the sheriff, accompanied by a French-Canadian...who was the interpreter. We gave the sheriff a full account of our first meeting with the [Spaniard]; not quite sure he was guilty, we told the sheriff our suspicion without accusing him directly. The sheriff would have liked us to impute this crime to Indians. He wanted us to war on them, but needed a pretext, and we failed to serve his purpose. We could not accuse these unfortunate innocents; an arrow tears apart the flesh while a knife cuts into it; the Indians would have robbed the victim of all his clothes, while the culprit, saw in these clothes only a sure way to accuse himself.

On his return trip to the coast, Andre had seen a group of Indian huts burned for no good reason by some irresponsible miners. Such actions and trouble stirred up by men like the sheriff inevitably led to conflict, and by early June, the San Francisco *Alta* was reporting that Indians were numerous, and troublesome, at Trinidad.

To the north, in the beautiful Willamette Valley of the Oregon Territory, Jesse and Lindsay Applegate decided to open a new route through to the Northwest. Arriving in Oregon with the Whitman party of 1843, the Applegates were mindful of the difficult route they had followed overland and wanted to make the way easier for future emigrants. This would help to encourage further immigration and provide a more favorable route of retreat should the area become a British possession.

Their primary concern was the route from the Humboldt River, south of Fort Hall, to the Willamette Valley. Well-armed and provisioned, the Applegates led a fifteen-man party east from The Dalles, Oregon, on June 20, 1846.

The party was gone for over three months, but when they returned to their homes they had opened a new route to Oregon. On the trip, the men had several brushes with Indians, but managed to avoid serious trouble. Two of the party had left the main group at different times and were presumed dead when their personal effects later turned up in the hands of Indians. At two points along the route, they discovered the remains of burned wagons or graves of emigrants whose identity would forever remain unknown. Both the Nevada Paiutes and the Modocs of Oregon and the northern edge of California were hostile to the invasion of their lands and evidently intended to destroy the white people at every opportunity.

The burned wagons and graves, along with the constant sighting of large war

■ Ruts of the Applegate Trail still show up eighty years later. *Author's collection.*

parties, made this improved route a potentially bloody one. At Fort Hall, that summer of 1846, the Applegate party had talked a wagon train leader into following them into Oregon by their new route. Although avoiding the Indian dangers of the old Oregon Trail along the Snake River, the Applegate Trail exposed emigrants to the Paiutes, Modocs, and Rogue River natives—a Hobson's choice if ever there was one. Still, the new road was more practical in other ways and was soon being used extensively.

Late in September of 1850, a wounded man rode into the settlement of

■ Jacksonville, Oregon, during the Indian troubles of the 1850s. *Jackson County Historical Society.*

Jacksonville in southern Oregon. He told a story of a desperate wagon train besieged by hordes of Modocs east of Tule Lake on the California border. The whole wagon train of some ninety people had been wiped out, only the one man escaping by hiding in some adjacent tules. A hastily organized volunteer group was soon on the trail, but found only a scene of carnage and burnt wagons at the massacre site. Ghastly, mutilated corpses of men, women, and children covered the area and the volunteers sadly buried. Young Ivan Applegate searched vainly among the corpses for a sign of life, but there was none. Death hung like an invisible pall over the area.

The small force of volunteers decided against trying to locate and attack the Indians. It was clear that future emigrant trains would have to be escorted through what came to be called northern California's "dark and bloody ground." Soon, heavily armed patrols were escorting wagon trains

■ Shasta Butte City, later Yreka, as it appeared in the early 1850s.
Siskiyou County Museum.

over the Applegate Trail and wresting control of the region from the natives. It was a climate well suited for an adventurer such as Ben Wright.

Born to Quaker parents in a suburb of Philadelphia, Benjamin Wright had traveled overland to Oregon in 1847 and was about twenty-seven years old in the summer of 1851. He had fought Indians on numerous occasions, but had lived among them as well and usually had a native woman companion. He had roamed over much of northern California and southern Oregon and knew the land and its peoples. When there was a dispute or a conference with the Indians, Wright was usually called to interpret. He was equally the first to be called when there was fighting to be done.

At this particular time, Wright was living at Cottonwood, a small mining camp some twenty miles north of Shasta Butte City, later renamed Yreka. Besides the continuous troubles on the Applegate Road, the Modocs had taken to horse stealing raids closer and closer to the settlements. It was common knowledge, also, that a band of white horse thieves in the area did all they could to lay their rascality at the feet of the Indians.

When some forty-six fine mules and horses were run off one night, the local miners and settlers formed a volunteer company to go after the thieves. A meeting was held at a local ranch and the men decided to invite Ben Wright to command the expedition. Wright showed up a few days later, bringing along several friendly Oregon Indians. He declined to take command of the party, but agreed to act as scout and guide. Samuel Smith was then elected captain and the twenty-two men were soon on the trail of the thieves.

On one of the first nights out, the Indians ran off the volunteers' horses, but they were quickly recovered, and the next day the search continued. When tracks were lost in some rocky country, the men made camp, while Wright and his Indians tried to locate the lost trail. By now, the volunteers were deep in Modoc country.

The following afternoon, the scouts returned with word that the Indian camp had been located on Lost River. They had viewed it from a distance and reported a rancheria of several hundred Indians who were herding large droves of stock nearby.

The volunteers were anxious to make an immediate attack, but Wright suggested a different plan. The scout proposed that they start early in the morning, ride by the Indian camp at a safe distance as if they were merely travelers, and then attack the unsuspecting natives at the break of the next day's dawn. The plan was agreed upon, and late the following afternoon the volunteers camped some eight miles beyond the Modoc camp. The natives were unaware of any danger.

■ Looking every bit the colorful character he was, Ben Wright could be ruthless in his dealings with Indians. *Oregon Historical Society.*

An hour after dark, Wright and his men silently checked their weapons and made ready to move out on foot. Five men were left behind with orders to bring the horses up at daylight. In a long column, the men disappeared like ghosts into the sage-covered plains.

Early the following morning, the men were on the outskirts of the Indian camp, but they had miscalculated. Instead of being poised in position for attack, they found themselves across the river from their quarry. After a quick consultation they decided to shoot across the thirty-yard-wide river, and as the sky lightened, the hidden men began picking out targets among the Modocs, who were just stirring. Volunteer Bill Fanning later wrote:

> One who had come out, untied a pony which was picketed within a stone's throw of the tent, and led him up in front of it, when Wright said in a low tone, 'We will commence by shooting that Indian.' Two of us who

were standing at his side fired, killed the savage instantly. The Indians came rushing out of their wickiups in confusion, and fought desperately for a while, having nothing but bows and arrows which were shot with great force and precision.... We fired as fast as we could load our rifles, reserving our revolvers at Wright's suggestion, to be used if we should come to close quarters. After a short resistance they took to their heels and deserted the village....

Just as the fight was ending, the men with the horses arrived and ferried their comrades across the river to the village. Sixteen dead Indians were found scattered about the camp, along with quantities of scalps within the wickiups. After burning the rancheria, the volunteers withdrew and set up camp several miles away.

After a few weeks scouting the area, Wright and his men were able to obtain a peace treaty with the Modocs. The Indians agreed to return what stolen livestock they had and stop molesting travelers if Wright and his men would leave their country. With winter closing in, and believing they had soundly whipped the Indians, the volunteers were more than ready to leave for home.

■ Schonchin was one of the few Modoc survivors of Ben Wright's poisoning incident. *Oregon Historical Society.*

That night, as they camped along Willow Creek, a shower of arrows fell among the volunteers, causing them to scamper for cover. During the confusion, the Indians also managed to stampede the stock, driving off some eleven of the volunteer's animals. Outgeneraled by the Modocs, the whites now voted to again go after the Indians rather than returning home. Sending two men back to town for supplies, Wright took the balance of the command after the fleeing natives.

The following day, there was some fighting when the volunteers caught up with the Indians. They killed several Indians, but most of them escaped into some nearby tules. The volunteers managed to recover some of their stock, but the weather was so bad they decided against pressing the attack. Returning to camp, they discovered another Modoc camp near the mouth of Lost River. Although tired and cold, the men still could not pass up another crack at the hated Modocs.

The volunteers decided to attack the village at eleven o'clock that night, and at the appointed time, Wright and his men walked their horses quietly down a stream bank. The village was on an island, and as the men arrived opposite the camp, they were seen by the inhabitants who quickly launched a cloud of arrows in their direction. Leaving five men to hold the horses, the rest of the volunteers jumped into the water and charged across the shallow, ice-cold river into the village. The Modocs scattered, but some thirty women and children were captured.

Leaving several guards for the captives, Wright and the balance of his men spent the rest of the night dodging arrows and searching out Indians in the tules. Two of the whites were badly wounded and several horses hit, but between fifteen and twenty Modocs were killed. Herding their prisoners ahead of them, the volunteers returned to camp on Willow Creek.

It was now early November and the weather was bitterly cold. The whites maintained their camp for the next few weeks, occasionally going out on patrols. Holding on to the prisoners was particularly difficult; the Indians made several attempts at escape. One night, as he was lighting his pipe by the campfire, Wright was pushed over by an escaping Indian. Jumping to his feet he chased the fugitive into the night, only to have the Modoc suddenly turn and punch him in the face. Shaking off the blow, Wright pulled his knife and a few moments later pulled the dead Indian into camp to serve as a lesson for the other captives.

The prisoners steadily maintained that their village had been innocent of any aggressions against the whites and that other Modocs across the river were the troublemakers. Finally, the captives agreed to lead the volunteers to the hiding place of the hostiles and again the small army prepared for a fight.

Up to this point, much of the fighting had been just across the state line, in Oregon, but now the volunteers crossed back into California and found themselves in the craggy bluffs and plains of the lava beds. Indian sentinels were soon discovered, and a running battle ensued as the whites closed in on the remote village.

Observing the advance of the volunteers, the Indians fled to a large cave from which they sent out several volleys of arrows. The volunteers took up positions outside the cave, but a steady volume of rifle fire had little effect on the embattled natives. To save ammunition and conclude the action as soon as possible, the volunteers built large fires at the mouth of the cave to smoke the Indians into the open. When the Modocs still had not surrendered some twenty-four hours later, the whites gave up. Cold, tired, and out of provisions, they headed for home and the comfort of their cabins.

• • • • •

·   With the establishment of the 1851 treaties at Camp Barbour on the San Joaquin River, the Indian commissioners decided they were experienced enough now to go their separate ways. Drawing lots, Redick McKee was allotted the northern portion of the state, Oliver Wozencraft drew the central section, and George Barbour would have responsiblity for the tribes south of the river. Barbour left for the Four Creeks country in May of 1851, while Wozencraft and McKee and his son John all left for San Francisco. As paymaster for the commissioners, McKee hoped to obtain the long overdue funds from Washington. Besides their salaries, the commissioners had run up thousands of dollars in operating expenses, and McKee was becoming worried. While in San Francisco, he mortgaged some of his own property to settle the outstanding debts and maintain a credit rating.

Although the funds still had not arrived by August, McKee and his retinue headed north. John McKee went along as secretary, accompanied by George Gibbs and a company of dragoons under the command of Major W. W. Wessels. Besides the seventy-odd men, there were 140 mules and horses and 160 head of beef cattle.

On August 20 and 22, treaties were concluded with twelve tribes of Indians inhabiting the Clear Lake region. Early in October, treaties were signed with the Trinity and Shasta Indians on the south fork of the Trinity River. Although there were strenuous objections from the settlers and miners of the area, a reservation was established at Scott's Valley and a treaty made with the local natives in early November. By the end of December 1851, McKee and his party were back in San Francisco.

■ The Indians and white settlers fought bitterly over the beautiful valleys of Northern California. One of the early Indian reservations was in Scott's Valley (below). *Peter Palmquist Collection.*

■ A group of McCloud River Wintu Indians, dressed for their war dance. Undated photo by Thomas Houseworth. *Smithsonian Institution.*

Elated with the success of his expedition, McKee modestly wrote his superiors, saying, "…I doubt whether ever, in the history of Indian negotiations in this or any other country, as much work has been done, as much positive good effected, and as many evils averted with such comparatively inadequate means…." Despite his optimism and the general belief of the commissioners that well-fed Indians were peaceful Indians, the troubles continued.

In February 1852, a group of Indians visited the McKinney ranch near Shasta City and stole some blankets and other items. The following day, nineteen-year-old Jim McKinney trailed the Indians, but failed to return home that night. When his mule came in alone, his father went to Major Reading's ranch and organized a posse of thirty miners and some friendly natives. Young McKinney was later found dead and decapitated. A report in the Sacramento *Daily Union* stated that the men then "…gave chase to the Indians, surrounded them and killed 30 without losing any of their own number." La   reports mentioned that two other Indians had been hanged and the heads of several others brought in by the posse.

At this same time, other armed groups of whites were searching for the killers of Captain Gilmore, a trader at Clear Creek. In June, George Gibbs wrote to Governor Bigler from Orleans Bar and noted the killing of a local miner the previous month. A quickly formed group of miners threatened to burn down a local Indian village unless the killers surrendered. When negotiations broke down, the village was attacked and burned, and several of the inhabitants were killed. In March, a miner was killed on the Shasta River, resulting in the reported slaughter of thirty or forty Indians in retaliation.

In view of the escalating troubles, an army post was established on Cow Creek near Reading's ranch in the spring of 1852. Fort Reading was garrisoned by fifty troops who were kept busy constructing barracks for the new post. Although it was intended to maintain the peace within a 200-mile radius, local settlers complained that the isolated fort did nothing to control the Indians.

In a letter dated July 2 at Shasta, a miner bitterly assailed the troops and government for lack of protection:

> For full three years this section of the state has suffered everything from the Indians. Last fall I was assured by Josiah Roop, our postmaster, that he knew of forty-seven men who had been murdered by the Indians in this neighborhood, and since that conversation I can count ten more, making fifty-seven, and within my knowledge they have stolen upwards of two hundred head of horses and mules, besides meat cattle and other property...

> These troops [Fort Reading] have now been fortified at their present point for some weeks, and men have been murdered, property stolen and destroyed, and hay burned upon Cow Creek, a few miles above them, all by the same Indians, and yet not a movement is made for protection.

An Army officer at the fort corrected what he considered inaccuracies in the letter and filled in some details:

> Concerning difficulties between the whites and Indians, it is...satisfactorily proved in many cases, that the whites are the aggressors. The Indians have been driven from their hunting and fishing grounds, from their fields of acorns and grasshoppers, and shot down like the deer...without provocation. Their squaws are stolen and abused, and they have no satisfaction for these wrongs done to them save to avenge them upon the white race. And for the exercise of this first principle of our nature, self defense, they are by white men indiscriminately shot down. Some tribes, doubtless, are exceptions to this rule, and have ever been hostile to the whites.

> The chief of the band of Indians on Clear Creek, states a short time before...the murder above referred to, that some white men had stolen

An Indian woman gathering acorns in Northern California. *Peter Palmquist Collection.*

some of his squaws and taken them off at night, and intimated by signs, that a white man would be killed.... When an Indian avenges an injury like this, a great ado is made and troops wanted—(if used it should be to punish the aggressors). Would such be the case in civilized society?

About the 15th of April 1852, a butcher named Anderson was found dead on the trail, six miles from Weaverville. He had been bringing a small herd of cattle to town when he was ambushed by Indians who reportedly nurtured a grudge against him. When Anderson's body was discovered, a posse was quickly formed and some thirty-six men rode out under the command of Sheriff William H. Dixon. The rancheria of the supposed murderers was discovered on the south fork of the Trinity River, at a place called Bridge Gulch. Checking their weapons, the volunteers prepared for battle. In its issue of May 1, the Shasta *Courier* gave a description of the ensuing fight:

> At midnight the company started from their encampment, Captain Dixon having divided his force into three parties, so as to come upon the Indians from different quarters and surround them. When the day broke, all parties were in the desired positions, and on the signal being given, the attack commenced. Each rifle marked its victim with unerring precision-- the pistol and knife completed the work of destruction and revenge, and in a few moments all was over. Of the 150 Indians that constituted the rancheria, only two or three escaped, and those were supposed to be dangerously wounded; so that probably not one of those engaged in the murder of the unfortunate Anderson now remains alive. Men, women and children all shared the same fate—none were spared except one woman and two children, who were brought back prisoners.

Early accounts of the fight at Bridge Gulch note that the Indian braves used their women and children as shields, assuming that the whites would not fire into them. This may or may not have occurred, but in any case there is no doubt that during and after the fight, women and children were butchered without mercy. Some ninety-three skeletons were counted on the battlefield several months later.

Franklin Buck, a Weaverville merchant, wrote to his sister on June 9 that the volunteers had brought in one squaw and a little boy. Later, a young girl just a few weeks old was brought to town by the Clifford family and raised by them. She grew up as Ellen Clifford and probably never knew Captain Issac Messec, one of the volunteers, who had saved her life that bloody morning at Bridge Gulch.

On July 9, 1852, a miner named Calvin Woodman was riding near Scott's Bar on his way to Yreka. He joined two Indians on the trail, and the three rode along together for a while, Woodman not noticing when one of the natives dropped slightly behind. Suddenly, a shot rang out and the miner dropped heavily to the ground. The two Shastas kicked their ponies and hurriedly galloped off down the trail.

A Mexican packer found the dying Woodman beside the trail and quickly raised the alarm in Yreka. The Indians had been identified as Shastas, and a posse under Deputy Sheriff Whipple headed straight for the Shasta village in Scott's Valley. In a fight at the village, Whipple was wounded and a mule killed. Two dead Indians were left on the field as the rest fled into the woods. Several other posses attacked neighboring rancherias, and rumors of depredations were everywhere. A Shasta *Courier* correspondent wrote:

> While I am writing, the citizens are gathering a party to go and dislodge them. Arms of all kinds are in requisition. Speaking of arms, I am of the opinion that there is no mining town in California...so destitute of firearms as Yreka. The Indians appear to be well armed from the fact that there have been persons in this place who have been so thoughtless as to trade their rifles to the Indians for horses and women.

Writing from Scott's Valley at this time, one Kendall noted that "...Mr. Steele has left this place for Yreka, accompanied by a number of brave men, with the determination of compelling the Indians to deliver up the murderers of Mr. Woodman or of exterminating the whole Shasta tribe."

Elijah Steele was widely respected by whites and Indians alike. He always treated Indians fairly and helped mediate their troubles. After counseling with regional native bands, he became convinced that the local Indians were innocent of Woodman's murder. Taking several hostage Shastas to Yreka as a precaution, Steele was authorized to organize a company and go after the killers who were thought to have fled to the Rogue River in Oregon. Organizing some volunteers, Steele and his men crossed the line into Oregon only to become embroiled in even more Indian trouble there.

During this time, Ben Wright aided the negotiations by acting as interpreter. He was living with an Indian woman, who divulged where the killers were hiding, and when Steele and his party headed north, Wright and several friendly Indians began their own search. Scarface, a Klamath traveling with Wright, became separated from the party near Yreka. A group of miners had heard that he had killed Woodman, and when they caught the grim-visaged Klamath near town, he was summarily lynched.

Wright and the balance of his Indians had meanwhile captured two natives, one of whom had confessed to the crime. A trial was held at the Lone Star ranch in Scott's Valley with a large crowd of local miners in attendance. Testimony established that the guilty Indian's father had been killed by white men some years before and the son had vowed vengeance. When the two passed Woodman on the trail, they shot him, although the Sacramento *Union* reported that "both stoutly denied that the other took any part in it."

The convicted Indian was hung from a butcher's scaffold, while his companion was released in a rare example of miner magnanimity.

It was about this time that a new company of volunteers was organized at Yreka to again escort the wagon trains across the most dangerous part of the Overland Trail. The company of some thirty men were well armed, provisioned and captained by Charles McDermit, sheriff of Siskiyou County. Heading east from Yreka, the volunteers galloped steadily through the pine-shrouded mountains and were soon well on their way towards Tule Lake and Bloody Point. The group passed one wagon train that had seen no Indians, and it was hoped more fighting could be avoided.

■ Elijah Steele was a lawyer, rancher, Indian agent, and friend to the Indians when few would defend them. *Author's collection.*

Riding down the emigrant trail beyond Tule Lake, the volunteers met a party of nine men who were packing into California. These men too had seen no Indians and after exchanging news for a few minutes were soon on their way. Shortly thereafter, however, at Bloody Point, the packers were ambushed by the Modocs and all but one were killed in the resulting fight. The survivor made his way to Yreka. Soon a new volunteer company was formed, with Ben Wright selected as captain.

Out on the emigrant trail, McDermit's force met two wagon trains heading towards Tule Lake. Detailing three men to guide and guard the

An unidentified Northern California Indian medicine man, in all his finery. *Peter Palmquist.*

two trains, McDermit and the rest of his party camped along the shore of Goose Lake to wait for the next train. From McDermit's perspective (not knowing of the slaughter of the packers), it looked as though there might be peace this fall after all.

The three volunteer scouts were guiding the trains past Bloody Point when suddenly a Modoc ambush killed all three and wounded several of the emigrants. The wagon train captains had the presence of mind to keep the wagons moving until they reached the plains, where they corralled for protection. Here they managed to keep the Indians at bay, after several attempts to fire the grass failed. Poorly armed and low on provisions, the emigrants could not move, yet were ill-equipped to withstand a long siege.

Ben Wright's new company of twenty-three volunteers had left Macklin's ranch on the morning of August 27. Near Sheep Rock, the men lost some of their pack animals and had to repack their remaining supplies on three mules. Wright's report of this first portion of the campaign and his request for aid is datelined September 2, 1852, at Bloody Point, the dreaded ambush spot on Tule Lake:

On Monday evening we reached the Natural Bridge on Lost River. Having seen fresh Indian signs through the day, I placed four spies (Indians) on a mountain about five miles south of camp in the night to look out for the smoke of their fires in the morning. They discovered one smoke a few miles off from the point that they were stationed and immediately proceeded to it and took four prisoners, three squaws and one buck. The buck told us that there was a large body of Indians across the lake [Tule Lake] near the emigrant trail, gambling with each other for the clothes and horses that they had taken from the 'Bostons.' We immediately proceeded to the designated point, moving with as much caution and dispatch as possible, leaving the regular trail in order to avoid raising a dust by which our presence might be discovered. About three o'clock in the afternoon we came to a body of emigrants encamped, whom, owing to our sudden appearance issuing from the low, swampy land and their own excited minds having been lately attacked; and expecting the attack to be every moment renewed, supposed us to be Indians. Could the good people of Yreka witnessed the rejoicing when it was known that we were friends instead of foes they would not grudge the assistance they have already furnished nor be slow to furnish all that is still required to protect the sick and travel-worn emigrants from the merciless savage. No man seeing what we have seen and having one drop of the milk of human kindness in his veins, could refuse his bottom dollar if required to prevent the repetition of such atrocities as have been committed at this place. Three of our own citizens were killed about twenty four hours before our arrival; Mr. Coats, Mr. Long and Mr. Owenby.

After meeting the emigrants we rested our horses a few minutes and then proceeded to attack the Indians who were collected in considerable force about two miles from camp and near the point at which they attacked the emigrants. On seeing us start for them, they paraded in sight, sixty-five strong, twelve on horseback and the others on foot. They came out on fair ground as if intending to give us a fair fight, but when we got within four hundred yards of them and advanced at full gallop in two companies, they broke for the tules. I then sent ten men under the command of Mr. Evans to a high point in the edge of the lake to make observations and to act as circumstances might direct. Our horses were then given in charge of five men and the remainder of the company, numbering about fifteen men, entered the tules on foot. We followed them about an hour and a half firing whenever we could get a sight of the red devils. About sixty shots were fired by our company and ten or twelve Indians killed. A number of women and children must have been drowned. Whenever we would shoot into a canoe they would all at once roll out into the lake. Three horses were taken. The others they had so effectively hidden in the high rushes that we could not find them. Having to wade into the water waist deep we got most of our ammunition wet and consequently had to give over the chase sooner than we otherwise would.

■ Siskiyou County Sheriff Charles McDermit. *Siskiyou County Museum.*

Fourteen men have been killed that we know of. The remains of eight have been found and buried.

Wright closed his report by asking for ten more volunteers and a refurbishing of his supplies. "…And for God's sake," he wrote, "don't be slow in responding to our call."

As Wright attacked the Indians, the rescued wagon train party quickly harnessed up and headed west. It arrived at Yreka about September 5, according to a correspondent of the Sacramento *Union*. The following day a wagon load of supplies was dispatched to Wright, with ten men leaving later that night as reinforcements.

Of the fighting in the tules, Bill Kershaw, one of Wright's lieutenants, noted that "we fought them for about three hours, when, night coming upon, we retired. Many of us fought in water to our armpits. In this engagement we must have killed as many as thirty or thirty-five of the enemy. The Indians themselves say we killed twenty. Our company sustained no loss whatever."

For the next few days, Wright and his men searched the area around the lake. They had found various items of clothing and some utensils in the Indian village and felt sure that murdered emigrant bodies were nearby. Their inclinations proved tragically correct.

■ Silas J. Day, one of Ben Wright's volunteers. *Southern Oregon Historical Society.*

"During this and the next day," wrote Bill Kershaw, "we found and buried twenty-one bodies, making with the one found in the tule the day previous, twenty-two. We also found various articles of women's and children's clothing, etc., indicating that entire families had been massacred. We found the body of but one female, however, but we were all of the opinion that more had been killed or taken captives. In one of the Indian rancherias we found the hair from a woman's head...."

Another volunteer party from Jacksonville, arriving about this time, found fourteen more corpses. All of the dead emigrants were terribly mutilated and the volunteers were visibly shaken by the discoveries. Parts of wagons and many personal effects of the slaughtered people were also found, but there was no way of knowing who they were or just how many had died. Thinking of their own families in the East, some of the volunteers sobbed as they buried the ripped and bloodied bodies in this vast and lonely new land.

Throughout the fall, Wright's men escorted wagon trains through the bloody corridor between Clear and Tule lakes. McDermit had sent his men as escorts with the trains, one and two at a time, until finally all of his command had returned to Yreka, when at the end of October, the last train was safely past the area of the Modocs' favorite ambush sites.

Throughout the past two months, Wright and his men had never had a decisive fight with their quarry. In the midst of most of their skirmishes, the Modocs had been able to flee to an island in Tule Lake where they were safe and secure. The whites resolved to somehow force a showdown. They knew that unless they could thoroughly whip the Indians and make them afraid to make war again, more emigrants would die in the spring and another campaign would be necessary. Too, the memory of the mutilated women and children haunted their thoughts. Wright vowed that he would not return a failure. Somehow, he must force a final showdown with the Modocs.

After sending three men to Yreka for supplies, Wright set out to negotiate with the natives. Old Mary, a friendly Indian woman, was induced to visit the Modoc village and invite them to a feast, during which a treaty would be discussed. After a few days, she was able to coax several Indians to the white men's camp, and they were feasted and treated well. Later, more Modocs came in and availed themselves of the free food until the volunteers were nearly out of rations for themselves. By the time new supplies arrived from Yreka, the Modocs were camped next to the whites and feeling quite at ease.

With the Indians lulled into a false sense of security, Wright informed the chiefs that if they would return the emigrant stock and other possessions, a treaty would be concluded and a grand feast held to celebrate the event. The Modocs agreed to the plan and while the stolen stock was being rounded up during the next few days, the volunteers and Indians mingled freely in both camps.

Wright and his eighteen men were in a dangerous position. Singly, and in groups, the Indians began bolstering the size of their camp until nearly one hundred were gathered along the river. The whites were badly outnumbered and were relieved when it was decided the Indians had had more than enough time to produce the stolen goods, and the matter would be brought to a head.

When Wright demanded an immediate accounting from the chiefs, he was given a few old guns and some broken-down horses. "We will give

■ Tule Lake, with Bloody Point in the distance, as it appeared about 1900. *Author's collection.*

no more," grumbled a chief, snarling in the same breath that his warriors outnumbered the white men and would as soon fight them as not. Old Schonchin, a head man, sniffed trouble in the wind and left with his people. A grim-faced Wright stalked back to the security of his own camp and into conference with his lieutenants.

With winter and snow due at any time, Wright had determined some weeks before to conclude the campaign, one way or another. Besides bringing freshly slaughtered beef, he had instructed his men to obtain a can of strychnine while in Yreka. Late that night, the beef was well-doctored with the poison, while Wright detailed several of his men to a strategic site overlooking the Indian camp. Two other men were sent across the river where they quietly took up concealed positions. With his men stationed and his plans made, Wright rolled up in his blankets and slept until dawn.

The Modoc camp was along the river's edge, and the water was quite low at this time. Above the Indian camp, on a shelf indicating the high water mark of the river, was the volunteers' camp. At dawn, Wright and his men were up and quietly moving into positions overlooking the Indian wickiups and shelters. The Modocs were stirring, and soon campfires were blazing. Grabbing the slab of poisoned beef, Wright dragged it over to the Modoc camp.

Wright was wearing a blanket with a hole cut in the center, as a poncho. As soon as he dropped the beef at the feet of a group of Indians, he gripped the butts of the two pistols in his belt. As the Modocs gathered about the beef and began cutting off chunks, Wright squatted by the fire and watched them eat. Under his poncho, he still held tightly to the butts of his two pistols.

It was some minutes before several braves appeared to have stomach cramps. When the pains apparently subsided, Wright realized that the poison was not working—weakened perhaps by the cooking of the beef. Before the Modocs could arrive at the same conclusion, Wright drew his pistols and shot two of the nearest Indians. Even as he fired, he was on his feet and running off to the side and out of his men's line of fire.

The men above the Indian camp fired volley after volley into the Modocs, then followed Wright in a charge. The Indians rallied for a moment, letting loose a flight of arrows into the attacking whites. Then, the volunteers were among them. Shooting right and left with their pistols, they drove the battered natives into the river. A few almost reached the other side when suddenly the previously hidden whites jumped up and poured another deadly volley into them. Very few of the Indians escaped the onslaught, and in a few minutes it was over. The cries of the wounded cut like a knife through the cold morning air.

Wright and his men walked among the fallen Modocs and quickly dispatched all survivors with a shot to the head or a knife to the throat. Neither women nor children were spared. Of the whites, Issac Sanbanch had been painfully wounded with an arrow in the back, and John Poland had been shot in the stomach. Bill Brown had taken wounds to the forehead and wrist. Over forty dead Modocs, some of the band's best fighting men, lay scattered about the stream edge or drifted silently down river. A score had been settled. The Modoc campaign was over.

Making litters for the wounded, the volunteers immediately packed up and headed for home. The Sacramento *Union* of December 4, 1852, briefly acknowledged the return of the "heroes":

> On the arrival of the party at Yreka, they paraded through the streets— the wounded being borne in litters—each of the party, consisting of 16 whites, 2 Indians, and a Negro, having...the muzzle of his gun decorated with a scalp taken from the enemy."

For a week, Wright and his men were feted by the townspeople. It was a drunken, grand carousal and after a few days Hallick, Burgess, and several others became disgusted and went back to work. Soon things were back to normal in Yreka. And, out on the plains, beyond Sheep Rock, the fighting propensities of the Modocs had been curbed for the present. In time, however, they would reemerge as a powerful threat to their neighbors.

The sporadic Indian outbreaks in the northern country prompted the founding of Fort Jones in Scott's Valley in October of 1852. Established by two companies of United States Dragoons, the post was later garrisoned by several infantry companies and played an important part in the Indian troubles of the area, until its abandonment in 1858.

And, Ben Wright had become a legend. Hailed by many as the brave savior of the emigrants, others came to know his darker side—a brutal killer of Indians, intemperate abuser of his Indian women, and a frontier enigma whose curious character has yet to be read. In later years, there were those who denied the poisoning story, but Elijah Steele, Dr. Ferrber who sold the poison, and even some of Wright's men knew the truth and spoke out.

While serving as an Indian agent in southern Oregon, Wright was later killed during the great Rogue River Indian uprising of 1856. According to all reports, his body was terribly mutilated.

CHAPTER 8 / SOURCES

UNPUBLISHED MATERIAL

U.S. Congress, 34th Congress, 3rd Session, Senate Executive Document 76:

Brevet Brigadier General E. A. Hitchcock to Colonel S. Cooper, March 31, 1853.

U.S. Congress, 35th Congress, 2nd Session, Miscellaneous Doc. 47:

Statement of W. T. Kershaw, November 21, 1857.

Elijah Steele to General C. S. Drew, November 23, 1857.

Office of the Secretary of State, California State Archives, Indian War Files, Sacramento:

James B. Holder to Governor John Bigler, July 12, 1852.

Benjamin Wright Report, September 2, 1852.

G. Ferris to Governor John Bigler, September, 1852.

NEWSPAPERS

San Francisco *Daily Alta California*, July 4, 1852.

Sacramento *Daily Union*, February 28, March 9, 25, July 9, 27, August 3, September 16, 30, October 4, December 4, 1852.

Shasta *Courier*, May 1, July 24, 1852.

The *Humboldt Times*, March 8, 1856.

The Oregonian, August 9, 16, 23, 30, September 6, 13, 20, 27, October 4, 18, 25, November 1, 15, 22, 1885.

PRINCIPAL PUBLISHED WORKS

Andre, Alexander. *A Frenchman at the California Trinity River Mines in 1849*. New York: The Westerners New York Posse, 1957.

Bledsoe, A. J. *Indian Wars of the Northwest*. Oakland: Biobooks, 1956.

Brown, William S. *California Northeast: The Bloody Ground*. Oakland: Biobooks, 1951.

Buck, Franklin A., compiled by Kathleen A. White. *A Yankee Trader in the Gold Rush*. Boston and New York: Houghton Mifflin Company, 1930.

Carr, John. *Pioneer Days in California*. Eureka, CA: Times Publishing Company, 1891.

Cox, Issac. *The Annals of Trinity County*. Eugene, OR: J. H. Nash, 1940.

Coy, Owen C. *The Humboldt Bay Region, 1850-1875*. Los Angeles: State Historical

Association, 1925.

Hart, Herbert M. *Pioneer Forts of the West*. Seattle: Superior Publishing Company, 1967.

Gudde, Erwin G. *California Gold Camps*. Berkeley: University of California Press, 1975.

Heizer, Robert F., editor. *George Gibbs' Journal of Redick McKee's Expedition through Northwestern California in 1851*. Berkeley: University of California Press, 1972.

_____, and Whipple, M.A., editors. *The California Indians*. Berkeley: University of California Press, 1973.

Kroeber, Alfred L. *Handbook of the Indians of California*. New York: Dover Publications, Inc., 1976.

Neasham, Ernest R. *Fall River Valley, an Examination of Historical Sources*. Sacramento: The Citadel Press, Inc., 1985.

Phillips, George Harwood. *Indians and Indian Agents: The Origins of the Reservation System in California, 1849-1852*. Norman, OK: University of Oklahoma Press, 1997.

Raphael, Ray. *Little White Father: Redick McKee on the California Frontier*. Eureka, CA: Humboldt County Historical Society, 1993.

Read, Georgia Willis, and Gaines, Ruth. *Gold Rush: the Journals, Drawings & other Papers of J. Goldsborough Bruff*. New York: Columbia University Press, 1949.

Riddle, Jeff C. *The Indian History of the Modoc War*. Medford, OR: Pine Cone Publishers, 1973.

Thompson, Colonel William (publisher). *Reminiscences of a Pioneer*. San Francisco, 1912.

Victor, Frances Fuller (Dorothy and Jack Sutton, editors). *Indian Wars of the Rogue River*. Grants Pass, OR: Josephine County Historical Society, 1969.

Wells, Harry L. *History of Siskiyou County, California*. Oakland: D. J. Stewart & Co., 1881.

OTHER SOURCES

Kelsey, Harry. "The California Indian Treaty Myth," *Southern California Quarterly*, The Historical Society of Southern California, Fall 1973.

Victor, Frances Fuller, "A Knight of the Frontier," *The Californian*, August 1881.

Chapter 9

GARRA

In the southern tip of the Mexican province of California, a deserting sailor was married to a Cupeno Indian
woman. Originally a native of Providence, Rhode Island, Bill Marshall had shipped out of Boston on a
whaling ship and in 1844 found himself in the harbor at
San Diego, while his ship took on supplies. Weary of life at sea, young
Marshall jumped ship and hid out in town until his whaler left port. Although small of stature, he was a good-looking young man and quickly
made friends in the old Spanish town. He fell in love with one of the local
beauties, but when she spurned him, Marshall left for the Indian country
to the northeast. Here, in 1846, he married the daughter of Jose Noca, a
Cupeno Indian, and set up a store at the village of Kupa.

Marshall found himself in a vast country of mountains and plains,
corridored by rocky hills and passes and alternating between forests and
wasteland. To the east stretched the Colorado Desert and to the west the
waters of the vast Pacific. It was a land of seemingly endless fertile valleys
interspersed with barren, rolling hills and brush-clumped flat lands. It was
also a lonely land, located 135 miles from Los Angeles and about half that
distance from San Diego. Large Spanish land grants spotted the area, but
the homes of the rancheros were few and widely scattered.

The three sons of Antonio Maria Lugo held the San Bernardino rancho
in the north. Between there and Kupa were the vast acreages of the San
Jacinto Nuevo y Potrero, the San Jacinto Viejo, the Pauba, the Pauma, and
the San Jose Del Valle ranchos. Dozens more of these huge land grants lay
to the south and along the coast, some worked by Americans married to
Californian women. William Wolfskill had planted an orange grove as early
as 1841, while a Scot named Hugo Reid owned the Rancho Santa Anita.
Isaac Williams had a half interest in the Rancho Santa Anna del Chino with
Antonio Lugo, his father-in-law.

The village of Kupa was also known as Agua Caliente, for the hot
springs nearby. The springs were located on the ranch of a former trapper

The village of Kupa, some years after the Garra troubles. *Los Angeles Public Library.*

named Jonathan Warner whom the Californios and Indians called "Juan Largo." Warner had traveled extensively in California, but finally settled in a beautiful valley some three miles from Kupa, on the road from Yuma. Here he farmed and raised livestock, besides operating a store for travelers.

Warner met young Marshall at Kupa and the two Americans, far from home, became friends. Marshall later gained the confidence of Warner to the extent that when Warner was away on business, Marshall would take charge of the ranch.

For centuries, this had all been Indian country, but weakened by years of domination by Spaniards and Californios, the Indians had been decimated by disease, their tribal units broken and destroyed. Still they roamed the land in various stages of bewilderment and alarm at the changes taking place.

There were around 20,000 Indians in southern California in 1770. The Yumas, or Quechan, and Chemehuevi populated the east on the Colorado River, and the Kumeyaay, Juaneno, and Gabrielino lined the coast. In between were the Luiseno, Cahuilla, Cupeno, Kamia, and Serrano, all overlapping by way of trade, culture, and marriage. By the mid-1840s, the original native population had been cut nearly in half.

In 1844, the Lugo family had retained Juan Antonio and his band of Cahuilla Indians to reside on their ranch as protection against other marauding tribes. Most other southern natives lived their traditional life as best they could, except when working on the ranchos of the Californios.

Jonathan "Juan Largo" Warner.
Los Angeles Public Library.

136

The Indians had no sooner adjusted from the mission days to the great rancho period, when they were confronted with yet another new development—the war with Mexico. The scattered fighting that took place in California occurred largely in the south, and the natives found it difficult to know just where their allegiance lay.

When General StephenW. Kearny marched overland from the Colorado River toward San Diego, he stopped briefly at Warner's Ranch, then pushed on towards the narrow San Pascual Valley. Here, on December 6, 1846, the Americans were met by a force of Californio cavalry under Andres Pico, and a brief, bitter clash took place.

The weary Americans were outmaneuvered by the fine Californio lancers, and Kearny lost some eighteen killed and as many wounded. The Californios suffered only one death. Kearny, wounded himself, positioned his men in a defensive position on top of a hill and asked for volunteers to ride to San Diego. A young naval officer, Lieutenant Edward F. Beale, scout Kit Carson, and an Indian crawled through the enemy positions and secured help after a desperate journey. Meanwhile, Pico's troops dispersed into the countryside.

After the battle, some eleven deserters from Pico's army hid out on the Pauma ranch. One of the more isolated ranchos, it was also the site of two Pauma Indian villages, governed by chieftain Manuelito Cota. The seventy-five Indians who inhabited the two villages greeted the arrival of the deserters with angry words of protest.

Various reasons are given for the unrest of the Paumas, including the recent killing of some Indians and the taking of horses by foraging Californio troops. Other sources state that General Kearny, while in the area, had led the Paumas to believe that the Americans would not now object to the killing of their former masters. Whatever the reasons, the events that followed are an indication of the confused emotions of the natives at this newest interruption of their lives.

The owner of the rancho, Jose Antonio Serrano, learned of the hostility of the Indians and warned his eleven wards to be on the alert. For some reason, the deserters ignored him and on December 10, when some Indians approached the house where they were staying, the Californios had not even posted a guard.

The soldiers were housed in an adobe located a mile or so from Serrano's main ranch house. One of the men was a brother of Serrano. The others included five men from San Diego, one from San Juan Capistrano and a young boy who had brought food to his father in the field. One of the San

Diegans was Jose Maria Alvarado whose wife, Lugardia Osuna, had earlier spurned the affections of Bill Marshall.

Manuelito Cota himself pounded on the door of the adobe where the deserters were staying that late December night. The Californios were armed and undecided about opening the door, when suddenly the latch was tripped and the room was full of Indians. In a moment the men were stripped and tied, then carried off to Kupa.

At the Indian village, a council of Paumas, Cupenos, and Luisenos debated on what to do. Most of the Indians wanted to kill the prisoners, but Cota and others insisted they be turned loose. The Pauma chieftain, suddenly alarmed at the situation, even tried to let the Californios escape once, but they refused, not believing they were in any real danger.

When they could not reach a decision, the Indians called in two whites who lived among them and asked them what to do. One of the men was a Californian named Yguera who had married a Cupeno woman. The other was Bill Marshall.

The prisoners must have realized as time passed that they were in serious danger. Antonio Serrano and Jose Aguilar had trailed the raiding party only to be chased back to the ranch by the Indians. Sending word of the trouble to the Santa Ysabel Rancho, Serrano asked the foreman, Bill Williams, to intercede for the captured soldiers. Williams rode to Kupa that night. Upon his arrival, he saw the prisoners tied up around a fire, but the Paumas refused to let him near them. Unable to strike a deal with the Indians, Williams returned and prepared to lead a rescue party, but even as he did so, it was already too late.

At Kupa, Marshall had noticed his old rival, Alvarado, among the

■ Manuelito Cota, a Luiseno chieftan, led the raiders at the Pauma massacre but tried to prevent the murder of the prisoners. *Title Insurance and Trust Company, San Diego.*

prisoners. He began talking to the council, telling them that the war would soon be over, that the Mexicans had no chance and now was a good time to gain favor with the Americans by killing the prisoners. By now, the Indians were excited and needed little convincing. Before any help could arrive, one by one the Californios were savagely murdered.

Jose del Carmen Lugo and Juan Antonio were detailed by the military commander of the district to punish the Paumas. They cleverly ambushed the hostiles in Temecula Canyon, and in Lugo's words "made a great slaughter." Some eighteen or twenty prisoners were turned over to Juan Antonio and his Cahuillas who promptly killed them. When remonstrated by Lugo, Juan Antonio replied that he had joined the expedition to kill Indians and if the Paumas had caught him, they would have done the same.

In all, thirty-eight hostiles were killed during the campaign. Marshall's advice had proved disastrous for the Paumas, but the storekeeper seems to have gone back to his shelves as though nothing had happened.

In January 1847, Lieutenant Colonel Philip St. George Cooke, commanding a 500-man unit of Mormon recruits for the Mexican War, arrived at Warner's Ranch. He described the locale as "a beautiful little valley, shut in by mountains or high hills on every side—the former are nearly covered with green shrubs amongst which the rocks show themselves, and are crowned with pine and cedar; the latter with oak and other evergreens...."

At Kupa, Cooke met Marshall and Antonio Garra, chief of the two Cupeno villages in Warner's valley. Garra was reportedly a Quechan by birth, but was raised as a mission Indian at San Luis Rey. The San Diego *Herald* once referred to Garra as "a man of energy, determination and bravery. As one of the principal chiefs, his power and influence over the Indians is almost unbounded."

Apparently, Cupenos had been among the Paumas when the Temecula Canyon battle had taken place. Garra asked Cooke if he and his men would accompany the Cupenos to the battle site so they could bury their dead. Cooke did so in exchange for some Indian guides and herders and Garra was able to bury his dead without fear of attack by rival Cahuillas.

Garra lived at Kupa in a large house where he reportedly read from his extensive library, called meetings, and generally lived the good life.

When the Americans occupied Los Angeles, Juan Antonio and some eighty followers rode into town to disclaim responsibility for a recent raid. At this time, the chief also asked that an Indian agent be appointed over his tribe. He insisted the agent be an American, however, since the Californios had always been their sworn enemies. In August of 1847, a former member of Cooke's Mormon Battalion was appointed agent of all the Indians in and around San Luis Rey.

Garra and his people were regarded as "mission Indians" and subject to pay county taxes even though they were not property owners. In 1850, the Cupenos, Luisenos, and Kumeyaay were assessed some $600 in taxes, which they dutifully paid, although even most whites regarded it as unfair. It was literally a case of taxation without representation—the Indians having no legal land of their own, or even an elected representative to look out for their interests.

When they were again assessed the following year, the San Diego tax collector, Sheriff Agostin Haraszthy, reported the Indians again paid with a minimum of objection. When General Joshua Bean arrived in the port city and announced that he did not think the Cupenos should have to pay a tax, he was overruled by the state attorney general, who insisted the natives must pay up.

The Cupenos were thoroughly confused by now and some of the captains were refusing to pay. Finally, most of the taxes were paid in cattle, but the Indians were upset that they must pay while their bitter enemies, the Cahuillas, were exempt. Juan Antonio and his people were considered "wild" by the government and therefore not subject to the tax.

Other news had further upset Garra and his people. They had heard of the treaties being made in the San Joaquin Valley to the north—treaties in which the Indians were being given their own land and cattle and supplies with which to live. All the southern Indians had looked forward to the arrival of the commissioners, and when word was received that Commissioner George W. Barbour was on his way south in early June, the Indians were jubilant. Juan Antonio and his people gathered at the Chino ranch of

Isaac Williams, who slaughtered two cattle a day to feed them. Cupeno and other Indians awaited developments. After waiting several days beyond the agent's expected arrival time, all the Indians became quite restless.

Barbour had in fact reached Los Angeles on June 16, but was without funds. Upon hearing of impending trouble in the San Joaquin, he headed north again on June 30. He had also learned that he and sixteen other commissioners had been reappointed Indian agents by Congress. The southern Indians were peaceable anyway, he reasoned.

After a brief stay in the valley, Barbour returned to San Francisco, where he received news that the southern natives were upset. Again he waited several months for funds to arrive, then in early October sailed for Washington, D.C. The following February, he resigned.

When the Indians were told the agent would not be visiting after all, they were disappointed and angry. Isaac Williams gave Juan Antonio some farm equipment and blankets in an effort to pacify him, but the Cahuilla chief could not understand why they were being ignored by the Great Father in Washington. The Cupeno and other groups were equally disappointed.

■ Sheriff Agostin Haraszthy.
Author's collection.

"The present warlike movement of the southern savages," commented the *Alta*, "may have been promoted by jealous and indignant feelings arising from the fact that the northern Indians have been treated with so much more consideration than they, by the agents of the U.S. government." The newspaper was right and this, coupled with the tax problem and a steady stream of emigrants through Indian country, proved to be more than Antonio Garra could bear.

Watching the hordes of emigrants passing through his land, Garra knew that the day of the Indian was fast disappearing. If he were to make war and turn them back, it must be now while there was still time. And it could not be just he and his handful of Cupenos who would fight. Somehow he must unite all Indians before it was too late.

After the Glanton tragedy at Dr. Lincoln's ferry, Captain Samuel P. Heintzelman and a detachment of troops were ordered to set up an army post near the ferry site. By March of 1851, the camp was established, but transporting supplies across the desert proved so costly that most of the command was removed in June. Lieutenant Thomas W. Sweeney and ten men were left behind at a small stockade some six miles below the junction of the Gila and Colorado rivers. The fort was called Camp Independence. Nearby, another ferry company was in operation.

The Yuma Indians were bitter over the Glanton incident and subsequent events, and had tried to scare off the latest ferrymen. "The white man and the Indian cannot live together," they declared. But the whites were always well armed and on their guard. The Indians were further dismayed by the presence of the troopers and wanted to know why Sweeney and his men had been left behind. At a meeting between the officer and the Yuma chiefs, angry words were exchanged and the Indians left in a sullen and hostile mood.

Early in November, seven men ferried their herd of sheep over the Colorado River and headed west across the desert. Some four miles from the river, they were stopped by a large band of Indians who demanded blankets and provisions. Suddenly, fighting erupted and five of the sheep men and some twelve Indians were killed. One of the escaping white men was able to reach the ranch of Paulino Weaver. Although wounded, he identified Antonio Garra as the leader of the hostiles.

The other sheep man, a German named Neagle, also managed to escape the massacre and made his way to Camp Independence late that night. Lieutenant Sweeney told him that the Indians had been there earlier and tried to bluff their way into the stockade. From descriptions, they were the same Yumas who had attacked the sheep men.

For the past few months, Garra had been engaged in trying to unify the southern Indians. He was probably on such a mission when he was caught up in the sheep man fight and the attempted invasion of Camp Independence. He was in communication with most of the local chiefs and had sent word to Baja California urging a coalition with the Indians there.

Garra even contacted his old enemy, Juan Antonio, and at a large feast asked him to join in the impend-

■ These Yuma warriors were fierce enemies of the encroaching white men, but they soon realized their day was over. *Author's collection.*

142

ing war. That wily old rascal must have thought the whole proposition rather shaky, but agreed to send a messenger north to try to enlist the aid of the San Joaquin Valley Indians. The Yokuts, however, had just signed treaties with the commissioners. They had no intention of going to war at this time. Despite his disillusionment with the Americans, Juan Antonio felt the same way.

Juan Largo Warner had been elected to the state senate in 1850, and found it necessary to be absent from his ranch for long periods of time. In his absence, Bill Marshall managed the Warner property. The treacherous overseer must have watched with interest as Garra's preparations for war hatched and matured. His reasons for allowing himself to be caught up in such an affair are obscure, and it is hard to imagine he could have so lost touch with reality as to imagine Garra had any chance at all with his war. It is entirely possible, however, that Marshall found himself in a situation where he must side with his Cupeno friends or die.

Garra returned from the Colorado on November 12, with the hot winds of war at his back. It was his plan, apparently, for the Yumas to wipe out Camp Independence, then attack San Diego itself. The Cahuillas and Cupenos were to strike at Los Angeles, while the Tulare Indians would pounce on Santa Barbara.

A letter from Garra to the prominent California Don Jose Estudillo indicated that Garra's plan entailed only the killing of Americans:

■ Early ferry on the Colorado River. *Williamson Railroad Survey Report, 1853.*

■ Quechan warriors, such as these photographed in the 1880s, accompanied the Yumas attack on the sheepherding party. *True West Archives.*

Senor Don Jose Anto. Estudillo,—I salute you, the time I told you what I thought of things; now the blow is struck; if I have life I will go and help you, because all the Indians are invited in all parts, and it is possible that the San Bernardinos are now rising— and now a man by the name of Juan Berro told me that the white people waited for me, for this I give these my words, and to be prepared for Tuesday to leave this for the Pueblo: and you will arrange with the white people and Indians, and send me your word, nothing more.

It was signed by Antonio Garra, dated Agua Caliente, November 21, 1851.

Garra's letter is difficult to understand, but seems to make two important points: that a large portion of the southern Indians were joining his uprising and that the native Californios were also involved in the war—certainly they were encouraging the Indians. Whatever the fine points of his meaning, the letter was a declaration of war.

After a war council at the Cupeno village of Wilakal, two bands of Indians went into action shortly after midnight on November 21. Chapuli, chief of the Los Coyotes Cahuillas, led the group which rode towards the Warner ranch. Young Antonio Garra, a son of the chief, led a second group of raiders who headed towards Kupa where three Americans were living while bathing in the hot springs for their beneficial effects. Old Garra claimed to be ill and was not involved in subsequent events.

Warned that an attack was imminent, Warner sent his family to San Diego where he planned to join them later. Except for several young Indian servants, he was alone that night when some two dozen yelling warriors began galloping around the ranch house. Leaping out of bed and grabbing his rifle, Warner ran to the door and saw Indians everywhere. Two horses tethered at the house had been cut loose, so he ran towards the barn. On the way, he managed to shoot two Indians out of their saddles, then dashed into the cover of the barn.

144

After sending a servant named Santos to parley with the attackers, Warner quickly saddled the only remaining horse and had his other servant scramble up behind him. When Santos failed to return from the parley, Warner galloped out of the barn door through a shower of arrows.

■ Warner's ranch buildings as they appeared many years after the Garra War. *Los Angeles Public Library.*

Young Garra's party of about six warriors arrived at Kupa and tied their horses in front of the alcalde's house. From there they went straight to the home of Bill and Dominga Marshall where three Americans—Piddler, Ridgely, and Slack, were staying. Barging into the Marshall home, Garra's men dragged the Americans outside. The men were stripped of their clothes, then murdered by Garra and his men.

After killing another American who was staying with Marshall's father-in-law, the Cupenos abandoned their villages and fled to the Cahuilla village in Los Coyotes Canyon, some two days away. Bill Marshall and a Californio named Juan Verdugo rode with them.

First news of the Indian war was announced by the San Diego *Herald* on November 27:

> Our city was thrown into high state of excitement on Sunday afternoon last, by the arrival of an express from Agua Caliente, the residence of Hon. John J. Warner, state senator, conveying the intelligence that the Indians, who are numerous in that vicinity, had risen and attacked his ranch, destroying all of his household property, and driving away his stock, consisting of late and valuable bands of cattle and horses…. Mr. Warner's house was surrounded by a party of Indians numbering 100 strong who…rifled the house of everything it contained, and are now in arms in the mountains, defying the Whites and boldly proclaiming their intention to massacre every white in the state.
>
> The Indians have since killed four Americans at the Springs, making a total of nine men murdered since the commencement of this unhappy outbreak.
>
> The same day, an express from Lt. Murray, the officer in command on the Gila, reached here, notifying the commanding officer of a hostile disposition being manifested by the Yumas and Cocopas, and of the killing of four whites by the Indians. On the following morning a message arrived from the residence of Don Juan Bandini, in south California, conveying the unpleasant news that the Indians of lower California had been invited in a conspiracy, having for its object the annihilation of the Whites. When it is

recollected that Warner's Ranch is distant from the point occupied by Lt. Murray, 130 miles, it will be seen that there is a probability that the entire Indian race, numbering some ten thousand souls, residing between Los Angeles and the Colorado River, are concerned in this outbreak....

Rumors of an impending uprising had been current for weeks, and lack of communication and distrust between the Californios and the Americans added to a panic that now alarmed much of the state.

Sheriff Haraszthy wrote to Governor McDougal:

I called on the captain of the organized Fitzgerald Volunteers in which every able-bodied man had voluntarily enlisted, but the whole county not numbering over one hundred able-bodied men, destitute of arms, horses, &c. cannot do more than defend the city of San Diego, where an attack is daily expected. Apprehensive that some white men are united with the Indians, the citizens united in a mass meeting, and ordered the city and country under martial law. The force of Antonio [Garra] is estimated at from 4 to

■ Jonathan Warner, standing second from left, with some of his Indian vaqueros. He was always a friend to the Indians and frequently spoke in their defense as a state legislator. *Los Angeles Public Library.*

500 men; but as it is just concentrating, and the tribe can muster within three days at least 3000 men, and Antonio having a large number of six shooters, rifles and other arms, with the use of which his people are well acquainted, your excellency will easily judge that our means are inadequate to resist a long time such a force.

After noting the death of the sheep men and the attacks on the military post on the Colorado, Haraszthy closed with a plea for aid:

Your excellency will see from the above that we are in need of volunteers from other counties, as all of our county are on duty and I fear Los Angeles County in the same distress. Consequently, the quickest way would be to send a steamer from San Francisco with sufficient force, arms, &c....'

146

Another letter written from San Diego and published in the *Alta* on December 3 was even more alarming:

> San Diego County is in a blaze from the Colorado to the Pacific. [Juan Antonio] is said to be in command of not less than three thousand Indians, which he has been over twelve months organizing; is now, and has done this within sixty miles of this town. He is allied with the Colorado Indians, and has invited the different tribes on lower California and Los Angeles County to join him.
>
> ...[A]ll the effective men...have gone to the relief of the detachment of troops at the mouth of the Gila; the whole country has concentrated at San Diego and formed themselves into a company which does not amount to fifty effective men; the town is under martial law, and all capable of bearing arms passed into service for the protection of the town against an antici-pated attack of hordes of Indians. Thus we now stand, with sentinels at every corner, business of all kinds suspended, easily stampeded, and scouts out to ascertain whatever facts they may be able.

Warner had returned to his ranch later on the day of the attack. On the way he encountered an Indian with some of his property and had to kill him when the straggler attempted to string an arrow. At the ranch, he sur-veyed the burned buildings and corrals. He had lost everything and later estimated the destruction at over $58,000. He quickly rode off to San Diego and safety.

Antonio Garra and his son had mobilized their forces at Los Coyotes Canyon, but they had nowhere near the strength estimated by the whites. Armed with a few guns, most of the Indians had only bows and arrows and lances, and their strength probably never exceeded two hundred fight-ing men. There was no turning back now, and Garra desperately sent out word for the surrounding tribes to unite with him in the war. All refused. On November 28, he wrote to Jose Joaquin Ortega, pleading for aid in the uprising:

> Some time I have been waiting here the answer to know clearly. For that this is not by will; it is for all in one. We have got to help with our lives, because we are invited to lose our lives. I sent a letter to Jose Estudillo—as yet he sends no answer. I also sent a letter above. I am here with the Cahuillas, and for this I say to you that you hasten to animate the Captains, before many Americans can arrive. Because here is Politano, also the People of Razon [Californios] and they are hurrying me to go there. For that I say to you, that you will arrange quickly, because it is for all that the damage has been done. They do not rise for anything but the Taxes —not for the mere wish of revolting. Nothing more.

Garra knew that every day the Indians held back from pressing the attack, the advantage was being lost. Again he wrote to Juan Antonio and pleaded for his help. "...If we lose this war," declared Garra, "all will be lost—the world." The Cahuilla chief again ignored the request and reiterated his friendship for the whites.

The uneasy whites had cause to be worried. A united Indian effort might have swept through the southern settlements as a hot knife through butter. The *Herald* noted:

> The people...on ranches south and east of this city, becoming alarmed at the hostile feelings exhibited by the Indians, are flocking to our town for protection...The town now presents the appearance of a fortified camp. Sentinels are on duty at every approach to the city, are pacing their lonely round; no Indian being permitted to pass without giving a good account of himself. The mayor of San Diego...has patriotically enrolled himself as a member of the volunteer company.

In Los Angeles, five commissioners were appointed at a mass meeting of the citizens to procure arms, horses, and supplies for an expedition against the hostiles. Able Stearns chairmanned a mixed group of Californios and Americans, including General Joshua Bean, Pio Pico, Augustin Olvera, and Francis Mellus. Sheriff Barton reported that a trip through the outlying districts had convinced him that the Indians were rising. He considered the situation desperate.

Pio Pico pressed the needed horses into service, and his brother quickly raised a force of fifty Californio cavalrymen. "...There is every possibility," commented the *Los Angeles Star* of November 27, "that in the course of the next forty-eight hours, two hundred men will be in the field."

Although enthusiasm and activity had helped forestall any panic in Los Angeles, a southern correspondent of the *Alta* confirmed that the Angelenos were really in no better shape than the San Diegans:

> There is not a cannon in this county, and as for muskets, there are not more than eighty good, bad and indifferent, in the county, except with the twenty U.S. soldiers at the Rancho del Chino. No small arms can be had, and there are but few in the county in the hands of private individuals. There is only about 300 pounds of powder in the stores for sale, and but little lead.

In San Francisco and the surrounding northern cities, there was great excitement and concern for their southern neighbors. Although sporadic skirmishing with Indians in the north took place, such affairs were usually quickly terminated by well-armed miners' posses. According to all reports, however, there was a serious danger that the Indians might well obtain the upper hand in the south because of superior strength and an unarmed citizenry. Such a circumstance was unthinkable, given the general attitudes held by the whites at the time.

148

"We will let those rascally redskins know," wrote a pioneer of those days, "that they have no longer to deal with the Spaniard or the Mexican, but with the invincible race of American backwoodsmen which has driven the savage from Plymouth Rock to the Rocky Mountains." The San Francisco *Alta* commented :

> The position of our Southern friends, appears extremely dangerous and imminent…. The impression appears well-founded that this attack of the Indians is but the precursor of a systematic and extended plan of operations against the whites, reaching from San Diego…to Santa Barbara in the north…. That whole country is, therefore, in a most exposed and perilous condition, without the men or other means to protect it against the…relentless savages.

Governor McDougal had only recently seen the settlement of the Mariposa war and he must have wondered when these Indian troubles were going to end. But Americans were already dead, and he quickly contacted General Ethan A. Hitchcock, commander of the United States Army Department of the Pacific. At the time, most of the California troops were on duty in Oregon, and few soldiers could be spared. The steamer *Sea Bird* was detailed to pick up fifty soldiers at Benecia and twenty more at Monterey and take them to San Diego under command of Major Frazier. These were all the available soldiers in the state.

At the same time, Governor McDougal authorized the formation of volunteer units in San Francisco. An advertisement in the *Alta* stirred up much interest and read as follows:

VOLUNTEERS, ATTENTION! HO! FOR SAN DIEGO!

> Patriots and adventurous young men, desirous of participating in the effort of the people of Southern California to drive from their soil hostile tribes of invading Indians, are requested to meet at the California Exchange, THIS DAY, (Sunday,) AT TEN O'CLOCK when preparatory measures will be taken to organize an effective cavalry company, for an expedition to the South, to leave on Tuesday.

It was dated December 7, 1851, and signed by Jno. W. Geary and John G. Marvin.

Marvin, fresh from his experiences in the Mariposa campaign, no doubt felt that his expertise in Indian fighting would prove valuable. Besides, there was as yet little in the way of California schools to superintend.

Calling themselves the San Francisco Rangers, the volunteers met officially on December 9, at the local California Guard armory. Geary was elected captain of the rangers and other officers were voted on and approved. That evening, Governor McDougal commissioned the officers of this group, and those of another unit known as the Aldrich Rangers. Both groups were to provide their own weapons and supplies and buy their own horses on arrival in the south. All, of course, expected to be well paid by the state, and the governor himself planned a trip to the seat of the disturbances.

Indian Agent Wozencraft, feeling that he should act in Barbour's absence, was aboard the *Sea Bird* with the U.S. troops heading for San Diego. He had been assured by General Hitchcock that if more troops were needed in the south, a hundred dragoons would be brought down from Port Orford.

In Southern California, events were moving swiftly. At Camp Independence, a topographical exploring party had arrived on November 30 following a difficult trip from Santa Fe. The group's scout had been wounded, and one of the soldiers of the escort had been killed by hostile

Indian Agent Dr. Oliver M. Wozencraft. *Author's collection.*

Yumas. By the time they reached the fort, they had been living on mule meat for several weeks and had engaged in several Indian fights.

At the fort, Lieutenant Murray and a detachment from San Diego had bolstered Sweeney's small force and made the worn-out exploring party as comfortable as possible. Two days later, a relief squad of soldiers under the command of Captain Davidson arrived, and preparations were made to abandon the post. Destroying the ferry and everything that could not be carried, the men started across the desert for San Diego.

Not intending to wait for an attack, the San Diego volunteers struck out for Warner's Ranch on November 27. Captain E. H. Fitzgerald was in command, and the men arrived at Warner's on December 1. From there they rode over to Kupa where they discovered and buried the dead Americans. All had been killed with their hands tied behind their backs. The village had then been burned to the ground.

Scouts sent out by the volunteers discovered a large force of Indians, together with much of Warner's livestock, located in Los Coyotes Canyon. Feeling that his force was inadequate for an attack, Fitzgerald bided his time in Warner's Valley. It was here on December 6 that he received news that Garra had been captured by Juan Antonio.

The Cahuilla chieftain had steadily ignored Garra's pleas for aid, yet being an Indian he was caught in the middle of events. The Mormons at San Bernardino had already accused him of being in league with the hostiles, while many of the Californios also mistrusted him. It was probably to settle the question of his loyalty once and for all that Juan Antonio sent for Garra early in December. And it was probably in the hope that the Cahuilla chief was finally ready to join his uprising that Garra rode to an Indian village some fifteen miles from Los Coyotes for a meeting.

Garra arrived at the rendezvous late at night with two of his men, one a Los Coyotes Cahuilla. The following day, Juan Antonio and Paulino Weaver, a local ranch man, rode in and confronted the three hostiles. Juan Antonio immediately ordered the Indians seized and stripped. He would have put them to death on the spot, but for the intervention of another Indian. Declaring the war over, Antonio sent word to the hostiles at Los Coyotes to disperse, then

■ Gabieleno Indians at San Gabriel. Carleton Watkins photo, ca. 1860s. Security First National Bank Collection.

escorted his prisoners to his village, located some three days away.

At Los Coyotes Canyon, there was panic when news of Garra's capture was received. Most of the Cupenos scattered to their villages, but Bill Marshall, Juan Verdugo, Jose Noca, and Santos, the Warner servant who had defected the night of the ranch fight, left for the coast. They were camped at Santa Isabel when a group of Fitzgerald's men took them into custody and returned with them to San Diego.

By this time, General Bean's Los Angeles volunteers were in the field, including a force of Californios under Andres Pico. A detachment of Mormons from San Bernardino was to meet them at Williams' Chino Ranch, and it was there they heard news of Garra's capture. Bean immediately rode to the Cahuilla village in San Timoteo Canyon. After much negotiating with Juan Antonio, he was finally able to obtain custody of Garra. By convincing the rebel chieftain that his son's only hope lay in surrender, Bean soon had the younger Garra in custody also. The Garra War, if the series of events could be styled as such, was over. The world, as Garra had known it, had indeed been lost forever.

After distributing presents and signing a new friendship treaty with Juan Antonio, Bean escorted his prisoners back to Chino. Here, on December 13, Garra dictated a statement, or "confession," as it was termed in the newspapers. In it he gave some personal information and recounted the attack at Warner's and the deaths of the American visitors at Kupa. The following excerpts seem to indicate he was telling the truth and trying to set the record straight:

> The two men named Bill Marshall and Juan Verde (Verdugo) had nothing to do with the transaction…. Neither have those men taken any part in the hostilities practised towards the Americans. They were entirely ignorant of what was done. I was advised by Joaquin Ortego and Jose Antonio Estudillo, to take up arms against the Americans. They advised me secretly, that if I could effect a Juncture with the other Indian tribes of California, and commence an attack upon all the Americans wherever we could find them, that the Californians would join with us, and help in driving the Americans from the country. They advised me to this course that I might revenge myself for the payment of taxes, which has been demanded of the Indian tribes…. This advice was given me by Juan Ortego, in his rancho. No other person was present at the time. I afterwards saw Antonio Estudillo, who advised me to the same effect, assuring me of the cooperation of the Californians, throughout the country.

> My men under arms have never exceeded 30 or 40 at any one time. I myself have had no communication with any other tribes than the Yumas and Cahuillas. The former agreed to join with me, but they subsequently refused. I only know of the readiness of the other tribes to combine and kill Americans from what Ortego told me. …In the affair with the men with the sheep, ten of my men were killed by the Americans.

Whatever Marshall's involvement might have been, it seemed clear that various Californios had helped instigate Garra's war against the hated Americanos. But to Garra it no longer mattered.

At San Diego, Major Heintzelman had received orders to proceed against the hostiles. Dr. Wozencraft had arrived with the army troops on the *Sea Bird* and he now joined the expedition which arrived at Santa Isabel on December 17. Here the command was joined by Captain Davidson, who had just abandoned Camp Independence. The combined force now numbered about a hundred men.

■ Southern California Cahuilla Indian village. The rectangular house construction suggests a date ca. 1870. Prior to that, circular homes, or Kish, were used. *Smithsonian Institution.*

On the morning of December 20, Heintzelman divided his forces and entered Los Coyotes Canyon from two different directions. They were quickly spotted by the Cahuillas who remained there—some one hundred strong—under their chief, Chapuli. According to one newspaper account of the action, the Indians thought the troops were an emigrant party and decided to attack. The San Diego *Herald,* however, stated that the Indians opened fire because they considered their positions impregnable. What-ever happened, there was a brief exchange of bullets and arrows and the Indians fled up the mountain side, leaving behind eight dead. The soldiers then fired the rancheria, while a detachment pursued the Cahuillas. No casualties were sustained by the troops.

Bill Marshall's wife was taken prisoner and convinced Heintzelman that the Indians would come in if the troops would stop chasing them. Within two days, most of the natives had been rounded up and four of them were put on trial for the killings at Kupa. The military tribunal found all four guilty. The condemned knelt at the edge of their graves in the pres-ence of eighty other Indians on Christmas morning and were executed by a squad of twenty soldiers.

Wozencraft was a witness to the proceedings and later wrote that "they [the Indians] all admitted the punishment to be just and well deserved. …To have done less after they knew we were aware of their guilt, would have been fraught with evil…."

The day preceding the execution, General Bean had escorted eleven prisoners to the Chino ranch, where another military tribunal was called to order. A state militia court composed of both Americans and Californios tried and executed young Antonio Garra and another Indian on December 27, 1851. It was decided there was not enough evidence to try the remain-ing Indian captives.

In San Diego, Bill Marshall and Juan Verdugo were hanged on the afternoon of December 12. Their trial had been conducted by yet another military tribunal, primarily because Marshall had been convicted largely through the testimony of Indians—testimony not admissable under civil law. Despite the elder Garra's declaration that Marshall was innocent, other Cupenos had insisted he was indeed involved in the various murders.

Tradition has it that after his conviction Marshall asked for an interview with the woman who had spurned him so many years before. Senora Lugardia de Muchada, who had remarried since her husband's death, visited Marshall and he begged her forgiveness for his involvement in her first husband's death.

On the gallows, Marshall asked to be forgiven also for his many transgressions but steadily maintained his innocence of the crime for which he was to die. When the trapdoor was sprung on the ex-sailor, the drop proved to be too short and he struggled horribly before he was pronounced dead.

By December 10, it seemed clear that arms, not troops, were needed in southern California, and Governor McDougal disbanded the two volunteer companies. With their fighting blood aroused and the promise of government pay in the offing, the men hesitated in abandoning the expedition. About forty of the volunteers insisted on maintaining their company and paraded about the streets declaring they would charter a boat for the south, anyway. No promises as to their legality could be made by McDougal, but he sanctioned the expedition, which sailed under the command of one Captain Haig.

■ These Mohave Indians at Fort Mojave in 1864 are still dressed in the grass skirts and rabbit skins of their pristine period. *Bancroft Library.*

The volunteer group landed at San Diego on December 30, and although there was no Indian fighting to be done, the men promptly distinguished themselves by fighting each other. After Haig and one of his men had twice fought with knives and pistols, a San Diegan and a volunteer had a duel, and if the army had not stepped in, "the streets of San Diego would have been drenched with blood," as one officer put it.

Antonio Garra was brought into San Diego on January 9, 1852, and put on trial the same day. Again, the tribunal was made up of state militia officers, with J. J. Warner acting as interpreter. Major McKinstry agreed to defend Garra on charges of treason, murder and robbery. The trial was a brief affair, and by early afternoon of the following day the Indian leader had been convicted of murder and theft.

Just after four o'clock on the afternoon of January 10, 1852, Garra was shot by a firing squad as he knelt at his grave. "…His whole deportment," noted the *Herald*, "evinced the brave man prepared to meet his fate."

Garra's "war," an insignificant affair by any standards, still managed to achieve a measure of respectability in the annals of California Indian troubles. Whatever the old Indian's short-comings as a leader, he dreamed of uniting a large segment of the state's natives in a war to sweep all the whites from California. It was a wild dream—a scheme that never could have succeeded even if he had somehow managed to destroy San Diego and Los Angeles. But the scope of his ambition was magnificent. And his admissions of guilt afterwards made it clear that he would rather die than live in a land where his way of life, and great dream, had failed.

■ A mounted Mohave Indian poses for photographer George Wharton James, ca. 1900. *Southwest Museum.*

Juan Antonio died during a smallpox epidemic in 1863. In his last years the old Cahuilla chieftain perhaps regretted not having joined in Garra's revolt. But by then, the dream had been all but forgotten.

CHAPTER 9 / SOURCES

Any modern study relating to the Garra uprising must acknowledge the fine work on Indian resistance in Southern California entitled *Chiefs and Challengers* by George Harwood Phillips. Mr. Phillips' book is carefully and thoroughly researched and is highly recommended to anyone interested in the problems, and politics, of the Southern California Indians during the 1850s.

UNPUBLISHED MATERIAL

U.S. Congress, 33rd Congress, Special Session, Senate Executive Document No. 4:

O. M. Wozencraft to Hon. Luke Lea, January 18, 1852.

Office of the Secretary of State, California State Archives, Indian War Files, Sacramento:

J. H. Bean to John McDougal, January 1, 1852.

NEWSPAPERS

San Francisco *Daily Alta California*, December 3, 4, 7, 9, 11, 12, 18, 1851; January 2, 1852.

The San Diego *Herald*, November 27, December 11, 18, 1851; January 17, 1852.

PRINCIPAL PUBLISHED WORKS

Bean, Lowell and Lawton, Harry. *The Cahuilla Indians of Southern California*. Banning, CA: Malki Museum Press, 1965.

Bonsal, Stephen. *Edward Fitzgerald Beale*. New York: G. P. Putnam's Sons, 1912.

Heizer, Robert F., editor. *Handbook of North American Indians, Vol. 8, California*. Washington D.C.: Smithsonian Institution, 1978.

Hill, Joseph John. *The History of Warner's Ranch and Its Environs*. Los Angeles: privately printed, 1927.

James, Harry C. *The Cahuilla Indians*. Los Angeles: Westernlore Press, 1960.

Morrison, Lorrin L. *Warner, The Man and the Ranch*. Los Angeles: privately printed, 1962.

Phillips, George Harwood. *Chiefs and Challengers*. Berkeley: University of California Press, 1975.

Robinson, W. W. *The Indians of Los Angeles, Story of the Liquidation of a People*. Los Angeles: Glen Dawson, 1952.

Whipple, A. W. *The Whipple Report*. Los Angeles: Westernlore Press, 1961.

Wilke, Philip J., Lawton, Harry W., King, Thomas F., and Hammond, Stephen. *The Cahuilla Indians of the Colorado Desert: Ethnohistory and Prehistory*. Ramona, CA: Ballena Press, 1975.

Woodward, Arthur. *Feud On The Colorado*. Los Angeles: Westernlore Press, 1955.

OTHER SOURCES

Guinn. J. M. "Yuma Indian Depredations and the Glanton War," *Historical Society of Southern California*, Vol. VI, Los Angeles, 1903.

Veeder, Charles H. "Yuma Indian Depredations on the Colorado in 1850," (deposition), *Historical Society of Southern California*, Vol. VII, Los Angeles, 1907-1908.

Chapter 10

MAJOR SAVAGE

When peace treaties with many of the tribes had been
signed at camps Fremont, Barbour, and Belt, it was hoped
the San Joaquin Valley and foothills could return to normal. The commissioners and agents had worked hard. Reservations had been established between the Tuolumne River
in the north and the Tule River in the south. The Indians
were instructed that they were to live on this land where
the Great White Father would feed, clothe, and care for them. As soon as
the treaties were ratified by Congress, schools, farming equipment, and
working stock would be supplied. For now, the natives were given token
presents of beads and clothes and were fed by the commissioners. Trading
posts were established on the reserves also, and in July 1851, Major Savage
opened his new store on the Fresno River, near Coarsegold Gulch.

Besides being a general store for both the local whites and the Indians,
the trading posts served as distribution points for ladling out government
supplies to the natives. Public roads ran through or near the reserves, and
soon there were scattered ranches, stores, ferries, and crude hotels along
routes. Almost all of these places served whiskey and were a constant source
of trouble among both whites and Indians.

In early April of 1851, Adam Johnston was called to the Merced River
to investigate reports of whiskey troubles on the reserve. Upon arrival, he
found that there were four tent saloons operating at various river crossings, the place at which he stayed being within 100 yards of an Indian
rancheria. On his first night there, Johnston became embroiled in a difficulty which he described in one of his reports:

> A young man, having first heated himself with liquor at this house,
> proceeded about 12 o'clock at night to the Indian rancheria and demanded
> a woman to sleep with for the night. Not being supplied as promptly as he
> expected, he set about appropriating the wife of an Indian to himself, when
> he was seized and tied by a portion of the Indians, while others ran to me to
> know what they should do with him. By the time I got out of bed, the man
> had broken loose from them and rushed into the tent, followed, or rather
> surrounded, by a large number of Indians.

Both parties were clamorous and noisy, the Indians telling me their story in Spanish and Indian, (all at a time) and the white man swearing lustily and loudly that he would massacre all the Indians.

Johnston was able to calm everyone down and the following morning assembled both parties for a parley. He assured the Indians that the man was drunk and did not know what he was doing and that it would not happen again. Finally both groups separated without further trouble. Local whites had assembled that morning also, and their grumbled oaths and threats made the agent wonder just what might have happened if he had not been there.

Quite naturally, saloon keepers had no compunctions about selling liquor to either Indians or white men. In December, a correspondent of the San Francisco *Daily Alta California* wrote that "I have just seen a gentleman who witnessed a fight yesterday evening...between the San Joaquin Indians, 'TomKit' chief, and the Kings River Indians, 'Pasqual,' chief. A number of each tribe had collected for the purpose of catching salmon, when a dispute arose, occasioned by liquor. Two or three were killed and several wounded."

Pahmit, a Dumna Yokut, helped build Fort Miller and lived to be over one hundred years of age. *Monna Olsen.*

Johnston urged that a military force be established permanently in the locality of the reservations to help the Indian agents enforce the treaties. The army and commissioners both agreed on the importance of troops in the valley. Captain Keyes, who commanded the commissioners'

Fort Miller as it appeared in the early 1860s. Most buildings were constructed of adobe, beginning with the arrival of Quartermaster Captain Thomas Jordan in 1853. *National Archives.*

escort, had orders to select sites for military posts while in the valley.

When Keyes headed south in May of 1851 as an escort to commissioner Barbour, he detailed Lieutenant Tredwell Moore to take charge of two infantry companies and establish an army post at the site of Camp Barbour, on the San Joaquin River. The commissioners and their army escort were located on the Kings River at the time, concluding treaties with the Four Creeks Indians.

Returning to the site of Camp Barbour, Moore's first act, according to the local Dumna Indians, was to drive the Indians from their rancheria and burn their huts. The soldiers pitched their tents, and Moore began planning his new post. Temporary structures were put up to house the low stock of provisions. Recently, Captain Keyes had sent eight wagons to Stockton for supplies, but the city had been destroyed by fire, and the supplies had burned with the town.

In a dispatch to the war department, Lieutenant Moore reported the establishment of his post on June 1, 1851. He named it Fort Miller, after the commanding officer at Benecia. He reported the location as being "on the San Joaquin River, 150 miles from Stockton, the nearest post office."

There was no immediate need for shelter as the weather was quite warm and the men would have all summer to prepare for fall. Moore did want to erect a wooden blockhouse as soon as possible, however, and he was soon sketching his plans.

Born in Ohio in 1825, Moore was appointed a second lieutenant in July of 1847 and served in Mexico during the war. He expected to receive his first lieutenant's commission at any time and was no doubt quite pleased to be a member of the escort during this historic, treaty-making trek.

When Moore began work on his blockhouse is not clear, but in September, a local miner noted in his diary that the soldiers were busy building a barracks. Moore's plans called for a structure measuring eighty by twenty-

■ An Indian shelter near Fresno, ca. 1890s. The native Californians quickly adapted to the white man's clothing, but were anxious to retain their own culture. *Fresno City and County Historical Society.*

The old, original Fort Miller blockhouse and barracks as it appeared prior to being moved. It was moved to avoid the flooding of the area caused by the construction of the Friant Dam, near Fresno. *Author's collection.*

four feet, with a room at either end and an open passage in the middle. Besides the four windows and two doors, there were to be loopholes lining the walls. Lumber was a problem, however. Captain Keyes noted that there was "scarcely any timber fit for building on the reserve. A coarse-grained pine, oak and cottonwood are the principal trees, the oak being brittle and in most cases more or less decayed at the heart." The pine would have to do.

Moore and his men rounded up as many of the local Indians as they felt were needed and supervised them in cutting down trees and hauling them to the building site. They were shown how to shape the logs with axes and carefully fit them together, for nails were scarce. Wooden pegs would have to hold everything together. Wood gathering was hard work, and it took many men to haul the logs. It was deemed "squaw" work, and the Indian men at first objected.

"Sometimes Indians don't want work," recalled Pahmit, a Dumna Indian who was there. "Soldiers make 'em work. Soldiers put two iron rings in oak tree, tie Indians hands to 'em. Soldiers take long black snake whip for whip mules. They whip Indians on back. They whip, whip, whip. Two, three Indians die—whip 'em too much." The Indians called the blockhouse that was taking shape "big wood house for fight," and they were made to understand just what it was for. It was late September before the first structure of Fort Miller was completed.

Above Cassity's Crossing, sometimes called Fort Washington now, another collection of tents was springing up which the inhabitants referred to as Rootville. The Yokuts watched the steady influx of whites with alarm and suddenly realized they would never stop coming. "Their land," wrote a correspondent from the San Joaquin, "which was solemnly guaranteed to them by a late treaty, is now overrun with miners, both Americans and foreigners, and the richest holes in the river wrested from them by the strong arms of the invaders."

Miner Robert Eccleston had watched the Fresno reserve and noted in his journal that "the Americans are working on the Indian Reservation and

162

determined to keep the Indians off by force who don't like it.... The traders are selling goods and liquor to the Indians...." Working a claim above Fort Miller, Eccleston and many other miners fully expected an Indian outbreak in the fall.

With the disbanding of the Mariposa Battalion in July, Jim Savage immediately began putting his trading empire back together and again sought to dominate the Indians. Lorenzo D. Vinsonhaler, who had been the official guide of the battalion, became Savage's partner, and the two men began trading operations between the Chowchilla and Kaweah rivers. Judge Marvin was appointed quartermaster of the Kings River reservation, despite his official position as state superintendent of public instruction. When Marvin and Savage saw how much freight was being shipped to and from the reserves, they became partners in a freighting operation also.

Savage estimated his losses during the war at over $25,000 and in October submitted a claim to the government for that amount. He had always considered himself a friend of the Indians, and it probably never crossed his mind that he took advantage of them. After all, he was teaching them to farm and even building an Indian school.

Savage once addressed Dr. Lafayette H. Bunnell:

> Doc, while you study books, I study men. I am not often very much deceived, and I perfectly understand the present situation, but let those laugh who win. If I can make good my losses by the Indians, out of the Indians, I am going to do it. I was the best friend the Indians had and they would have destroyed me. Now that they once more call me 'chief' they shall build me up. I will be just to them, as I have been merciful, for after all they are but poor ignorant beings, but my losses must be made good.

Bunnell reminded Savage that he was surrounded by lawless men who were anxious to further their own interests at any cost—men who were quite capable of "cutting your throat." But Savage only smiled and reminded the doctor that he could take care of himself.

One of the men working for Savage exemplified the lawless characters to whom Bunnell referred. Little is known of Joel Brooks, and he first appears in the records as a member of the Mariposa Battalion. Brooks once guided one Gwinn H. Heap from Tejon Pass to Fort Miller, a trip Heap later recalled when asked about Brooks' character.

> He boasted to me that he had killed more Indians than any other man in California, frequently after they were captured and made prisoners. He had been expelled from all the settlements neighboring on the upper San Joaquin as a notoriously bad character, and soon after he left me at Fort Miller the inhabitants of Millerton threatened to hang him if he again made his appearance in their town.

Brooks later claimed that Savage cheated the Indians, although few would believe him:

> My instructions from Savage were that when I delivered cattle on the San Joaquin and Kings River, and to other more southern Indians, I was to take receipts for double the number actually delivered…and when to Indians on the Fresno, to deliver one-third less than were receipted for. I also had orders to sell all beef I could to miners, which I did.

This was beef sold by rancher John C. Fremont to the government to be provided to the Indians through the Indian traders. Although Brooks probably lied, there was so much fraud and misconduct in the Indian service that he was correct in spirit, if not in substance. Captain E. D. Keyes recalled the following incident:

> About ten years subsequent to the treaties…a herdsman who had been employed by contractors to furnish beeves to these Indians on their reservations declared to me, as a solemn truth, that he had delivered, and had receipted for, one and the same old Toruno [stag] twenty-seven times. The weight of that beast was entered in the accounts and paid for at figures varying from 1,000 to 1,100 pounds. That old stag…would break loose invariably the night after he was receipted for, and return to the corral to which he was habituated and where he was always well cared for.

Just as informal were the means by which all these cattle distributions took place. In a conversation with an Indian office official the following year, Dr. Wozencraft displayed a particularly naive handling of his duties as agent. When asked what proof he had that the Indian traders had issued beef to the Indians, Wozencraft replied that he had no other proof than the word of the traders themselves:

> "Have you not ordered beef to the amount of 1500 head to be delivered between the Fresno and Four Creeks, without ever having been in the Four Creeks region?"
>
> Answer: "I have never been to the Four Creeks region, but have ordered the beef."
>
> "How many Indians do you suppose the Four Creeks country to contain?"
>
> Answer: "I do not know."
>
> "If you do not know, how could you determine the amount of cattle necessary for their subsistence?"
>
> Answer: "From what was promised them by the treaties."
>
> "How do you know that the Indians of the Four Creeks ever received any of that beef?"
>
> Answer: "Nothing, further than that I was told so by the traders at the Fresno. I have no proof of it."

"Do you not know that, in some instances, the traders who issued and the contractors for the supply of the beef were the same men?"

Answer: "I do."

"Were the contracts made by you verbal, or written?"

Answer: "With Mr. Norris my contract was simply a verbal one; with messrs. Savage and Haler [Vinsonhaler] it was, on my part, the acceptance from them of a proposition, which I understood was the same as a contract."

Several years later, Wozencraft repudiated this testimony and gave a more detailed explanation of the circumstances. His testimony, still a picture of loose and sloppy handling of Indian supplies, did little to enhance the public view of the Indian office. Wozencraft's reputation was further damaged when rancher Isaac Williams charged that the agent wanted a kickback for giving him the contract to supply cattle to the Indians.

Despite the dire predictions of trouble that fall, nothing happened. A letter from the San Joaquin in early December 1851 noted that the Indians were peaceable on the river around Fort Washington and were busy catching salmon. One thousand, one hundred and eighty head of cattle were reported as having been distributed among the tribes on Kings River and in the Four Creeks country since August. The winter would be peaceful after all.

At the time of the creation of Mariposa County in 1850, it was understood that as the situation arose, other counties would be created out of that vast territory. The recent Indian war had called attention to the Four Creeks country, and much interest was shown in that area because of its farming and stock-raising potential. A notice in the Stockton *San Joaquin Republican* in early March requested that questions concerning the Four Creeks be sent to Major Savage at his trading post on the reservation. By that spring a minor real estate boom was developing.

Other factors contributed to the opening up of the valley. William Campbell and John Pool established a ferry on the Kings River, while others were located on the San Joaquin and other crossings. The single, most important factor of the boom, however, was a bevy of out-of-office politicians in Mariposa County. Here was a chance to get in on the ground floor of a rich and developing area.

Savage and others pushed an act through the legislature creating Tulare County out of the southern portion of Mariposa. It became law on April 20, 1852. The act provided for a commission of four men, with Savage in charge, to hold elections on July 10 and organize a county government. After leading a large group of men south, the trader set up polling places at Pool's Ferry and the Woods cabin. When the election results were in, Martin Lewis, president of the commissioners, reported that Major Walter H. Harvey had been elected county judge, William Dill was the new sheriff, and the other county offices were all duly filled. The new county could boast of no village or town, and the county seat was designated as the tragic Woods cabin.

In April of 1852, Savage had taken young Dr. Lewis Leach as a partner in his trading post. Savage was again an important figure in the area, both among the whites and Indians. Besides his mining and trading activities, he was engaged in extensive farming ventures, utilizing Indian labor. "Major Savage," noted a Stockton newspaper in May, "has just come over with a large number of Indians and has given new life to everything in the neighborhood. He bought wagons, ploughs, seeds, provisions, etc. and the quantity of work he has gone through...has astonished everybody.... The Indians all love him, to all appearances, and still he manages them in such a way that they also fear him as much."

Late in April 1852, a party of eight prospectors left Coarsegold Gulch and headed for the high country looking for "color." There had been no trouble with Indians since the late war and prospectors felt it was now safe to travel anywhere in the mountains. It was known, however, that the Yosemite Indians had left the Fresno River reserve nearly a year ago and returned to their old haunts. The prospectors entered Yosemite Valley on the morning of May 2 and fanned out, looking for both game and mineral deposits. Young Steve Grover stayed behind in camp to care for the stock and prepare dinner.

A short time later, Grover was horrified to hear war whoops, guns being fired, and the yells of his companions. Soon two members of the party came running into camp drenched to the skin from having waded through Bridalveil Falls Creek. One of the men had been wounded by several arrows, and Grover held off the pursuing Indians while the men caught their breath. In a moment, the rest of the surviving whites returned to camp, and it was determined that three men by the names of Sherburn, Tudor, and Rose had apparently been killed.

The Yosemites surrounded the camp, but the miners successfully held them at bay with their rifles. Finally, the whites were able to make a break and began climbing a rock bluff while the Indians swarmed below, showering them with arrows. "The valley seemed alive with them," wrote Grover later, "on rocks, and behind trees, bristling like demons, shrieking their war whoops, and exulting in our apparently easy capture."

The white men had all panicked by now, most of their weapons having been dropped in the flight. Grover's hat had been shot off, he had lost his pistol, and several arrows had pierced his clothes. As the men huddled together beneath a projecting rock, which provided some cover from the clouds of arrows, the Yosemites began rolling boulders down on them from above. They could see old Chief Tenaya below in a clearing, directing his men. With only two rifles remaining to the party, the whites were sure they had only moments to live. However, a lucky shot killed a sub-chief, and the Yosemites suddenly withdrew out of sight. "Our feelings toward the 'noble red man' at this time can better be imagined than described," recalled Grover.

By now it was dusk and the battered miners hugged their niche in the cliff until midnight, then ventured out into the flat land. Terrified that the Indians would pounce on them at any moment, they climbed out of Yosemite Valley and in five days were resting in Coarsegold Gulch.

Grover's brother formed a party of men and started for Yosemite Valley to retrieve the remains of the lost miners. Only the bodies of Sherburn and Tudor were found, and they were buried where they had died. Six days later, Rose turned up in Coarsegold and reported he was the only survivor of the group. Interestingly, he immediately sold the mine he had owned jointly with the two dead men, and foul play began to be suspected.

Meanwhile, at Fort Miller, Lieutenant Moore had been apprised of the

▦ Grover's prospecting party took shelter from the Indians in the rocky cliffs beside Bridalveil Falls, shown here in a view from the 1860s. *Yosemite Museum.*

hostilities and quickly reported to his superiors. "I will start in pursuit of them on Monday next," he wrote on June 12, "and endeavor not only to punish the Indians who were engaged in committing the murder, but also remove the tribes to the reservation set aside for them by the commissioners last year."

Moore was short on supplies, but after sending to Benicia for more, he took most of his command into the mountains. According to a report in the *Alta* on July 2, only a sergeant, four privates, and several sick men were left behind. When their comrades rode out, they barricaded the gates to keep out the Indians and hoped for the best. Moore's first report on the expedition was written from the headwaters of the Merced on July 8:

> ...[I]mmediately on my arrival scouting parties were sent to scour the country in all directions, many deserted rancherias were found, but no Indians. The friendly Indians we had with us as guides are of the opinion that the entire tribe had crossed the Sierras. Major Savage with a party of Indians struck a fresh trail leading from the valley towards the headwaters of the San Joaquin, his provisions given out he was obliged to return. On the 1st I took with me a party of twelve men and taking major Savage's trail soon came to a heavy trail. This we continued to follow, and on the morning of the 4th crossed the main ridge of the Sierras. I encamped about noon and sending out scouts I received information that there was a rancheria some four miles distant. By dividing my party I was enabled to take them so completely by surprise that before they were able to move they were entirely surrounded. Prisoners were taken—six men. The remainder women and children. One of the prisoners acknowledged that they saw the murder of the whites on the Merced, but denied having participated in it. A number of trinkets, together with some clothing was found which fully implicated their participation in the division of the murdered men's property, if not in the murder. The men I then ordered to be shot which was done in the morning of the 5th. From the women taken I have learned that it was a general thing and that nearly the entire tribe was present at the murder.

> "Lt. McLean started for the Yo-cemity Valley on the 1st with ten men with instructions to destroy the rancherias and provisions there, he succeeded in finding a large quantity of acorns which were destroyed. One of his men (Riley) was severely wounded, receiving two arrow shots on the night of the 4th while on post as sentinel. Lieut. McLean arrived this morning having accomplished the destruction of as much property...as could be found. Riley, the wounded man died last night...."

Guide Joel Brooks volunteered to execute the Indian prisoners. In a second report dated the following day, Moore related that the Indian women captives told him the Yosemites had fled to the Mono country, and Moore was determined to go after them. In the course of the campaign, Moore did discover Mono Lake, on the east side of the Sierra, but he failed to bring in the stubborn Yosemites. Lieutenant McLean had returned to Fort Miller by early August, and Moore followed with the balance of his command a few days later. Brevet Major George W. Patten had recently arrived at the post and was in charge at this time.

Some important developments took place that early winter and spring of 1852. Adam Johnston was dismissed as agent, and the Indians lost a friend whose place would be difficult to fill. He had traveled widely and worked hard, but his subordination to the commissioners had discouraged him. It all seemed so hopeless. When his disillusionment began to be reflected in his work, he was discharged. In 1856, he was still trying to collect back pay and expenses.

George Barbour, too, had resigned in February. Although eighteen treaties had been secured and an uneasy peace prevailed, there was still little in the way of an Indian program in California.

On March 3, 1852, a federal act creating an Indian superintendent of California was enacted, and Edward F. Beale was named to the post. Beale, it will be remembered, was one of the men who made the desperate journey to San Diego after the battle at San Pascual. He was a personable and energetic naval officer and saw much duty carrying dispatches across the country. It was Beale who carried the first California gold samples to Washington and when it became likely he could secure a political appointment, he resigned his naval commission early in 1851. The Los Angeles *Star* editorialized that Beale's appointment was the best that could be made.

McKee and Wozencraft remained as agents, while Benjamin D. Wilson of Los Angeles was appointed the new agent in the south.

■ Lieutenant Nathaniel C. McLean. *Army Military History Institute.*

But the most significant and far-reaching event of the period was the rejection of all eighteen treaties by the United States Senate on June 1. This was largely a result of strenuous objections by many California newspapers and private outrage that so much prime land had been given to the Indians for reservations—land coveted by much of the white population.

The Indians' case had not been helped by the fact that the commissioners had been allotted $25,000 for the expenses of their duties, but had spent or committed the government to more than $700,000.

"Though we might have been disposed to overlook a little stretch of authority on the part of the commissioners in the face of the meagre appropriation of Congress," groaned the *Alta*, "we should not like to have it supposed that we can even tacitly assent to such extraordinary proceedings as appear to have taken place."

■ Lieutenant Tredwell Moore, first commander of Fort Miller. *Army Military History Institute.*

At least now there could be no more complaints about white encroachments on the reserves or the dispensing of liquor on Indian property since, as of June 1, the Indians had no property in California. One can only speculate as to the feelings of a people who had been given a bit of their own land by a distant Great White Father with one hand, while he later took it away with the other. It was late in July before news of the treaty rejection reached California.

Judge Marvin was in San Francisco in early July and passed on some news of the San Joaquin to a local newspaper:

> A number of squatters have settled on the Indian reservation on the Fresno with the hopes that the Indian treaties may not be confirmed. It is the intention of some of them to engage in farming. Major Savage is now threshing his barley...he had nearly two hundred acres and employed two or three Americans...and a number of Indians with sickles in cutting it, giving the Indians the gleanings for their labor.... He has fifty or sixty acres of wheat, twenty-five acres of corn and twenty-five acres of potatoes, all doing well.

Besides the Indian laborers in his fields, Savage had brought Chief Pasqual and most of the men of his Choinumni tribe from the Kings River to help in the construction of a large, adobe home, trading headquarters and hotel on his farm. "The house will be two stories high, surmounted by an observatory, telescope, etc.," reported the *San Joaquin Republican*. Savage was once again "King of the Tulares," and kings did not live in rude shacks and tents.

While both Savage and the troops at Fort Miller were in the mountains chasing the Yosemites, an incident on the Kings River threatened to engulf the foothills in another bloody war. On July 1, a group of Choinimni Indians under Chief Watoka visited the ferry of Campbell, Pool and company where Mr. B. F. Edmunds was the only man on duty. The property consisted of a cabin which served as a combination saloon, trading post, hotel, and cafe, and a ten- by thirty-foot boat on a rope which did duty as the ferry. Watoka showed Edmunds a paper given to him by Savage, which stated that the ferry was located on land given to the Indians by the commissioners and no white man must set foot on it without permission. During the discussion, several other whites arrived and the Indians left, "threatening to kill them all if they were on the reserve at their return," noted the Sacramento *Union*.

This alleged threat was the basis for the events that followed, but just why the Indians waited so long after the treaties had been made to claim the land on which the ferry operated is not clear. The ferry had been in operation for many months by this time. Perhaps the real reason for the Indian visit was suggested by a newspaper correspondent writing from the San Joaquin. Fish was a staple in the Indian diet and the ferry was destroying the native fisheries above. Watoka was merely protesting this newest incursion on Indian rights by the ferrymen. Also, it was known that Savage was interested in running off the traders at the ferry so that the local Indians would trade with him.

Leaving some travelers in charge of the store, Edmunds and William Campbell rode north to secure aid from the miners along the San Joaquin. Events now moved swiftly, as chronicled by a correspondent of the *Alta*:

> The people here are expecting every day to have the devil to pay with the red-skins. A few days ago a man keeping a store and ferry on Kings River came into our camp under whip and spur, stating that he had been warned by…the Kings River tribe to leave immediately—that the next time they warned him, they would kill him. Very soon there was a party numbering twenty-eight men, mounted, and armed to the teeth, who left here for the river to investigate….

Campbell, Edmunds, and Major Walter Harvey collected a large group of men and galloped back to the ferry. Leaving a portion of the volunteers at the store, the balance struck out for the Indian rancheria after dividing into two groups—all under Harvey's command. The party rode into the native village and a parley was held, although few details were revealed in the various accounts of the incident.

One participant wrote that:

> Had they confined themselves strictly to this object [investigation] there is no doubt but the whole affair might have been settled to the satisfaction of all parties, for I believe it to be the desire of the Indians to preserve the treaty. But, instead of making any inquiries regarding the threat, the whole

party rode into the rancheria and after a few words had passed, the import of which I didn't understand, they commenced firing upon and killed about 25 or 30 of them.

Major Harvey, in his account of the affair, stated that the whites had merely asked the Indians to accompany them back to the ferry where matters could be discussed. "The chief refused to go," he wrote, "and immediately the warriors began gathering up their bows and arrows with every evidence of hostility. We thought it better at this juncture, to convince them that we were ready for war if they desired it, and at once fired upon them, and after a fierce conflict of some minutes, they fled to the mountains, leaving some of their number dead upon the ground..."

With most of the Indian men of the village away helping build Savage's home on the Fresno, it was feared by other Indians hearing of the incident that many of the dead were women and children. The fact that only one of the whites "received a slight wound in the arm..." made it all the more likely that a slaughter had taken place. None of the accounts of the "fight" offers any estimation of just how many Indian men were involved in the action.

At Savage's farm on the Fresno, Pasqual heard news of the trouble and feared the worst. He complained bitterly to Savage:

> What shall we do? We try to live on the land the commissioners gave us, in friendly relations with the white man, but they kill our women and children, and if we flee to the mountains, they hunt us, and we have no place on the lands the commissioners gave us or in the mountains. Where shall we go and what shall we do? When the commissioners gave us the United States flag and our papers they told us it would protect us, but now the flag is all stained with blood, and our papers are all bloody, and who shall wash it off? We are poor and weak—the whites are rich and strong—and we pray for mercy.

Disgusted at Harvey's action, Savage did what he could to pacify the natives. Most newspapers condemned the attack and Dr. Wozencraft immediately wrote Governor John Bigler, pleading with him for help in "preventing the recurrence of similar outrages, and preventing a war." When the governor did not bother to answer, the agent tried to secure federal warrants from the U.S. attorney, but was informed that no laws applied in the case. Before a civil action could be initiated, Harvey was elected county judge and further efforts seemed futile.

When General Ethan A. Hitchcock, commander of the U.S. Army Department of the Pacific, received news of the incident, he quickly dispatched troops to the area. He had been preparing to send a patrol of dragoons to reinforce Lieutenant Moore anyway, but he now sent Brevet Major

George W. Patten and an infantry detachment to Fort Miller also. As senior officer at the post, Patten would now be in command, but after leaving a token force at the fort, he left for Kings River. His report, dated July 26, related the results of his meeting with the Indians:

I left Fort Miller on the morning of the 22 instant at which time Lieut. Moore was still in the mountains in pursuit of the hostile Indians. The tribes in the vicinity of Fort Miller are in an unsettled condition owing on the one hand to the expedition of Lieut. Moore into the mountains and on the other side into the recent, and unprovoked attack of certain citizens under the command of Major Harvey upon the peaceful rancherias upon Kings River. At the time of the attack, their chief, Shasta, with his people [men] was employed at the plantation of Major Savage, building him an adobe house.

General Ethan Allen Hitchcock seems to be pondering California's Indian troubles. *National Archives*

Not an arrow was fired by the Indians until the attack was made by the whites, and then apparently more in fear than in anger. The result is this—The Indians wish to know whether they are to be protected or not by the government on their own reserves—They have lost confidence in the whites and deem the Americans their general enemy.

Shasta says that the flag which he has raised above his ranch, the United States Flag, is bloody and that the stains must be wiped out—that if it is not done, and that soon, he will take his people and go into the mountains and weep.

Yesterday, the 25th instant, I promised to meet the tribes in council (some five thousand) but have sent them word that I would return by the 15th of August at which time Major Savage informs me that there will be a gathering of some ten thousand Indians at which meeting will be discussed the ultimatum—they demand the arrest of the murderers of their innocent people—and if something is not done in regards thereto and that speedily, in my opinion a general war with the whole of the tribes is unavoidable.

The tribes have still confidence in the troops, but distrust all others, and with this statement I would call respectfully the attention of the Commanding General to as strong a display of troops in the vicinity of Kings River on or about the 15th of August as can possibly be made. I am quite assured it will save...blood.

Upon his return to Fort Miller, Patten sent for Major Savage and asked him to go to the Four Creeks and explain the situation to as many Indians as possible. Within three days, Savage had visited some twelve to fifteen different tribes and villages and asked the Indians to keep the peace. An

Although kicked out of West Point, Walter Harvey somehow acquired the title of "Major." He was a special Indian agent on occasion and almost went into the ferry business with Savage.
Maurine Anderson, Annie Mitchell Room, Tulare County Library.

observer reported that "never was an audience at Divine service more strict and orderly." According to a report in the *San Joaquin Republican* of July 21, it was at this time that Savage and his party learned that two braves and one squaw had been killed in the Harvey raid, while six or eight others had been wounded. This seems more likely than the higher casualty figures reported earlier. In any case, Savage was undoubtedly relieved that more had not died.

The Indians promised not to make any moves prior to the grand council called for August 15, but they were clearly confused and did not know where to turn or whom to trust. They wanted to believe in Savage, but had he not turned against them in the war? The soldiers seemed to be their only hope and this assurance was echoed by all fair-minded observers of the scene. The *Alta* editorialized that "a strong military force should be stationed on Kings River to check—not so much the natural propensity of the savage Indians to commit errors and offenses, as to prevent the dastardly outrages on humanity and keep in restraint, the brutal passions of a class of ruffianly white men."

Savage returned to his farm and hoped for the best. He had a genuine concern for the Indians and he denounced the actions of Harvey on several occasions. He forgot the Kings River troubles momentarily when local Indians stole a large portion of his unripened melon and corn crop. On August 12, the Sacramento *Daily Union* printed a letter posted from near Fort Miller:

> The mortality among the Indians on the Fresno has been very great. Doctor Leach, assisted by Major Savage and others, administered medicine to over seven hundred on Wednesday. Several have died every day for ten days past. I stayed at the ranch one night this week, and the howl of the Indians all night long made the welkin ring with unearthly noises. The cause of the mortality on the Fresno is attributed to eating unripe melons and green corn.

A detachment of ninety dragoons under Major Fitzgerald was reported in Stockton in early August, and word rapidly spread that they had come to arrest Harvey and his volunteers. Actually, they were part of the show of force which was to convene at the Four Creeks on the 15th, but Harvey became quite concerned.

Savage and Judge Marvin, meanwhile, left the Fresno River Indian Farm and headed for the Four Creeks and the great council. They stopped at Campbell and Pool's ferry on the morning of August 16 and had breakfast in Campbell's store and saloon. A few moments later, several shots were fired and coveys of jays and mocking birds scattered from the branches of nearby trees.

Savage's friend, John G. Marvin. *Mary Etta Segerstrom.*

On August 26, the *Alta* reported some startling news; "Major Savage was killed on Monday last, in a fight with some Americans. It is not known yet who killed him, but the rumor has it that he was shot three times." Savage had been reported killed before, but a few days later the San Francisco *Herald* published a confirming article giving some details on his death.

There had been no love lost between Harvey and Savage, and when the two met in Campbell's store that August morning, there was bound to be trouble. Savage had heard that Harvey had referred to him as being "no gentleman." When Savage asked about his remark, Harvey admitted it was true. After a bitter exchange of words, Savage knocked Harvey down several times, dropping his pistol from his waistband in the process. Judge Marvin reached to pick the weapon up, while also trying desperately to disarm Harvey. Most accounts agree that Harvey now saw his chance and quickly drew and shot the unarmed Savage several times. The "King of the Tulares" crumpled to the floor and was dead in a few moments.

The *Herald* correspondent wrote:

> The night he was buried the Indians built large fires around which they danced, singing the while the mournful death chant, until the hills rang with the sound. I have never seen such profound manifestations of grief. The young men, as they whirled wildly and distractfully around in the dance, shouted the name of their father that was gone, while the squaws sat rocking their bodies to and fro chanting that mournful dirge until the very blood within one curdled with horror at the scene.

Despite Savage's death, the grand Indian council was held, and a report concerning the outcome of the meeting was published in the Sacramento *Daily Union* on August 30, 1852:

We understand a report has been received from major Patten, the commanding officer at Fort Miller, of the 23 inst., stating that he met the Indians in the Great Council at the Four Creeks a few days previous and that the chiefs promised faithfully to keep the peace. Francisco, a chief in regards to whom the whites are in much fear, was particularly earnest. Major Patten says, in his protestations of friendship, and as a guarantee, has delivered as a hostage his little daughter, 12 years old, who is now in the rancheria of the chief, Tomquit, immediately under the guns of Fort Miller.

The display of force, says Major Patten, at the Four Creeks, the impetuous charge of the dragoons, together with the rapid fire of the infantry, and the simultaneous roar of the guns 'that thunder twice,' [howitzers] produced an effect which will not soon be forgotten.... It is to be hoped that the white settlers in the country will consult their real interest and not themselves create an Indian war.

The incident of the child hostage offered by Francisco is interesting in the light of a report which appeared in the Los Angeles *Star* on October 16:

Two of the chiefs of the Tulare Indians have been in town during the past week, endeavoring to seek redress for some alleged aggressions committed by their white neighbors. They say that some white people have encroached upon their grounds near the Four Creeks, and have taken prisoner several of their children. Mr. Wilson, to whom their complaints were made, dismissed them with the promise that he would look into the matter and would use his endeavors to see them righted.

Wozencraft was not at the gathering, but he wrote that "several companies of soldiers were ordered to be on the ground. Provisions were ordered to be furnished them when they should assemble in council, and thus display to them the power to punish, and at the same time the humanity to befriend them."

In the same report Wozencraft noted Savage's death:

The cutting off from life and usefulness of a human being is deplorable under all circumstances, but the more so when it falls on one like Major Savage—a man of untiring energy, and a will to direct it aright, through and by which he had gained a singular influence over the Indians. Indeed, his controlling power was almost absolute, and, so far as we could judge, that influence was directed to the amelioration of their unfortunate condition....

Whatever the agent's judgment, Savage was gone, along with one more hope for the natives. He was buried along the Kings River, but in 1855,

■ Dr. Lewis Leach served with Savage in the Mariposa Battalion and was the trader's friend and business partner. *Author's collection.*

San Joaquin Republican, January 25, 1854.

Dr. Leach removed the body to a site on the Fresno River. Here a large, imported granite shaft was erected to the memory of a man who was already a legend and whose motives are argued to this day.

A particular touch of irony was the fact that Savage had, the previous year, scheduled a visit to his family in Illinois. He had planned, also, to attend the great British World's Fair then being held in London, following his visit to Illinois. His passport applications have recently been discovered in the governor's *Applicants-Procedure Book*, in the California State Archives. Savage had been too busy to leave, however, and an unkind fate had made other plans.

For the time being, the Indians fled to the mountains. Because of the treaty rejection, their beef rations had been discontinued, and they hoped to be able to stockpile some food for the winter. Despite the council, trouble was expected.

Not all of the Yokuts were disturbed at Savage's death. Pahmit, the Dumna who lived well into the twentieth century, was a grandson of Tomquit and recalled those troubled times vividly: "Major Savage go 'way. He go Kings River. White man there shoot Major Savage like our man shoot 'em [here recalling Savage's bullet-catching trick]. Major savage die. Ha! Ha!—why he not catch 'em bullets?"

But, if no well-defined peace existed in the foothills of the San Joaquin, at least there was no war, and the ravines and mountain canyons echoed to the sounds of the miners' picks and sluice boxes.

Chief Tenaya was still living with the Monos in 1853. There are several versions of his death that summer, with one member of his tribe insisting that he was killed during an argument over a particularly hard-fought Indian game.

A Yosemite woman who had lived in the valley prior to its discovery was Maria Lebrado Ydrte, who died on April 21, 1931. Whether she was a daughter,

James Savage's grave and monument have been moved several times over the years. It can still be seen in the hills of eastern Madera County. *Madera County Historical Society.*

or granddaughter, of Tenaya—or related at all—is not clear. Local tradition placed her age at 109 years. She was the last of the full-blood Ahwahneechees who had made the great valley their home since the dawn of time when the Great Spirit led them there from a distant place.

Sickened by the death of his friend and partner and disillusioned by frontier justice, or the lack of it, John Marvin returned to Sacramento and his duties as superintendent of schools. The legislature had been dragging its feet in appropriating funds to initiate an educational system, and Marvin was anxious to implement his ideas, as well as to impress the Democratic Party. He offered to donate his salary as quartermaster of the Mariposa Battalion to the state to start the school program rolling. And the legislature, inundated with financial and other troubles, was no doubt eager to accept.

CHAPTER 10 / SOURCES

UNPUBLISHED MATERIAL

U.S. Congress, 33rd Congress, Special Session, Senate Executive Document 4:

Adam Johnston to Luke Lea, April 11, 1851.

Captain E. D. Keyes to Colonel G. W. Barbour, May 21, 1851.

Captain E. D. Keyes to Captain F. Steele, May 1, 1851.

O. M. Wozencraft to John Bigler, September 9, 1852.

O. M. Wozencraft to Edward F. Beale, September 9, 1852.

Edward F. Beale to Luke Lea, December 14, 1852.

National Archives, Records of the Office of Indian Affairs, Record Group 75, California Superintendency, M234:

L. D. Vinsonhaler and James D. Savage to Adam Johnston, May 3, 1851.

George W. Barbour to Luke Lea, July 28, 1851.

P. T. Herbert and O. M. Wozencraft to Robert McClelland, August 6, 1853.

National Archives, Records of the Office of Indian Affairs, Record Group 75, California Superintendency Special Files, M574:

Joel Brooks to Edward F. Beale, September 21, 1852.

Statement by G. W. Heap, April 5, 1855.

National Archives, A.C.P. Files Colonel Tredwell MOORE, Record Group 94:

Military History of Colonel Tredwell Moore, May 18, 1876.

National Archives, Records of the 10th Military Department, Record Group 210:

Captain E. D. Keyes to Captain F. Steele April 22, 1851.

National Archives, letters received, Fort Miller, California, Record Group 393:

Lieutenant Tredwell Moore to Captain E. D. Townsend, June 12, July 8, 9, 1852.

Office of the Secretary of State, California State Archives, Indian War Files, Sacramento:

Major G. W. Patten to Asst. Adjutant General, July 26, 1852.

Leonard, Charles Berdan, "The Federal Indian Policy in the San Joaquin Valley, Its Application and Results," unpublished Ph.D.. thesis, University of California, 1928.

Supervisor's Minutes Vol. A, 1852, Court of Sessions, Mariposa County, California.

NEWSPAPERS

San Francisco Daily *Alta California*, September 26, December 8, 11, 1851; July 2, 9, 19, August 26, 1852.

Sacramento *Daily Union*, July 10, August 12, 30, 31, 1852.

The Fresno Bee, April 21, 1931; February 12, 1956.

San Francisco *Herald*, September 3, 1852.

San Joaquin Republican, March 3, June 23, July 4, 7, 9, 10, 11, 17, 20, 21, 24, 28, 1852.

Los Angeles *Star*, October 16, 1852.

PRINCIPAL PUBLISHED WORKS

Anderson, George E., Ellison, W. H., and Heizer, Robert F. *Treaty Making and Treaty Rejection by the Federal Government in California, 1850-1852*. Socorro, NM: Ballena Press, 1978.

Bingaman, John W. *The Ahwahneechees*. Lodi, CA: End-Klan Publishing Company, 1966.

Chamberlain, Newell D. *The Call of Gold*. Mariposa, CA: Gazette Press, 1936.

Crampton, C. Gregory, editor. *The Mariposa Indian War, 1850-1851: Diaries of Robert Eccleston*. Salt Lake: University of Utah Press, 1957.

Ferris, Daniel F. *Judge Marvin and the Founding of the California School System*. Berkeley: University of California Press, 1962.

Keyes, E. D., *Fifty Years Observation of Men and Events*. New York: Charles Scribner's Sons, 1884.

Kroeber, A. L. *Handbook of the Indians of California*. New York: Dover Publications, Inc., 1976.

Latta, Frank F. *Handbook of Yokuts Indians*. Santa Cruz, CA: Bear State Books, 1978.

Mitchell, Annie R. *Jim Savage and the Tulareno Indians*. Los Angeles: Westernlore Press, 1959.

Russell, Carl P. *One Hundred Years in Yosemite*. Yosemite, CA: Yosemite Natural History Association, 1968.

Wood, Raymund F. *California's Aqua Fria*. Fresno, CA: Academy Library Guild, 1954.

OTHER SOURCES

Ellison, William H. "The Federal Indian Policy in California, 1846-1860," *The Mississippi Valley Historical Review*, June, 1922.

English, June. "James Smith: A Pioneer in Kings River Transportation," *Fresno Past & Present*, September 1969.

Journals of the House and Assembly and Senate of California, Second Session, Sacramento, 1851.

Chapter 11

SHASTA

The desultory beginnings of California Indian policy began to gradually evolve under Superintendent Beale. Having taken office in March of 1852, Beale was recommending various programs with which to control the native population as early as the following September. Utilizing the present reservations set up by the commissioners, as well as creating new ones, Beale proposed they be occupied by a military post with a resident Indian agent. The local natives would be invited to live on the reserve subject to the discipline and instruction of the agent. The expense of the troops would be borne by the product of the Indians' work, and the reservations themselves would be subject to relocation where an increase of the white population made such a move necessary.

Beale's plan had merit. Although he obviously adopted some of his predecessor's proposals, for better or worse, these first stumbling steps toward a firm Indian policy in California was the beginning of the Indian reservation system in the United States.

Beale believed that the Spanish mission method, without the religious emphasis, was a good starting point, and he wanted to teach the Indians to work and support themselves. At the same time, he wanted to give them the security of their own land. These would be small reservations, involving no permanent treaty obligations and obtained by a simple agreement with the government that could be abrogated at any time. General Ethan Allen Hitchcock went on record as firmly in accordance with the project. It was a choice between either Beale's plan, he reasoned, or the removal and systematic extermination of the Indians.

Beale's plan was adopted in Washington and an appropriation of $250,000 was allotted for setting up the reserves. After visiting Washington and reporting the needs of the native population, Beale returned home in August of 1853 and set about putting his new plans into operation. He was to learn quickly that politics, broken promises, and ugly Indian-white contacts throughout the state would result in two steps backward for every positive step forward.

When Commissioner Redick McKee made his trip north in the fall of 1851, he concluded four treaties and established a reservation in Scott's Valley. In his report to his superiors, he hailed the success of his mission in glowing terms, but trouble plagued the northern frontier in spite of, and because of, McKee's expedition.

John McKee, the agent's son, had been secretary to his father during the expedition. He had gone into partnership with a political hack and opportunist named James Estell, selling cattle for distribution to the Indians. Later, the elder McKee would become involved in a bitter dispute over the alleged irregularities of these cattle deals.

McKee also had much trouble in establishing the reserve in Scott's Valley. Local settlers were bitterly opposed to giving the Indians this land, especially since some of them would be dispossessed in the process. When Fort Jones was established in the valley by two companies of dragoons in October of 1852, it was hoped further Indian troubles could be averted. This was not to be the case, however.

At a treaty-making session on the Klamath River, McKee employed an interpreter named Robert Walker, a local ferry operator. Walker had had trouble with the local Indians before, even though he often had to depend on them for aid during high water. After McKee passed out a supply of trinkets and cattle to a large gathering of local natives, he proceeded with his usual speech. When he finished, he turned to Walker and directed him to translate.

Walker was not one to pass up such an opportunity. Instead of making a literal translation of McKee's speech, Walker added his own touches. He told the Indians they must do whatever he said or they would be destroyed. McKee would return in a few months with many more presents and until that time they must help him with his ferry. When McKee left the area, however, he was never to return, and after many months helping Walker with his ferry, the Indians probably guessed the truth.

McKee had barely returned to San Francisco when he received news from the north of Indian troubles. In February, two men living on the west

■ Edward F. Beale, the first California Superintendent of Indian Affairs. *California State Library.*

side of Eel River, near Humboldt Bay, were murdered and their house robbed. Owing to high water, it was several weeks before news of the murders reached the settlements, but groups of volunteers were hastily assembled at Eureka and other settlements. A rancheria of unsuspecting Wiyot Indians, living on the bay, was pounced upon and several Indians were killed. The posse then rode up the Eel River and killed some fifteen other natives—all without making any effort to discover just who the guilty Indians were.

About this same time, at a place called Happy Camp, an Indian boy was suspected of stealing a knife and was shot down, and his body was thrown into the river and allowed to float downstream. When the Indians became exasperated and threatening, an alarmed ferry operator got together another group of volunteers, and two villages and some forty Indians were destroyed. Some women and children fled to Scott's Valley, where John McKee was acting as temporary agent. From these Indians and several whites who participated in the actions, young McKee put together the report which was sent to his father.

The elder McKee was upset at the hostilities—not only for humanitarian reasons, but because he was anxious that his northern mission be considered a success. Pompous and ambitious, McKee was seeking permission at that time to return to Washington and such a trip was not likely if the Indians were on the verge of war.

On April 5, 1852, McKee wrote a long letter to Governor John Bigler, blaming the troubles on the whites and noting that the settlers felt justified in any action against the natives because of the opposition in the press and legislature to the treaties. Calling for the strongest possible action on the part of the governor and the military, McKee pleaded that measures be taken "...to vindicate the laws of the country, as well as of humanity, and...bring some of these desperadoes to punishment."

Governor Bigler was a vain and unprincipled politician who always based his decisions on which way the political winds were blowing. McKee was fortunate that at least Bigler saw fit to answer his letter and not ignore it as he had the pleas of Wozencraft over the Tulare troubles. But perhaps Wozencraft had, in fact, been lucky in that matter.

Writing under date of April 9, Bigler delivered a stinging rebuke to McKee for taking the part of murdering savages over his own kind. After talking to the legislative representatives of the counties involved, the governor had been assured that, far from the whites being to blame, the Indians in the past few months had murdered 130 whites and destroyed some $240,000 worth of property.

Shocked by the governor's reply, McKee quickly realized that in a contest between white taxpayers and non tax-paying Indians, the latter had little chance. McKee quickly sent off a rebuttal and although the pen war continued for some time, he got nowhere. Between this dispute and his conflict with General Hitchcock, McKee became a troublesome and ineffective representative. When he clashed with Beale over their respective authority, he was dismissed early in 1853. Bitter that he had not been appointed superintendent over Beale, McKee could at least now return to Washington. When he died in 1886, he was still trying to collect money he felt the government owed him from his years as an Indian agent in California.

A continuing series of Indian forays now assured a future of blood and violence along the streams and mountain canyons of the north. In May 1853, the theft of twenty-four oxen brought forth an avenging posse which attacked the offending village near Red Bluff.

That spring too, a small band of Indians stole five horses from a rancher in Shasta Valley. Quickly gathering a posse of fifteen men, including several members of Ben Wright's old command, the rancher took the field in pursuit of the thieves. Locating a village near a place called Squaw Valley, the volunteers quietly surrounded the Indian camp late that night. It was a small rancheria—about six men with their families in as many crude wickiups.

The whites waited until dawn and then opened fire when the first yawning Indian made an appearance and shot down the remainder as fast as they scrambled from their shelter. In a few moments, the slaughter was complete. Three of the stolen horses were recovered and returned to the grateful owner.

A constant tension now existed between the whites and the natives, and neither knew when the other would strike next. In the fall, Chief Shasta Bill and his band of Shastas came down to a favorite spring near Yreka where they performed "medicine" to increase their fishing catch. It was an annual affair, but since there had been so much trouble the chief asked two nearby whites if it was safe for the Indians to camp in the area. They were told that it was probably all right, but to be careful since the whites on the river were all very suspicious of the Indians.

When the Indians began performing their dance, the sounds were heard by a nearby settler named George Heard. Jumping to the conclusion that the natives were performing a war dance, Heard furiously rode to Yreka and spread the alarm. In town, a heavily armed group of volunteers promptly formed and were soon headed toward the Indian camp. Shasta Bill and his men saw the approaching whites and guessed what had happened. After a brief skirmish in the brush during which one of the whites shot another, the Indians fled without firing a shot. No attempt was made by the Shastas to retaliate for the unprovoked attack.

• • • • •

Tucked away in the columns of frontier California newspapers are accounts of the brutal incidents which drove the native inhabitants to war. The following appeared in the *Butte Record* in December of 1853:

> Mr. McGeary of Adams & Co.'s Express, informs us that he saw an Indian boy, as he came up in the stage, three days ago, lying dead on the roadside, near Oak Grove, in Butte County. He had a bullet hole in his forehead. He was last seen, when alive, in company with a packer, and was then quite sick. It is supposed that the packer killed him in order to be freed from the trouble of taking care of him.

A typical cause of trouble was reported in the Sacramento *Union* in its issue of November 23, 1853:

> Mr. Pierce, a packer, missed some of his animals one morning a week or two since, on the Trinity, and after searching ineffectually for some time, returned to his camp. Soon after he observed several Indians approaching, and jumping to the conclusion upon the instant, that the Indians had stolen his animals, he shot two of them dead. In a very few hours hereafter he found his animals in the immediate vicinity of his camp. The consequence has been that since that time the ranch men in the valley have lost a large number of animals; and the ultimate result will be the further loss of life on both sides.

Earlier that year, the *Union* had noted the desperation of the settlers in the constant warfare that had been engendered:

> The Indians have committed so many depredations in the north of late, that the people are enraged against them, and are ready to knife them— shoot them—or inoculate them with the small pox, all of which have been done.

> Some time since the Indians of Colusa County destroyed about five thousand dollars worth of stock belonging to Messrs. Thomas & Toombs; since which time they have had two men employed at $100 per month to hunt down and kill the Diggers, like other beasts of prey.

Only occasionally is there uncovered a hint of sanity in Indian-white relations. At Indian Valley, in the mountains to the east of Bidwell's Bar, one William Carr was in the store of J. T. Taylor talking with George Rose, a local blacksmith whose antipathy toward the Indians was well known. The men both purchased some supplies, then Rose, who was quite drunk, walked over to the fireplace and lit his pipe.

Sitting at the fireplace were a young Indian and his father, neither paying any attention to Rose. Suddenly the white man pulled his pistol and

An unidentified ambrotype from the 1850s of a scene thought to be in northern California. Two Chinese stand on the porch among the white inhabitants of what is possibly a boarding house. Four Indian women stand in front of the steps, while two Indian men stand to the right. *California Historical Society.*

killed the young Indian for no apparent reason. The father would have been killed also had he not been saved by Carr.

Rose was allowed to go home, but the following morning he was arrested and brought back to the store. Here a court was appointed, a jury impaneled, and Rose was given a "long and impartial trial." Found guilty by his peers, the blacksmith was actually hanged on December 18, 1853.

"Living amongst Indians as we do in these wild Mountains," wrote Carr in a letter to the *Butte Record*, "some steps have to be taken for the protection of our families. We have hitherto lived at peace, and hope so to continue. Indians must not be shot down as dogs, by a reckless, drunken man who has nothing to lose—nothing to care for—nothing at stake…."

But Indian Valley was the exception in the scarred and ugly Indian-white relations in California. Along the Klamath River, near Cottonwood, where Ben Wright lived, a group of "squaw men" camped with their Indian women during the winter of 1853-54. Gamblers and frontier riffraff such as those who had caused much of the trouble in the state, several of these men had been on the Wright campaign against the Modocs. The Indian women of these men belonged to Shasta Bill's band who made their headquarters in a cave about twenty miles above Cottonwood.

When the women left one day because of ill treatment, they were followed by their furious masters to the cave of Shasta Bill. The white men's demands for the return of their "property" were received by a grim group of Indians who were ready to fight. They told the whites to leave them alone. Muttering threats, the "squaw men" retreated to town.

In Cottonwood, the "squaw men" spread the word that they had been threatened by the Shastas after discovering some stolen stock at the cave. A volunteer group was quickly formed, and when they returned to the cave, a brisk fight took place. Four of the posse were killed as the Indians drove the whites off a second time.

Leaving their dead behind them, the battered volunteers limped back into town amid great excitement. A messenger was dispatched to Fort Jones for aid and on January 18, Captain Henry M. Judah rode into Cottonwood with a command of twenty-six men of the 4th Infantry. Accompanying the troops was a small group of volunteers from Yreka.

A Klamath River Shasta tribesman.
Peter Palmquist.

Captain Judah, like many of the frontier soldiers, had seen service during the war with Mexico. He was thirty-three years old at this time, liked his liquor, and seems to have been erratic in his official behavior. Young Lieutenant George Crook, who was also along on this expedition, saw much of Judah in the next few years and later referred to him as "an unmitigated fraud." Like other army officers, however, Judah had a genuine sympathy for the plight of the Indians.

At Cottonwood, Judah's forces were augmented by another group of volunteers led by Captain R. C. Geiger and Ben Wright. The weather was bitter cold and snow was falling as the men headed towards the cave. The volunteers made up the rear guard and soon had lagged so far behind they were lost to view.

Late that night in camp, one of the civilians offered to go back and look for the stragglers. He returned with the alarming news that Indians had wiped out the whole force. An army patrol, headed by Lieutenant Crook, backtracked in search of the victims, but turned up only a drunken crowd of packers who followed the soldiers back to camp. Riding in about an hour later, a drunken Captain Judah had to be lifted from his horse. The rear guard slowly dribbled in, all of them in the same condition as the army commander.

The following day the soldiers and their hung-over auxiliaries again moved out towards the Indian stronghold. Captain Judah was quite ill—suffering "delirium tremens," as Lieutenant Crook phrased it. At the cave, the bodies of the previously slain white men were found frozen and partially devoured by wolves. The command set up camp nearby in deep snow, with temperatures often dropping to as low as twenty degrees below zero. Still, neither the volunteers nor the soldiers had learned the truth about how the trouble had originated.

The Shastas had fortified the cave in the meantime, making their position nearly impregnable. Judah at first advocated a direct frontal assault by the volunteers, but since he was still on the sick list, Lieutenants Bonnycastle and Crook would have to lead the charge. It was a grim Bonnycastle who bluntly told Judah that if he survived the attack he was preferring charges against his commander. It was a tense moment.

Suddenly Judah had a better idea. He dispatched Lieutenant Crook to Fort Lane, Oregon, to procure a howitzer for the attack. Leaving a squad of men to watch the cave, Judah and the balance of the volunteers went into camp about five miles away.

On January 26, Captain Andrew J. Smith and a fifteen-man detachment of the First Dragoons arrived, accompanied by Lieutenant Crook. Smith had brought a howitzer with him, but he was disturbed after having talked to some nearby settlers concerning the origin of the trouble. Nevertheless, the troops and volunteers proceeded to the cave where the howitzer was placed in position. Captain Geiger and some of his men took up positions on top of the cave. Just after cautioning his men not to expose themselves to the Indian fire, Geiger himself was shot and killed.

■ Lieutenant George Crook.
National Archives.

Several howitzer rounds only succeeded in scattering the volunteers on top of the cave. After several more ineffectual rounds were lobbed into the mouth of the cave, the Shastas asked for a parley.

Early the next morning, Captain Smith and a local settler named Eddy went up to the cave and talked to Shasta Bill. The chief revealed the truth about the origin of the trouble and reported that three warriors, two women, and three children had been killed. The disgusted Smith told the Indians to stay in the cave until it seemed safe, as he was sure they would be massacred if the "squaw men" had their way.

"What justice can be expected," wrote Captain Smith in his report of the incident, "of a community that will furnish poison and approve of its being administered wholesale to the Indians: just such characters were the instigators of this affair." Here Smith was referring to the earlier Wright campaign during the fall of 1852.

Sickened by the needless deaths of whites and Indians alike, Captain Smith ordered the troops to return to their respective posts. He watched with further disgust as the volunteers appropriated the Indian ponies as they left.

• • • • •

A. M. Rosborough was born about 1815 in South Carolina and arrived in Siskiyou County in 1853. In Yreka, he established a law firm with Elijah Steele and J. Berry, although all three had various other interests. Rosborough was a kindly, intelligent man, and friends recalled in later years that he could talk for hours on almost any subject. He took an immediate interest in the Indians and became the subagent for northern California in August of 1854. His territory was vast and mountainous and he spent much time in the saddle in the course of his duties. The Indians loved and trusted him and during all his life sought his aid and counsel.

Rosborough's friend, Elijah Steele, was also a man of the finest character and a friend to the Indians. Born in New York in 1817, Steele had come to California in 1850 and, aside from his law practice, operated a cattle ranch in Scott's Valley. Steele furnished beef to the Indians for the government, but he often did so whether or not he received payment. On a bill submitted to Rosborough, Steele noted that he hoped payment for the beef would be allowed, but "if not, no charge is made as humanity required the issue."

In March, Lieutenant Bonnycastle was in charge at Fort Jones while Captain Judah was away. Ever since the fight at the Shasta cave in January, the "squaw men" and other Cottonwood citizens had complained of the hostile intention of the Shastas. The Indians had several times petitioned the troops to allow them to live at the fort under army protection.

On March 26, Lieutenant Bonnycastle left the fort with Elijah Steele as interpreter.

The two men met with Shasta Bill at the cave, where the chief told the officer that he did wish to live at the fort, but that several of his people were ill and he would have to come in later. Cautioning the chief that he must in no way molest the whites, Bonnycastle led his men back to Fort Jones.

"On reaching the Klamath Ferry on my return," wrote Bonnycastle in his report, "I found several of the lower class of the Cottonwood population there, for the purpose…of getting into a disturbance with the Indians in the event of their being with us. This however, I presume to have been mere talk, as these men were of the party attacking the Indians in January, and as at that time they did some pretty good running and very little fighting, there was not much danger of their attacking the same Indians when under the protection of a few well armed soldiers."

There was still a good deal of unrest on the northern borders, much of it attributed to a roving band of Indians under the leadership of one Tipsha Tyee, sometimes called "Tipsy" by the whites. The Yreka *Mountain Herald* of May 20, 1854, notes that a pack train had been raided and one of the packers killed, while some stock had also been stolen. The Shasta *Courier* related how four Indians were brought into a Trinity River mining camp and executed after confessing to various murders and the contemplated plunder of a local pack train.

On March 29, the Sacramento *Union* reported a pitched battle north of Yreka between a large band of Indians and regular troops. Sixty or seventy Indians were reported killed, while several officers of the troops were wounded and five privates killed.

In early May, Lieutenant Bonnycastle was informed that a Shasta In-

■ A Karok warrior of the Klamath River country. His reed armor would be very effective against arrows, but not bullets.
Siskiyou County Museum.

dian named Joe had attempted to rape a white woman living between Yreka and the Klamath River. Her husband had arrived just in time and the Indian had fled, presumedly for the protection of the cave. An army officer and Agent Rosborough went to the cave and talked to Shasta Bill about the incident. The chief was angry at Joe but wanted to make sure Joe would not be lynched before he would turn him over to the authorities. Later, another Shasta chief assured Lieutenant Bonnycastle the white woman had not been hurt. "It was with some difficulty," wrote the officer, "that I could make him understand that the intention was almost as culpable whether successful or not. Indeed, the Indian could not see why I spoke of the offense as being of such magnitude when their squaws are constantly run down, sometimes by men on horses, and raped...."

Shasta Bill promised to bring Joe to Fort Jones in three days, but when the time elapsed and the Indian did not appear, Bonnycastle and a squad of troops took to the field. The officer took along a group of Deschute (Oregon) Indians as scouts and trackers. Indian emissaries again promised that Bill and his Shastas would come in with Joe, but while he was waiting, Lieutenant Bonnycastle received word of an attack on a pack train and he quickly headed for the scene of the trouble.

Convinced that Tipsy and his band had attacked the pack train, the troops were soon at the site and trailing the attackers across the Siskiyou Mountains. When the trail led straight to Shasta Bill's cave, Bonnycastle was sure that they had been guilty of the attack. The troops and Indians had covered twenty-five miles of the roughest imaginable country in just three days.

At the cave, Bonnycastle found a local "squaw man" named James P. Goodall who gave the officer the news that Tipsy and two others had gone to the cave to ask Bill and his Shastas to join in war against the whites. Instead, to prove their good faith, Bill and the Shastas killed the hostiles as reported in the Sacramento *Daily Union* on June 3. They had taken the scalps into Yreka and asked Goodall to return with them so as to prevent the troops from attacking them. Bonnycastle met with the Indians and was promised that Goodall would bring Joe into Yreka the following day. The officer then rode into town.

During the meeting with Rosborough at his office the next day, Lieutenant Bonnycastle was surprised when Captain Goodall showed up without the much-promised Indian. After giving him a severe dressing down,

Stereo view by Louis Heller of the rugged Siskiyou Mountains, ca. 1870s. *Siskiyou County Museum.*

the officer made Goodall promise to return immediately for Joe, and he started back to the cave that night.

Acting on the spur-of-the-moment, Goodall convinced not only Joe, but all the Shastas to return with him to Fort Jones. The captain claimed some twenty years experience with southwestern Indians, had an Indian wife, and believed that with fair treatment the natives could be responsible citizens. He probably was not involved in the events that followed, but one way or another word of the returning Indians was received in Cottonwood.

Headed by Goodall, the Shasta caravan made its way towards Fort Jones, stopping on the evening of May 24, 1854, at the Klamath River. After setting up camp, Goodall accompanied his wards down to Dewitt's Ferry where the Indians wanted to bathe. It was a quiet and beautiful evening. The Indians believed that soon they would all be safe.

Suddenly, a group of white men emerged from the brush and trees across the river. Leading them was E. M. Geiger, brother of the volunteer killed in January at the cave fight. With the whites were the Deschute Indians who had been hired for the afternoon. Other whites emerged on the opposite bank, all heavily armed. The first shots wounded Shasta Bill and two others, and two other Indians were killed instantly.

"A white man named Stuart," wrote Bonnycastle in his report, "went up to Bill for the purpose of scalping him, while yet alive, but Bill struggled with him, got his knife away, when that man after having beat him about the head with his pistol, shot him several times, after which he was scalped by a man named Brickey I understand. When not yet dead he was thrown into the Klamath River."

The "squaw men" had had their way after all.

Most of the Shastas escaped and even managed to kill one of the whites during the fight, but the Deschutes plundered the Shasta camp and stole four children. Bitter and vowing vengeance, the Shastas retreated again into the mountains.

Both Rosborough and Lieutenant Bonnycastle were concerned that the Indians would begin raiding isolated settlers and never again believe the word of a white man. Sending several Scott's Valley Indians as mediators, Bonnycastle informed the Shastas that he would do all he could to retrieve their children and punish the men involved in their chief's murder. He also told them that he would have nothing to say if they retaliated against the murderers, but that they must not take vengeance on any innocent people.

Strangely enough, two Shastas did come into Yreka to talk with the agent and the army officer. The Indians agreed that not all whites were bad and that they would try to bring their band into Fort Jones for protection.

Bonnycastle and Rosborough, meanwhile, did all they could to prosecute the guilty parties, but were never able to obtain more than three names to work with. Geiger quickly fled to San Francisco where he took the first ship east. The others probably did the same. Along the Klamath and its tributaries, the miners were relieved that another Indian scare was concluded.

During the summers of 1853 and 1854, southern Oregon settlers had maintained a company of militia in the Modoc country to insure the safety of emigrants. During the latter year, a fifteen-man volunteer group was organized in Siskiyou County also, as many men of the area had families traveling the overland route to join them. There were several skirmishes with Modocs, and near Warner's Rock, a band of Paiutes was destroyed. In the fall, the volunteers returned home after a successful campaign.

In October of 1854, Rosborough could write to his superiors that "since my last letter, the Indians through the northern part of California have continued to be at peace with the whites." The agent had worked hard for peace and traveled hundreds of miles over rough country to help make the country safe for both races. It was a thankless job, and he looked forward to resigning the following year to concentrate on his legal practice. It was winter now and snow covered the plains and valleys of Northern California. Perhaps peace would continue.

General John E. Wool, the new commander of the Department of the Pacific, was even more optimistic. In a report published in the *Alta* in December, General Wool noted that "no disturbance of any importance has occurred...since I assumed command some ten months since. In that time only one white man and five Indians have been killed...."

General Wool was either naive or very poorly informed on the Indian difficulties of his territory. He, like others in both the army and Indian department, was more concerned with making himself look good than in issuing detailed, and accurate, reports.

■ General John E. Wool assumed command of the Department of the Pacific in 1854. *National Archives.*

CHAPTER 11 / SOURCES

UNPUBLISHED MATERIAL

U.S. Congress, 33rd Congress, Special Session, Senate Executive Document 4:

E. F. Beale to Luke Lea, December 14, 23, 1852, January 3, 1853.

Redick McKee to John Bigler, April 5, 12, 1852.

John Bigler to Redick McKee, April 9, 1852.

Redick McKee to General E. A. Hitchcock, April 7, 1852.

U.S. Congress, 35th Congress, 2nd Session, House of Representatives, Miscellaneous Document 47:

E. Steele to General C. S Drew, November 23, 1857.

A. M. Rosborough to General C. S. Drew, November 23, 1857.

National Archives, Records of the Office of Indian Affairs, Record Group 75, California Superintendency, M234:

Captain A. J. Smith to Colonel G. Wright, January 31, 1854.

Lieutenant J. C. Bonnycastle to General John C. Wool, May 28, 1854.

James P. Goodall to Thomas J. Henley, August 30, 1856.

National Archives, Records of the Office of Indian Affairs, Record Group 75, California Superintendency, Special Files, M574:

E. F. Beale to Luke Lea, November 22, 1852.

Accounts of Superintendent Edward F. Beale, California Superintendency, 1852-55.

Redick McKee, claim for compensation for expenses and losses resulting from service in California during 1850-53, 1852-87.

National Archives, Records of the War Department, Department of the Pacific, Record Group 98:

Lieutenant J. C. Bonnycastle to Colonel G. Wright, March 26, 1854.

Captain Henry M. Judah to Colonel G. Wright, January 31, 1856.

NEWSPAPERS

The San Francisco *Daily Alta California*, July 4, 1852; December 24, 1854.

The *Butte Record*, December 17, 31, 1853; February 18, 1854.

Sacramento *Daily Union*, March 5, May 7, November 29, 1853; March 24, April 4, May 20, 27, June 3, 1854.

Yreka *Mountain Herald*, May 20, 1854.

PRINCIPAL PUBLISHED WORKS

Boatner, Mark Mayo. *The Civil War Dictionary*. New York: David McKay Company, Inc., 1959.

Bledsoe, A. J. *Indian Wars of the Northwest*. Oakland: Biobooks, 1956.

Bonsal, Stephen. *Edward Fitzgerald Beale*. New York: G. P. Putnam's Sons, 1912.

Heitman, Francis B. *Historical Register and Dictionary of the United States Army*. Washington, D.C.: Government Printing Office, 1903.

Heizer, Robert F., editor. *George Gibbs' Journal of Redick McKee's Expedition through Northwestern California in 1851*. Berkeley: University of California Press, 1972.

_____. *The Destruction of the California Indians*. Santa Barbara, CA: Perigrine Smith, Inc., 1974.

Kroeber, A. L. *Handbook of the Indians of California*. New York: Dover Publications, Inc., 1976.

McBeth, Frances Turner. *Lower Klamath Country*. Berkeley: Anchor Press, 1950.

Schmitt, Martin F., editor. *General George Crook, His Autobiography*. Norman, OK: University of Oklahoma Press, 1946.

Thompson, Gerald. *Edward F. Beale & The American West*. Albuquerque: University of New Mexico Press, 1983.

Wells, Harry L. *History of Siskiyou County, California*. Oakland: D. J. Stewart & Co., 1881.

OTHER SOURCES

Ellison, William H. "The Federal Indian Policy in California, 1846-1860," *The Mississippi Valley Historical Review*, June, 1922.

Rosborough, Alex J. "A. M. Rosborough, Special Indian Agent," *California Historical Society Quarterly*, Vol. 26, 1947.

Chapter 12

HENLEY

When Superintendent Beale returned to California after his initial authorization to inaugurate his reservation program, he set to work immediately. Holding a meeting at the Tejon Pass in late August 1853, he discussed his plans with groups of Indians and various army officers who had traveled throughout th' state. All agreed that the Tejon region was ideally suited for location of the Sebastian Reservation. From the Tejon, Beale struck out across the valley to an experimental farm he had set up the previous year on the San Joaquin River. He had assembled a group of local Indians and helped them to initiate a farming venture in an effort to see if they could support themselves. Beale was enthusiastic when he saw how they had learned to plow, reap, build corrals, and tend gardens. On the new Tejon reserve, things would be done on a much grander scale, and the Indian situation could begin to normalize itself.

As he began surveying some 50,000 acres of an old Spanish land grant in the Tejon for his Sebastian reserve, Beale was at the height of his career as superintendent and seemed on the crest of great achievements. The San Francisco *Alta* speculated that the Indian difficulties were over:

> Five years after the first [reservation] settlement is made and put into successful operation, the Indian affairs in California will cease to be an item of expense to the General or State Government; all hostilities will be over; the whites will be entirely free from annoyance by the Indians: the Indians will be transformed from a state of semi-barbarism, indolence, mental imbecility, and moral debasement, to a condition of civilization, Christianity, industry, virtue, frugality, social and domestic happiness and public usefulness.

A Los Angeles *Star* editorial lyrically stated "...[I]f transforming a race of savages into men and teaching them the arts of civilization, can render a man's name and character immortal, that of Lieut. Beale is destined as one of the brightest in history."

The new Sebastian Indian Reservation was off to a good start. By February, 1854, many Indians, including a few from as far away as Nevada

County, had gathered there. A report in the *Star* in June noted that some of the crops being produced were wheat, barley, corn, pumpkins, potatoes, and beans. At this time there were over 3,000 acres under cultivation and some 400 laborers in the fields. Over ten miles of irrigation ditches carried water to all the fields.

A road was built into the mountains, and the Indians cut and hauled out timber with which to construct buildings. Seven rancherias, containing a transitory population of some six hundred people, were on the reserve under the chiefs Juan Viejo, Meterina, Jose, Zapatero, Antonio, and Stanislaus. Along with local Kitanemuk Indians were many southern Yokuts, such as Tachi, Yowlumne, Tulumne, and others.

■ Samuel Bishop was a prominent rancher in the Tejon area and later in Inyo County where a town is named after him.
Santa Clara Historical Society.

Writing from the reserve in early July, a traveler noted that the crops were worth between $3,000 and $4,000 at Los Angeles prices. "The Indians are arriving daily in small parties," wrote Patrick Connor, a visitor, "and are immediately reported to Mr. Bishop, the worthy superintendent of the farm, who is not long in finding them employment. A more happy set of beings it has never been my lot to see; and although each tribe speaks a different dialect, such a thing as a fight or quarrel has never happened among them...."

Sam Bishop was a Virginian by birth and had come to California during the Gold Rush of 1849. Beale had first met him at the experimental farm on the San Joaquin where Bishop tended a ferry and worked as a mechanic. He reportedly was living with an Indian wife at the time.

Beale was impressed with Bishop and hired him on the spot to manage the Indians at the Sebastian Reservation. It was a good choice. The new overseer instructed the Indians in farming techniques and supervised the construction of villages. Various bands were moved from other locations and in Beale's absence, Bishop had charge of the reserve.

But there was soon trouble in Beale's paradise. Early in 1854, political opposition to Beale developed, for the most part as a result of the superintendent's own carelessness. Although later resolved satisfactorily, much of Beale's $250,000 appropriation was unaccounted for in the spring. This proved disastrous and Congress not only slashed the next year's appropriation, but had Beale removed from office. A new superintendent, one Thomas J. Henley, took office on July 15, 1854, and ushered in a dark and shameful period of California Indian affairs.

Henley had been maneuvering for position in the Democratic Party for many years. Born in Clark County, Indiana, in 1808, he was a prominent farmer-lawyer who served his area both as state legislator and congressman. He edited a Democratic newspaper which supported Martin Van Buren for president and, like his candidate, he was a strong believer in the spoils system.

After joining the Gold Rush in 1849, Henley participated in the state's constitutional convention, where he placed fourth in the contest for first U.S. senator

Thomas J. Henley, the most controversial of the early California Indian superintendents, took disgraceful advantage of his office. *Indiana Historical Society.*

from California. A noted orator and party stalwart, Henley was elected president of the first Democratic Party convention in 1851 and delivered the California vote to Washington the following year. Besides serving in the state legislature, he was prominent in banking and real estate in the Sacramento area. Prior to his latest appointment, Henley had been postmaster at San Francisco. One newspaper darkly hinted that "Mr. Beale's place was needed for some other person," and this seemed to be the case.

The *Alta* commented on the "good deal of discontent" over Beale's removal and noted that "...the Indians are leaving Tejon. A few days ago almost fifty left—they were followed by Mr. Bishop. Rather than be taken back they showed fight. The cause is said to be the removal of Mr. Beale."

Upon assuming his duties as superintendent, Henley visited the Tejon reserve and assessed the situation. There were still many Indians there and although he believed the prosperity of the place had been overstated, the system still seemed the only solution to the Indian problem. After spending a month at the reservation, Henley left several assistants in charge and headed north up the San Joaquin Valley to visit the other reserves.

Because Beale's accounts had been so garbled, Congress had cut the Indian appropriation from $250,000 to $125,000 and the number of reserves from five to three. This disturbed Henley. He was a politician accustomed to thinking in terms of power. Five reserves meant more appointments, more prestige and larger appropriations once he had established a record to fall back on. The cutbacks were a problem, but not insurmountable. Meanwhile, he had no intention to merely follow in Beale's footsteps. He determined to establish a new reservation in the north.

Henley became acquainted with a young rancher on the Sacramento River named Henry L. Ford. A native of New England, Ford had come to California in the early 1840s and taken part in both the Micheltorena campaign and the Bear Flag Rebellion. In the latter uprising he had served as a lieutenant during the only fight of the affair and is generally credited with suggesting the bear designation for the group's flag. Ford had married Susan Wilson, daughter of California's first Indian agent, General John Wilson, and Henley had probably met Ford through his acquaintance with General Wilson.

In considering where to establish his new reserve, Henley availed himself of Ford's knowledge of the country. The rancher agreed to select a site for the new venture, having in mind the territory to the west of his Colusa County ranch. With a party of six men, Ford left Tehama in August of 1854 and scouted the hills between the Sacramento River and the coast range. Ford met with a group of Nomlaki Indians on Thomes Creek, and the natives agreed to reside there should a reserve be established. The Indians complained bitterly of a gang of Mexicans who kidnapped Indian women and children while they were out gathering seeds for food. Ford was well aware of the brutal practice.

Ford selected a triangular piece of land between Elder and Thomes creeks and reported to Henley early in September. The superintendent was so pleased with the rancher's work that he appointed Ford subagent of what was named the Nome Lackee Military Reservation. Ford was sympathetic toward the Indians and began settling his affairs in order to devote more time to his new work.

Nome Lackee as it appears today. *Photo by Pat Jones.*

Simmon P. Storms, the young rancher, trader, and Indian agent, was the right man, in the right place, at the right time, but found himself caught up in politics and Indian wars. *Peter Shearer.*

Besides the Nomlakis, Henley planned to take other Indian groups out of contact with the whites and move them to the new reserve. Since he had had numerous complaints concerning the poor condition of the Maidu, in Nevada County, Henley decided to move them to Nome Lackee and put on a show in the process. A local rancher and Indian trader named Simmon P. Storms was familiar with the Indians between the Bear and Yuba rivers. The superintendent contacted him upon his arrival at Grass Valley, and the two men got along well from the start.

Born in Venezuela in 1830, Storms had joined his mother in Massachusetts when he was in his early teens. He was only nineteen when he left Boston in March of 1849 and joined the rush for gold to California. Unlucky as a miner, he began ranching late that same year. Storms took the time to get to know the local Indians and got along well with them. Perhaps he had lived among Indians in South America. In any case, his ability to speak Spanish seemed to aid him in quickly mastering the local Indian languages.

These local Indians had been involved in the brief war following the raid on Holt's Mill in May 1850. Chiefs Weima, Buckler, Poolal, and others had signed a treaty with General Green at that time, but it was unofficial and no one paid any attention to its terms. An Indian agent for the district covering Yuba, Nevada, Sierra, and Placer counties, estimated that some ten thousand Indians occupied this area in 1849, while only thirty-eight hundred remained by December of 1854. Smallpox had killed many.

In July 1851, Commissioner Wozencraft made a treaty with Weima and some five other Indian bands at a camp on the Yuba River. Storms served as interpreter. The terms of the treaty awarded them a portion of land twelve miles square, with the army post Camp Far West occupying one corner.

■ Labled only as "Maidu Headmen with Treaty Commissioners," this half-plate ambrotype was perhaps taken at the time Wozencraft made his treaty with Weima and other Maidu chiefs in July of 1851. In any case it is a pristine image of California Indians in the very early days of the great Gold Rush. *Courtesy George Eastman House.*

Wozencraft made the usual promises of so many fat bulls, mirrors, knives, and bolts of cloth, as well as tools and school teachers. A report by one who accompanied the expedition noted that "when these conditions were interpreted by Mr. Storms, who by the way speaks their language with great 'fluency,' they all collectively and individually responded 'Ugh, good.'"

In a letter to the *Alta* in October 1851, Wozencraft noted that Weima and the other chiefs were still waiting patiently for the fruits of their treaty with General Green. Impressed by the friendly relations between Storms and the local Maidu, Wozencraft appointed him agent for the area. Storms continued in that position under commissioners Beale and Henley.

Henley made arrangements to hold an Indian council at the Storms Ranch in September 1854. Named "The Hermitage," the ranch featured a hotel and saloon, as well as a large arena where both whites and Indians found entertainment on holidays. "Sport at Storms Ranch," reported the local newspaper, "called together quite a concourse of people last Sunday. Races, shooting, games…." Bull and bear fights, Indian foot races, and dog racing were some of the sports the locals enjoyed.

Henley invited all the Democratic Party stalwarts to his big show. Senators Weller and Gwin were present, as were James Denver, Sam Brannan, and other dignitaries. General John Wool attended as representative of the army.

The meeting took place on October 2, and Storms served a fine meal to the assembled dignitaries. Many miners and settlers from the surrounding country gathered for the show also, and Chief Weima and some twenty-five Indians assembled in the center of the arena. Storms introduced them individually to the crowd.

■ General John E. Wool was one of the guests at Henley's big Indian gathering. *National Archives.*

Colonel Henley then explained to the natives how he wanted to move them to another area to avoid contact with the whites. There, the government could take care of them and teach them to care for themselves. There they would be safe and at peace.

As Storms interpreted, the Indians grumbled among themselves and shook their heads. They did not believe the white men. General Green had lied to them. Wozencraft had lied to them. Some of them had even gone south to live at the Tejon, but when their friend Beale had left, they had returned home. Weima then made a comment that the *Nevada Democrat* referred to as "one of the most sensible things said on the occasion:...."

"Why do you not remove the Chinese. The Indians are better than the Chinese and you allow them to remain among you. Remove the Chinese first—then we will go."

But Henley was equal to the occasion. He told the natives they would be allowed to examine the new reservation and help in the planting of crops. The superinten-

■ Storms had a large arena constructed on his ranch where he held meetings, bull and bear fights, races, and various other amusements for the surrounding Indians, settlers and miners. *Peter Shearer.*

EXTRAORDINARY
Attraction!
ONE THOUSAND
INDIANS
With their War Implements, Squaws, Papooses, &c.

WILL ASSEMBLE

At Storms' Rancho,

On the Illinoistown road, six miles from Grass Valley and 6 1-2 from Nevada, on the afternoon and evening of Monday, July 19, 1852, for the purpose of

Celebrating their Annual Feasts and Fancy Dances.

This will be one of the largest Indian collections that has ever taken place in California, and

To those who have never witnessed any thing of the kind,

IT IS WELL WORTH
The Ride.

Storms' Rancho. July 11, 1852.

CAPT. WEYMEH.

dent added that if the whites of the area did not object to the continued Indian presence, they could stay. A committee of attending whites quickly assembled and voted for the Indians' removal, and settled that matter. During voting, senators Weller and Gwin spoke to the crowd on things politic.

The Nome Lackee Reserve was already well along in being prepared for the arrival of the Indians. A two-story frame building was being constructed for the white employees, including a kitchen and storehouse. Log quarters for the Indians who worked on the project were nearly ready, as well as stables and a council building for the chiefs. The reserve itself consisted of thousands of acres of rich land, including many small valleys of several hundred acres each. The plan was to situate the different tribes in their own separate valleys, to avoid any troubles due to language and custom barriers.

A variety of white employees were hired, including farmers, teamsters, carpenters and masons, both to construct buildings and teach the natives. Most, of course, were good Democrats. The wife of a local rancher, Mrs. Mary Ann Jennison, was hired to instruct the Indian girls in sewing. By December 1855, there were twenty-nine whites employed at Nome Lackee under Subagent Ford.

' The *Grass Valley Telegraph* chronicled the removal of the Nevada County Maidu:

> We learn that 'King Weima,' notwithstanding the effort to retain him here, has consented to take up his abode at the reservation. Nearly all the able bodied members of the tribe are also to go there. Mr. Storms has been untiring in his efforts to accomplish this end, and it is in the main, through him, that the matter has been brought about. "Several wagon-loads of Indians...passed our office yesterday.

In one of his first reports concerning the new reservation, Superintendent Henley wrote to the commissioner of Indian affairs in Washington on December 8, 1854:

> There are now about nine hundred Indians at that place having come in from all the surrounding country for a distance of fifty miles, most of them of their own accord.... They have erected their own huts for the winter and are very industriously engaged in gathering acorns, grass seeds and wild oats for their winter's provisions. They are very contented and seem to want nothing but protection from the Spanish kidnappers who have been engaged in stealing and selling their children.

Besides the local and Nevada County Indians, a group of natives from Trinity County were brought down, bringing the total on the reserve to around one thousand. This was more than Henley had wanted initially, but he made plans to accommodate them. Rations consisted of three pounds of wheat or barley per person a day—"Quite enough," wrote Henley, "and is more and better food than they have heretofore been accustomed to. We are giving the Indians no meat, not even those who work."

The kidnapping of Indian women and children was a continuing problem. Subagent Ford and a party of men were out on the headwaters of Stony Creek rounding up Indians for the reserve, when they came upon a band of Mexican kidnappers. Thirteen captive Indians were no doubt greatly relieved when the Americans rode up and disarmed their captors. On the way back, the slavers made a break in a brush-choked canyon, and when one of the party closed in, they opened fire with a pistol that had been concealed. One of the Mexicans was shot off his horse, but he managed to escape with his companions. Most of the rescued natives were brought into the new reserve by the agent and his men.

Henley's instructions to Ford as to how to conduct the reservation were detailed in a letter of November 30, 1854:

> The business at your reservation will be conducted as follows: Rations will be issued by the commissary to the white men in your employ according to the regulations of the U.S. Army, as far as practicable.
>
> You will report to the clerk every evening the work done during the day…and report same to me once a week. The plow teams must be put in charge of one man who should be responsible for the labor of all persons in his charge.
>
> You will be allowed one teamster for every two plows and two yokes of oxen to each plow…three harrows should be placed in charge of one man. One farmer will be allowed for sowing the grain.
>
> For hauling wood and getting out timber, one man will be allowed to superintend Indians who perform that labor.
>
> Strict economy and vigilance must be required….

Henley closed his instructions by noting that no more Indians should be encouraged to come onto the reserve, although all who came in must be provided for.

Simmon Storms had been hired by Henley to direct the removal of the Nevada Indians to Nome Lackee. He had no trouble, to speak of, with his own Indians. Other native groups, however, were not so easy to deal with as Storms detailed in a report written in May of 1855 from Nome Lackee:

> I arrived here yesterday with between sixty and seventy Indians—men, women and children. I have had more trouble than I expected to have in collecting the Indians. If it were not for a few bad white men the Indians would all come out of the mountains willingly. The better class of citizens

of Yuba and Nevada Counties have wished for the removal of the Indians to a proper location, for their present condition is, indeed, pitiful…. There are many traders selling them whiskey with which, of course, they are frequently drunken. First I had a lot of Indians at Empire Rancho, all willing to come to the reserve, but during my temporary absence, some trader sold whiskey to them, causing fights…so that nearly all left…[another] reason why the Indians did not like to go with me then was that their great 'crying time' was coming off and they wanted to be present.

The following October, Storms was back in Nevada County again removing some one hundred fifty natives who had either stayed behind previously or had returned to their home land. "It was sad," commented the *Marysville Herald* on November 1, "to see old, white-haired Indians looking for the last time at their old grounds."

During the summer of 1855, Captain E. D. Keyes visited the new reserve and reported huts being built and a variety of crops under cultivation. Keyes counted some one thousand natives living there, although most of these were women and children. The agent in charge stated that most of the males were out hunting.

Reports concerning the early reservations are difficult to assess since the reporters were often trying to make themselves look good to their government superiors. A report in the *Alta*, written early in January 1857, seemed to indicate that Ford was doing a competent job:

> Nome Lackee appears to be the most flourishing and prosperous of any of the reserves…. On these lands are some three thousand Indians. They have cultivated about one thousand acres of land and it is estimated that it has produced fifteen thousand bushels of wheat, besides corn and vegetables….

• • • • •

However, even as Henley initiated his new reserve, the Indians were again preparing for war in the Klamath country. The trouble had originated, as it had many times before, somewhere along the Klamath River. The *Humboldt Times* of January 27, 1855, gave the following report of the incident:

> The facts are, as we are informed, that about the 10th of December a ruffian in attempting to commit an outrage upon the person of an Indian woman, who was accompanied by an Indian boy, the woman clung to the boy and the white man drew his revolver and shot the boy down, who later died from the wound…. The man, after bullying around for some time, left for parts unknown. The Indians, thinking to get revenge, killed an ox that had formerly belonged to this man, but learning that he had sold it, they offered to pay the present owner the value of the steer, which was refused.

The Indians became frightened and by their conduct filled the minds of the miners with suspicion. The miners tried to disarm the Indians without paying the value of the guns, and upon the Indians refusing to surrender them, the miners burned the Indian ranches, with their winters supply of provisions, which they defended...."

Earlier, the miners first suspected trouble when the Indian women and children were reported leaving for the mountains. In a growing panic, the whites deserted their diggings along the rivers and congregated in the larger camps and towns. On January 6, the miners at Orleans Bar held a public meeting and voted to do all they could to stop any traffic in arms to the Indians. It was also agreed that the Indians would be given until the 19th of the month to surrender their weapons. After that date, any native caught armed would be shot.

A group of Karok Indians, under Chief Red Cap, flatly refused to surrender any arms. When the deadline expired, a company of miners formed and marched to the Red Cap rancheria. A brief parley resulted in an exchange of gunfire, and the natives drove the whites from the field. Two miners were reported killed and several others wounded. The Karoks disappeared into the forests to prepare for war.

As rumors of impending hostilities traveled through the canyons and along the river banks, dispatches were sent to Superintendent Henley and Brevet Lt. Colonel Robert Buchanan at Fort Humboldt, on Humboldt Bay. Skirmishes between volunteer

■ Isolated Northern California mining camps were rallying points for volunteer groups during Indian troubles. *Siskiyou County Museum.*

groups and Indians were reported near Trinidad, and several prospectors were killed near Orleans Bar. Other casualties resulted in the miners of the Klamath sending out calls for help to nearby mining camps along the Salmon River, in neighboring Trinity County.

In February, Captain Henry Judah and a twenty-five-man detachment of troops set up camp at the mining camp at Weitchpeck Bar, located at the junction of the Klamath and Trinity rivers and named after the local Indians. Judah had recently been transferred to Fort Humboldt because of his intemperance. Lieutenants Crook and Bonnycastle had become thoroughly disgusted with his behavior during the Shasta cave expedition. When they returned to Fort Jones, the junior officers demanded that Judah put in for transfer, and he quickly complied.

At Weitchpeck, Judah found angry groups of miners clamoring for a war of extermination against all Indians, friendly or hostile. It was with

A Karok warrior, pictured in 1894, armed and dressed as he might have been during the fighting in the 1850s. *Smithsonian Institution.*

great difficulty that the officer was able to make the miners agree to a policy of protecting all local natives who would give up their weapons and remain in their villages. Judah was greatly relieved when Captain F. M. Woodward and a company of volunteers from Union arrived to help keep the unruly miners in check. Just as Judah was preparing to move against the hostiles, he was recalled to Fort Humboldt leaving the situation in the hands of the now numerous volunteer companies.

By this time volunteer groups from Humboldt, Shasta, and Trinity counties were in the field. Captain Woodward and his men were from Union, on Humboldt Bay, while Captain Chesley Woodward and his brother William each led groups of miners from the Salmon River. At Big Bar, a sixty-man company formed under the leadership of William Young, while two other companies under captains Flowers and Lufkin were mustered into service.

During the first week in February, Agent Rosborough arrived at Orleans Bar, where the volunteers were now encamped. He found the various companies quarreling among themselves. Besides groups from different counties, the companies varied as to the type of men enlisted. William Young complained bitterly of the situation in a letter to a friend:

> We have 3 companies of men out in pursuit of Indians. The two
> Woodwards have a company, each of which are pulling against the interest
> of this County. All the men that has any interest on this river or in the county

A scene at the mining camp of Weitchpeck, with a pack train being unloaded at a store. *Author's collection.*

belong to my company. I think it is a damned shame that the interest of people living on this river should be trampled on by men belonging to other counties. I have organized a company of the best men in the county, rejecting all that are not good, also refuse those that do not belong to the county....

The Weitchpeck Indians wanted to remain friendly with the whites, and when Captain F. M. Woodward decided to make a tour of inspection of two nearby rancherias, several Weitchpecks went along as guides. The natives at the first rancheria informed Woodward that a number of Red Cap's band were concealed nearby and had offered to guide the whites to their hiding place. Suspecting treachery, the Weitchpecks refused to go along,

Indian Agent Alex Rosborough. *Author's collection.*

but Woodward and his men accompanied two new guides into the forest.

After following the guides on what seemed to be a false trail, the volunteers suddenly found themselves fired upon from ambush. Woodward shot the guide in front of him, while one of his men was able to shoot one of the ambushers. The whites quickly retreated, miraculously having suffered no casualties.

The following day, the Union volunteers and Captain Chesley Woodward's men from Salmon River returned to the Cappell and Moreno villages previously visited. They attacked without warning, and the Union men killed twenty warriors and took eighteen prisoners, while the Salmon River company killed six natives and took five prisoners. The volunteers reported only one man wounded.

While the volunteers were attacking the two villages, some of the more irresponsible miners on the Klamath had attacked a friendly village and set it afire. This action was condemned by the decent class of miners and at this time most of the volunteer groups went into camp to wait for word from the government, and for supplies. In a letter to Agent Rosborough, Captain Young of the "Big Bar Rangers" again complained of the actions of some of the volunteers:

> ...No fighting has been done since your departure. C. Woodward's company has gone down the river—started soon after you left. I have had no news from him since they left. Wm. Woodward's company still remains where you left them just below my house. They have singled out all the squaws compelling them to sleep with some man every night. This causes great excitement—the bucks complain daily of it. Their acts since you left have been disgraceful. If you remember, one of the squaws had a child while you were here. Since then the child has died—the same afternoon one of the men of the party says now I will have a squaw to sleep with—same day of the death of the child, beat the squaw until she could not walk because she would not consent to sleep with him. This shocking state of affairs people cannot tolerate long. Something must be done.... The conduct of those two companies has been more disgraceful since you left ...."

In a report to Superintendent Henley written from Weitchpeck on February 22, Rosborough noted that the only reason the hostile Indians had not committed more atrocities was that they knew the peaceful Indians would be the ones to suffer for it. Friendly whites did what they could to protect the peaceful natives, but it was impossible to guard them every moment. Rosborough begged for U.S. troops, or even a deputy U.S. marshal, to insure some stability in the area:

> There is no law on this river, not a single constable or justice of the peace on the river.... The sure knowledge that there was legal authority on the river...would stop the lawless.... If something was not done, and that soon, I am certain that you will hear terrible news from this region.

Earlier, Rosborough had worked desperately to avoid more bloodshed. The Hoopa Valley Indians and the Weitchpecks had both offered to fight Red Cap's band to prove their loyalty and avoid further attacks on their own villages. Captain Young went down river and brought up other Indians willing to fight the hostiles, but none of these native allies were used.

Rosborough had done all he could. For some time he had indicated a desire to leave the Indian service and in March, S. G. Whipple was appointed in his place. Rosborough practiced law in Yreka and was elected a county judge in 1856. All his life he was a friend to the Indians, and they always trusted him. He was an important negotiator during the Modoc War of 1873 and died in Oakland in 1900.

The new agent went right to work and prevailed upon Colonel Buchanan at Fort Humboldt to return Captain Judah to the troubled area.

The officer's first action was to dismiss the bickering volunteer companies and send out word to the Indians that a "big talk" would be held on April 7. A large attendance of friendly Indians was present to hear Judah demand that hostile Indians who had killed white men and made war be punished or surrender.

After the council, Indian difficulties subsided. Judah and his thirty-man detachment were constantly in the field, always just one step behind the hostiles. Friendly natives kept up the pressure also, and within a few weeks, some sixteen of Red Cap's band had surrendered, with one being killed.

Late in May the *Humboldt Times* reported the murder of two friendly Indians at the mouth of the Salmon River, but further bloodshed was somehow averted.

■ Fort Humboldt, near Eureka in Humboldt County, played a major role in the Northern California Indian troubles. *Fort Humboldt State Historic Park.*

When Captain Judah was again recalled to his post, a Captain Jones replaced him in the field. Agent Whipple and Jones concluded that the establishment of a reservation would be the practical way to conclude the troubles and selected a site along the Klamath River. Beginning at the river's mouth, the new reserve was a mile wide from each side of the river and extended some twenty miles upstream. The harried members of Red Cap's band were eager to accept their new home and the peace it seemed to offer, and the Klamath Reservation was brought into the system.

As two drunken Indians rode along lower Humbug Creek in late July 1855, they met a miner named Peterson on the trail. When Peterson questioned them as to where they obtained their liquor, one of the natives pulled a pistol and shot him. As he fell from his horse, Peterson drew his own weapon and shot the Indian in the stomach. The Indians then fled, galloping off towards the Klamath. The incident was witnessed by another white man and soon word of the shooting was being spread among the mining camps. Another war seemed imminent.

Several volunteer groups were organized, but they had little luck finding Indians. Of the several that were captured, two escaped and one was discharged by a local justice of the peace at Humbug. While the companies had been in the field, the Indians made a raid along the Klamath which was chronicled in the *Humboldt Times* of August 11:

> On the 27th the Indians killed ten men and wounded two others on the Klamath near Scott's Bar. They killed three at work at Buckeye Bar, four packers at Peckham's ranch and between there and Buckeye they killed five more and wounded two. Two of the murderers were hung on the 31st at Yreka and the negroes who furnished them with guns were lynched.

Some eleven men met their death that night when the Indians swept down the banks of the Klamath. The whites claimed the natives had been planning hostilities for some time, but whether this was true or whether the Peterson shooting and subsequent events had touched off the raid is not known. However, the whites reacted predictably, killing every Indian they could find.

The Indian who had been exonerated at Humbug was escorted back to the Klamath by several whites. After learning of the bloody raid, the whites promptly shot their prisoner and threw his body into the river. Another Indian, found walking along a creek, was dragged into Humbug where he too was promptly shot and his body heaved into a mining shaft.

At Yreka, two hapless Shastas were found walking through the willows below town and were promptly arrested and thrown into jail. These were the two "murderers," noted by the brief August 11 account in the *Times*. Released after a night in jail, the two Indians were immediately pounced upon by a mob and hanged from pine trees on the main street of the town. Not content to merely relish the strangling figures, several brutes climbed the trees and, sitting on the limb from which the rope stretched, pulled the dying Indians up and down several times. At this, many of the crowd left in disgust.

With their blood lust up, the mob, now numbering some two hundred men, headed for several buildings occupied by Negroes who had been accused of harboring Indians and selling them whiskey and ammunition. As members of the mob were preparing to break down a door, the owner of the property, George Tyler, jumped into the doorway with a pistol in his hand. Tyler growled that whoever touched the door of his house would die if it was the last act of his life. The mob quickly decided that Tyler was taking matters entirely too seriously and accordingly dispersed and headed for the nearest saloon. This was apparently the basis for the exaggerated *Times* story that local Negroes had been lynched.

At Fort Jones, Captain Judah equipped a cavalry patrol and headed for the Klamath. He had no sooner left the post than ranchers in the Scott's Valley area began gathering to "exterminate" the Indians there. Assistant Surgeon F. Sorrel, in command of the fort in Judah's absence, took the Indians under his protection and warned off some armed whites who had gathered. On August 1, Sorrel took in nineteen other Indian women and children who had been rescued by humane whites at Scott's Bar. The men of the band had either been killed or were in hiding. Sorrel also received word that fifty Shasta women and children were threatened with death at Hamburg Bar on the Scott's River, but he had his hands full at the fort and did not feel he could divide his small force.

When Judah returned to Fort Jones later in the month, he found the post under severe threat by whites who wanted to kill the Indians gathered there. "I have openly and freely told the citizens," reported Judah, "that the reserve should be held inviolate and if they attempt to interfere as they have threatened, it will be with a full knowledge of the reception prepared for them."

The officer's patrol to the Klamath accomplished little other than to establish that many of the volunteers had committed acts "too shocking for repetition" and were men "who would appropriately ornament the gallows." Judah brought charges against several whites who had taken an Indian boy from a house, told him to run, and then shot him down, but with so much country to cover, there was little he could do to prosecute the charges.

At the mining camp of Deadwood, just west of Yreka, an Indian working a claim with some Kanakas was murdered by a prowling white posse. A gang of forty drunks from Humbug City raided a nearby rancheria and managed to murder an old man and two boys after tying them up. Two other old Indians were killed, one a woman, before the crowd returned to town herding several Indian women and "squaw men." The justice of the peace turned them all loose.

Five volunteer companies were formed, one containing some sixty men from Scott's River. The groups quickly took the field against the hostiles, who were reported to be carrying with them the Indian who had been wounded by Peterson. The Indians were trailed to the Oregon border, the whites at one point getting so close to the fleeing Indians that they captured some of the Shasta ponies. Crossing the summit of Siskiyou Mountain and descending Applegate Creek, the volunteers soon made camp at the Fort Lane Indian Reserve. Convinced that the Indians they were tracking were here, the whites were certain that all they had to do was demand their quarry. Captain A. J. Smith, however, had other ideas.

When the five volunteer captains explained their mission and asked for the Indians, Smith refused. Two of the wanted Indians were in the post guardhouse at that time and Smith feared that if he gave them to the Californians, the Oregon Indians would go on the warpath in protest. When the volunteers threatened to take the natives by force, Smith had them removed from the fort grounds.

The whites actually made plans to attack the fort, but Bill Martin, who commanded the Scott's River volunteers, finally realized just how ridiculous the situation had become. The men all returned home and resumed their mining operations.

The two Indians in the Fort Lane guardhouse were later returned to Siskiyou County, but no evidence could be produced against them and they were released. Both were shot and killed as they left town and their bodies hurled into an abandoned mining shaft. The Humbug War was over.

CHAPTER 12 / SOURCES

UNPUBLISHED MATERIAL

National Archives, Records of the Office of Indian Affairs, Record Group 75, California Superintendency, M234:

P. E. Connor to Jarvis Scofield, February 22, 1854.

H. L. Ford to Thomas J. Henley, September 4, 1854.

Thomas J. Henley to Edward P. Beale, September 15, 1854.

Thomas J. Henley to G. W. Manypenny, October 14, December 7, 8, 1854.

Thomas J. Henley to H. L. Ford, November 30, 1854.

A. M. Rosborough to Thomas J. Henley, February 22, 1855.

Simmon P. Storms to Thomas J. Henley, May 25, 1855.

Captain Henry M. Judah to Thomas J. Henley, August 28, November 1, December 13, 1855.

General John Wool to Thomas J. Henley, September 15, 1855.

Thomas J. Henley to Captain Henry M. Judah, December 29, 1855.

National Archives, Records of the Office of Indian Affairs, Record Group 75, California Superintendency Special Piles, M574:

Voucher No. 41, statement by Edward F. Beale concerning S. A. Bishop.

National Archives, Records of the War Department, Department of the Pacific, Record Group 98:

Asst. Surgeon F. Sorrel to Bvt. Major B. D. Townsend, August 2, 1855.

Captain Henry M. Judah to Bvt. Major E. D. Townsend, August 23, 1855.

Beard, Estle, to the author, March 27, May 17, 1978.

Jones, Pat, to the author, August 10, 1977.

Kirkland, Olin C. "A Historical Study of Military Operations in Humboldt County, California, 1851-1870, unpublished paper in Special Collections, Humboldt State University Library, 1960.

NEWSPAPERS

San Francisco *Daily Alta California*, October 10, 1851; July 1, 14, August 5, 17, October 2, 6, 27, November 8, 1854; May 26, October 15, 1855.

Sacramento *Daily Union*, July 13, 28, 1851; September 27, 1853; December 30, 1854.

Grass Valley Telegraph, May 25, July 6, 1854; October 10, 1855.

Grass Valley Union, July 20, 1963.

Humboldt Times, October 14, 28, 1854; January 20, 27, February 3, 10, 24, March 3, April 28, June 9, 16, August 11, 1855.

Los Angeles *Star*, June 17, 1854; June 30, 1855.

Marysville Herald, November l, 1855.

PRINCIPAL PUBLISHED WORKS

Bancroft, Hubert H. *History of California*. Vol. VI, San Francisco: The History Company, Publishers, 1887.

Bledsoe, A. J. *Indian Wars of the Northwest*. Oakland: Biobooks, 1956.

Casebier, Dennis. *Fort Pah-Ute, California*. Norco: Tales of the Mojave Road Publishing Company, 1974.

Coy, Owen C. *The Humboldt Bay Region, 1850-1875*. Los Angeles: California State Historical Association, 1929.

Heizer, Robert F., editor. *The Destruction of the California Indians*. Santa Barbara: Peregrine Smith, Inc., 1974.

_____ and Whipple, M.A., editors. *The California Indians*. Berkeley: University of California Press, 1973.

Kroeber, A. L. *Handbook of the Indians of California*. New York: Dover Publications, Inc., 1976.

Latta, Frank F. *Handbook of Yokuts Indians*. Santa Cruz, CA: Bear State Books, 1978.

Rice, William B. The *Los Angeles Star, 1851-1864*. Berkeley: University of California Press, 1947.

Victor, Francis Fuller (Dorothy and Jack Sutton, editors). *Indian Wars of the Rogue River*. Medford, OR: Josephine County Historical Society, 1969.

Wells, Harry L. *History of Siskiyou County, California*. Oakland: D. J. Stewart & Co., 1881.

OTHER SOURCES

Ellison, William H. "The Federal Indian Policy in California, 1846-1860," *The Mississippi Valley Historical Review,* June 1922.

Rogers, Fred. "Bear Flag Lieutenant—Henry L. Ford," *California Historical Society Quarterly,* June, September, December 1950.

Rosborough, Alex J. "A. M. Rosborough, Special Indian Agent," *California Historical Society Quarterly,* Volume 26, 1947.

Chapter 13

TULE RIVER

Once the Indian troubles had seemingly subsided, civilization advanced swiftly in the San Joaquin Valley. In newly-formed Tulare County, the hub of the Four Creeks area, the first meeting of the Court of Sessions was held in October 1852. This was the governing body in California counties at this time and combined both legislative and judicial duties. The meeting was held in the tragic Woods cabin and consisted of Walter Harvey, who had recently been elected county judge, William J. Campbell, and Loomis St. Johns.

Ironically, the first arrest and inquest trial in the fledgling county was that of Harvey for the killing of Major Savage. Harvey was easily acquitted, however, after appointing his murderous friend Joel Brooks to serve as judge.

Settlers and cattlemen were arriving in Tulare County, even at this early date. Included among the newcomers were the lawyer and land speculator Colonel Thomas Baker and Nathaniel Vise and his family. Vise had given up part of his claim to provide the ground upon which to found a town, and already crude shacks, tents, and cabins were scattered along the barely discernible streets of the village called Visalia. A millrace and gristmill had been constructed during 1853, using mostly Indian labor. Nathan Baker opened a store and the first saloon quickly made an appearance. There were only a half dozen children in Visalia, but a school was initiated that same year.

The Indians had materially aided in the building of the community. Telamni, Wolasi and Gawia, as well as Chunut, and Tachi from the Tulare Lake area, had helped plant the first crops, hauled logs for construction, tended stock and worked as servants. The two races seemed to get along well and reason prevailed.

When an Indian boy disabled a work oxen by shooting him with an arrow, the settlers and Indians held a meeting, and trouble was averted. The boy was fined fifty buckskins, and both sides concurred that the punishment was just.

As if to emphasize this new-found harmony between the races, the first grand jury met in early July 1853 and brought a true bill against one Samuel Lago. It was a unique case for California at this time, for Lago was charged with "the crime of attempting an assault with intent to commit murder on two Indians."

The trial was held in William Dill's saloon on August 22, and testimony took most of the morning. Lago plead not guilty, but five white men appeared against him, and a jury found him guilty that afternoon. He was sentenced to two years in prison and assessed for the cost of the trial. It was an incredible incident, all the more so when it is considered the jury deliberated within sight of the spot where Woods and his men were buried. A new era seemed to be dawning in the valley. Perhaps common sense and reason would secure the peace after all, although there had been occasional flurries of trouble in the area.

During the summer of 1852, two members of old Tomquit's Pitkachi band had wandered past the boundaries of the Jenny Lind claim, just below Rootville, later called Millerton. A miner named David B. James ordered the two Indians to "git" and punctuated his anger with several pistol shots. Immediately all the Indians working along the San Joaquin vanished into the surrounding hills.

Three days later, the Indians suddenly reappeared. A miner working the Jenny Lind looked up and saw a nearby hilltop covered with painted and armed Pitkachis and Dumnas, led by a drunken Tomquit. The old chief was naked and armed with a battered cutlass, and he yelled at the miners to turn "Brigham" James over to him. The natives were careful, however, to stay out of range of the white men's pistols.

A miner yelled at Tomquit to come over and get James if he wanted him, and for a time the groups yelled back and forth. Eventually, peace was secured and this was apparently the last serious trouble in the hills surrounding Fort Miller.

In February of 1853 six Americans traced a stolen horse to an Indian village on the Chowchilla River. Dismounting, the whites walked into the village and tried to make the Indians understand that they were looking for a missing animal. To all their questions, the natives kept answering, "No sabe." When one of the whites, a man by the name of Starkie, thought he detected a hostile movement, he shot and killed the Indian leader. A moment later, Starkie fell, pierced by several arrows. When the Indians tried to cut them off from their horses, the whites made a hasty retreat, abandoning the wounded Starkie.

Several days later, another posse surrounded the village, but the Indians had fled. After destroying the rancheria and all food stores, the whites returned home.

The Fresno River Reserve, or Indian Farm as it was usually referred to, was established between the San Joaquin and Fresno rivers by the Camp Barbour Treaty in 1851. Savage had lived here with his collection of Indian wives and conducted his farming and trading enterprises. Another serious incident on the Fresno River Farm in May 1855, threatened the peace of the valley. A man named Williams attempted to punish an Indian boy who did not feel like working. The boy was insolent and when Williams tried to force him to work, a group of warriors knocked him down. Seizing a rifle, Williams shot and killed one of his attackers. Everything happened so fast, Williams was able to flee to Fort Miller before the startled natives could recover.

The Indians sought out Lorenzo Vinsonhaler and demanded justice in the matter. He pacified them as best he could, but by the time Subagent D. A. Enyart returned from the fort, the Indians became frightened and fled to the mountains.

First reports of the affair appeared in the Stockton newspapers and consisted of wild stories of stolen cattle, burned stores and hundreds of armed Indians looking for blood. The day following the shooting, Enyart and twenty soldiers pursued the natives into the hills. After several days, the Indians tired of the chase and begged to be allowed back on the farm. Enyart let them return peaceably and soon reported the incident settled.

In a letter to the Stockton *San Joaquin Republican*, Enyart wrote that the major difficulties in the whole affair were those stirred up "by persons de-

An undated drawing of Fort Miller made by a private soldier. *National Archives.*

■ An Indian woman gathering acorns in the Sierra Nevada. *Jeff Edwards Collection.*

lighted with the flare-up, and hoping to be rid of the Indians forever."

• • • • •

Elisha and Samuel Packwood had settled along the Tule River in 1853 or '54. The family had first come west in 1846, and had lived in Oregon and operated a store at Culloma and a dairy at San Jose. The Packwoods brought Durham cattle to the valley and settled just south of the Four Creeks where the family name was given to a creek and to the road between their ranch and Visalia. With the Packwoods came several brothers-in-law and their wives and children.

A son of Elisha Packwood was stirred by the palpitations of young love during the spring of 1856. White women were still a scarce commodity in the valley, and the object of young Packwood's attention was a comely Yokuts maiden. The two were married after the Indian fashion, and to celebrate the occasion, young Packwood contributed a yearling calf from his father's herd. There was a grand wedding feast that was enjoyed by all.

Young Packwood's intentions were good, but his timing was particularly inopportune. The settlers, from Packwoods north to Fort Miller, were beset by rumors of Indian trouble. The reasons for their apprehension stemmed, as usual, from their own rash acts. Early in February, Sam Jennings wrote to Superintendent Henley and related how a young Indian boy had been murdered by an eighteen-year-old white man. When the killer was tried and acquitted at Woodsville, the Indians became quite upset.

Soon Indians were shooting arrows into cattle, and several Indians were shot "while trying to escape" from a white posse. Writing from Fort Miller in early May, a correspondent noted the developing unrest:

> The settlers of Four Creeks have been alarmed quite often of late by rumors of intended attacks by the Indians in the mountains at the head of the Cahwia, Tule River and Deer Creek. These Indians having threatened to 'fan out' the pale faces, and take possession of the valley again. This they might have intended, but I am satisfied that the valley Indians were not linked in with them. Their chief, Gregorio, has been on to Washington, and knows the power of the American people; and knows it would be folly to commence war with us…. But, as I have stated, there was a good deal of excitement among the settlers, and when some one brought in news that a

The foothills east of Visalia, where the Indian troubles began. *Jeff Edwards Collection.*

steer had been stolen from somewhere by the Diggers, the excited population thought that they were laying in provisions preparatory to commencing hostilities. The blood of an American ox had flowed and the Americans raised the cry of war! War!

By early May, the *San Francisco Herald* had magnified Packwood's contibution of a yearling calf into a herd of five hundred cattle driven off by the natives. Rumors had been rampant before, but now they were really flying!

Nathan Dillon, Wiley Watson, and several other prominent Visalians were anxious to learn just what had taken place and they questioned some of the local natives. When the truth became apparent, they were horrified that such an incident could be magnified into the wild stories now being circulated.

The men hurried back to town but found that matters were already out of control. At a meeting of local settlers, Dillon disclosed what had really happened, but no one would listen. It was decided to attack, rather than talk to the Indians, and a volunteer company of some sixty men was formed. Captained by one Foster DeMasters, the volunteers quickly made plans to seek out the Indians on the Tule River.

Meanwhile, groups of whites were already patrolling the perimeters of town. At a rancheria, they told a group of valley natives to give up their arrows and move closer to town. In the foothills, a group of mounted whites rode through a village of Yokodos yelling and shooting and driving the terrified natives into the swamps.

When a whiskey-inspired mob of thugs conceived the idea of destroying a friendly village near town, David James and others brought the natives to Visalia where they could be protected.

221

Nine men under John Williams were detailed to follow a group of Tejon Indians who were heading south towards White River, while the balance of the volunteers headed up the north fork of the Tule River. Campfire smoke soon disclosed the Indian position but to the surprise of the whites, it was quite strategically located and fortified. Besides breastworks of rock and brush, the Indians had located their fort in the midst of dense chaparral thickets where any attacking force would have to advance over rough and open ground. In addition to this unforeseen situation, the whites also had no idea just how many natives they were up against. Later reports mentioned five to seven hundred, but such figures were usually exaggerated. Quoting a letter from the Fresno Indian Farm, a San Francisco newspaper reported:

> They are in a valley about a mile long and a half mile wide, that is very thick with brush. It is impossible to ascertain the number of Indians, but there is quite a strong party of them. The Americans went up close, but could only see an Indian now and then in the brush, and would fire. The Indians would return the fire with a volley of arrows. They were unable to dislodge them without losing half their men, so retired and sent an express to Fort Miller for aid….

Williams and his men had meanwhile kept on the trail of the Tejon Indians and had surprised them in camp at dawn of the second day. The Indians had women and dogs with them and it was highly unlikely they were a war party. Nevertheless, as the dogs heralded the approaching whites, an Indian ran up a small hill to look around and was shot dead. Charging through the camp, the volunteers killed five natives and scattered the rest. After burning the camp, the men headed north to join DeMaster's group on Tule River.

According to a work report from the Sebastian (Tejon) Reserve, Williams' group had attacked a group of Tejon Indians who had been visiting in the Four Creeks area. The Tejon Indians were now all terrified that the whites would come there.

■ An old log fort said to have been constructed at the time of the 1856 troubles. *Jeff Edwards Collection.*

■ Rock defenses constructed by the Indians. *Jeff Edwards Collection.*

A May 1 report by Fort Miller's commander, Lieutenant James Stewart, gave an account of the confused state of affairs:

> I was waited on this afternoon by three gentlemen of Tulare County: Mr. Jennings, Indian agent or subagent at Four Creeks; Mr. Campbell, in charge of the Indian farm on Kings River; and Mr. Wallace, bringing a communication....
>
> It appears that last week a single cow, if I mistake not, was killed by an Indian or Indians and at a meeting of the citizens it was the wish of the majority (about two-thirds) to demand the aggressor or aggressors of the chiefs: but some of the citizens insisted upon punishing the Indians collectively, and for this purpose organized a company and gave pursuit....
>
> Day before yesterday some friendly Indians consulted a white friend of theirs as to their safety during the then state of excitement, and they were assured that so long as they remained peaceable they would be in no danger. Unfortunately, within one hour of this they were attacked by a party of whites, six of them killed, several more wounded, and the balance dispersed. Another party of friendly Indians had five killed, several wounded, and the others dispersed, and one of the gentlemen mentioned a third case of the same kind. The number of hostile Indians encamped at the head of Tulare Valley may not, therefore, be overstated.
>
> These events have caused great excitement and no little anxiety on the part of the more peaceable inhabitants, who are anxious to avoid all hostilities, thinking such hostilities unnecessary.
>
> Under these circumstances, I have ordered Lieutenant Livingston to leave tomorrow morning, with a detachment, for the Tule River. A copy of his orders is enclosed....
>
> These gentlemen informed me that the 'war party' [whites] were going to send or had already sent an express to Sacramento, to petition Governor Johnson for arms. They left here this evening hoping to be able to allay the excitement around their homes....

Other sources confirmed the attacks on friendly Indians. The San Francisco *Bulletin* reported:

> The poor devils were frightened out of their wits, but had enough left to strike out straight 'shirt-tail' for Campbell's reservation on Kings River,

at least those on the Kaweah above Woodsville. Those down nearer the lake hid in the tules. Old Gregorio, the Capitano Grande of the lake Indians, came up on Kings River, and told a farmer there (and he told me) that he did not want to fight, and offered to give up every bow, arrow, knife, hatchet, sharp stick and other deadly weapons in his camp, and to go anywhere the Americans wanted—(he could not have done it, for I know several that wanted him and all his tribe to go to the devil.)...At last accounts they had killed 15 Indians.

When Williams and his men rejoined the main body of volunteers, they heard the story of the first skirmish. Besides sending a courier to the governor, DeMasters had also sent Wallace to Fort Miller, Millerton, and Coarsegold to ask for help. Williams himself was sent south to Keyesville for additional volunteers. With no idea just how many Indians he was up against, DeMasters did not mean to take any chances.

The Keyesville reinforcements were the first to arrive, bringing the white force up to a total of 140 men. Tulare County Sheriff W. G. Poindexter apparently took command at this point and decided he had enough men to make another assault. Again the whites advanced on the Indian positions, having learned from the first skirmish that the natives had few, if any, guns.

■ Thomas Baker was prominent among those who tried to prevent the 1856 Indian hostilities around Visalia. *Author's collection.*

As soon as the whites were in arrow range, the battle began. It was another brief skirmish, the whites firing into the thickets as they tried to dodge the clusters of arrows which zipped around them. Three volunteers, including Loomis St. Johns, were wounded, and several Indians were seen to drop in the chaparral. Suddenly, the whites began falling back, and the Indians pursued them with wild war cries. Once out of the open ground, the whites turned and again drove the natives back with their rifle fire. The second battle ended with the Indians still holding their ground.

For the next several days, the volunteers stayed in camp, with only small groups going out to search for and destroy any native food stores that could be located. They had decided to wait for further reinforcements before attacking again, but meanwhile some strategy was being planned.

Certain now that the Indians had no guns, the volunteers were still less than excited about the next attack. A frontal assault seemed the only choice, and charging into those flights of arrows could be dangerous, as the three casualties discovered. Billy Lynn, one of the Keyesville volunteers, had an idea. Why not form a special assault brigade of ten or twelve men who would bear the brunt of the Indian arrows while the rest of the troops followed close behind. This special force would wear protective clothing and, with luck, would not be hurt by the native missiles.

Lynn's idea seemed to make sense, and wagon covers and other materials were procured and fashioned into long, protective, padded vests. As the assault team held its first muster, the members were jokingly dubbed the "Petticoat Rangers" by their fellow volunteers.

Meanwhile, a portion of the volunteers returned to Visalia, and they were in an ugly mood. Having been whipped twice by the hostiles, the men vented their wrath on a group of local Indians who were camped in town under the protection of the "peace party." When Nathan Dillon, Wiley Watson, and Judge Thomas Baker objected to the men's actions, the volunteers insisted that the Indians must be removed to the Kings River farm or they would be killed. Reluctantly, Baker and the others hired teams and provided provisions for the trip north.

A steady stream of reinforcements began arriving at the volunteer camp on Tule River. John Hunt brought in a group from Coarsegold Gulch, while Ira Stroud rode in at the head of a detachment from Millerton. A cavalry troop from Fort Tejon arrived also, and when Lieutenant LaRhett Livingston arrived with twenty-five troops and a small howitzer from Fort Miller, the men again prepared for action. With this strong force of soldiers and civilians, the whites were now eager for a final fight.

Lieutenant Livingston assumed command of the various units and it was decided that the volunteers would make another assault on the Indian

■ Another view of the Indian rock fortifications during the 1856 Visalia troubles. *Jeff Edwards Collection.*

fortress at daybreak. This time the Yokuts were to be annihilated by a simultaneous attack on the front, rear and both flanks.

To familiarize himself with the terrain and locate a position for the howitzer, Livingston and his men and a group of volunteers ascended a large rock formation overlooking the Indian positions.

It was the evening of May 13, and the weather was brisk in the Sierra Nevada. The army officer wore his heavy cape as he stood atop his promontory surveying the rough, mountain scenery around him. As he gazed down on the Indian positions, the natives saw him too and sent a flight of arrows in his direction.

■ John Barker was one of the volunteers in the 1856 fighting. *Author's collection.*

"We saw the arrows strike him several times," wrote John Barker, one of the volunteers, "but they could not penetrate the cloak and being shot from an angle below they simply stuck in the cloak and slipped up and hung there. It seemed as though one must have stung him for he commenced to swear, and ordered his men to charge the breast work. Upon this we all went in and in about ten minutes we had it all our own way...."

■ Lieutenant LaRhett Livingston, from Fort Miller, commanded the Tule River volunteers, along with his own twenty-five-man force. *Army Military History Institute.*

The sudden sight of Livingston and his men above them had prompted the flight of native arrows. The soldiers rushed the flank, and when the other volunteers made a frontal assault, the battle was quickly over. John Barker reported forty Indians killed; some Tejon Indians later corroborated this report, adding an "equal number" of wounded.

Billy Lynn's armored troops were never put to the test. "The 'Petticoat Rangers,'" reported the *Bulletin*, "were upon the field, but effected nothing, as their padded garments only served the purpose of sleeping accommodations."

The soldiers and volunteers had swept through the brushy fortress and chased the natives up the valley and into the mountains where their women and children were hidden. After pursuing them for several days, the whites returned to the valley, leaving several scouting groups to prevent further Indian raiding. To all intents and purposes, the Tule River War was over.

Despite the patrols, fast-moving Indian raiders swept down onto the plains and foothills at night and commenced a series of depredations. Thirteen houses were reported burned along the creeks and rivers of the area, while many cattle were killed or driven off. Orson Smith's $30,000 sawmill was destroyed, along with a reported 100,000 board feet of lumber, although few took the latter figure seriously. Saddles were reported stolen from Packwood's station, also. The settlers began to wonder just what kind of can of worms they had opened. A little Indian killing was one thing, but a war....

Meanwhile, Edward F. Beale was back at home in California. He was a political animal and after a defeat always seemed to land on his feet. Although from a prominent Eastern family and related to the Porters and Farraguts of naval fame, Beale had already made a name for himself on the California frontier. He had been considered something of a success as the first California superintendent of Indian affairs, despite his early replacement, and he had gained some degree of gratification for his rough handling in the East at the time of his removal.

When he had returned to Washington to try to straighten out his tangled affairs, Beale had at first been further humiliated by the federal commissioner of Indian affairs, G. W. Manypenny. The commissioner saw fit not only to publicly accuse Beale of being a defaulter, but to publish several anonymous newspaper stories to that effect in one of the administration organs, the *National Star*. Soon, however, Beale had the great satisfaction of not only being completely cleared of any irregularity in the use of government funds, but of meeting Mr. Manypenny in the doorway of a Washington hotel one day. Beale slapped him twice in the face, then after a brief brawl, the commissioner walked away.

In California, Beale had traveled over much of the state as superintendent, as a government surveyor, and with the army. He had seen the rich, agricultural opportunities that were available. Gold was only the tip of the iceberg. Real fortunes were to be made with the land.

After leaving the Indian service, Beale spent much time in the Tejon area, mostly at and around the fort which had been established in August of 1854. Fort Tejon was now garrisoned by a dragoon company under Brevet Lieutenant Colonel B. L. Beall. In surveying the Tejon territory, Beale had become familiar with the area and the various Spanish land grants which comprised the best property. It was good land, ideal for stock raising and just waiting to be developed.

With Sam Bishop as a partner, Beale purchased some 48,000 acres of one of the grants and moved his family to the Rancho La Liebre. In a few years the two men became wealthy and widely respected in Southern California. Beale gained further prominence through his use of camels in the California deserts and by building a wagon road across the Mojave Desert. But he was always casting about for more land. President Lincoln appointed him surveyor general for California and Nevada in 1861, but did not reappoint him when his term was up. Reportedly, the president was concerned at Beale's inclination to become "monarch of all he surveyed."

In the spring of 1856, Beale was asked by Governor J. Neely Johnson to investigate the Indian troubles in Tulare County. Superintendent Henley was in Washington at the time, and Beale was known to have friends among the natives of the area. As an added inducement, the governor bestowed the rank of brigadier general of the state militia upon the rancher. General Wool also empowered Beale to utilize federal troops in making either war or peace with the rebellious natives. Beale must have enjoyed this slap in the face of the powers who had previously removed him from office. He also jumped at the opportunity to steal a march on Henley.

Proceeding to Visalia, Beale learned that William Campbell had pursued the Indians into the mountains and finally convinced them to come in. Beale arranged a conference with some ten or twelve chiefs and discussed the Indians' troubles with the help of Gregorio, the English-speaking Tachi chief. He told the natives they must live on the reserves or he would make war on them. After getting them to agree to wait for the arrival of Superintendent Henley, Beale distributed presents and dismissed them. Only Gregorio and the other Tulare Lake Indians were permitted to return to their old homes.

According to a report in the Los Angeles *Star*, the Indians were inclined towards peace, but they were starving. It was a drought year, the game was scarce, and the streams were dry. All the Indians' acorn supplies had been destroyed by the whites during the recent fighting. The Indians reiterated that they had only stolen stock to feed their families.

In a report to the governor on July 12, Beale listed seven buildings and a sawmill as destroyed by the Indians, and seven horses and seventy-five to one hundred head of cattle having been stolen. He had insisted the Indians stay either in Yocole Valley or on the Kings River farm until Superintendent Henley arrived. Bill Campbell was furious at Beale's imperious actions. "Beale would take pleasure," grumbled Campbell, "in running the Department into heavy expense."

Martin B. Lewis saw the problems as stemming from the usual lack of government Indian policy and action. "But when these unfortunate people are to be counseled and instructed by Mr. Jennings, Lieut. Beale, the war party, the peace party, Mr. Campbell and others, each party advising or directing them according to their own notions of policy, or for effect, as they may choose, how are they [the Indians] to know what to do?"

After a trip to San Francisco, Beale returned to the Tejon and his ranching activities. He had solved nothing at the Four Creeks and only postponed a festering situation. Henley, of course, was furious when he learned of the governor's, and Beale's, actions. In Washington, defending himself against charges of malfeasance, Henley certainly did not need this sort of situation to make him look even worse.

Trouble again erupted in early August, this time on the Kings River. When a settler near Campbell's Indian farm accused the natives of stealing a horse, a group of local whites quickly collected a posse and visited the Choinumni camp. The whites insisted the horse must be returned, or all the Indians would be killed. The chief, Watoka, said he would find out if any of his people stole the animal and, if need be, make up the loss from his own herd of horses. The whites, however, were adamant. Either the stolen horse was returned or all in the village would die. The minute the whites left, Watoka and his people fled to the mountains.

As soon as they heard the Indians had left, a troop of twenty volunteers collected and began to follow the Indians' trail. Early on the morning of August 12, they came upon the native camp and in a surprise attack killed three men and one woman. The other Indians scattered into the surrounding terrain, while the whites proceeded to destroy everything in the camp. Appropriating seven Indian ponies, the volunteers then headed north toward Dry Creek.

Barracks at old Fort Tejon. *California Department of Beaches and Parks.*

The following morning, the volunteers were positioned around another Indian camp on Dry Creek, about twelve miles from Fort Miller. The inhabitants had been warned, however, and the whites stormed into an empty village. Again, the camp was destroyed.

The battered Indians straggled into Fort Miller, and before long, the

events of the past few days were known.

Lieutenant Livingston reported from the fort:

Mr. Campbell, in charge of the Kings River Indian farm, knew all this and did not notify me of it. The whites probably used endeavors to prevent his informing me, as he says they did. I knew nothing of it til the Indians came in for protection. It was the intention of the Whites to kill all the Indians. These are a well disposed band of Indians; raising some grain and vegetables, and not interfering with the whites, that I have ever heard of. ...Before going against these Indians, they gave Mr. Campbell notice that he must remove every Indian from the Indian farm before a specified time, or they would kill them. Mr. Campbell did not inform me of this either, but removed the Indians to this river, and visited me only this morning [August 17]. Many Indians have come into the fort, and many more will come. There are not supplies here to feed them all, and with at least a nominal Indian agent on either side, they are very poorly provided for. Many of the Indians who ran to the mountains were those that were brought to the river during former troubles in Tulare County.... The acts of the whites...seem...utterly lawless.

The commanding officers of posts, are not authorized, as I understand it, to make purchases for the support of Indians, where there is a well organized Indian department, whose business it is to attend to the welfare of Indians. The Indians must be fed and collected in suitable spots, or they must be allowed to go to the mountains where they can collect their own food. In this latter case, every theft or evil that is committed will be charged to their account, and they will be hunted and shot down. Several men on Kings River have worked many Indians, reaping a considerable pecuniary benefit thereby, and, in return, treated them worse than slaves....

The Indian agents have never fed or attended to one-tenth part of the Indians, here. Still the whites appropriate their country and drive them from it....

Lieutenant Livingston's report underscored both the deterioration of the Indian department and changing attitudes of the Tulare settlers. Although the Indians had proved their worth as servants, farm hands, herders, and general unskilled workers, they were a storm center of growing problems in the valley. Any stock that turned up strayed or missing were automatically blamed on the Indians. It was always the Indians. But even more important was the land. Whites wanted the Indian reserves for their own. They wanted

Visalia in 1863, seven years after the "war." *Jeff Edwards Collection.*

to graze their stock where the natives camped and fished and gathered seeds and acorns. It was no longer Indian country. The Yokuts had to go.

Superintendent Henley visited Campbell's farm and the Fresno River Farm at the end of August. It was a quick trip and accomplished nothing. Evidently, Henley just wanted to be able to claim that he had visited the scene of the recent troubles.

Lieutenant Loesser wrote the following report from Fort Miller:

A Yokuts warrior of more peaceful times. *Jeff Edwards Collection .*

The Indians from Kings River were on this river at the time of his visit and were not taken back to their own homes until three days ago (October 25). I did not see Col. Henley, I learned from his sub-agent, Mr. Campbell, that he said "he did not intend doing anything with the Indians till after he saw how the next election went."

At the time Col. Henley passed near this place many Indians were here, and wished very much to see him. Among them was the mountain tribe that the whites had the late disturbances with. The number was, in all, five hundred…

231

All the Indians in this country, as far as I can learn, are in a state of great destitution.

Henley could not have talked to Campbell and not known the Indians were at Fort Miller. Furthermore, he had corresponded with both Beale and the governor and knew the Indians were expecting a visit from him. Still, he did nothing. Clearly, he was not going to interfere with the whites on the Kings River.

An article in the Stockton *San Joaquin Republican* disclosed that the settlers understood the message of Henley's inaction:

> Mr. Pool informs us that the Indians recently driven to the mountains, have not returned [to the farm], nor will they be allowed by the whites to do so. The families which were left when the braves were driven off, were, as before stated, taken by the agent over to the San Joaquin, and remain there. The settlers very generally have combined, and are determined that the Indians shall not return to their old haunts.

In a report dated September 12, Agent Campbell brought Henley up to date on the situation. Patterson's stolen horse, the original cause of the trouble, had been brought in by an Indian. According to Watoka, the mare had been stolen by Paiutes, and not by a Choinumni at all. "Yet," wrote Campbell, "the people of Kings River refuse to deliver the seven animals which they took from the Indians after the fight." He reported the whites also threatened the Indians with extermination if they returned to their homes in the foothills of Kings River.

In August, Henley assigned Alonzo Ridley as a special agent to restore peace and see that the Indians had food. Ridley was also to seek a site for a new Indian reserve near the Four Creeks area. The following year, the Tule River reserve was established, and many Indians between Tejon and Visalia were sent there. Others refused to go, setting the stage for the final chapter of the San Joaquin Valley Indian troubles.

CHAPTER 13 / SOURCES

UNPUBLISHED MATERIAL

Congress, 34th Congress, 3rd Session, House Executive Documents:

> Lieutenant J. Stewart to Captain D. R. Jones, May 1, 1856.
>
> Adjutant General William C. Kibbee to General John E. Wool, May 14, 1856.
>
> Captain D. R. Jones to Adjutant General William C. Kibbee, May 14, 1856.
>
> Lieutenant LaRhett Livingston to major W. W. Mackall, August 17, 1856.
>
> Lieutenant Lucien Loesser to Major W. W. Mackall, October 28, 1856.
>
> General John E. Wool to Lt. Colonel L. Thomas, November 3, 1856.

U.S. Congress, 35th Congress, 2nd Session, Document 114:

> Topographical Memoir of the Department of the Pacific, March, 1859.

National Archives, Records of the Office of Indian Affairs, California Superintendency, Record Group 75, M234:

> Samuel Jennings to Thomas J. Henley, February 5, 1856.
>
> M. B. Lewis to Thomas J. Henley, May 16, 1856.
>
> Thomas J. Henley to Alonzo Ridley, August 13, 1856.
>
> William J. Campbell to Thomas J. Henley, September 12, 1856.
>
> Alonzo Ridley to Thomas J. Henley, September 23, 1856.

Office of the Secretary of State, California State Archives, Indian War Files, Sacramento:

> Edward F. Beale to Governor J. Neely Johnson, July 12, 1856.

NEWSPAPERS

San Francisco *Daily Alta California*, February 4, 1853; May 6, 12, 21, 26, 1856.

The *Daily Evening Bulletin*, May 5, 16, 23, June 12, 1856.

Sacramento *Daily Union*, May 31, September 15, 1856.

San Joaquin Republican, July 9, 19, 1855; September 25, 1856.

Los Angeles Star, May 10, 1856.

Visalia *Times Delta*, April 12, 1952; June 25, 1859.

The *Humboldt Times*, July 7, 1855.

PRINCIPAL PUBLISHED WORKS

Barker, Captain John (William Harlan Boyd and Glendon J. Rodgers, editors). *San Joaquin Vignettes*, Bakersfield, CA: Kern County Historical Society, 1955.

Bonsal, Stephen. *Edward Fitzgerald Beale.* New York: G. P. Putnam's Sons, 1912.

Briggs, Carl and Trudell, Clyde Francis. *Quarterdeck & Saddlehorn: The Story of Edward F. Beale, 1822-1893.* Glendale, CA: The Arthur H. Clark Company, 1983.

Cullimore, Clarence. *Old Adobes of Forgotten Fort Tejon.* Bakersfield, CA: Kern County Historical Society, 1949.

Hart, Herbert M. *Old Forts of the Southwest.* Seattle: Superior Publishing Co., 1964.

Heizer, Robert F., editor. *The Destruction of the California Indians.* Santa Barbara, CA: Peregrine Smith, Inc., 1974.

_____. *They Were Only Diggers.* Ramona, CA: Ballena Press, 1974.

History of Fresno County. San Francisco: Elliot and Company, 1882.

Latta, Frank F. *Handbook of Yokuts Indians.* Santa Cruz, CA: Bear State Books, 1978.

Mitchell, Annie R. *The Way It Was.* Fresno, CA: Valley Publishers, 1976.

Phillips, George Harwood. *Indians and Indian Agents.* Norman, OK: University of Oklahoma Press, 1997.

Small, Kathleen. *History of Tulare County.* Chicago: Clark, 1926.

Thompson, Gerald. *Edward F. Beale & The American West.* Albuquerque: University of New Mexico Press, 1983.

OTHER SOURCES

Leonard, Charles Berdan. "The Federal Indian Policy in the San Joaquin Valley, Its Application and Results," unpublished Ph.D. thesis, University of California, 1928.

Mitchell, Annie R. "Tule River Indian War of 1856," *Los Tulares,* Bulletin of the Tulare County Historical Society, March 1966.

Stewart, George R. "The War on Tule River," *Overland Monthly,* January 1884.

Chapter 14

ACHOMAWI

For years there had been trouble along Pit River. Stretching across the northeastern corner of California, the Pit branched off from the Sacramento River and for some miles formed a portion of the Lassen Trail route. The Achomawi Indians roamed the length of the river, its name originating from the pits they dug to trap game. Their enemies, the Modocs ranged to the north, while the Atsugewi, the Yana, Okwanuchu and Paiutes ringed their flanks.

A Hudson's Bay party headed by John Work passed through the area in 1832 and found the Achomawi friendly and quite shy. By 1849, however, the native disposition had undergone a change, festered undoubtedly by the increasing white emigration. Joseph Goldsborough Bruff, while camped in the area during October 1849, noted in his diary that "the Indians about here and all along Pit River, several days march below, are known to be most hostile, occasionally murdering people, and continually shooting and stealing the animals."

A few days later, Bruff made note of several messages posted along the trail warning of recent Indian attacks. On October 6, he noted finding the grave of a man killed the previous day. Sticking in the mound of the grave was an arrow bearing the cryptic message, "This is the fatal arrow." Other bodies were discovered and Bruff noted the dead animals and destroyed wagons along the trail.

Late in June 1850, six emigrants from Ohio were killed along the west bank of the pit in a night attack by the Achomawi. All were men, traveling without families. The party had left the main wagon train and pushed on ahead because they were low on provisions. On the night of the 27th, the men stayed up late talking and, finding all quiet, decided to bed down without a guard. About midnight, a shower of arrows fell on the camp, and Sam Kaufman was hit in the forehead and killed instantly. Three others were struck also, and the terrified men huddled together for the rest of the night, trying to ease the pain of the wounded.

At dawn, the men discovered their horses and mules had all been killed or wounded by arrows. They stayed in camp, waiting for their wagon train to come along, but about eight o'clock that morning, a group of Indians suddenly appeared. By signs and gestures the natives seemed to be trying to get them to leave, but the whites insisted on waiting for their train. A short time later, a larger group of Indians surrounded them. In a few moments the helpless whites were stripped of their clothes and slaughtered on the trail. Only George Stuck survived the attack by jumping into the river and swimming to the other side, where he hid in some bushes. When a wagon train arrived later, he was rescued and taken to the settlements.

In a diary note of June 30, Bruff made a brief reference to the tragedy and noted that many emigrants had run out of supplies on the trail. "They were reduced to starvation, and the Pit River Indians had killed several of the party, and stolen what animals the hardships of the travel had spared. These who arrived here are from Ohio...."

From 1850 forward, miners swarmed deeper and deeper into the northern California country. At French Gulch, the first quartz mine was worked in Shasta County at a time when much of the country bordering the juncture of the Sacramento and Pit rivers was becoming overcrowded. The miners' horses and the muddying and diverting of the streams of the area scared off game and destroyed the Indian fisheries. Writing home from French Gulch in July of 1851, young Edward Henry commented on the crowds of miners and the resulting Indian troubles:

The beautiful and primitive Pit River Valley was a scene of massacre, mayhem and murder in the 1850s. *Author's collection.*

...There is thousands here that is not making their board hardly and some that is doing very well...making from two to eight dollars a day clear of expenses....

The Indians are very troublesome. They are stealing and killing men every day. On the third of July there was a company of men, fifteen in number, went out to give them a chase. They hunted in the mountains three days so last Sunday they got over on Pit River and they came across three squaws and one papoose. They took them along a short distance. The Indians saw them and they gave the boys a brush. They commenced howling like a passel of Kiowas and then they gave a war whoop and on they went. They surrounded them. They had a pretty good captain who understood the Indians and got his men on a little hill so that the Indians could not get above them.... There they stood and fought them about one hour. ...There was but two of the boys wounded, one in the hip and one in the shoulder. ...on Monday last the citizens of Shasta made up fifteen hundred dollars for volunteers to go out and fight the Diggers. On Tuesday they made up forty two men...when the men are out burning their rancherias, they [the Indians] are here stealing mules and shooting men....

Both the parties referred to by young Henry were commanded by Captain B. F. Harvey, who claimed to have killed some sixty natives in his first attack and about fifty a week later, in a second foray. A letter from Shasta dated July 15 noted that the town was nightly harassed by the Indians who were attempting to rescue their captured women and children.

In February 1852, the Sacramento *Union* reported a well-armed, forty-two-man expedition being out for two weeks along the Pit River. About thirty male Indians were reported killed, twenty-two villages were destroyed and seventeen prisoners were brought in. Several whites had been reported killed in the area, as well as numerous attacks on wagon trains. In June, another expedition reported killing some "ten or fifteen Indians" who had stolen some stock and fled to the Pit River.

The next few years saw a steady increase in Indian troubles in the Shasta area, most of them culminating in raids against the Achomawi in the Pit River Valley. In November of 1854, the Sacramento *Daily Union* commented on the deteriorating Indian-white relations in the north:

Unless the Pit and McCloud River Indians are attended to before spring, much valuable stock will inevitably be lost by our citizens, and perhaps the lives of many whites. We again call upon our Superintendent of Indian Affairs to see to this. It can as well be done now as any other time. Make a trip amongst these tribes. Indian agents are supposed to be mountaineers—men willing to forgo the luxuries of the cities for a short time, and live in the mountains. Our subagent possess all these qualifications, and is ever willing and ready, but we repeat, is unauthorized and without means. They might as well send a man to kill grizzly bears with a pop-gun.

■ "Black Mouth," a chief of the McCloud River Wintu. Joaquin Miller lived with the Wintu in the 1850s. *Author's collection.*

The local Indian subagent was ready to try to make peace with the Achomawi, but apparently could get no cooperation from the Indian department. Colonel Henley, other than publishing some newspaper articles on the subject, did nothing.

With the great influx of miners into the northern country, roads became increasingly important for supplies and communication. In 1851 Colonel James L. Freaner was given permission by the legislature to build a road from Yreka to the Sacramento Valley via the Pit River. With a party of four, Freaner set out to establish his route and soon vanished into the wilderness. He was never heard from again. It was quickly assumed he had been killed by Indians, and the Shasta *Courier* seemingly confirmed his fate in August of 1852:

> Late from Yreka—Colonel Freaner—Dr. Thompson, who left Yreka on Monday last, has informed us that Col. Freaner has not yet been heard from. His favorite mule had been taken from an Indian and brought in. An Indian squaw of the Shasta tribe, who was taken captive some months ago by the Pit River Indians, has recently made her escape, and states that the Pit River Indians shortly before her escape, murdered a party of 5 well armed and well mounted white men. It is supposed that these men were Col. Freaner and party.

It was 1855 before another effort was made toward establishing a road. That year a Yreka saloon owner named Samuel Lockhart piloted a wagon train from Yreka through the Pit River Valley and down to Red Bluff, the head of navigation on the Sacramento River. It was an important accomplishment. The Indians must have known that it meant more whites coming through their country and perhaps even settling in the Pit River and Fall River valleys.

Lockhart knew well the importance of his road. Little is known of his background other than his being recalled by acquaintances as a Southern gentleman, prejudiced, but educated and kind. He must have had some good qualities since he formed a partnership with the highly respected Judge

Rosborough, the Yreka attorney and Indian agent. In the spring of 1856, the two men established a ferry over the Fall River at a place just before it entered the Pit and another across the latter river a short distance away. Traffic along the road picked up quickly, and the Indians anxiously watched the lines of wagons, riders, and pack trains that heralded the continuing invasion of their land.

In May, a representative of the California Stage Company surveyed the road with the intention of establishing a stage line between Red Bluff and Yreka. That spring too, Z. H. Rogers and his partner, Adam Boles, moved sawmill machinery into the Fall River Valley by ox team. They set up camp about midway between the two ferries. Lockhart's twin brother, Harry, was also working with him at the upper ferry. Scattered ranches and farms were beginning to appear in the surrounding country now as the settlers crowded ever closer to the two valleys.

By August 1856, a regular line of stagecoaches was running between Yreka and Shasta. Toward the end of the month, Jared Robbins was driving

his empty coach on the down trip towards Shasta. After leaving the Pit River station, located at one of the ferries, Robbins trotted his team along a chaparral-lined stretch of road when suddenly a shower of arrows made a pincushion of the coach, wounding both him and several of his horses. Whipping his team into a run, Robbins had traveled a short distance when the coach broke down and he was compelled to stop in the road. In a matter of minutes, the Indians would be on him, and Robbins worked frantically to cut the team loose from the coach.

"During the time he was unhooking the team," recorded the Shasta *Courier*, "no less than eighteen arrows were shot at him. He managed, after being shot, to ride one of the horses to Jack Hill's ranch. An express was immediately sent from there to this town—a distance of over forty miles—for a physician, who left immediately."

■ Jared "Curly Jerry" Robbins (right), and his twin brother, Dan. Both were stagecoach drivers. *Author's collection.*

Robbins was badly hurt, but recovered. The coach was completely destroyed by the Indians, who turned out to be Atsugewi and not Achomawi, as was first assumed. Although the California Stage Company abandoned

A Concord stagecoach in Northern California in the 1850s. *Trinity County Historical Society.*

its services after this experience, regular travel along the road continued.

At Fort Jones, Captain Judah had once again assumed command. When news of the attack arrived, Judah took a patrol of about thirty men and headed for the scene of trouble. At the ferry, the officer found Lockhart to be "perfectly conversant with the state of Indian affairs in that vicinity." In his report, the captain noted that Lockhart could give no reason for the Indians' "recently developed hostile feelings towards the whites." After some local friendly Indians had identified the Atsugewi as the guilty parties, Judah proceeded to seek them out.

Scouting the territory around Hat Creek for several days, Judah had no luck locating the hostiles. He managed to secure a local Indian chief as a guide, however, and surprised an encampment of Atsugewi on September 6. A chief and five Indians were killed, but Captain Judah declined to chase the natives into the rugged surrounding country. Instead, the patrol returned and again set up camp near Lockhart's ferry.

Captain Judah felt his expedition has been a success, and writing his official report from Fort Jones on September 9, the officer penned that "I trust that their pursuit by troops through a country where they had never been seen before in connection with what punishment I was enabled to inflict upon them may, through fear of a second visit, influence them to relinquish their attempts at plunder upon those who travel upon the road." The officer also reported that two missing teamsters were presumed to be dead.

Other whites moved into the valley that summer of 1856. F. S. Whitney and N. D. Fowler worked for Lockhart raising hay and herding stock. A young

A typical river ferry of the period. *Author's collection.*

240

■ Established in October 1852, Fort Jones was a collection of several log buildings in Scott's Valley, housing a thirty-man infantry company. *Author's collection.*

man named Daniel Bryant also worked for the Lockharts, as did a man noted only as being a German named John who tended the ferry.

To the northwest, between Yreka and the Pit River country, a young man named Cincinatus Miller lived a precarious existence. A teenager at the time, young Miller performed odd jobs in the shanty mining towns, sometimes working in the mines. He lived with the Indians for a time and was camping with a group of Shastas during the winter of 1856-57 when several of his Indian friends left for a visit to the east. In about a month, they returned, saying they had been visiting in the Pit River Valley.

"After the usual Indian silence," Miller wrote later, "they told a tale which literally froze my blood. It made me ill. The Indians had got into a difficulty with the white men of Pit River Valley about their women, and killed all but two of the settlers. These two they said had escaped to the woods, and were trying to get back through the snow to Yreka...."

Miller's story was garbled, but was essentially true. Lockhart's men had treated the Indians badly the previous summer and had reaped the whirlwind. N. D. Fowler later told Miller and others how the trouble had originated. Two Shasta Indians had taken up residence in the Pit River country and married Achomawi girls. Reportedly these two Shastas were friendly toward the whites and often gave them game and helped in other ways. But it was lonely in the valley and the whites looked longingly at the Indian girls.

One day, as one of the Shastas was watching the whites mowing hay, he was shot and killed from behind. The wife of the murdered Indian was then seized and carried off to the white men's camp. In the evening, the other Shasta returned and asked where his friend and wife were. He was led into the woods and murdered also, and his wife dragged off by the brutal ranch hands.

The Shasta *Republican* noted other outrages attributed to the whites at the time, including the shooting of an Indian for stealing a box of matches. "Mr. Lockhart," noted the newspaper, "stated, with apparent gusto, his poisoning achievements during last summer while living in Pit River Valley. According to his own story, a number of the Indians of that section of the country were treacherously poisoned by him. Since hearing of the above conduct we have lost our wonder at the untimely fate of the settlers of Pit River Valley...."

Piecing together what happened, it appears that despite their brutal behavior, the whites were unaware of any danger, and some of them decided to winter in the valley. Whitney and Fowler went to Yreka for the Christmas holidays. Sam Lockhart and several others headed south for Red Bluff, where they would obtain supplies. They left a peaceful and snow-covered valley.

Whitney and Fowler left Yreka about the 25th of January 1857 and made their way through deep snows to Lockhart's place. Expecting a hot meal and warm welcome from their friends, the two found desolation and ruin instead. The ferries had been destroyed and the houses burned down. Other property had been destroyed also, and all stock had either been killed or driven off.

"The sad, terrible fact," wrote Judge Rosborough to the Shasta *Republican*, "that the inhabitants had all been butchered by the Indians burst fully upon them. Being well armed they kept the Indians at bay...." Continued Rosborough:

■ Henry M. Judah was technically a good officer, but his drinking made problems for himself and everyone else. *National Archives.*

Seeing Indians running in different directions, (as they supposed to procure reinforcements to attack them) they turned back and keeping the Indians at a distance by presenting their guns at them, they arrived at the nearest ferry, where they had left the raft, but finding it was gone they turned down the river to try and wade it at a wide, shoaly place. By this time the number of Indians had increased to fifteen. Being weak already from hunger and hard walking on snow shoes, they did not think they could wade the deep, swift stream without drowning. So they kept down the river to the forks at the great falls. Here they found an old Indian and asked him to bring them across the river in an old canoe. He consented with an alacrity that made them suspect that he would turn them overboard with the canoe (as it is reported they did to Freaner and his party). They got into the canoe, and as the old Indian got in, Whitney took the paddle from him, at the same time presented his revolver at his breast and told him to sit still, and while in this position Fowler paddled the canoe across the stream…."

The two men camped that evening near the ashes of another settler's cabin on the river bank. The Indians watched them closely, but after dark they stirred up their fire, then managed to slip down to the water. Traveling all night, they escaped from the valley and headed north for Yreka. The heavy snows made for extremely difficult travel and when they ran out of provisions, the fleeing men were forced to eat their pet dog.

When young Cincinatus Miller heard of the Lockhart massacre, he took two Indian friends and made the journey over to Fall River Valley. It was

the middle of March by now and still a difficult trip. Entering the valley, Miller saw many Indians in the distance and proceeded cautiously down to the first ferry site, or so he later claimed. The three companions then left and headed north for the settlement at Soda Springs.

As Miller left the valley, a party of eighteen men headed by Sam Lockhart arrived in search of survivors. Lockhart was very concerned about his twin brother Harry, and since no bodies had been found, he hoped some of the whites might have escaped. A look around quickly convinced them that the whites were probably all dead. Being short on provisions, the men headed north for Yreka to raise a volunteer company to settle with the Indians. Lockhart, meanwhile, left behind a quantity of flour well seasoned with strychnine.

■ Cincinatus Hiner Miller as a young man. *California State Library.*

On the road, Lockhart and his party came upon Miller plodding along on his mule. When Miller told them about the massacre, he was told that they had already been there and that he must accompany them to Yreka. Upon arrival in town, the boy was questioned by Lockhart and the others who suspected that he had somehow been involved in the massacre. Only the interference of Judge Rosborough saved the young man from a swearing and drunken Sam Lockhart.

"No doubt the judge, who is really, I think, a good man at heart, did save my life," recalled Miller some years later. "But somehow, I cannot feel any great gratitude toward him for that, under the circumstances."

In noting the return of Lockhart's expedition, the Shasta *Republican* of March 14 noted that:

> ...[T]he company captured a boy, about eighteen years of age, and information was derived from him which led Mr. Lockhart to hope that his brother was yet alive. The boy stated that all had been killed except him, and that he was some distance up the river, in the keeping of a tribe of Indians....

Alexander M. Rosborough was a highly respected lawyer, judge, businessman, and friend to the Indians. *Siskiyou County Museum.*

The implication from the newspaper account is that Miller lied to Lockhart in an effort to gain time and to calm the man down. Evidently his stalling worked and the boy was allowed to sleep.

After spending the night under guard, Miller was told by Lockhart that he must join the expedition that was being organized to return to the valley. His association with the Indians being generally known now, Miller realized he had no choice in the matter. Two men escorted him to where the volunteers were camped.

"This was the rudest set of men I ever saw gathered together for any purpose whatever," Miller recalled later. "There were perhaps a dozen good men, as good as there were in the land; but the rank and file were made up of thieves, bar-room loafers, gutter snipes, and men of desperate character and fortunes. They growled and grumbled and fought half the time."

Lockhart and Judge Rosborough rode over to Fort Jones and requested an immediate military campaign into the Pit River country. When Captain Judah demurred because of the weather and deep snow, Lockhart reportedly flew into a rage, and Rosborough had difficulty in preventing his shooting the officer.

Under the command of one Gideon Whitney, the Yreka volunteers entered the Pit River area on the first of April, while Lockhart pushed on to Red Bluff to raise another company. In his absence, the men again searched the area in hopes of finding a survivor, or at least some of the bodies of the vanished men. The Shasta *Republican* reported the first news of the expedition when four of the party came out for supplies:

They state that on Wednesday, the 1st. inst., the body of one of the settlers massacred by the Indians had been found. The body was identified as that of a German, who had been in the employ of Mr. Lockhart. It seems that his throat had been cut, and after he had been entirely stripped of his clothing, his body had been thrown in the river, with a log chain fastened to his legs. The body had apparently risen to the surface only a few days before it was found.

In a rancheria a human skull was found, supposed to be that of an old man who had gone to the valley in company with Mr. Rogers.

…When the party from Yreka first arrived in the valley, they saw about four hundred Indians. Since that time the Indians have scattered, and have been occasionally seen in small parties. On one night, two Indian scouts were seen near camp by the guards, and were shot. One was killed, and the other escaped with severe wounds. There is but one pass out of the valley which is free from snow, and that is closely guarded. As the Indians are much disinclined to travel upon the snow, the whites expect to hem them in in such a manner as to be enabled to make an effective assault upon them. Those who came out for provisions expect that the attack will have been made before they return.

Just when the first contact was made is unclear, but early in April, there was a brief skirmish in which neither side apparently suffered any casualties. Locating the Indian camp a short time later, the whites planned an attack which was briefly described in a journal kept by young Miller:

The Indians were about one hundred and fifty strong. Our party was eleven in number. Whitney attacked the enemy at break of day with five persons, including himself, while I took the remainder of our party and lay in ambush and met the enemy as they retreated. Fifteen of the Indians were slain and eighteen taken prisoners, all of which were turned free as they were squaws and children, except one warrior which was hung.

On April 13, Miller penned, "Took 5 squaws and one buck. Hung the buck and freed the squaws…" Miller offers no other detail on these two hangings, but many years later while riding along Pit River with a friend, he was moved to briefly reminisce:

It was near here that the white men hung the Indian chief. He tried to convince them that he was not a party to the massacre, but it was no use. They placed the rope around his neck, and over the limb of a tree, and just before he was pulled up from the ground he motioned to his daughter to approach. She was tall, well muscled, her bosoms curved, her long, black hair hanging over her shoulders. The Indian chief said not a word, his form erect, but with his arm outstretched he pointed towards the north. The Indian maiden turned and without a sigh or tear walked away, silently, to the north.

Lockhart had meanwhile grown impatient in Red Bluff and told his new group of straggling volunteers to follow him to Pit River where they would join forces. Arriving in the valley before his men, Lockhart apparently lost his head and began shooting at the first Indians he encountered. He quickly found himself besieged on a hilltop, behind a hastily constructed rock fort. He reportedly held out for several days before his Red Bluff volunteers arrived and rescued him. Lockhart and his men then joined Whitney's forces and made final plans for an assault on the Indians.

Lockhart and Whitney disagreed as to who should command the combined forces, and when Whitney resigned, a man named John Langley assumed command—probably as a compromise candidate. By about April 23, the Achomawi had been located, and a final fight took place which Miller briefly chronicled in his diary:

> Thirty-nine Indians were left dead on the field. None of the whites were hurt. A number of prisoners, all of which were turned free except the children, sixteen of which were taken into the settlements by the volunteers.

The Sacramento *Union* noted the return of the Indian fighters in its issue of May 20, 1857:

> The Pit River volunteers have returned to Yreka, carrying with them a number of children who were presented to different families in that place. The *Union* says that some of them are bright little specimens and no doubt will be of much benefit to those who raise and care for them.

Besides the prisoners taken, the volunteers reported killing fifty-nine Indians and wounding many more. Miller commented sadly that he "was glad when we broke camp to return. We had found the valley without a white man; we left it with scarcely an Indian."

With the Indians hiding in the mountains, Lockhart reestablished his ferry business, but this time he built at a site where only one ferry would be necessary. Early in May, the road was again open and freight wagons were making the trip between Red Bluff and Yreka. By late May, Captain Judah and a detachment of troops were in the valley to insure the safety of the settlers.

Lockhart brought in more stock and constructed several public buildings. He seems to have abandoned his Yreka business entirely and concentrated on what looked to be a lucrative enterprise. He also reportedly resumed his vendetta against the Indians, training an Indian boy to report to him any Achomawi thought to be involved in his brother's death. Several years later he told Judge Rosborough that he had killed all but one of Harry Lockhart's murderers. Later, Sam Lockhart drifted north to the Owyhee area of Idaho, where he was killed in a gunfight during a mining dispute in 1868.

Young Miller was glad to get away from the brawling volunteers. He later claimed one of them tried to ambush him as he rode away. There was no love for the ragtag boy who admittedly had lived with the Indians and was still suspected of somehow being involved in the massacre. When he returned to Yreka many years later, it was as Joaquin Miller, the far famed "Poet of the Sierras" and the toast of two continents. And he did what few pioneers of his day would do when he acknowledged the paternity of a young Indian girl and took her home to be raised by him in civilization.

When Captain Judah left Fort Jones in mid-May and moved south to patrol the Red Bluffs road, he headed two companies of the 4th Infantry, mounted on mules. Mounted infantry is awkward enough, but poor equipment and Judah's frequent imbibing from his high-proof canteen made the trip nearly intolerable. Noted Lieutenant Crook:

> It was as good as a circus to see us when we left Fort Jones. Both companies were mounted on mules, with improvised rigging, some with ropes, and others with equally, if not worse makeshifts to fasten the saddles on the mules…. Many of our men were drunk, including our commander. Many of the mules were wild, and had not been accustomed to being ridden…. The air was full of soldiers after the command was given to mount, and for the next two days stragglers were still overtaking the command.

Once in the valley, scouts quickly located an Indian village and Judah prepared for an attack. With Crook insisting that the village was deserted, Judah led the troops in a wild charge that must have resembled something out of a Mack Sennett comedy. Crook recalled that as he looked back over the field he had crossed he could "see the men 'hors-de-combat,' riderless mules running in all directions, men coming, limping, some with their guns, but others carrying their saddles…."

■ The placid Pit River hid many secrets of the Indian "wars" of the 1850s. *Troy Tuggle.*

Captain Judah had seen enough. The village had indeed been empty as Crook had insisted, and the commander decided there were not enough Indians around to worry about. Besides, he was anxious to return to his new bride back at the post. Leaving Crook in charge of sixteen men of D Company, Judah again headed north. His junior officer was probably relieved to see him go.

Left to his own resources, Crook continually sent out both day and night patrols seeking to locate the hostiles. He had a number of minor skirmishes, but it was late in June before he had his major confrontation.

An article in the Siskiyou *Chronicle* blamed the Indians for becoming bolder and harassing the stock that belonged to Lockhart and his men:

> A very large number of cattle has been driven into the valley where there is the best pasture in the country. The Indians had succeeded in driving off eighty head into the country east of the valley. Lieut. Crook started in pursuit as soon as the fact was ascertained. Being in advance with five or six of his men he came suddenly upon the Indian camp, where they had killed some of the cattle and were feasting. He opened fire on them at close quarters, and killed five of them before they got out of reach. The Indians returned the fire with arrows, and Lieut. Crook received a wound in the thigh, the flint point penetrating about five inches and remaining in the wound.

Although the arrow was reportedly poisoned, Crook's wound was more painful than serious. After sending a report to Fort Jones, he went into camp along the river. Captain Judah dispatched 1st Lieutenant Hiram Dryer and twenty-five men to proceed at once to Crook's aid. An assistant surgeon accompanied the detachment which reached Crook's camp on June 16.

Being senior officer now in the valley, Dryer immediately began sending out scouting parties in search of Indians. He occasionally discovered sign, but was unable to track them in the rugged country. On June 22, Dryer moved the army camp since it was located close to the ferry and "the number of whiskey shops was becoming too numerous...."

On the 24th, Dryer sent the surgeon and fourteen men back to Fort Jones when supplies began running low. Taking twenty-six men, he then left on a three-day scouting expedition down the west bank of the river, where he had been informed the Indians were gathering in a large valley. After prowling about the hills and valleys all day, the soldiers finally discovered fresh tracks made by three Indians.

"We trailed them for some time before we overtook them," wrote Dryer in his report. "The man we killed. The woman and child were not molested. I then returned...to my camp that night."

When twenty head of cattle were reported stolen on the 26th, Dryer sent Lieutenant Crook and twelve men out to locate the stock and chastise the thieves. Two days later, Crook returned after having seen "much Sign," but no Indians or stock. When Lieutenant Dryer was ordered back to the fort, he departed on June 29, leaving Crook again in command.

About this time a detachment of the First Dragoons under Captain John Gardiner arrived in the area. The dragoons were from Fort Reading and were in the valley for the purpose of establishing an army post. The site was to be on the Fall River, a short distance upstream from where it joins the Pit River at Lockhart's ferry. It had been decided that Fort Reading would be abandoned and the new post would take its place. Soon plans were being sketched for what Gardiner proposed to call "Fort Crook" in honor of the recently wounded officer.

In August, the Shasta *Republican* reported Fort Crook was "rapidly improving in the way of buildings. The houses are built of logs and before winter arrives these will be comfortable quarters for the troops and animals…."

There was continuing trouble with the Indians, however, despite the presence of the troops. In early July, the Yreka *Union* published the following notice concerning developments in the Pit River Valley:

> Mr. Jenner came up in company with four loaded teams and a peddler's wagon, he reports the road in good condition, except one difficult hill. Near the junction of Fall River with Pit River, Mr. J. saw the body of a white man hanging to a tree; the body was considerably mutilated and the stench was so offensive he could not go near it. The ferry boat at Lockhart's is completed, and there is no difficulty in crossing the river. Quite a village is growing up at the crossing; there are two 'rum mills' and a considerable number of tents and canvas houses. The soldiers stationed at Pit River have frequent skirmishes with the Indians; they go out in small bodies of four or five men; if a larger body goes out it is very difficult for them to get upon the Indians without being discovered. Lt. Crook, who was wounded in the thigh some time ago, with an arrow, is much better and is able to walk about. The head of the arrow was in his thigh some six days.

Crook's first report to Judah, since resuming command at Fort Jones, was dated July 8, 1857:

> I have just returned from 10 days scout. I had a most satisfactory engagement with the lake Indians on the 2nd inst.—killing some 18 dead and

wounding as many more (most of the latter mortally). Capt.. Gardiner is here building quarters on the site selected by you—he has orders from head-quarters to take command of my detachment and to send it back to Fort Jones when he can dispense with its services, so he gave me orders to re-main until further orders. The Indians are getting very bad, they killed old Dikeman, a couple days since.

Crook had been anxious to get back in the field, and the moment Dryer left, he galloped out of camp in pursuit of the hostiles. Following up the Indian sign he had seen, Crook pursued the natives and stolen stock through incredibly rough, rock, and lava country. "No one but an Indian could have driven those cattle through this country," he was to write later. Through good scouting and careful surveillance, he spotted smoke from an Indian camp and worked his way up close. Crook sent two groups of his men be-hind the camp, and the re-maining soldiers waited for the Achomawi to be chased into their fire. Crook re-called in his memoirs:

■ This 1870s photograph shows a Pit River Indian family struggling to survive in a white man's world. *California Historical Society.*

> We met the Indians piling out of the rancheria, running from the attack of the other two parties. They were all yelling, women and children and all. Bucks were imitating wild beast 'war whoops,' and a worse pandemonium I never saw before or since. We met them face to face, so close that we could see the whites of each other's eyes. The yelling and screeching and all taken together made my hair fairly stand on end.

> We killed a great many and after the main fight was over, we hunted some reserved ground, that we knew had Indians hidden.... One or two faced us, and made a manly fight, while others would attempt to run. There was but one squaw killed.

Having found quantities of beef in the Indian camp, Crook was satis-fied he had attacked the guilty parties. After a brief rest back

250

A winter scene at Fort Crook in 1857. *Oregon Historical Society.*

at the base camp, the soldiers again took the field and trapped a large number of Indians in a secluded valley. Crook personally killed several Indians, but the fighting was so scattered it was difficult to tell just how many natives had been hit.

Captain Judah, meanwhile, was furious that the dragoon captain had assumed command of Crook's troops. He immediately ordered Crook to return to Fort Jones and sent a steaming communique to Gardiner, who promptly preferred charges. Crook stayed in the valley however, and eventually Judah cooled off. During the squabbling, Crook kept after the Indians and his relentless pursuit was noted in the Sacramento *Union* of September 1, 1857:

> Already he has induced a number to come in and sue for peace and it is expected that what remains of the tribe will surrender. He has pursued them into their rugged mountain fastnesses, through brakes and tules, and routed them with great loss, on the part, of the Indians: and the severe lesson—the first that they have ever received—has taught them that a peace is worth keeping. It is believed that Lt. Crook's small command has killed as many Indians in the present campaign, as were killed…on Rogue River in 1856, and he merits a like honorable recognition.

With Fort Crook garrisoned by a company of dragoons and the Indians battered and bruised from the constant prodding of the past few months, the Pit River Valley was considered secure, and Crook was recalled to Fort Jones. "As we marched through Yreka," wrote the future famous general, "we were treated as heroes."

In the mountains, the Achomawi looked about and wondered just what to do. It was September and the leaves were turning. They had had little time to prepare for winter, and no food had been stored. The game had been scared off in the mountains, and whites occupied the valleys. Some would starve that winter. Others went down and camped by Fort Crook for protection against Lockhart and other whites who would kill them if they could.

Soon the winter snows would blanket the land, and food would be impossible to find, and the little children would be crying. Life was hard.

CHAPTER 14 / SOURCES

Ernest Neasham's work on the Fall River Valley is a good starting place for any study of that region. The writings of Joaquin Miller have been used with care since he is often unreliable as an historian. Nevertheless, his published contemporary diary and at least one contemporary newspaper account are enough evidence to place him on the scene. Also, his service record with Lockhart's volunteers is indicated in the California State Archives. His *Unwritten History* is a mixture of fact and fancy, yet if used carefully, there are episodes that can be verified from other sources.

Although spelled "Pitt" River in most of the early accounts, I have utilized the original and modern spelling with one "T."

UNPUBLISHED MATERIAL

National Archives, Records of U.S. Army Continental Commands, Department of the Pacific, Record Group 393:

Captain Henry M. Judah to Major W. W. Mackall, September 9, 1856; June 14, July 5, 11, 16, 1857.

Captain Henry M. Judah to Lt. Hiram Dryer, June 13, 1857.

Captain Henry M. Judah to Lt. George- Crook, July 11, 1857.

Captain Henry M. Judah to Captain J. W. Gardiner, July 11, 1857.

Lt. Hiram Dryer to Captain Henry M. Judah, June 22,, July 6, 1857.

Lt. George Crook to Captain Henry M. Judah, July 8, 1857.

Henry, Edward, letter to family, in manuscript collection of California section, California State Library, Sacramento.

NEWSPAPERS

San Francisco *Daily Alta California*, July 23, 1851; February 17, April 16, May 27, July 6, 1857.

San Francisco *Bulletin*, September 1, 1856.

Shasta *Courier*, August 7, 1852.

The *Sandusky* (Ohio) *Clarion*, September 23, 1850.

Stockton *Daily Argus*, March 10, August 6, 1857.

Sacramento *Daily Union*, February 17, June 26, August 10, 1852; March 29, 1853; November 10, 1854; August 3, 1857.

Weekly Butte Record, February 21, March 7, June 27, July 11, 1857.

Shasta *Republican* December 13, March 14, 1856.

Sacramento *State Journal*, September 20, 1856.

Humboldt Times, September 20, 1856; March 7, 1857.

PRIMARY PUBLISHED WORKS

Barry, W. J. *Up and Down or Fifty Years Colonial Experiences in Australia, California, New Zealand, India, China and the South Pacific.* London: Sampson Low, Marston, Searle & Rivington, 1879.

Boggs, Mae Helene. *My Playhouse Was a Concord Coach.* Oakland: Howell-North Press, 1942.

Giles, Rosena A. *Shasta County, California.* Oakland: Biobooks, 1949.

Hart, Herbert M. *Pioneer Forts of the West.* Seattle: Superior Publishing Company, 1967.

Kroeber, A. L. *Handbook of the Indians of California.* New York: Dover Publications, Inc., 1976.

Miller, Joaquin. *Unwritten History: Life Amongst the Modocs.* Eugene, OR.: Orion Press, 1972.

Neasham, Ernest R. *Fall River Valley: An Examination of Historical Sources.* Sacramento: The Citadel Press, Inc., 1957.

Powers, Stephen. *Tribes of California.* Berkeley: University of California Press, 1976.

Read, Georgia Willis, and Gaines, Ruth. *Gold Rush: the Journals, Drawings & other Papers of J. Goldsborough Bruff.* New York: Columbia University Press, 1949.

Richards, John S., editor. *Joaquin Miller: His California Diary Beginning in 1855 and Ending in 1857.* Seattle: The Dogwood Press, 1936.

Schmitt, Martin F., editor. *General George Crook: His Autobiography.* Norman, OK: University of Oklahoma Press, 1947.

Wagner, Har. *Joaquin Miller.* San Francisco: Har Wagner Publishing Co., 1929.

Wells, Harry. *History of Siskiyou County, California.* Oakland: D. J. Stewart & Co., 1881.

OTHER SOURCES

Kardell, Margaret Guilford. "Joaquin Miller: Fact and Fiction," *The Californians*, November/December 1991.

Chapter 15

NOME CULT

Located some ninety miles north of San Francisco, Mendocino County began attracting settlers in the early 1850s. The area was untamed and beautiful, a country of tree-shrouded hills and valleys, and was quickly seen as being particularly adapted to stock-raising and farming. The coastal areas were settled first, then gradually the interior lands were explored and claimed.

Pierce and Frank Asbill were of English lineage and had arrived early in California with their parents. Farmers and hunters, the brothers settled on the northern California coast, at Bodega Bay. Together with a man named Jim Neafus, Pierce and Frank had originally left their Missouri home for Mendocino County because of a mix-up over horses. The three were young men, tough and far from home.

Early in May 1854, the Asbill party met up with Samuel Kelsey and two others who were locating a wagon road from Trinity County, south to San Francisco. The two groups met at the ranch of George Armstrong and agreed to join forces while traveling north. Kelsey and his men had marked their trail and were returning to their mines in Trinity County.

The two groups followed the eastern fork of the Russian River to Potter Valley, then crossed various ridges and mountains to the South Bel River. Passing over the main ridge between the south and middle Eel Rivers, the men came to a hollow in the mountains where they decided to camp. Pierce Asbill named the place Eden Valley, after a name he recalled from the Bible. The Asbills, like most of the party, were illiterate.

The following day, the men camped on the middle Eel River. While out looking for strayed horses, Frank topped a rise and suddenly saw in the distance a great, round valley. The date was May 15, 1854, and Asbill was soon leading his companions down into the vast, tree and brush-spotted hollow.

Frank Asbill named his discovery Round Valley. It was a beautiful place that spring—20,000 acres of green and wild fields dotted with oak groves with the forested hills and distant, snow-capped peaks making a splendid backdrop for the scene.

The Yuki were the original inhabitants of this great, natural basin and called themselves Ukumnom, meaning "in the valley." The Wailaki were their closest neighbors to the north, while other Yukian groups were to the west. Over the mountains to the east were various Wintun groups, principally the Nomlaki. South were the Pomo, whose land stretched down to the shores of Clear Lake.

Living in much the same manner as most California Indians, the Yuki built their shelters along the fringes of the valley. Seed grasses, clover, and berries were abundant, while wild game and acorns made the place a primeval paradise.

Riding northwest across the valley floor, the explorers ran into a large gathering of Yukis along a stream where the present town of Covelo is located. The whites were heavily armed with rifles and navy-model Colt revolvers. The Indians had no concept of the invaders' firepower and were armed only with their bows and arrows. Suddenly the two groups were face to face.

What started the trouble is not clear, but Sam Kelsey needed no excuse to shoot an Indian following the events at Clear Lake. In a moment, the air was full of arrows and great clouds of gun smoke.

No match for the white man's weapons, the Indians fled into the surrounding hills, leaving a reported thirty-two bodies along the stream bed.

After reloading and rounding up their scattered animals, the white men moved across the valley and pushed on to the north. They next camped some twelve miles away at a place they named Summit Valley. Several days later, the party broke up, the Kelsey group going on to their mines and the Asbills setting up camp to trap for the winter.

In the spring of 1855, Pierce Asbill struck out for the Sacramento Valley, looking for a trading post. He was able to sell his winter's catch of pelts at Kingsley's place at the Red Bluffs, where he met a Mexican with horses to trade. The two men made a unique agreement. For each Indian girl furnished, the Mexican would trade three horses, the exchange to be made the following year at a specified place. After shaking hands with the vaquero, Asbill headed for Bodega Bay and a visit with his parents. Later he rode north to rejoin his brother and Neafus at Hetten Chow.

The three young men returned to Round Valley that summer of 1855. They were a nervy trio and feared nothing. They were heavily armed, but estimates of the Indian population at that time in the valley and its immediate vicinity ran to some twelve thousand.

The men set up camp and began hunting, keeping an eye out for Yukis. They managed to capture two Indian boys and "gentled" them to help out around camp and taught them to use firearms. With the aid of their helpers, an Indian girl was coaxed into their clutches—mainly through the medium of some beans and syrup. The hunters soon had a group of thirty-five girls ready for the journey to the "Land of beans and syrup."

The Asbills met the Mexican vaquero at the appointed rendezvous, the exchange was made, and they rode off with their new horse herd toward Potter Valley.

Superintendent Henley had become increasingly concerned with the wholesale kidnapping of Indians in California. In 1852, Beale had personally rescued a group of Indians who had been kidnapped from Clear Lake and sold to a rancher. The *Alta* commented in 1854 that "abducting Indian children has become quite a common practice. Nearly all the children belonging to some of the Indian tribes in the northern part of the state have been stolen. They are taken to the southern part of the state, and there sold."

In September of that same year, the Sacramento *State Journal* also commented on the practice:

■ Round Valley was an idyllic haven in the Mendocino wilderness, but the white man's greed quickly turned it into a battleground. *Mendocino County Historical Society.*

We learn from Col. Henley…that he ascertains from the Indians that there is a band of about twenty Mexicans who traverse the coast range from the vicinity of Bodega to Shasta, and who follow no other occupation than that of stealing Indian children for the purpose of selling them, and that in a number of instances they have not scrupled to take the life of the parents, when it becomes necessary in securing the children. These Mexicans travel through different parts of the mountains on horseback, and when they find the squaws and children away from the men gathering the seeds and roots on which they in part subsist, they ride down upon them and catch the children with the riata, as they would a calf. These children are then brought to this city, San Francisco, and sold to the farmers throughout the country where a tale is told of their being orphans, or some other plausible story, and they are sold at prices varying from one to two hundred dollars….

Col. Henley has made application to Gen. Wool for troops to put a stop to these outrages on the Indians.

That same month, Henley hired Major William McDaniel as an attorney for the California Office of Indian Affairs. On a list of Indian service employees, McDaniel's duties were detailed as "to prevent and prosecute kidnapping." His salary was $100 per month, plus an additional fee for prosecuting his cases. When he wrote to General Wool requesting aid, Henley also asked for "a pair of Colt's pistols," since the kidnappers were well known as desperate characters. Wool refused any aid in the matter without an order from the president. Both Jefferson Davis, secretary of war, and the head of the Department of the Interior refused Henley's request for troops also, claiming such cases were a civil matter. In April of 1855, Henley wrote to his superior in Washington, describing the difficulties of the situation:

I enclose herewith the reply of Genl. Wool to my request for assistance in capturing some Spaniards under indictment for kidnapping Indians and who cannot be arrested by the sheriff. The object of soliciting the aid of the soldiers, who have nothing to do, is to avoid the expense of hiring men to assist in making the arrests. The danger and expense of pursuing these robbers into their mountain retreats is too great a burden on the civil authorities, and without such assistance as I have solicited I know of no means of effectually stopping the infamous practice of kidnapping and selling Indians. Citizens who aid in arresting Spaniards for this crime are in danger of assassination by these desperadoes and it is difficult to induce anyone to engage in it.

Henley was able to arrest and prosecute several Mexican kidnappers in Napa County, even after the district attorney refused to become involved in the case. McDaniel's fee for the successful prosecution was $500, which the presiding judge later testified was well worth it, since kidnapping in

■ A Yuki Indian village in the Mendocino Mountains. Photograph ca. 1860s.
Mendocino County Historical Society.

that area was effectually "broken up" due to the prosecution. Of course, no such thing had actually been effected. Between 1852 and 1867, it is estimated that some three thousand to four thousand Indian children were kidnapped in California.

In May of 1855, a letter bearing the names of fifty-one coastal settlers in Mendocino County was received by Robert White, a special Indian agent. White had farmed near the coast since 1852 and was friendly with the Indians. The petition complained of Indian theft and depredations for the past two years. A lack of food in the back country had driven the natives to the coast where they robbed homes and reportedly pillaged farmers of both livestock and crops. All that was needed to solve the problem, the letter went on, was a schooner-load of potatoes "…and paying some attention to them, generally. No answer or inaction was to be regarded by the settlers as a refusal…and a war of extermination [would] be entered into, by a set of men maddened by the losses of several years labor and a prospect of the same for the future."

White lost no time in writing Henley, explaining the situation. He suggested he be allowed to hunt game for the Indians so as to feed them and keep them from going to the coast to fish and steal. In an addendum to the letter, White noted that three Indians had been stolen from a local rancheria by a man named McDonald—"a woman and two boys had started for home, with them, by a by-road, and [he] intends to sell them, or trade them for cattle, which has been much practised of late."

Kidnapped Indian children as depicted in the *Overland Monthly*. When a white kidnapper insisted in court he was just finding homes for orphans, the judge asked how he knew they were orphans. "I killed their parents myself," responded the defendant. *Author's collection.*

In a letter to Henley dated August 20, White related that he had visited the victimized Indian tribe and discovered that the kidnapped natives had escaped and returned home. He had learned of another mass kidnapping, however, and succeeded in recapturing thirteen Indian women who had been taken by two white men and a large force of Indians. White apprehended the kidnappers, who were from Clear Lake and pretended to be elk hunting and claimed to know nothing of the stolen Indians. White let the two men go, but after learning they had killed an old Indian woman and injured a small boy, he again started in pursuit. He had lost too much time, however, and was not able to catch his quarry.

Writing on September 1, 1855, White detailed to Henley how he had successfully hunted for the Indians and prevented any further problems created by hunger. He reported killing twenty-three elk, 216 deer, and seven bears, all of which he distributed as best he could. Trouble had been averted in the area for the present.

Henley had promised to visit White in late August and was probably already thinking in terms of locating an Indian reservation in Mendocino. Much of the coast and interior valleys was yet unpopulated and he knew any new reserves should be located in the north. At the time, he was constantly receiving petitions from settlers, and recommendations from his agents, to remove Indians from the vicinity of white villages. As if this were not enough, Henley was beginning to be criticized for both inaction and his political activities. The *Humboldt Times*, in June of 1855, remarked:

> Rumor has it that there is such an office, and that it is embodied' in the person of one Thomas J. Henley. He has been written to, beseeched and entreated to take some steps to relieve our section of the troublesome Indians that infest it. Our rancheros have all been compelled to drive their stocks into the immediate vicinity of the towns. Not a pack train leaves this place unless doubly manned and armed, to resist the attacks of Indians. ...Our citizens will be compelled to take up arms and exterminate every Indian against whom suspicion is directed. ...We hope that Col. Henley can be induced to lay aside intrigue and "compromise" and at-

tend to the interest of the whites and the wants of the Indians, instead of making the office a political machine and of affording to his political favorites opportunities for speculation.

It was becoming more and more apparent that whites and Indians must be kept separate if there was to be peace.

In June, Henley received a report from Edward Stevenson, a special agent in El Dorado County. After listing the number of natives in the locality at about 1,750, the agent noted that the condition of the Indians was "wretched in the extreme." He wrote that the "…[S]quaws in this county lead a life of prostitution, contracting disease and disseminating it among the Indians, the horrible consequences of which no language can portray. I have found some 50 that were dying with this awful disease, they are all fond of the 'fire water' and get beastly intoxicated every opportunity they have…. I think there will be no trouble in removing them to reservations…."

■ Edward A. Stevenson, a good Democrat, was first a special Indian agent, then later served at Nome Lackee in Tehama County. *Idaho Historical Society.*

In another report the following December, Stevenson described visiting a rancheria and conversing with a chief on the subject of removing the Indians to a reserve:

He answered me in quite good English saying that he was in favor of that course because he was satisfied that if they remained where they were they must all starve or fall victim, to that fatal disease that the white men had brought among them, but says that 'I shall die before their removal can be accomplished therefore it matters little to me.' I asked him his reasons for thinking so when to my surprise he showed me his legs which were covered with ulcers peculiar to the disease I have referred to. He asked me if the Big Chief of the white men would cure them of this dreadful disease if they went to a reservation. I told him yes, and although I had no power or instructions from you to expend any money for medicine or medical treatment, I took him to a doctor and paid him for his prescription out of my own pocket which I have done in many other cases…. In one camp…I found nine squaws so far advanced with this disease that most of them were unable to walk.

Although he still maintained the farms at Kings River and on the Fresno, Henley at this time had only the two full-fledged reservations: Nome Lackee and the Tejon or Sebastian Reserve. Nome Lackee had received some good press and seemed to be going well, but Henley was a politician and ambitious. Too, the constant complaints and requests for

Indian removals from contact with the white settlements made it imperative there be more reserves.

In July of 1855, he had sent Commissioner Manypenny an estimate for the cost of maintaining two more reservations for a period of three months. To his surprise, he was given permission to go ahead with the two new projects and his appropriation was raised by some $200,000. Now he was getting somewhere. Now he had power.

In late September of 1855, Henley sent H. P. Heintzelman to look over some land in the vicinity of Cape Mendocino. Heintzelman's favorable report resulted in the establishment of a new Indian reservation there the following May. Planning and preliminary work was initiated at once.

The previous summer a Yreka judge named Peters had written Henley seeking an Indian agent post for a friend. In the course of his letter, Peters had mentioned a rich and beautiful valley in the Eel River country, just east of the new reserve. Noting that the place, called Round Valley, contained some thirty thousand acres and was one of the loveliest valleys in the world, Peters thought its isolated locale would make it perfect for an Indian reserve. He wrote, however, that the natives there were "numerous and hostile."

When questioned by Henley, some of the Indians at Nome Lackee said they were familiar with this valley. In June he sent Simmon Storms and a party of men north to explore the site as a possible location for yet another Indian farm.

Storms had been depressed lately. After coughing up some blood one day, he had seen a doctor who verified what he must have known. Perhaps the trip would take his mind off the diagnosis. Taking along George White, Charles Bourne and Dryden "Buck" Lacock, Storms picked out some Nome Lackee guides and headed for the valley. He found it to be a beautiful place and named it "Nome Cult," a Wintun Indian name meaning "West Tribe." He took possession of it for the government and reported that "of all the places I had ever seen, this was the place for an Indian reservation...."

Storms and his party camped in the valley on their first day there and within half an hour some two hundred Indians had gathered on a knoll near them. Storms sent an interpreter to arrange a parley, and six of the Indians returned to the white men's camp. One of them, a chief, offered Storms his bow and arrows. He was told to keep his weapons—that they were here at the order of the Great Captain to teach the Indians how to work and live among white men. Storms found the natives to be much the same as other California Indians he had known. Their reticence and hostility, he quickly learned, was the result of losing women and children to white men. At first, the Yuki stole some knives and cups, but when Storms scolded the chief, everything was returned.

The following day, about two hundred Indians returned to the white men's camp. Of these, only a few had any weapons. The natives were told how the Indians at Nome Lackee lived and worked, and the Yukis seemed pleased and agreed to work at anything if only their families would be protected from the kidnappers.

"I think that in the valley and mountains around," observed Storms in his official report, "there are at least five thousand Indians and that the valley can be made to support twenty thousand or more. It is the best place for Indians I ever saw. I

■ Simmon Storms was a friend to the Indians, but quickly became enmeshed in the schemes of his friend and employer Thomas J. Henley. *Peter Shearer.*

did not see a sick Indian or one afflicted with the Venereal. I think they are generally a better looking set of Indians than those at the Nome Lackee Reserve. Most of the squaws tatoo, the men do not."

Leaving three men behind, Storms left the valley on the morning of June 16. He was convinced that the site would be an ideal Indian farm and felt sure Henley would agree. On his way out, he met several parties going in and warned them that the government had already reserved the valley for its own use. "They will probably go elsewhere," he noted.

In Southern California, the Indians had been consistently ignored since the termination of the Garra incident. They had never forgotten the promises Wozencraft had made them, and although they frequently complained of a lack of attention, they remained peaceful. Isaac Williams, John Warner, and others felt a responsibility towards the southern natives and had helped them when they could. But the Indians never forgot the unfulfilled promises of the white men.

Paulino Weaver, the rancher who had helped capture Garra, had interpreted for Wozencraft and promised to look after the Cahuillas. In January 1855, Weaver had visited with Henley while traveling between Sacramento and San Francisco. He told the superintendent of the broken promises and Indian complaints, and Henley had promised to visit his southern wards as soon as possible. Weaver made the mistake of telling the

Cahuillas of Henley's promised visit, and again the Indians waited in vain for a government agent to show up. That summer Weaver wrote to Henley again and reiterated the Indian complaints of broken promises: "I believe that unless immediate steps are taken with these Indians, there will be trouble here."

Still unable to get away, Henley detailed Special Indian Agent Walter Harvey to visit the Cahuilla and Yuma Indians. Harvey, it will be remembered, had led the raid on the Kings River rancheria in 1852 and later shot and killed Jim Savage. Originally appointed by Beale, Harvey's credentials consisted primarily of being a loyal Democrat and out of a job.

The agent duly visited the southern Indians and reported on his trip late that year. "They entertain no hostile feelings against the Americans," he wrote, "nor have I any reason to believe they ever will...." Harvey said nothing of any Indian complaints of broken promises.

If he even made the trip, Harvey must have been talking to another group of Cahuilla Indians. Lieutenant William Winder of the Third Artillery conducted a patrol into Cahuilla territory in April of 1856, and although he found the Indians quiet, there was constant friction as the whites steadily encroached on the Indian land. Again Juan Antonio complained of the broken promises—all the more so since the native crops had failed that year. Without government help, the Cahuillas would be forced to steal cattle for subsistence.

■ A Cahuilla Indian home in the Southern California desert country. *Los Angeles Public Library.*

"I am of the opinion," wrote Winder, "that it would be cheaper to issue beef to these Indians than to fight them, at all events, until some superintendent of Indian Affairs is appointed who will attend to the duties pertaining to his office.... For many years these Indians have been in the habit of cultivating their fields without fencing, but at present the cattle of the whites overrun and destroy their crops, and they have no means of redress...."

Henley did write to Washington for authorization to provide the southern Indians with assistance in order to help preserve the peace. He also suggested appointing Juan Antonio and Manuel Cota as special Indian agents, with no powers, but at a nominal salary. It was an attempt to buy the peace, but the move never materialized.

Some food supplies were issued to the Yumas and Cahuillas, but since there was no immediate trouble, the southern Indians were quickly forgotten in the activity and problems of the new reserves being established in the north.

Captain Henry Ford had shown so much energy as subagent at Nome Lackee that Henley placed him in charge of the new reserve on the Mendocino Coast. Arriving in November of 1856, Ford immediately began construction of various dwellings and headquarters structures. Two separate farms were established with Bob White as general overseer and in charge of the gardens. The following year, Ford could report over three hundred fifty acres of crops under cultivation and over forty thousand pounds of fish being dried.

In casting about for a successor to Ford, Henley assigned Edward Stevenson of El Dorado County to take charge of Nome Lackee. Earlier Henley had hired Vincent Geiger as special agent for the Sacramento Valley Indians. Although living in Sacramento, and spending only some time at Nome Lackee, Geiger quickly saw the advantages of being connected with a reservation.

Having arrived in California during the summer of 1849, Geiger was another of the Democratic party faithful seeking his political place in the sun. For a time he ran a newspaper, but it failed when he lost a contract for lucrative state printing business. He was prominent in party councils and had been on the State Democratic Committee in 1854 and 1855. His appointment as agent seems to have been purely political, with Henley and the party awarding the position to one of their own.

Simmon Storms was meanwhile making progress as subagent at the new Nome Cult Farm. Supplies were brought in and buildings erected as the agent and his men prepared for winter. As a precaution, Storms erected a log fence around his first cabins, and in late July, they were better able to defend themselves when the Indians attacked. The cause of the trouble is not known, but Storms noted that the natives "threatened our lives and killed some stock." With the aid of several settlers and some roving mountain men, many of the Indians were killed and the balance driven off.

Storms kept busy bringing in supplies, although the new reserve would be almost totally dependent on Nome Lackee for subsistence that winter.

In October, he traveled to Marysville to set up the machinery for removal of the local Indians there. "We have no doubt that it will be in accordance with the wishes of a large majority of this community," noted the Marysville *Daily Herald*. "They are a wretched set of creatures and their condition in regard to all physical and moral wants is most miserable."

The following month, Superintendent Henley met General Sutter at Yuba City. Sutter had been appointed special agent for the Indians in the vicinity of his Hock Farm residence, and the two men met with Marysville officials and the local press prior to holding a council with the natives. The recent bad publicity surrounding his trip to Washington needed cushioning, and Henley no doubt sought all the press attention he could get on his new endeavors.

At the council, Sutter spoke in Spanish, while Captain M. D. Dobbins translated, telling the Indians of the benefits awaiting them at the new reserves. The Indians agreed to go, but wanted a month's delay, which Henley granted. In the interim, many of Sutter's Indians pleaded with their master to let them live on with him and die on their own land. The old Swiss pioneer finally gave in, even though he had originally asked for the removal to save his wards from the baleful influence of "civilization."

■ Distribution of rations on the Mendocino coastal reservation as depicted in *Hutching's California Magazine*, 1858. *Author's collection.*

"Gen. Sutter will be a faithful guardian to the Indians who remain with him," wrote Henley to the home office in Washington, "many of whom were his companions in this country long before its occupation by the Americans and fought with him in the contest which acquired California."

Exactly one month later, however, the Marysville Indians were rounded up for the trip to Nome Lackee. The local police force aided the Indian agents, holding the natives at the station house as they were brought in. From Marysville, they were taken to Yuba City, then on to the reserve.

"It seems hard," commented the *Herald*, "at first thought, to remove the poor creatures from the homes of their fathers, but the act is warranted both by justice and humanity. The influence of civilization have during the last seven years more than decimated their numbers...."

Whatever the newspaper rhetoric, Henley received some good publicity, the town got rid of a lot of drunken nuisances, and Captain Dobbins received over $8,000 for removing some six hundred Indians a distance of about a hundred miles.

At Nome Cult, Storms busily prepared for winter. A labor report for a day in July notes that "Lacock started with Capt. Ford's party to lookout a road to Eden Valley—Farr with 4 Indians getting out timber—Kalburgh with 20 Indians mowing and putting up hay [grass]—6 Indians ditching—2 hunting, killed 4 deer."

The winter of 1856-57 was particularly severe, causing much hardship in northern California. Violent snow storms, rain, and flooding were common. "The sky was a water sieve and the earth a sponge," commented the *Humboldt Times*. Storms led a succession of Indian pack trips

■ A modest monument marks the site of Nome Lackee Reservation today. *Photo by Jim Secrest.*

across the mountains to Nome Lackee that winter for supplies. "On several occasions I nearly lost my life," he recalled later. "...[O]ne Indian was frozen to death, two men drowned in the Eel River and several mules were lost...."

When Storms or others made the occasional trek over the mountains for supplies, it was usually the occasion for a prolonged drinking and gambling bout at Nome Lackee. In May of 1857 Henley received a letter from the rancher husband of Mary Ann Jennison, the sewing instructor at the reserve. Jennison complained of the frequent drinking and gambling of the employees. He accused Agent Stevenson of gambling extensively, both on the reserve and in town, and maintained he was often drunk and disagreeable to both employees and Indians. After an investigation, Henley decided to remove Stevenson and appoint Vincent Geiger in his place.

In the spring, the new Round Valley reserve was again the scene of much activity. Early in June, the *Red Bluff Beacon* noted that Storms and four other white men, together with thirteen mounted Indians, were on their way to McCorkle and Smith's ranch to take charge of six hundred head of cattle for use at Nome Cult. This stock and the cattle and hogs brought in by various settlers the past fall were to seriously change the atmosphere of the valley.

About fifteen settlers had come into the valley in the fall of 1856. The following spring, the first of many others began arriving. The Wilsey brothers drove in a herd of cattle, as did some others. Wesley Wilsey had been in the stock business with Henley in Indiana and had driven a cattle herd across the country in 1853. The two men were apparently partners in a cattle ranch in San Mateo and later a milk farm near San Francisco. Wilsey and his brothers, along with other friends of Henley, were invited to take up claims in the area, not only because it was virgin country, but because more settlers meant safety from the hordes of Indians. However, the livestock being brought in was to initiate the very trouble Henley sought to avoid.

Already the guns of the whites had scared and driven off much of the natural game of the area. The ranchers and the reservation employees were gathering the rich valley grasses as forage for their stock, not caring that these same grasses were a staple ingredient of the Yuki diet. Also, the ranchers' hogs fed on the native acorns, the other staple food of the Indians. It was the same old story that had been repeated a thousand times throughout the state. Drama, as inevitable as in a Greek tragedy, was beginning to unfold.

As the number of settlers increased, most of the agency employees also hastened to take up claims in the valley. Buck Lacock, Simmon Storms, Charles Bourne, and others began setting up ranches utilizing Indian labor. Henley himself was a silent partner with Storms and Bourne in some thirteen hundred acres. He also had an interest in a large horse herd that had been brought into the valley. Henley was so taken with the area that he brought two sons, who had been employed in his San Francisco office, to set up ranches also. Late in the year, he informed his friend, Judge Serranus C. Hastings, of the opportunities in the north, and the judge took up claims totaling nearly all of nearby Eden Valley.

Hastings lived in Benecia at the time and was prominent and well known. He had been the first chief justice of the State Supreme Court, as well as attorney general in 1851. He and Henley were political cronies who had campaigned together, and they engaged in both banking and

Serranus C. Hastings, real estate speculator, attorney general, and first chief justice of the State Supreme Court. *Author's collection.*

extensive land speculations as partners. As often as not, Hastings would list himself as being a land speculator rather than a judge or lawyer, and he was quick to see the potential in the rich, northern country.

Another force had been slowly evolving in the valley—a class of men who were also a part of every Indian problem of the period. Early settlers characterized these rootless hunters, stock herders, and mountain men as "floaters" and "buckskin gentry," men who had no investment or family interests to worry about. They were callous and indifferent in their dealings with the Indians. They treated the native inhabitants brutally, whipping and abusing the men and taking the women as concubines. Storms and the other agency people knew what was going on, but found there was little they could do in the lawless wilderness in which they found themselves. Many of the troublemakers were criminals and fugitives from justice, seeking anonymity in the wilderness. They mingled freely with the settlers in the valley.

The shadow of war hung over the rushing streams and forests of northern Mendocino. The kidnapping of Indians and continual influx of settlers, coupled with the frequent cruel treatment of the natives, insured that the problems now evolving would not be easily solved.

Surly and resentful at what was happening, the Yuki began to appropriate the white men's cattle as a food source, bringing even more grief down upon their heads. "In 1856," recalled Buck Lacock, "the first expedition by the whites against the Indians was made, and have continued ever since; these expeditions were formed by gathering together a few white men whenever the Indians committed depredations on their stock; there were so many expeditions that I cannot recollect the number; …we would kill, on the average, fifty or sixty Indians on a trip."

Other settlers were reported killed, while stock continued to be taken by the Yuki. "This will, of course, continue," wrote Henley to his superiors in October of 1857, "until the force of the whites is sufficient to overwhelm the Indians and exterminate them or drive them to the reservations…."

With his own investments at stake in the area, Henley either had to justify what he knew was taking place, or call in the army to take charge of the Indian situation. He was in a dangerous position, both politically and investment-wise, but he was soon to be distracted by other trouble that was brewing in the San Joaquin Valley.

CHAPTER 15 / SOURCES

Any history of Mendocino County's Round Valley area would have been eminently more difficult to research without the help of the late Estle Beard of Covelo. Mr. Beard was a retired cattleman and historian of the area whose exhaustive research into government archives, newspapers of the period, and local family history resulted in a vast collection of material which he very generously shared with others. *Genocide and Vendetta,* Mr. Beard's book (in collaboration with the late Lynwood Carranco), was published in 1981 and is recommended as the superlative early history of the Round Valley area.

UNPUBLISHED MATERIAL

U.S. Congress, 34th Congress, 3rd Session, Document 123:

Lieutenant William A. Winder to Captain R. S. Burton, April 29, 1856.

National Archives, Records of the Office of Indian Affairs, California Superintendency, Record Group 75, M234:

Thomas J. Henley to G. W. Manypenny, October 14, 1854, April 9, 1855, April 7, 14, December 4, 1856.

Major General John Wool to Thomas J. Henley, March, 1855.

Fifty-one settlers to Robert White, May 1, 1855.

Robert White to Thomas J. Henley, May 13, 1855.

Edward A. Stevenson to Thomas J. Henley, June 18, December 31, 1855.

J. Montgomery Peters to Thomas J. Henley, June 24, 1855.

Paulino Weaver to Thomas J. Henley, August, 1855.

Thomas J. Henley to Hon. John A. Sutter, February 13, 1856.

W. H. Harvey to Thomas J. Henley, February 23, 1856.

Thirteen Russian River settlers to Thomas J. Henley, March 20, 1856.

S. Jenison to Thomas J. Henley, May 26, 1856.

Simmon P. Storms to Thomas J. Henley, June 26, 1856.

Report of labor at Nome Cult, commencing July 21 and ending August 10, 1856.

Thomas J. Henley to James W. Denver, October, 1857.

Estle Beard to the author, 1970-1978.

Garrett, Gary E. "The Destruction of the Indian in Mendocino County, 1856-60," M.A. thesis, Sacramento State College, copy on file in Office of the Secretary of State, California State Archives, Indian War Files, Sacramento.

NEWSPAPERS

San Francisco *Daily Alta California*, December 8, 1852.

Sacramento *Daily Union*, August 29, 1851.

Sacramento *State Journal*, September 29, 1854.

Humboldt Times, April 19, 1856.

Marysville *Daily Herald*, October 14, 25, November 25, December 1, 24, 1856.

Red Bluff Beacon, June 10, 1857.

PRINCIPAL PUBLISHED WORKS

Beard, Estle and Carranco, Lynwood. *Genocide and Vendetta*. Norman, OK: University of Oklahoma Press, 1981.

Heizer, Robert F., editor. *The Destruction of the California Indian*. Santa Barbara, CA: Peregrin Press, Inc., 1974.

Hislop, Donald Lindsay. *The Nome Lackee Indian Reservation: 1854-1870*. Chico, CA: Association for Northern California Records and Research, (no date).

Keller, John E. *The Saga of Round Valley: The Last of the West*. Fort Bragg, CA: Mendocino County Historical Society, 1976.

Kroeber, Alfred L. *Handbook Of the Indians of California*. New York: Dover Publications, Inc., 1956.

Potter, David M. *Trail to California, the Overland Journal of Vincent Geiger and Wakeman Bryarly*. New Haven, CT: Yale University Press, 1967.

OTHER SOURCES

Appendix to the Journals of the Senate of the Eleventh Session of the Legislature of the State of California, Sacramento, 1860.

Beard, Estle. "The Settlement of Round Valley," *Mendocino County Historical Society Newsletter*, Vol. 3, No. 6; Vol. 4, No. 1 (no dates).

Jones, Pat. "Simmon Pena Storms—Right Man, Wrong Time," *The Californians*, November/December, 1988.

Rogers, Fred. "Bear Flag Lieutenant—Henry L. Ford," *California Historical Society Quarterly*, June, September, December 1950; March, June 1951.

Secrest, William B. "The Old War Horse of the Democracy: The Rise and Fall of Thomas J. Henley," *The Californians*, November/December, 1988.

Tassein, A. G. "Chronicles of Camp Wright," *Overland Monthly*, July, 1887.

Chapter 16

WHITMORE'S FERRY

Thomas Henley had early perceived the necessity for a physician on the Indian reserves. Deserting Spanish soldiers and runaway neophytes from the missions had introduced venereal diseases among the natives of the great central valley fifty years earlier. Contact with the Californians, and now the Americans, had made the problem much worse. Already weakened, the Indians were much more susceptible to the other diseases spread by the white man. Writing to the commissioner of Indian affairs in Washington in August of 1854, Henley made an urgent request:

> There is great necessity for a physician at the Tejon Reservation. Venereal diseases prevail among the Indians and deaths are of frequent occurrence from that cause. ...I can think of nothing more important than employing a physician to reside permanently on the reservation and devoting his time and attention to the amelioration of the condition of these people. The expense would be but little...

To his credit, Henley soon had doctors attached to each of the reserves. Dr. Lewis Leach was hired for the Fresno reserve as early as February of 1855. Pay ranged from $1,250 to $3,000 per year, but liquor, disease, rape, and the increasing prostitution of many Indian women made the doctor's work a nightmare. The commandant at Fort Miller underscored the problems in a report to Benicia in 1857:

> The medical officer at this post having reported to me the prevalence of venereal disease among the troops of this command, I have the honor to make the following report to the Col. commanding the Dept. for the information of the Indian Department—if necessary. The Indians that have for years lived in the immediate vicinity of this post have during that time been in constant intercourse with the worst class of whites to be found in any country. They have contracted disease—to them the most fatal—and are constantly furnished by the whites with liquor so that every day an observer may see a dozen Indians reeling drunk. The civil law as administered here seems wholly inoperative, not only to the protection of the Indians, but the punishing of the whites. All are diseased and from such

constant intercourse with whites it must go on increasing.... I am continually obliged now to quell disturbances among drunken whites and Indians to prevent serious results. All disturbances are caused by introduction of liquor among them and intercourse with their women. ...The Indian agents have done nothing towards bettering their condition.... I would recommend that they be taken to the Fresno Indian Farm, fifteen miles from here. It is only by a move of this kind that they can be saved from complete annihilation....

E. D. Keyes, who had commanded the troops in the valley during the treaty making of 1851, returned in 1858 to attend a court martial at Fort Miller. Keyes had become acquainted with several of the Indian chiefs along the San Joaquin River and wanted to see them again. "I inquired for several individuals whom I remembered," he wrote later. "I was told that they were nearly all dead, victims to drunkenness, and that of the whole number I then saw in such full activity (some 1,200 natives) not above fifty remained."

Pahmit, the Dumna Indian who lived well into the twentieth century, also recalled those dark years of the late 1850s: "Not many Indians left. Lots Indians die whiskey; lots Indians die bad white man's sickness. Just a few Indians left.... White miners still whip Indians; still shoot Indians...."

By 1858, conditions were much the same all over the state. Although Henley and his agents continued to make promising reports concerning

The site of old Fort Miller, as it appeared in 1914, shows many of the adobe buildings still in place and being used by the owner. *Laval Company.*

the reserves, the constant newspaper notices of Indian fights, drunken natives, and the widespread prostitution of Indian women made the public wonder about the value of the reservations. Clearly, they were not doing the Indians any good.

In August of 1849, young John Ross Browne landed in the sprawling, gold-mad port of San Francisco. As an officer of the United States Revenue Service, Browne was charged with the impossible task of devising a means of preventing the mass desertion of naval personnel to the gold fields. In 1854, he was appointed a special agent of the United States Treasury Department with the responsibility of examining the collecting and dispersing of federal funds. California, so far from Washington, was ripe for exploitation, and that was exactly what was happening.

J. Ross Browne, the government investigator, made herculean efforts to clean up the California Indian department. *California State Library.*

The Gold Rush of 1849 was followed by what California historian Richard Dillon has quite aptly referred to as "the graft rush." Politicians, ballot box stuffers, thieves, thugs, and every variety of get-rich-quick con men and merchants had soon manipulated the new state into chaos. Depressions, vigilante uprisings, and corruption on a wide scale were the result.

Browne investigated any institution where government money was involved and early began keeping an eye on the new Indian reservations. The agent was in a difficult position. In politics, he was a Democrat, and all the officials he investigated were of the same party. Yet, he never faltered, reporting all wrongdoings he encountered and the devil take the hindmost.

Beale's efforts at the Tejon impressed Browne at a time when there still seemed to be hope for the Indian. "True," Browne wrote, "it cost a great deal to get started,...but a considerable crop was raised and there was every reason to hope that the experiment would prove successful."

As late as December 1854, Browne was still optimistic and after a visit to Nome Lackee, wrote his superior that "I am well convinced that there could not be a better system devised for the improvement...of the Indians on this coast."

An essential part of Browne's job was to read men and he did not like what he saw in Tom Henley, the new superintendent. "Nearly all men with whom I have come in contact, are more or less corrupt," he once wrote his wife. He recalled how the Sacramento *Daily Union* had accused Henley of throwing undelivered mail into the trash when he was postmaster at San Francisco. He remembered, too, Henley's hurried trip to Washington in 1856 to defend himself against newspaper charges of inefficiency, defaulting on, and speculating with government funds.

At the Tejon the following year, Browne obtained a series of affidavits from agency employees accusing Henley and others of selling reservation property for their own profit. Alex Godey stated that government blankets meant for the Indians were instead being sold to whites. Sam Dummer testified that he had seen government flour, intended for Indian use, sold to private parties. Patrick Connor recalled having once bought some provisions at the Tejon, but later discovered his payment had been used to settle a private debt of Henley's.

In digging deeper, Browne learned that nearly all Indian agency employees were engaged in private ranching enterprises. In a letter to Commissioner of Indian Affairs Charles E. Mix, in October 1858, Browne made some specific accusations:

> At this very time it is well known that Mr. J. R. Vineyard, the agent at the Tejon, owns several thousand head of sheep on that reservation, which are herded by Indians...Messrs. White and Simpson, at Mendocino, have become wealthy by their stock speculations. Mr. Ford owns both stock and a stock ranch; S. P. Storms owns stock at Nome Cult; and indeed, it would be difficult to find an agent or employee who is not engaged to some extent in the stock business.

Browne had already reported on Henley's extensive stock ventures in Mendocino County and at San Mateo.

Abuses on the Tule River Indian reserve were also ferreted out by the agent. Alonzo Ridley had been sent to establish the reserve on Tule River after the 1856 troubles. Ridley built a large adobe house, planted orchards and vineyards, and leveled many acres of land—all with Indian labor and supplies from the Tejon. At the time this work was being done, the land itself was already filed on with school warrants by a clerk at the Tejon and other parties. Someone was either going to have a nice ranch courtesy of the government, or else sell the improved property at a handsome sum to the government.

Farther north in the valley, at Millerton, Browne encountered incredibly sloppy business dealings between local merchants and the agents on the Fresno farm. Goods were being receipted for as having been delivered to the Indians without agency employees ever having seen them. Except for the fraud involved, it did not really matter if some of the supplies were delivered or not so far as the secret agent was concerned. Browne charged that, although exorbitant prices were paid for agency supplies, much of it was worthless: clothes that ripped out at the seams at the slightest strain, blankets so thin they could do double duty as windows and medical supplies that had been culled from the discards of drugstore back rooms across California.

It was becoming increasingly apparent that despite large appropriations of money and glowing reports from the superintendent, the reservations were a failure. "The Fresno farm," wrote Browne, "costs government some twenty or twenty-five thousand dollars per annum. It has not been of the least benefit to the Indians for the last few years."

Browne himself, despite the concern for the natives which seems so obvious in his reports, saw nothing wrong in buying two Indian children at Nome Lackee to help out at his family home in Oakland. This, of course, was perfectly legal at the time.

The Fresno Indian farm had been established during the summer of 1854 on the farm of Captain Lorenzo D. Vinsonhaler. The doughty captain was a survivor of Fremont's disastrous fourth expedition and later had been a partner with Savage in his trading post. Vinsonhaler had been the guide of the Mariposa Battalion and Captain Keyes recalled that he was a good one. "His ability to find paths appeared to me almost miraculous," recalled Keyes. Vinsonhaler was also hired to "take charge of the farm," while D. A. Enyart was appointed special Indian agent.

■ The Adobe Ranch of Lorenzo Vinsonhaler, who died in 1857, was the site of the Fresno River Indian farm. This view is from the early 1880s. *From* History of Fresno County.

It had been quickly established that beef was much too expensive to feed the Indians as had first been done under the commissioners. Writing to his Washington superior in December of 1854, Henley stated that he "was determined to retrench this enormous and…useless expenditure." Wheat and barley was to be the staple reservation fare, supplemented by whatever crops of vegetables were raised. The Indians were also to continue hunting game and gathering as much acorns and seeds as possible.

A Tachi medicine man, from a photograph taken in the 1920s.
Jeff Edwards Collection.

In his first report to Henley, Enyart noted that he had some four hundred and forty Indians on his farm. There was no food on hand, and acorns had been quite scarce that year. Crops were planted, however, and the following year a harvest of five hundred acres of wheat, seven hundred acres of barley, and two hundred acres of corn and vegetables was expected. In addition, Enyart was preparing to take a group of Indians up the Fresno River and put them to work mining in November 1854. It was a typical report, full of high figures and higher expectations, neither of which ever seemed to materialize.

Jim Savage had estimated years earlier that some six thousand Indians lived on or about the shores of Tulare Lake, a vast, tule-shrouded runoff for the Four Creeks area. About sixty miles long, Tulare Lake was situated in the heart of the San Joaquin Valley, between the Tejon and the Kings River. Savage's estimate was high, but there were at least three valley tribes living in the area whose culture revolved around the lake. They lived in tule huts, built tule boats, and depended on fish, roots, grasses, and the abundant game of the area for food. An early settler reported catching a thirty-six-inch-long lake trout that weighed some thirty pounds.

The Wowol, Chunut, and Tachi, natives who held the lake territory, were close neighbors and friends with the Nutunutu and Wimilchi who inhabited the shores of Kings River. It was a good life for the Indians, and many managed to avoid the reservations because of the abundance of food in the area. In 1856, Campbell, the Kings River Indian agent, wrote to Henley that "the people on Kings River near the lake are well satisfied with the position of the Indians—they make no complaints in regard to them."

But by 1858 this had changed. An article in the *Visalia Weekly Delta* in December of the following year noted that the country along Kings River was filling up quickly with farmers' homes no more than a half mile apart. The foothills of the coast range, on the west side of the lake, had also attracted many ranchers. Suddenly, the Indians were a nuisance. The elk and antelope were being scared away and killed off, and livestock grazed on the native seeds and tule roots that formerly subsisted the natives. Soon local ranchers' stock was reported missing and provisions were being stolen from homes. It was an old story.

In late October of 1858, Justin Esrey, B. J. Hickell, Ben Andrews and other local ranchers held a meeting. It was determined that all the lake Indians would be rounded up, their homes destroyed, and their winter food supply burned. The natives would then be forcibly removed to the Fresno River Indian farm. "These Indians," noted the ranchers, "and a community of stock-growing people cannot inhabit the same country."

But not all local settlers agreed with Esrey and his crowd. Henry and Anderson Akers ran hogs on the Kings River and often foraged them on the shores of Tulare Lake. They had come to California in 1852 and lived among the Indians for many years. "I never knew one of them to steal anything from me or any of my neighbors," Henry Akers recalled. "I have heard of them stealing stock, but I do not believe there was any foundation to such stories."

However, there undoubtedly was periodic stock-raiding and stealing at that time. A petition by the settlers noted that some mission Indians were living in the area "who are all daring and expert marauders." Possibly they were responsible for much of the theft. J. Ross Browne, who had been in the neighborhood, wrote of "petty depredations committed upon their property by the Indians who were constantly lounging about their places...." Whatever the magnitude of the offenses, the settlers moved swiftly—and mercilessly.

"Most of the stockmen wanted the Indians out," recalled Henry Akers. "I don't know why, because they didn't hurt a thing down there and it was theirs, anyway. They [the settlers] asked Anderson and me to help, but we refused. We thought the Indians should be left where they were."

The roundup began early in November of 1858, but just how many whites were involved is not known. Both Indian and white accounts refer to soldiers, or cavalry, as being involved in the roundup. A check of the records of Fort Tejon and Fort Miller, reveal no such actions by the army at the time. It is known, however, that Ben Andrews, and probably most others of the group, belonged to the Millerton militia unit. They had apparently donned their uniforms to overawe their quarry, both white and Indian. The ranchers were well armed, some being equipped with cavalry sabres. Several wagons accompanied the expedition, also.

The posse galloped into the several Indian villages on the lake and quickly rounded up all the inhabitants they could find. Burning their huts and destroying the stored native food supplies, the whites were swift, thorough, and brutal.

■ A ferry on Kings River, pictured some years after Whitmore's ferry was in operation. Whitmore's craft was about sixteen by sixty feet, built originally for a man named George and later bought by Whitmore. *Author's collection.*

"They beat the Indians with whips and hit them with their swords and ran their horses over them when they would not go," declared Yoimut, a Chunut woman whose parents lived through the roundup. "Some Indians were shot because they ran away. My mother said she saw twelve Indians killed, but the rest had to go anyway."

Henry Akers substantiated Indian accounts of what happened. "The way in which the cavalrymen handled the Indians was as brutal as could be. None of the Indians wanted to go and few of them had any idea what was going to be done with them if they went. A white fellow named Mann was killed because he tried to help his Indian wife hide. No one ever knew," continued Akers, "how many Indians were killed or crippled at the lake. I would not be surprised if they killed fifty or more. I am surely glad that none of my family had anything to do with it."

Captured Yokuts were driven to Whitmore's ferry on the Kings River where they were held under guard while more Indians were rounded up.

When most of the lake Indians had been accounted for, the posse swept into several rancherias along the river and gathered up the Indians who lived there. It was a time-consuming job and over a week was taken in raiding the villages and locating natives who had tried to hide in the tules and brush.

Gregorio, the Tachi chief, fled the round up and made his way to the Fresno reserve where he told Agent Martin B. Lewis what was happening. It was the first Lewis had heard of the trouble. An estimated seventy warriors from the various lake and river rancherias escaped the posse and hid in the tules. There was little they could do. Choking back their feelings of helplessness, they tried to keep a distant watch on their families at Whitmore's ferry.

> **The Southern Indians.**
> A correspondent of the Mariposa *Gazette* defends Judge Lewis, the Indian agent of that vicinity, from the charges recently made against him. He charges the people with great cruelty in forcing the Indians upon the Reservation where the agent has no means to support them, and where they must suffer. The writer says, also, that 12 or 15 Indians who were driven away from their homes by the settlers to the Reservation, escaped, and have either starved or frozen to death in the vicinity of the lake.

■ *San Joaquin Republican*, January 12, 1859.

When he heard Gregorio's story, Lewis did not know quite what to do. He had seen much of frontier life as a soldier under Sam Houston and as adjutant of the Mariposa Battalion. In 1856, he had been one of the commissioners when Fresno County was created and also served as a judge and justice of the peace. He was a friend to the Indians and often defended them in court. He knew full well how little chance the natives stood if the whites decided to move them out of the lake area.

"There…always has been a war going on between the white people in the neighborhood of Kings River Indian farm," wrote Lewis to Henley, "about the Indians in that vicinity and it is only necessary for one party of whites to be satisfied that they have the advantage and they will pitch into the Indians."

On November 11, Lewis sent Gregorio back to his people with a note to Whitmore. The agent knew the Fresno farm was probably the destination of the Indians, and he asked the ferryman to do what he could both to help the natives and to fill him in on the situation. But by that time the roundup was complete and the Indians were being herded toward the Fresno.

Gregorio said the Tachi prayer for those of his people who had been killed; "You are going to another land. You will like that land. You shall not stay here." The prayer also applied to those of his people who would now have a new home at the Fresno farm, since Agent Lewis had made it very clear there was no food for them on the reserve.

Yoi-mut, the Chunut woman, remembered her parents telling her that it took about ten days to round up the Indians. "The ranchers did not let them take time to carry any grub," she recalled. "Then it took four days to drive them to the Fresno River reservation. My mother and father both went.... All this time the Indians only had a few things to eat. They ate a few mussels from the river and a few tule roots. Some Indians caught a few salmon along the river and ate them raw.... About 10 Indians died on the way. Three or four babies were born during the trip...."

On November 14, Lewis wrote Henley of the "arrival at the farm on the 13th inst. under the escort of seven armed and equipped white men, of some two hundred nearly destitute Indians.... It is truly unfortunate for these suffering people," continued the agent, "that they should have been driven from their homes where they had a bountiful supply of subsistence for the season. It is however their fate, and they will not be permitted to return. The men who had the Indians in charge treated them very kindly and conducted themselves with propriety whilst here."

As usual, not enough food had been raised the previous year to accommodate the farm Indians alone, much less two hundred additional natives from the lake. It was a drought year and what acorns there were had been utilized by the hog ranchers. Lewis managed to get together some one thousand pounds of wheat and four hundred pounds of beans which he sent over to the Indian camp.

Esrey, Andrews, and the other ranchers presented Lewis with a petition listing their grievances and noting that "no violence was used in capturing these Indians. They have been kindly treated.... We also state that this is the last time their peaceable removal will be attempted and that should they return they will surely be harshly dealt with. As abide with us they shall not!"

Anxious to avoid further bloodshed, Lewis went to the lake with some wagons and rounded up what remaining Indians he could find. It was bitter cold, and the tule fog made it difficult to even keep his wag-

■ A posed view showing Indians building a tule boat. The tall tules in the background hid some of the Indians during the lake roundup. *Arthur Barr Productions.*

ons on the road. All but seventeen natives agreed to go with him, the others saying they preferred to "die in the lake with their relatives who had already perished with hunger and cold."

By December 23, Lewis had transported all the lake and river Indians to a spot on the San Joaquin River, where they set up camp. The agent wrote Henley that he had rescued not less than three hundred Indians "who were threatened with extermination."

Upon his return to the Fresno, Lewis found that the "vigilantes" had deposited another group of Kings River Indians on his reserve. A writer in the *Mariposa Gazette* in early January decried the whole episode:

> All the evidence of theft or wrongdoing by the Indians is vague and indefinite...against the irreparable injury they are now sustaining at the hands of their more enlightened neighbors. An element of jealousy and dissatisfaction with two or three individuals who are supposed to be benefitted by the presence of the Indians, may also have entered largely into the motives.

At Tulare Lake, the ranchers kept a wary eye out for Indian stragglers who tried to sneak back to their old homes. They meant business. The lake people would not be allowed to return.

Lucius Whitmore had come to California about 1850. A carpenter by trade, he probably helped J. S. George build a ferry on the Kings River in 1854. Late in 1856, Whitmore bought the ferry and it became a profitable venture, due to the ever-increasing traffic of wagons, stagecoaches, and travelers in the valley.

The ferryman seems to have gotten along well with the natives and by the late 1850s had an Indian wife and several half-blood children. He naturally had no sympathy with the ranchers who had removed the Indians and did what he could to aid the Indians, as Agent Lewis requested.

In early February, a squad of local ranchers again swept through the tules and rounded up some returning Indians. Furious that their threats had not been taken seriously, the ranchers were in no mood to put up with any interference. When they rode up to the ferry this time, they insisted that Whitmore's wife and children be included in the roundup. The ferryman adamantly refused and hurried his family into the house. A rancher followed, and moments later a shot was heard. The Sacramento *Union* of February 10 reported:

> L. A. Whitmore, formerly owner of Whitmore's Ferry on Kings River, was recently shot in his own house by Dr. Workman, one of the leaders of the Lower Kings River anti-Indian men, backed by ten or fifteen of his party for no other cause as yet known than to gratify the evil passion of a

■ An Indian tule shelter built in the Tulare Lake area. *Smithsonian Institute.*

mob. Serious fears are entertained that the lawless disposition and interference of a few men on Kings River, who have arrayed themselves against the helpless digger Indians, will force the employees and Indians to abandon the Kings River Indian farm.

Dr. Pleasant Workman fled the area but later returned and was tried and acquitted. The ferry was sold at public sale in July of 1859, but it is doubtful if Whitmore's Indian family benefitted from the proceeds.

The Tachi chief, Gregorio, faded into the obscurity of Indian life of the time. In 1846 he had been a member of Fremont's California Battalion and had accompanied him east when that controversial officer was charged with insubordination. Gregorio and another Tulare Indian had lived at Senator Benton's (Fremont's father-in-law) farm in Kentucky and cared for the explorer's favorite horse until he formed his fourth expedition in the fall of 1848.

Gregorio was one of the lucky survivors of Fremont's disastrous winter crossing of the Rocky Mountains that year. An Indian companion and ten others perished on that terrible trip, a trek linked by several of the survivors to cannibalism. Tough and used to hard living, Gregorio had his most exciting moment when he turned a stampeding buffalo herd away from the party's camp.

Back in California, Gregorio lived with the Fremonts for several years as a servant. Later he returned to his people on the lake and told of the wondrous things he had seen—the river boats, locomotives, the strange Indians on the Great Plains, and the teeming cities of the white people. He had seen the roads and the buildings and the vast numbers of the white race who were always in a hurry and on the move.

Soon, all of California would be like that. Soon, there would be no room for the Indian in the San Joaquin Valley.

CHAPTER 16 / SOURCES

UNPUBLISHED MATERIAL

National Archives, Records War Department, Department of the Pacific, Record Group 98:

Lieutenant LaRhett Livingston to major W. W. Mackall, March 9, 1857.

National Archives, Office of Indian Affairs, Record Group 75:

Thomas J. Henley to G. W. Manypenny, August 29, October 14, December 7, 1854.

Statement of Mechanics, Laborers & Employed on the Fresno Indian Farm, California, commencing September 12, 1854 and ending June 30, 1855.

D. A. Enyart to Thomas J. Henley, November 3, 1854.

J. Ross Browne to G. W. Manypenny, December 1, 1854.

William F. Campbell to Thomas J. Henley, September 12, 1856.

J. Ross Browne to Charles E. Mix, October 8, 1858.

Justin Esrey, B. A. Andrews, W. G. M. Kinney, A. M. Net, B. J. Hickell, W.A. Tull to M. B. Lewis, November 14, 1858.

M. B. Lewis to Thomas J. Henley, November 14, 21, 1858, December 27, 1859.

J. Ross Browne to James W. Denver, January 18, 1859.

Leonard, Charles B., "The Federal Indian Policy in the San Joaquin Valley," unpublished thesis, University of California, 1928.

Mitchell, Annie, to the author, November 9, 1977: newspaper data and biographical material on L. A. Whitmore.

NEWSPAPERS

San Francisco *Daily Alta California*, December 20, 1858.

Mariposa Gazette, January 7, February 11, 1859.

The *Placerville Mountain Democrat*, May 31, 1856.

Visalia Times Delta, August 4, 1935.

Sacramento *Daily Union*, October 27, 1856; December 20, 1858; February 16, 1859.

Visalia Weekly Delta, December 3, 31, 1859; January 14, 1860.

PRIMARY PUBLISHED WORKS

Brandon, William. *The Men and the Mountain*. New York: William Morrow & Company, 1955.

Browne, Lina Fergusson, editor. *J. Ross Browne: His Letters, Journals and Writings.* Albuquerque: University of New Mexico Press, 1969.

Dillon, Richard H. *J. Ross Browne, Confidential Agent in Old California.* Norman, OK: University of Oklahoma Press, 1965.

Egan, Ferol. *Fremont, Explorer for a Restless Nation.* Garden City, NY: Doubleday & Company, 1977.

Heizer, Robert F. and Whipple, M. A., editors. *The California Indians.* Berkeley: University of California Press, 1978.

Heizer, Robert F., editor. *The Destruction of the California Indian.* Santa Barbara, CA: Peregrine Smith, Inc., 1974.

History of Fresno County , San Francisco: Elliot & Co., 1882.

Hull, Donna M. *And Then There Were Three Thousand.* Fresno, CA: published by author, 1975.

Keyes, E. D. *Fifty Years Observation of Men and Events.* New York: Charles Scribner's Sons, 1884.

Kroeber, A. L. *Handbook of the Indians of California.* New York: Dover Publications, Inc., 1953.

Latta, Frank F. *Handbook of Yokuts Indians.* Santa Cruz, CA: Bear State Books, 1977.

_____. *Tailholt Tales,* Santa Cruz, CA: Bear State Books, 1976.

Meighan, Clernent W. and Geiger, Maynard, editors. *As The Padres Saw Them.* Santa Barbara: Santa Barbara Mission Archive Library, 1976.

Smith, Wallace. *Garden of the Sun.* Fresno, CA: California History Books, 1960.

OTHER SOURCES

Browne, J. Ross. "The Coast Rangers," *Harpers New Monthly Magazine,* August 1861.

Report of the Commissioner of Indian Affairs, accompanying the Annual Report of the Secretary of the Interior for the Year 1854, Washington, 1860.

Chapter 17

JARBOE

With the establishment of the Nome Cult Indian farm in Round Valley, settlers began taking up land in the surrounding country almost immediately. Judge Hastings, and a rancher named H. L. Hall claimed all of nearby Eden Valley. Jackson Farley settled in Long Valley in May of 1857, along with Bill Frazier and several others. Ranchers and farmers lived in Redwood, Potter, and Scott's valleys, and all were raising crops and herding cattle, sheep, and hogs, which forced the Indians back into the mountains.

Simmon Storms felt very much at home in Round Valley. Besides being overseer at the Indian farm, he was building up his own place now, stocking it with cattle and sheep and beginning work on his hotel and store. With his Nevada Indians as the nucleus of his work force, he felt that he was doing quite well indeed. He saw nothing wrong in appropriating lumber and other supplies from the reserve for his own use. Superintendent Henley was doing the same thing. Both men obtained all the Indian labor they needed from among their wards on the reserve.

Storms was married in San Francisco, November 18, 1857. Quite probably, Sarah Stevens Storms had been the first white woman in the valley, arriving with her brother from Massachusetts. Young Henry Stevens went to work on his brother-in-law's farm, and was no doubt intent on making a place for himself in this new land.

Early in 1858, Henry Stevens, William Mantel, and a Nevada County Maidu Indian named Lucas drove a band of Storms' cattle down to Sonoma. The return trip to Round Valley, however, was to end in tragedy.

On Monday, February 22, the three men arrived at the south fork of the Eel River and found it to be a raging torrent. Tying their clothes to their saddles, the men rode into the water. Young Stevens lost control of his mount in midstream and his companions saw the horse's head go under. Mantel and the Indian watched helplessly as Stevens and his horse rolled over and over while being swept downstream. In a moment, both had disappeared, and Mantel and Lucas knew their companion was dead. After a difficult crossing themselves, the two men were chilled to the bone. They built a fire and camped beside the river that night. Both men dreaded the arrival at Storms' ranch, since they well knew how close young Stevens was to his sister.

"The next day," Storms wrote in a letter to Henley, "they came to the middle fork of Eel River, found that much higher than the other. In swimming their horses across, the white man's horse got lost in some drift wood [and] he swam down to him to get him out, when a party [about 20 in number] of Indians, who I suppose, had been watching them come down to the bank & shot him full of arrows. Lucas was about 100 yds above him...and...got away from the Indians and arrived at Bourne's that night...."

"As you may imagine, this is an awful blow to my dear wife to lose her brother. I don't think I ever saw brother and sister think as much of each other as they did...," continued Storms. "I hardly know how to tell his father of this sad news...."

In a work report dated March 8, Storms notes that a Round Valley posse had gone out and avenged Mantel's death by killing twelve Indians, although he gives no details of the incident.

H. L. Hall had come into Eden Valley in the summer of 1858, bringing in 320 head of stock for Judge Hastings and Henley. Besides running stock for the judge and superintendent, Hall operated his own farm, utilizing Indian labor whenever possible. When in need of supplies from one of the settlements, Hall and other ranchers made up a pack train of Indians and traveled to Sonoma, Bodega, or sometimes Tehama. One of these processions was noted by the editor of the Sonoma *County Journal* in April of 1860:

■ Henry Stevens, brother-in-law of Simmon Storms. *Peter Shearer.*

A Novel Pack Train—...[T]he party consisted of ten Indians, all the way from Long Valley, Mendocino county,' and were in the employ of Mr. Eland, who came down to procure a supply of groceries, provisions, clothing, etc. They belong to the Kipooma [probably northern Pomo] tribe. The train was supplied by I. D. Cross. Each one was packed with a load of about 125 lbs., which he has to carry 140 miles. The distance will be traversed inside of six days. This was their first trip to town, and their astonishment, surprise, and curiosity can be better imagined than described...."

Hall at one time employed thirteen Indians to pack goods back to his farm, promising each a shirt as payment. It was an eighty-mile round trip, and when the Indians returned with the supplies, Hall informed them that he had not yet received the shirts. When the natives complained, Hall whipped several of them, and they all fled.

In December, a friendly Yuki told Hall that one of his horses had been killed by Indians. Quickly rounding up some of his stock herders— Chesley "Texas" Vaughn, Charles McLane, and J. W. Smith—Hall rode over to where eighteen or twenty Indians were in camp. The whites galloped up and began shooting, killing between six and ten Indians, the balance fled into the surrounding brush and trees. One Indian was trapped in his wickiup and when ordered to come out, refused to do so. Hall then set fire to the hut and the native was shot down as he ran from his burning shelter.

"I think there was one or two squaws killed," recalled Tex Vaughn. McLane agreed, stating that "…I think one or two squaws were killed unintentionally." When the whites searched the camp, they reported finding horse meat, beef bones and hog's hair. Like so many Indian-hunting posses, Hall's men had shot first and looked for evidence later. Rancher William Pollard, who also worked on the reserve, once commented that cattle meat and hides in an Indian camp did not automatically make the inhabitants thieves: "have seen a great many cattle in the hills this winter that have died a natural death, as there was no signs of them being killed. The Indians eat these dead cattle, and the hides, and horns, and remains…might be found in an Indian rancheria without being evidence that the Indians had killed the cattle…."

Other ranchers testified that Indians frequently asked for the remains of dead stock. Still, by blaming the Indians, the ranchers could later make claims against the government for restitution.

By the summer of 1858, the Nome Cult farm had taken on the look of a prosperous, small community. Twenty log houses sheltered the Nevada Maidu and Yuba Indians—the Yuki still preferring their native shelters. There was a large storehouse, a building for the white employees, and a separate home for Storms and his wife. Some ten miles of fences surrounded a good harvest of wheat, rye, corn, and vegetables, and there were large corrals for the stock. The appearance of the farm gave little indication of the developing troubles in the area.

But there were other changes in the valley. That same summer, Storms commented that "venereal prevails to a considerable extent here among the Indians…whiskey is furnished to the Indians [and] it is impossible for me to prevent it…."

In November a gang of enraged settlers galloped up to Storms' house and demanded he produce a band of Indians who had been killing stock.

The agent had the suspected natives brought in from the hills and had an interpreter question them and point out the guilty Indians. When the designated men broke and ran, eight were shot down and a survivor hanged.

The same month, the Nome Cult Farm in Round Valley was elevated from being a subsidiary of Nome Lackee to a full-fledged reservation.

Other troubles plagued the reserve and were frequently mentioned in reports. As the settlers moved about the valley, they repeatedly tore down reserve fences, trampled crops, and often fed their stock on food raised by the Indians. Indian women were also constantly being stolen from the farm, since this was much easier than running one down in the mountains.

By late 1858, a total of four white men had been reported killed in the area by the Indians, while hundreds of natives had been killed by settler posses and in personal encounters. When Ben Arthur caught five Indians stealing supplies, he herded them off to the reservation. En route, one of the natives broke and ran, and when Arthur scuffled with him, he was attacked by the others. Arthur knocked two of the natives down and shot and killed another. He then resumed the trek to the reserve.

As a result of settler complaints and constant trouble on the reserve, a detachment of Sixth Infantry arrived in the valley in January 1859. The twenty-three soldiers were under the command of young Second Lieutenant Edward Dillon, who set up camp near reservation headquarters. Another small detachment of troops remained in Eden Valley under the command of Brevet Major Edward Johnson, who was in charge of both army units. Seeing the situation from a detached viewpoint, the two officers quickly determined that it was the natives, and not the whites, who needed protection.

Major Johnson had barely set up camp when a posse of local ranchers galloped up and dismounted. George White, the leader, told the officer that he was out hunting a band of Yukis who had camped next to his house one night and disappeared the next day with some hogs and other property. When he told Johnson he intended to kill the Indians when he caught them, the officer

■ Ben Arthur, one of the first settlers in the Round Valley area, saw much of the Indian troubles. *Ken Cornish.*

glared at him fiercely. If he heard of any such thing occurring, any whites involved would be arrested. After listening to the rancher's tales of past expeditions, Johnson told him there was to be no more indiscriminate Indian killing. The government would undoubtedly pay for any stock killed by Indians, if the ranchers would just be patient. The two men parted amicably, but each felt the other was decidedly wrong in his thinking.

■ George White, an early rancher in Round Valley, participated in much of the violence against the Indians. *Author's collection.*

Lieutenant Dillon had his baptism by fire in early February. One day, Jessie Henley and several Indians were skinning an ox on the reserve. Henry Brizantine, a local hard case, was standing nearby and without warning picked up a club and beat one of the natives senseless. The Indian had formerly worked for Brizantine, and the two had quarreled. Brizantine said the Indian had drawn a knife on him, but several witnesses stated that the Indian only had a knife in his hand because he was helping skin the ox. At the victim's and Storms' complaint, Dillon arrested Brizantine and quickly became aware of the polarization that existed in the valley.

The next day, twenty-five settlers galloped up to the army camp and demanded the release of the prisoner. Dillon told the mob he would fire into them if any attempt at rescue was made. As the two groups were arguing, Brizantine seized an opportunity to escape, and the young officer was off the hook.

"I did not attempt to arrest the prisoner again," Dillon noted in his report, "although he was in the valley, because I thought it proper to await further instructions…as it would be extremely hazardous with my small force at that time…."

In his report of the affair, Storms noted also that a few days earlier an Indian woman had been taken by force from the reserve. The perpetrator was apprehended and "kept under arrest for two days when he was released as no white man had witnessed the kidnapping. Just so long as [white] people are allowed to remain in the enclosure [valley], just so long shall we have trouble…."

As the valley became a steadily worsening battleground, Superintendent Henley found himself again under attack. The San Francisco *Daily Morning Call*, in commenting on the recent "Mint rascalities" uncovered by J. Ross Browne, added a long and bitter tirade against the superintendent and his management of Indian affairs.

The paper angrily demanded to know why such huge sums of money had been expended on the natives and still they remained naked and often starving on the reserves. "With good motives and justifiable ends," concluded the article, "we have directed the attention to the Commissioners to the general subject of Indian affairs, trusting that they will thoroughly sift the whole matter and put an effectual check upon the frauds that have been perpetrated in the name of the 'Poor Indian.'"

Henley was furious. That same day, February 19, 1858, deciding that the best defense is a good offense, he wrote to Commissioner of Indian Affairs Charles Mix, in Washington. Besides accusing the newspaper of attacking all federal officeholders in general, Henley invited the commissioner to have J. Ross Browne investigate his superintendency. It was a bad mistake. The treasury agent was soon poking his nose into every nook and cranny of Henley's burgeoning empire.

Browne found questionable practices and suspicious goings-on everywhere he looked on the reserves. On March 2, he and Henley traveled to the Mendocino Reservation, where the special agent made a number of startling discoveries. At the mouth of the Noyo River, he found a large new sawmill erected within the boundaries of the reserve. This was a private business owned by a man named McPherson, who claimed to have in-

■ An unidentified daguerreotype in the collection of a descendant of Simmon Storms. It was probably taken at Nome Cult Reservation in the late 1850s. Storms is thought to be the figure fourth from the left in this very rare California Indian image. *Peter Shearer.*

vested some $30,000 in the enterprise. Knowing it had always been the superintendent's purpose to separate the whites and Indians, Browne asked why the mill, and its attendant white workers, had been allowed to be located on the reserve. Henley responded that the mill was going to be built somewhere on the river and it was better to have it under his control.

Riding about the reserve, Browne saw that a store and hotel had also been erected. The store doubled as a saloon, and the agent strongly suspected Henley of being the silent owner. Travelers had to stay somewhere, commented the superintendent, and besides, it was "a small affair." A man named Dodge was the owner of record.

Within the native rancherias, Browne saw only a small percentage of the Indians reported to be living there. Subagent Ford had reported the previous August that some three thousand four hundred natives were living on the reserve, yet Browne estimated not more than three or four hundred were there during his visit. The Indians he did see were in a deplorable condition, all suffering from either illness or lack of food.

When Henley and Browne met with a group of thirty-five Indians in front of headquarters, the chief complained bitterly. "One word expresses their suffering," wrote investigator Browne—"hunger."

Browne was dumbfounded. Over a million and a half dollars had been expended to date in conducting the California superintendency and yet here were Indians apparently starving when crops had been raised, natural food had reportedly been gathered, and thousands of dollars had been expended hauling other provisions to the various reserves. And, in talking to other reservation employees, Browne was really startled.

Teamster Frank Warren testified that his horses were being starved to provide fodder for the teams hauling lumber to build the McPherson mill. Other employees stated that Indian food was being diverted to feed the mill workers, while carpenter L. F. Hinckley said that he worked on the mill while still drawing pay as a reservation employee. Bob White told Browne that Indians had actually died of starvation during the winter. G. L. Canning, the reservation clerk, testified that much of the reservation supplies had been given to the men engaged in building the mill. By this time, Browne strongly suspected Henley of having an interest in the mill himself. Other employees and witnesses refused to testify.

Back in San Francisco, his notebook bulging with information and affidavits, Browne wrote to his superiors that the evidence to date strongly suggests that Henley and his cronies were diverting Indian funds for their own use. He vigorously recommended a thorough further investigation.

In early August a special agent of the Interior Department named Godard Bailey arrived in San Francisco. After a tour of the two Mendocino reservations with both Browne and Henley, including interviews with everyone concerned, Bailey concurred in nearly all of Browne's findings. Henley's financial affairs, he concluded, were so confused and manipulated as to be impossible to sort out.

"If Colonel Henley had accepted office for the purpose of defrauding the government," wrote the agent, "he could not have devised a system better calculated to baffle investigation than that which obtains in every branch of the business of this Superintendency...."

Henley meanwhile fought back as best he could. He claimed inclement weather, resulting in supplies not being delivered to Mendocino, as the reason Indians were starving, but Browne and Bailey dug up vouchers proving food had been delivered—enough for many more Indians than were actually present. When witnesses recanted their testimony, Browne proved that they had later received a pay raise from Henley.

In a fourteen-page letter to Commissioner Mix in September, Henley found it impossible to explain his tangled financial affairs and business enterprises. He could only fall back on politics. "Knowing as I do," the letter closed, "personally the heads of the department, I have the most implicit confidence in whatever may be their judgement...." Now he could only wait and see. Meanwhile, all funds had been held up by the commissioner since June and would be for many months more.

Browne had particularly complained of Henley's assorted relatives, friends, and political cronies on the government payroll and recommended that all funds to "Special Agents" be stopped. He had quickly seen through this catchall office being used for political, as well as personal, payoffs.

The problem was exemplified by a petition received from eleven citizens of Tehama County. The petition charged that the agent at Nome Lackee, Vincent Geiger, was a drunkard who was living with a prostitute and who allowed his employees to rape Indian women—even in the presence of their husbands. Venereal disease was rampant, and the reserve was known locally as "the government whore house." At the same time, Geiger was accused of selling reservation crops for his own benefit as well as appropriating government materials.

■ George Henley, son of the superintendent, was another of the Round Valley ranchers.
Author's collection.

Finally dismissed from government service in July of 1860, Geiger remained active in politics. In October of 1863 he killed a man in Red Bluff during a drunken brawl and fled the country. Reportedly he died in Chile in 1869.

Troubles between the whites and Indians meanwhile became progressively worse. Early in March, a rancher named Gibson complained to Lieutenant Dillon that the Indians had taken some of his hogs. Taking ten men, Dillon found the trail and tracked the thieves to a hut near the forks of the Eel River. After surrounding the structure, Dillon had his interpreter yell to the inhabitants to come out, that they would not be hurt and would only be returned to the reservation. Several women emerged, but two men refused to leave the shelter. When one of the soldiers was ordered to try to knock down the hut with a pole, he was seriously wounded by an arrow. Dillon then fired the hut and shot the two Indians as they fled the burning structure.

"I do not blame the Indians, however," wrote Dillon in his report, "for I suppose they expected to be killed anyhow…as they have been deceived before…."

The following day, H. L. Hall and a group of men rode up to Dillon's headquarters on the reservation. Hall raged that the Indians had killed three cows and one of Hastings' stallions worth a thousand dollars. Dillon had nothing but contempt for Hall, but told him that he would go out after the Indians only if Hall and his men promised not to take matters into their own hands. Hall insisted that he only intended to bring the Indians in to the reserve and suggested that Dillon take some men down one side of the river, while his party patrolled the other bank. This plan was followed, but after seeing no Indians and being unable to cross the river, Dillon and his men returned to camp.

In a report dated March 23, 1859, Dillon reported that Hall had gone back on his word. "They have been for nearly two weeks hunting Indians and…it is currently reported here that 240 Indians were killed and I have been told by as reliable a man as there is in the valley that one of the party has said they killed that number."

When Hall returned, he made the mistake of asking Dillon what he intended to do about the matter. The officer told him he would do nothing to help him and he could expect no sympathy from him if the natives killed every head of stock in the valley. "He said," wrote the officer, "that the citizens intended to organize a company to go out and hunt the Indians to extermination, and I have no reason to doubt that it will be done."

In his report of the 23rd, Dillon also noted the rape of a young Indian girl on the reservation by a settler, and the killing of another Indian by Thomas B. Henley "because he looked like a bad Indian." Henley, a son of the superintendent, ranched in Round Valley with his brother, George. Both had worked for their father for years, but now were devoting full time to farming. Henley had also brought three Indians to the reserve, and Dillon sent word to the mountains that they had better all come in or be killed by the settler posses. In the next few days, nearly one hundred Indians reported in at the reserve, but it was an uneasy respite.

In April, Judge Hastings and a group of herders brought a thousand head of cattle into Eden Valley. The judge was appalled at the bloody state of affairs and the loss of his cattle and stallion. In conferring with Henley and other neighbors, he was informed that the soldiers were ineffectual against the Indians—that they actually took the part of the natives against their own kind. Other settlers told the Indian side of the story, but the judge found it difficult to think beyond the loss of his stock and future trouble. He was making a large investment in Eden Valley and something must be done.

Hastings quickly learned that both the military and most of the settlers disliked his foreman, Hall. He heard disquieting stories of Hall's Indian-killing expeditions—of his chasing them from their huts and poisoning their food. He was told that Hall insisted even the children be killed during his merciless forays. "A nit would make a louse," was the way Hall put it. Judge Hastings thought it expedient to fire his foreman immediately, which he did.

The jurist had no intention of putting up with Indian depredations, however, and he sent letters to his friend Governor Weller and General N. S. Clark, commander of the Department of the Pacific. He asked the army just what the disposition of troops was in the state, inquiring if any could be spared for duty in Mendocino.

To the governor, he complained of the inaction of the army and his stock losses. The settlers could not afford to continually take time off to fight Indians and the judge proposed organizing a volunteer group to be paid by the state. "I am attacked," wailed Hastings, "by the Indians in the front and the tax assessor in the rear." Many other petitions from ranchers in the area substantiated Hastings' complaints, although conditions were exaggerated outlandishly.

In March 1859, Colonel Henley was notified of his dismissal as super-intendent of California Indian affairs. He was replaced by James Y. McDuffie, who was to assume office in early June. Henley's empire had come tumbling down with a crash that made the Democratic Party cringe and his enemies cheer.

As usual, the Indians suffered most in this chaotic period, both during the investigations and later. Large cutbacks in employees on the reserves had been made. Storms saw the handwriting on the wall and resigned his position to work his ranch, hotel, and other interests. No Indian funds had been available since the preceding June, and Henley was being besieged by creditors, as well as his own agents who wanted to know how they were supposed to buy goods or pay their bills. The ex-superintendent would soon be sued by the hordes of merchants who had been caught up in the scandals.

Henley himself was no doubt relieved that the ordeal was finally over. He was through in politics, but he had not done too badly at that. Besides his ranches in Mendocino and San Mateo counties, he had a dairy farm outside San Francisco, interests in various other ranches, and several stores.

No doubt he had other irons in fire, also. Whether from a sense of self-banishment or a love of the wild, northern country, he wanted to stay in Mendocino, and after settling his affairs in San Francisco, he moved permanently to Eden Valley.

The ex-superintendent fully agreed with Hastings that a volunteer company should be raised to protect the ranchers' interests. Buck Lacock was approached by Henley to captain the proposed volunteers, who he hoped would eventually be funded by the state. Both Henley and Hastings agreed to guarantee the salaries of Lacock and his men until they were paid by the state, but Lacock shrugged and declined the offer. He, and other settlers, were to testify later that they did not trust either Hastings or Henley.

■ Serranus C. Hastings contributed greatly to the Round Valley Indian troubles. *California State Library.*

Casting about for another captain, the two prominent ranchers selected a tough local stockman named Walter S. Jarboe. Little is known of Jarboe, but he had a reputation locally as an Indian hater and reportedly had led an expedition the previous year which had killed sixty or more Indians at the Mendocino Reserve on the coast. Recently he had been wounded by an arrow while wiping out an Indian village, and he no doubt jumped at the chance to get paid for his murderous forays.

In a petition signed by Henley and twenty-eight settlers, Judge Hastings recommended Jarboe as the man to lead a volunteer force against the Indians. The petition claimed that at least twenty whites had been killed and some $40,000 worth of stock had been killed locally. Both figures were, of course, exaggerated. It was further claimed that persons traveling through Indian country were attacked "at sight." Governor Weller passed the petition along to the army for investigation. Major Johnson and Lieutenant Dillon were well aware of the situation, and after looking into the charges, Johnson replied to the governor in a report dated May 1, 1859: "The Yukas have not been, for the last two years, nor are they now, at open war with the whites; But the whites have waged a relentless war of extermination against the Yukas, making no distinction between the innocent and guilty."

■ Dryden "Buck" Lacock came to Round Valley with Simmon Storms and was an early rancher and Indian fighter. *Author's collection.*

The report went on to state that only two whites, not twenty, had been killed and they had deserved their fate; that it was generally believed that some six hundred Indians had been killed the past year, and that only a small fraction of the stock reported stolen or killed by the Indians had actually met that fate. On the contrary, much of the stock that had been reported stolen had since been found, or had died of natural causes.

Major Johnson further noted that it was untrue that white men were attacked "on sight" by the Indians. "I have repeatedly sent single expressmen through the country who have encamped in the Indian country without molestation," he recalled. The report related a series of bloody massacres in which the settlers had wiped out large groups of Indians. "The Indians, and not the whites, need protection," noted the major. The army report emphatically dismissed the atrocity reports and enclosed a counter petition from other Round Valley residents denying the outlandish tales of Indian troubles.

Not content with the army report, Governor Weller asked that Captain F. F. Flint of the 6th U.S. Infantry proceed to the scene of trouble. Flint's report indicated there was indeed an Indian problem, and he recommended formation of a volunteer group. As strong political figures and big taxpayers, Henley and Hastings were undoubtedly making their power felt with both Flint and the governor. Still, Weller held back in authorizing the volunteers.

Hastings and Henley agreed to become responsible for provisions, and Jarboe set out to put his company in shape. Lacock had previously organized a group and Jarboe now had merely to see to their outfitting. In this he had his own peculiar ideas.

It had already been decided that the volunteers would be fed with Hastings beef for which the judge would later bill the state. Jarboe and Bill Robertson, one of his men, were observed butchering a steer. They used no scales. The men simply guessed the weight of the beef, and when the steer was judged to weigh four hundred pounds, Jarboe told Robertson to put down seven hundred, as the state had to pay the bill, not them. The captain also told Robertson to charge the rangers six bits every time they ate at his place.

Jarboe also made an interesting proposition to rancher William Scott. He suggested that Scott supply the volunteers with "liquor, cigars, oysters, sardines, crackers, white shirts, and cards." The plan was that Jarboe would not be involved in the sale of these items, but that Scott should charge a good price, and the profits would be divided between the two of them and Robertson. Jarboe also offered to cut Scott in on his beef-weighing scheme. And so preparations for the coming campaign moved right along.

It was not until July 11 that Jarboe called his men together and drew up an official roster of the volunteers. They called themselves the "Eel River Rangers," and seventeen men were recorded as being members. Included were H. L. Hall, W. J. Hildreth, Charles Bourne, Bill Robertson, and others who had been active in campaigning against the natives. The men met in Eden Valley and, with the blessings of Hastings and Henley, began scouting the country.

By the middle of August, Jarboe was making his presence felt in the mountains. He had attacked several rancherias, killing a reported fifty Indians, including men, women, and children. He had also taken a number of prisoners, who were delivered to the coast reservation.

Hoping to involve the military and lend authority to his own actions, Jarboe wrote a letter to Major Johnson on August 13. Noting that he had proof of the cattle-stealing activities of a group of Indians, Jarboe wanted to show Major Johnson the camp and have the situation "taken in hand" by the army. He sent the letter by messenger to Johnson's camp.

Jarboe's letter, with Major Johnson's terse reply scribbled at the bottom, can still be found in the California State Archives. "I received," wrote

Jarboe, "a verbal reply from the major by my messenger...stating I was not worthy of notice and he (Major Johnson) wished the Indians would kill me."

The major was well aware of Jarboe's activities and complained of his actions in a letter to the governor. He noted that in their last attack on a rancheria, the rangers had killed six men, four women, and four children. Weller was disturbed by the letter and wrote Jarboe telling him that "women and children must under all circumstances be spared."

Despite any reservations he might have, on September 6, 1859, Governor Weller wrote Jarboe giving his official authorization for the rangers. A twenty-man force was sanctioned, and Jarboe was admonished to try to cooperate with the military, buy provisions at the lowest possible price and report "from time to time."

Jarboe immediately replied, stating that he had "mustered into the service of the state of California, 20 men mounted on horseback and armed with rifles and pistols, accustomed to warfare and frontier life." In the report, Jarboe told of his recent activities, noting that he had to date killed sixty-two Indians and taken approximately forty-eight prisoners. He listed the names of the rangers and suggested that with forty men in the field he could do his job much faster. Jarboe had been wounded in the shoulder on August 14, and one of his men had been arrowed in the neck. Neither man's wounds were serious, however.

On the 25th of September, the rangers had a fight near the forks of the Eel River, Jarboe reporting twenty-five Indians killed and twenty prisoners taken. Three freshly killed horses were discovered in the camp. On the 28th, Jarboe reported capturing thirty more Indians without firing a shot.

Early in October, word was received that John Bland, a former ranger, had been killed by some Wailaki Indians. There are several versions of Bland's death, but all generally agree he was captured and burned to death. Some settlers maintained that Bland was killed after whipping some Indians who had broken into his cabin, but army reports added more to the story. A young Indian girl, "better looking than most," had attracted Bland's attention, and she had been stolen from her people. After living with Bland for two months, the girl escaped, but Bland tracked her back to the Nome Cult Reserve. That night, Bland broke into the building where the girl was confined and again carried her off. Numerous reports of similar occurrences lend credence to this story. The girl once more escaped her captor, and it

■ Major Edward Johnson tried desperately to curb the Indian violence, with little success. *National Archives.*

was while Bland was again tracking her in the mountains that a band of Wailakis found him.

When Jarboe heard of Bland's death, he asked for assistance from the military detachment in Round Valley. Lieutenant Dillon still would have nothing to do with him and wrote back saying that he must "respectfully decline to cooperate with you against the Indians."

Undeterred by Dillon's latest refusal of aid, Jarboe again took to the field. On the 12th of October, the rangers found the Bland's remains when an Indian woman guided them to the spot. That same night Jarboe and his men attacked an Indian rancheria about twenty-five miles north of Round Valley. After a typical ambush in which eleven male Indians were killed, the rangers took six warriors and twenty-seven women as prisoners. According to Jarboe's report, these Indians confessed to killing Bland and also to stealing a number of horses.

On the way to the reservation, Jarboe stopped to camp in Eden Valley. At midnight his prisoners escaped and only fourteen of them were recaptured. After this incident, Jarboe tied all his captives together until they were delivered to the reserve.

Jarboe attacked another Indian village on the 23rd and, after killing nine, took thirty prisoners. On the 25th he surrounded a village containing some seventy Indians. These he persuaded to surrender and all were taken to the Mendocino Reserve. In his report of October 28, Jarboe noted that one of his men had been discharged for "improper conduct with a squaw."

During November, Jarboe kept up his relentless pressure on the Indians. W. T. Scott was induced to join the rangers, but after five days he had had enough. He later recalled that Jarboe's orders were to kill all male Indians. The first Indians they came upon were unarmed and gathering acorns. Despite Jarboe's orders to his men to get close enough to be sure of killing them, one of the natives escaped. After seeing two other Indians ambushed in the same way, Scott quit the volunteers in disgust.

Jarboe split his command on November 18, taking ten men to Long Valley, while Benjamin Birch took eight men to Round Valley to look into complaints there. Attacking a rancheria on the south Eel River, Jarboe's group killed three warriors and took six prisoners. Birch and his men attacked a village at dawn and killed nine of the inhabitants. As in previous reports, Jarboe noted that a "lot of beef was found in their huts which established their guilt."

It was a bitterly cold northern California winter, and the rangers had by now built several crude cabins to use as winter headquarters. The camp was located a few miles south of Round Valley on a promontory still known as Jarboe Ridge.

Despite the rain and snow, the rangers stayed doggedly on the trail of the hapless natives. On November 24, five horses were reported killed and Indians were seen butchering them. Jarboe sent Birch and a detachment of men to scout the area, and late that night, they located a large rancheria. The rangers were discovered approaching the camp, but they quickly charged in among the wickiups, killing several Indians and capturing nine squaws and children.

Birch had an interpreter with him, and the captured women told him that the guilty Indians were camped half a mile away in another canyon. Taking the prisoners along, Birch and his men pounced on the other Indian camp and, after a bloody fight, reported killing eighteen warriors. Some of the stolen horse flesh was reportedly found in the camp. With no one to guard them, the prisoners all escaped during the fight and the tired and hungry rangers returned to headquarters empty-handed.

Governor Weller had become increasingly disturbed at both the official and newspaper reports of the fighting in Mendocino. In another letter to Jarboe he warned the ranger captain not to "wage a war of extermination against a whole tribe…try to punish only the guilty."

Photograph of an unidentified Indian village in Mendocino County. Jarboe and his men were ruthless in ambushing and killing the inhabitants, then burning the rancheria. *California Department of Parks and Recreation.*

In his sixth official report, written on December 3, Jarboe took great pains to allay the governor's fears. "All attempts made to get them to come in and have a friendly talk with a view to entice them to cease their depredations and become friends...have so far proved utterly fruitless." Jarboe added that the "Indians roaming in that region...are without doubt the most degraded, filthy, miserable, thieving set of anything living that comes under the head and rank of human being."

Warming to his subject, Jarboe continued his report, noting that "They are so inferior in intellect, so divorced of feeling that they stand by coolly and unmoved and see their companions shot down by scores without evincing the least symptoms of sorrow and boldly avow their determination to continue their hostilities and kill our citizens and attack them so long as they live. ...They have had repeated lessons taught them since my company has been organized.... It seems that however cruel it may be that nothing short of extermination will suffice to rid the country of them, to make them cease their thieving and murderous course." After again complaining of the lack of cooperation from Lieutenant Dillon, Jarboe concluded his report.

Not content with Jarboe's merciless forays, other ranchers were also leading attacks on the natives. Jackson Farley took a group of forty ranchers out for a period of twenty-two days. Evidently, they killed every Indian they came across, although Farley claimed to have taken twenty-two prisoners. His total of slain Indians was recorded at between one hundred fifty and two hundred.

Early in December, Jarboe sent Birch and eight men out along the Eel River to hunt Indians who had reportedly been killing stock. Coming upon a small rancheria of several huts, the rangers quickly surrounded the largest shelter and called upon the inhabitants to surrender. During the resulting fight, the Indians fought back desperately, even after the shelter had been fired. Seven natives were either shot down as they fled from the burning hut, or died in the flames. The rangers, as usual, sustained no casualties. The three prisoners, who were taken, managed to escape several nights later.

At about this same time, Jarboe sent Lieutenant Bill Poole out for a scout around the south fork of the Eel River. Coming upon a large band of Indians, Poole ordered an attack and expected the usual rout as the Indians fled for their lives. To his surprise, the Indians stood their ground and loosed volley after volley of arrows. Jarboe was to report later that this group of Indians was the remnant of several rancherias that had been "chastised" by the rangers on former occasions. Not used to such resistance, the rangers were startled for a moment, but rallied and pressed their assault. Poole received an arrow in the thigh, but continued to fire. Two other rangers were also wounded by arrows.

The Indians kept up an "unearthly" war whoop during the engagement and fought until nearly all were dead or wounded. Jarboe reported thirty Indians killed in this most desperate fight of the campaign.

This battle seemed to indicate that many Indians were resigned to their fate and had determined to die fighting. They faced a Hobson's choice of starvation, ranger bullets in the mountains, or a more lingering fate on the reservation. Disease and hunger stalked them on the reserves, while their women were being abducted and Indian food and property was being stolen by unscrupulous government agents.

It is not hard to believe the story of an army officer of the time who recalled an Indian coming to him for protection. "You ask us to come on the reservation," said the native, "and tell us that we will not be molested. We

Account of Indian Slaughters, etc., in the North.

Round Valley, Cal., October 15, 1861.

Editor Bulletin:—As there will probably be various versions of the late Indian difficulties in this region, I hasten to give a connected account of them, as your paper has such an extensive circulation throughout the State.

For some time past an armed band of Indians have been prowling about the mountains in the Coast Range, killing cattle and any unprotected traveler who might fall in their way. Two weeks ago, a company of men from Long Valley sallied out to chastise these Indians. While on their route to Round Valley, they found the body of a man, partly consumed, in the ashes; also a dog, wearing a collar on his neck, was found dead, shot by an arrow in the eye. This was at the forks of Eel River. Eight citizens of Round Valley joined this party, which has not yet returned. These Indians have driven a large amount of stock from Long Valley, have burned one house there, and set fire to another, and have threatened to exterminate the settlers in Long and Round valleys. Within a few weeks horses, cattle and hogs have been missed from various ranches in Round Valley. On the 10th instant, cattle and hogs were taken from the north end of the valley, and on the night of the 11th a band of 40 mares, with a fine stallion, valued at $1,000, were driven from the same place. Eight carcasses were found within half a mile from the Valley.

A party of 10 white men, under command of Captain Charles Baume, with 50 picked Indians—of the Pitt River, Hat Creek and Concow tribes—from the Nome Cult farm, followed the trail of the Indians about 14 miles, when they camped for the night. At intervals along this trail they found the bodies of 31 horses. The next morning, they left their horses at the camp and walked about 10 miles, over a rough trail, crossing Eel River twice. On descending a steep bank, near the bed of the

San Francisco *Bulletin*, October 23, 1861.

304

have been there, and our brothers, our wives, and our children have been killed. We do not know in whom to believe; we have lost faith in everything but death."

Others told much the same story. Rancher William Pollard recalled how a terrified Indian came up to him one day and asked why "the whites punished and drove off and killed those that behaved themselves, in place of those that were doing the devilment."

On the order of Governor Weller, Jarboe disbanded his rangers early in January 1860. They had done their work well, and the troublesome Indians were either on the reservations, scattered, or dead. On February 18, Jarboe reported to the newly elected governor, John G. Downey, giving a brief summary of his campaign. He reported twenty-three engagements, resulting in the death of 283 warriors and the capture of 292 prisoners.

Jarboe's report included more than just a recital of his deeds. It was also a bill to the state for services rendered. For the five-month period of ranger service, Jarboe submitted a bill for $11,143.43. Considering the value of the dollar in those days, the rangers had done quite well for themselves.

But Jarboe and his men had focused the attention of the state on their "war" in Mendocino County. Newspapers had noted the carnage, some merely reporting the action, but others denouncing the ruthless destruction of human lives. The state legislature formed a Joint Special Committee on the Mendocino Indian War and dispatched an investigative group north. By the middle of February, depositions were being taken at Ukiah, Round Valley, and at individual ranches in the Eel River country. All of the characters involved in the troubles were allowed to tell their own version of the events of the past few years. Testimony was so contradictory that little was established at the time, beyond the fact of the extreme factionalization of the Round Valley area.

An examination of the settler depositions, given the perspective of time, points clearly to the fact that the whites wanted the Indians removed, one way or another, from what they considered was grazing land for their stock. These ranchers had been trying to drive out the Indians for years, blaming every head of stock that strayed, was lost, or died of natural causes on the natives, in an effort to involve the military in the trouble.

Lieutenant Dillon investigated reports of Indian theft time and again, only to find them false. He noted that, contrary to settler claims that over $100,000 worth of stock had been killed by the Indians, the sworn list of taxable property in the valley had only amounted to about $30,000. "This glowing absurdity," he wrote, "needs no comment...."

In revenge, and to stave off starvation, the Indians probably finally did take to killing stock, feeling that they might as well enjoy the fruits of what they were being punished for.

In their depositions, the settlers made no effort to cloak the bloody treatment afforded the natives. Ben Arthur testified that when he discovered an Indian boy had been stealing from his cabin, he rigged up a booby trap whereby the boy was shot and wounded during his next attempt at robbery. A few days later, he found the boy lying wounded in front of another rancher's cabin. "I spoke to him," testified Arthur, [but] "he refused to answer me and laid still; I then shot him in the head and killed him."

The laconic Jackson Farley was more subtle in reporting an attempt to punish some Indian stock thieves. When the Indian agent did not give him satisfaction, Farley took a posse out. "Those Indians are there yet," he bragged. "They are not killing any stock now that I know of."

Some ranchers related other aspects of the troubles. W. T. Scott testified that although he had lived among hordes of Indians in nearby Scott's Valley, they never bothered his stock nor did he feel any danger. "These Indians often visit my house," he recalled. "I have treated them kindly, and in a conciliatory manner, and to this fact I attribute the safety of my stock from Indian depredations."

Other ranchers testified in much the same vein and were corroborated by the army officers stationed in the area. An article in the San Francisco *Daily Alta California* in October 1859 called attention to an old man named Armstrong who was living alone on a ranch on the south fork of the Eel River. He ran about six hundred head of stock, and although his nearest neighbor was forty miles away, "the Indians never trouble him."

The ranger actions, however, had left much to be desired, whatever their motives. Jarboe and his men mounted their campaign in the fall so as to be able to track the natives to their winter quarters. It was bitter weather and the men deserved much credit for their determination. Their methods, however, were something else. The very fact that in twenty-three engagements only five rangers were slightly wounded says volumes as to how the group operated. It seems clear the rangers took no chances and all of Jarboe's "attacks" were in reality bloody ambushes in which men, women, and children were frequently shot down without warning.

In order to further establish credibility for his actions, Jarboe lied in his report to the governor. He repeated the fable of nineteen citizens having been killed up to the time his rangers had been organized. This figure was

refuted by army reports, settler depositions, and even by people sympathetic to the ranger actions.

Jarboe was always careful to mention in his reports that carcasses of cattle and horses were found in the Indian camps he attacked. Plainly, he could not have discovered the dead animals until after the attack, which substantiates the fact that the rangers shot first and asked questions later.

A majority of the state investigating committee came to this conclusion: "In relation to the recent difficulty between the whites and Indians in Mendocino County, your committee desires to say that no war, or a necessity for a war, has existed, or at the present time does exist. We are unwilling to attempt to dignify by the term 'war' a slaughter of beings…who make no resistance, and make no attacks, either on the person or residence of the citizen."

In the opinion of the committee, if all of Round Valley had been set apart for the Indians, instead of just the northern portion, trouble could have been averted. Perhaps they were right, but it no longer mattered to the Yuki and Wailaki. Jarboe's rangers and dozens of other posses had seen to that. Although the committee recommended laws that would protect the Indian in California, little was ever done. On the contrary, that very year an indenture law was enacted which made it possible for a white man to keep an Indian as a virtual slave.

Lieutenant Dillon, writing to a superior in May of 1860, gave a final report on the tragedy in Round Valley:

It might have been supposed that the settlers, being satisfied that it is the intention of Government to reserve the entire valley, would have stayed the hands of slaughter…. But not so. Several parties have recently been on expeditions against him, and only a short time before leaving I was informed by an Indian that a large camp near the forks of Eel River had been attacked on the day previous, and that he alone had escaped. The monster Hall, so frequently reported for his atrocities, was said by the Indian to have been of the party. This man of devilish attributes, assisted for a time by Jarboe's company, has well nigh depopulated a county which but a short time since swarmed with Indians.

Only a day or two after this attack, a man named Dodge fell upon an Indian and, with a hatchet literally chopped him to pieces. The only charge against the Indian was that he had stolen a knife. The same day…a wretch named Vaughn, alias Texas…violated the person of an Indian woman…in the presence of a white man.

When a mix-up of commas and periods in a legislative report made it seem as if Major Johnson were accusing Colonel Henley and his sons of killing Indians on the flimsiest of pretexts, the ex-superintendent was furious. "I have never killed an Indian in my life," he snorted, and referring to Johnson, noted that the officer "…too, is perfectly guiltless of having killed an Indian, though stationed in a country where, within the past two years, fifteen or twenty white men have been killed…." The critical differences separating the two sides was emphasized by an item in the *Sonoma County Journal* on March 30:

> It appears that young Henley challenged Lieutenant Dillon to mortal combat, through a note dispatched by the hand of Captain Storms. Dillon refused to receive the note; whereupon Storms made him acquainted with its contents, and demanding to know whether or not the lieutenant considered Henley a gentleman….

Although white tempers gradually simmered down, the Indian troubles were to persist for some years in northern Mendocino. But the story was told. The actors in the raw and bloody scenes of 1856 to 1860 lived out their lives, little realizing the devastating import of their actions in the drama of Round Valley.

Colonel Henley, his political career destroyed, spent the rest of his life on his Mendocino ranch. Tradition has him conveniently losing all his superintendency records while trying to cross a rain-swollen Eel River one spring. He died on his ranch of "softening of the brain" in 1875, his sons continuing to work the land in quiet obscurity.

Simmon Storms resigned from the Indian service during the summer of 1859 and built a race track to add to his Round Valley enterprises. The 1860 census lists his real estate and property values at over $100,000, but he later sold out and engaged in business in Central America, where he died of tuberculosis in 1865.

■ Jackson Farley probably killed more Indians than any of the other ranchers, and he had the scalps to prove it.
Author's collection.

308

■ This view of the Nome Cult reservation was taken in the 1880s and shows an ox team standing in front of one of the agency buildings. *Rena Lynn.*

Lieutenant Dillon and Major Johnson both fought through the Civil War as Confederate officers, while Walter Jarboe died unexpectedly in March of 1865 at Ukiah. Perhaps surprisingly, Jarboe's widow gave her indentured Indians their freedom shortly after her husband's death.

Jackson Farley was living at Cahto in 1899. "Uncle Jack" insisted to a reporter that he never killed any Indians, but had "stopped" a good many. The newsman was startled when the old man showed him a collection of nearly fifty scalps, plus a razor strop and a chair made from "Indian hide."

Judge Hastings became eminently successful and died a millionaire philanthropist. In 1878, he endowed a San Francisco law school with $100,000. A kind fate ignored the selfish part he played in a cruel and senseless Indian war and made the Hastings School of Law his monument.

CHAPTER 17 / SOURCES

The authority on northern Mendocino County history was the late Mr. Estle Beard of Covelo. Mr. Beard graciously shared his vast knowledge and research materials with the author for many years, and our ongoing exchange of information has shed light on many dim aspects of those faraway times. The generous, late Pat Jones of Chicago Park was also most helpful, as was Peter Shearer. Jarboe's War is one of the few well-documented Indian episodes of California history, primarily because of the legislative investigation and the resulting documentation which followed.

UNPUBLISHED MATERIAL

National Archives, Records of the office of Indian Affairs, California Superintendency, Record Group 75, M234:

Thomas J. Henley to Charles E. Mix, February 19, March 5, September 13, 14, 1858.

Simmon P. Storms to Thomas J. Henley (work report) March 8, 1858.

J. Ross Browne report to the U.S. Treasury Department, April 19, 1858.

J. Ross Browne to Commissioner of Indian Affairs, May 4, July 2, 1858.

Simmon P. Storms (statement), August 11, 1858,

J. Ross Brown to Charles E. Mix, October 16, 1858,

Godard Bailey to Charles E. Mix, October 27, 1858,

Thomas J. Henley to James W. Denver, December 18, 1858,

Simmon P. Storms to Thomas J. Henley, February 15, 1859,

Thomas J. Henley to J. Ross Browne, June 16, 1859,

Lieutenant Edward Dillon to Major W. W. Mackall. May 16, 1860,

Petition, Tehama County citizens to Secretary of Interior, 1859,

Office of the Secretary of State, California State Archives, Indian War Files, Sacramento:

Petition of nine Eel River area residents to Governor John B. Weller, April 24, 1859.

Serranus C. Hastings to John B. Weller (two petitions) April, 30, 1859.

Petition of 30 Mendocino settlers to Governor John B. Weller, June 10, 1859.

William Robertson to Governor John B. Weller, July 11, 1859.

Walter Jarboe to Major Edward Johnson, August 13, 1859.

Major Edward Johnson to Major W. W. Mackall, August 21, 1859.

Governor John B. Weller to Walter Jarboe, September 6, 1859.

Walter Jarboe to Governor John B. Weller, September 16, October 1, 16, 28, December 3, 5, 20, 1859.

Walter Jarboe to Serranus C. Hastings, October 7, 1859.

Lieutenant Edward Dillon to Walter Jarboe, October 8, 1859.

Walter Jarboe to Lieutenant Edward Dillon, October 8, 1859.

Walter Jarboe to Governor John G. Downey, February 18, 1860.

Beard, Estle, to the author, 1970-1978.

Garrett, Gary E., "The Destruction of the Indian in Mendocino County, 1856-1860," M.A. thesis, Sacramento State College, copy on file in California State Archives, Sacramento.

Jones, Pat, to the author, 1972-1980.

Thompson, Elsa, to the author, September 4, October 23, 1970.

Richardson, Viola, Mendocino County Clerk, to the author, July 23, 1970.

NEWSPAPERS

San Francisco *Daily Alta California*, April 13, September 24, 1857; October 14, December 20, 1858; October 14, 1859.

The *Daily Evening Bulletin*, January 14, 1860.

The San Francisco *Daily Morning Call,*, February 19, 1858.

San Francisco *Examiner*, January 29, 1899.

Sonoma County Journal, July 29, August 19, October 7, 1859; February 17, March 30, April 13, 1860.

Colfax Record, April 13, 1978.

PRINCIPAL PUBLISHED WORKS

Bancroft, Hubert H. *History of California, Vol. VI*. San Francisco: The History Company, Publishers, 1887.

Browne, Lina Fergusson. *J. Ross Browne: His Letters, Journals and Writings.* Albuquerque: University of New Mexico Press, 1969.

Dillon, Richard H., *J. Ross Browne; Confidential Agent in Old California*, Norman: University of Oklahoma Press, 1965

Heizer, Robert F., editor. *They Were Only Diggers*. Ramona, CA: Ballena Press, 1974.

_____. *Destruction of California Indians*. Santa Barbara: Peregrine Smith, Inc., 1974.

Hittell, Theodore H. *History of California, Vol. III*. San Francisco: H. J. Stone & Company, 1898.

History of Mendocino County, California. San Francisco: Alley, Bowen and Company, 1880.

Kroeber, A. L. *Handbook of the Indians of California*. New York: Dover Publications, Inc., 1953.

Potter, David M., editor. *Trail to California: The Overland Journal of Vincent Geiger and Wakeman Bryarly.* New Haven, CT: Yale University Press, 1945.

OTHER SOURCES

Appendix to the Journals of the Senate of the Eleventh Session of the Legislature of the State of California, Sacramento, 1860.

Beard, Estle. "The Settlement of Round Valley," *Mendocino County Historical Society Newsletter,* Vol. 3, No. 6, Vol. 4, (no date).

Browne, J. Ross. "The Coast Rangers," *Harpers New Monthly Magazine,* August, 1861.

Potter, Elijah R. "Reminiscences of the Early History of Northern California, and of the Indian Troubles," manuscript in the Bancroft Library, Berkeley.

Rogers, Fred. "Bear Flag Lieutenant—Henry L. Ford," *California Historical Society Quarterly,* June, September, December, 1950; March, June, 1951.

Tassein, A. G. "Chronicles of Camp Wright," *Overland Monthly,* July, 1887.

Chapter 18

HUMBOLDT BAY

North of Mendocino County, up the Eel River and beyond to the Mad River country, there was sporadic trouble
interrupted only by the bitter weather of 1856-1857. In February of 1858, a black man was camped with his Indian
woman near Angel's ranch in Humboldt County. Known
to history only as "Leroy," he was a typical tough frontiersman of the period and lived a wild, free life not much
above the level of the Indians. His mate was either a Mad River or Redwood Indian, the white names for the Whilkut and Chilula who peopled
the area. When the woman decided to leave her paramour, Leroy objected,
and the two quarreled violently. Two Indian relatives took up the woman's
cause and jumped Leroy one day at his camp. Fighting for his life, he managed to kill both his assailants, but was badly wounded. Leroy had lost a
lot of blood when he later dragged himself into the Angel ranch.

A posse was quickly organized, and a nearby Indian rancheria was
threatened and made to return the contents of Leroy's plundered camp.
Reportedly, it was discovered at this time that these same Indians had killed
two whites who had disappeared the previous year. When the whites left
the rancheria with Leroy's goods, both groups were bitter and threatening
war.

Late in June, a white man was shot down on the Trinity Trail, and a
short time later two packers were ambushed and one of them dangerously
wounded. The latter shooting was noted by an army officer as originating
in the stealing and selling of an Indian woman by the two whites. Whatever the origin, volunteer groups were soon in the field. Leading a party of
sixteen, John Bell attacked a rancheria on Grouse Creek, killing several warriors. While leaving the area, Bell was ambushed and one of his men was
killed. Not knowing how many Indians they were up against, Bell and his
men retreated back to camp, only to find the natives had been there ahead
of them. All their stock and supplies had been stolen, and Bell led his exhausted party to Pardee's ranch to await reinforcements.

On the 2nd of August, another group of volunteers struck the trail of these same Indians, but again the whites were decoyed into an ambush. Mr. Winslet, leader of the posse, was shot through the thigh but led his men in a charge against the Indian positions. A running fight took place and one Chauncy Miller was shot dead before the whites pulled back to Pardee's.

As the volunteers licked their wounds, they were disturbed at the thought that, although some Indians had been killed, two whites were dead in the fighting, also. This was not the usual scenario, and they did not like it. Too, many of the Indians had guns now, not merely bows and arrows. When reports were received that whites were selling guns to the hostiles, the volunteers could only exchange curses. Actually, unless they could obtain some official status from the governor, they would not even be paid for their risks!

In the frontier settlements at Eureka and Union on Humboldt Bay, taxes were levied to pay the costs of war. Governor Weller, inundated by settler petitions for protection, wrote to the commander of the Department of the

Pacific and asked for troops, but was told none were available. Undaunted, Weller sent state Adjutant General William C. Kibbe north to Weaverville. There he was to organize a volunteer company. As if to emphasize the sorry state of affairs, in mid-September a settler named Boynton was killed just ten miles from Union, and it was on the next day that Indians drove off the inhabitants of Pardee's ranch.

Fort Humboldt had been established on the bay in January of 1853, and was at this time was under the command of Major Gabriel J. Rains. Like so many of the frontier army officers, Rains disliked being forced into Indian fighting if he could avoid it. He knew whites had been killed, but he also knew that most trouble originated with white men who treated Indians like dogs and believed they should all be exterminated. He was roundly criticized for his inaction, but was determined to keep a low profile. When the town of Union itself had an Indian scare, Rains could no longer dodge the problem and a thirty-six-man detachment was stationed at Pardee's ranch for escort duty.

■ Major Gabriel J. Rains, Fort Humboldt's commander, was later a Confederate general during the Civil War. *The National Archives.*

In Trinity County, General Kibbe enlisted a seventy-man company at Weaverville, and another eighty-man group at Big Bar. This latter unit was under the command of Isaac G. Messec, a veteran of the Texas border wars as well as the northern California Indian troubles.

Captain Messec engaged in his first fight near Pardee's place late in October of 1858, when he killed four natives and took several prisoners. Keeping up the pressure, Messec and his men tracked the Indians to their winter quarters, where more were killed and twenty-six captured. Shortly after this, some eighty more Indians were captured as Messec hounded them from one locale to another. After a number of brisk engagements, Messec suddenly found himself in the uncomfortable position of being outnumbered by his prisoners. He was relieved in February, after sending 121 of his prisoners from Humboldt Bay by steamer to the Mendocino Reserve.

■ Captain Isaac Messec was a Mexican War veteran and noted northern California pioneer. *Siskiyou County Museum.*

Superintendent Henley had done his best to ignore all the Humboldt troubles and hoped they would somehow dissolve. His annual report, written at the height of the troubles, said that "it is gratifying to be able to state that a condition of uninterrupted peace prevails among the Indians in every portion of the state...."

The weather in January and February of 1859 was particularly severe, and in the mountains, the Indians could do little more than try to stay sheltered. Only limited fighting occurred, and when the volunteers finally surprised a rancheria, the starving Indians sullenly surrendered.

General Kibbe obtained the services of some friendly Hoopa Indians who initiated a partially successful conference with the hostiles at Big Lagoon. On March 15, a second group of 160 prisoners boarded a ship and were taken to Mendocino. With nearly three hundred Indians removed to the reserve and nearly one hundred killed in the field, on March 20, Kibbe declared the war at an end. The volunteers were disbanded and went back to work, but they anxiously awaited word on compensation for their efforts.

In early April, Governor Weller sent a message to the legislature asking for not only the pay authorized by law, but an additional allowance because of the "great hardships" endured by the troops. "A just and liberal spirit on the part of the state will always secure volunteers when Indian disturbances occur," he concluded. A bill was quickly passed and $52,000 was appropriated, enabling General Kibbe to pay off his troops in full in May 1859.

But even as the volunteers were being paid, Governor Weller was again the recipient of sheaves of petitions from settlers in the northern end of the Sacramento Valley. From Red Bluff to Tehama, stock was reported stolen and killed and around-the-clock guards were being maintained to prevent Indians from firing the ripening grain fields. Weller was frustrated at the unending Indian problems, and he dispatched a letter to General Clarke of the Department of the Pacific.

The trouble had originated several years earlier in the antics of a brutal class of settlers who were continually stirring up Indian troubles in the state. Captain Henry Judah had reported one such incident in a letter to a superior in April of 1858. A man named Bill Macon had killed several Indians and stolen and then discarded a number of native women at his claim on Butte Creek. When Macon disappeared one day, his partner, a man named Corby, organized a posse and pounced on the first Indian hut they found. Five Indians were inside, and the whites dragged one out and roughly questioned him about Macon's disappearance. When the native professed ignorance about what they were talking about, he was tied up and thrown in some bushes.

When the next Indian was dragged out of the hut, he already had the drift of what was going on. "Seeing he was in a tight fix," reported the *Red Bluff Beacon*, "without any means of extricating himself, and having concealed in his clothing a pistol, he resolved to sell his life as dearly as possible, and accordingly commenced firing at his captors, wounding one, it is supposed mortally. At the first report of the pistol, a man who was left to watch the Indian that was tied in the bushes, fired and killed him, after which the whole party...returned to the cabin and shot the other three...."

Macon's body was later found and Corby died from the wounds he had received in the encounter. Both men were described as "dissolute" and of "low associations," but this and other incidents initiated a series of Indian raids and caused the deaths of at least five whites.

■ Captain Henry M. Judah.
Natonal Archives.

Captain Judah had determined that the hostile Indians were Yahi, who ranged the eastern side of the Sacramento River, in the rugged country of Antelope and Mill creeks. By May of 1859, the situation was clearly out of control.

One of the petitions received by the governor described the actions of a white posse:

> A few weeks since, a party of whites, to recover some stock the Indians had driven off, pursued them into the mountains and surprised a rancheria in which there were a few bucks and a greater number of squaws and children, and we are pained to say that in the heat and excitement of the attack, the whites, exasperated with the recollection of the many injuries they had suffered from these Indians, commenced then and there a war of extermination, by shooting down the women and children. And it is since then these Indians have commenced the fearful work of burning houses. And, but…days ago, the plains at the foot of the mountains opposite the village of Tehama were fired by the Indians….

On the night of May 11, the house of former Nome Lackee Agent Edward Stevenson was burned, resulting in the deaths of his wife and five children. A young Indian house servant was blamed, but before an investigation could be held, the distraught Stevenson took the boy from a courtroom and lynched him. A few nights later, another house was burned.

Weller's letter to General Clarke resulted in the arrival of Captain F. F. Flint at Tehama, commanding Company A of the 6th Infantry. As they disembarked from the river boat, the soldiers caused quite a bit of excitement in the waterfront village. Some of the local Indian fighters went down to take a look at their competition.

"Hi Good and I went to see them after they had made camp," reported Bob Anderson, "and both of us came to the conclusion that they might be successful in an open country, but that there was little chance of their capturing any Indians in the hills."

Anderson and Good had the soldiers pretty well pegged. A report by Captain Flint in July noted that he and his men had "thoroughly examined" the Indian country, but had never seen either Indians or a sign of them. Several letters complaining of the inefficiency of the soldiers were received by Governor Weller so that in early July he sent General Kibbe to Tehama to determine if a volunteer force was needed.

■ Captain Robert Anderson saw much northern California Indian fighting in the 1850s and 1860s. *Author's collection.*

Kibbe, no longer an obscure state militia official, but a successful Indian fighter of the late Humboldt County war, paraded about, questioning locals and writing reports to the governor. About the middle of July, he traveled to Mendocino County and reported on the troubles there, then returned to Tehama. Under instructions from the governor, he proceeded to organize another volunteer group to deal with the hostile Indians.

Unimpressed with the military, the local citizens raised a purse of $3,000 and placed it in the hands of a local merchant who was to supply a separate volunteer group. Accordingly, Bob Anderson, Hi Good, John Breakenridge, and five other local settlers set out to locate the Indians. They were equipped for a two-month campaign and traveled on foot because of the rugged terrain they planned to cover. Anderson and Good were veterans of several campaigns, while Breakenridge had been killing Yahis since 1853. The weather was boiling hot as the men struck out towards the brushy and rugged Sierra foothills.

■ Left to right: Sandy Young, Jay Salisbury, Harmon "Hi" Good and an Indian known as "Ned." Good was later murdered by Ned, who was, in turn, shot and killed by Sandy Young. Sometime later, Young disappeared and was presumed killed by Indians. *Native Daughters Museum, Oroville.*

Kibbe heard of the intended expedition and was anxious that he would not be upstaged. He sent Captain William Byrnes to take over command of the group, and the volunteers willingly accepted another member to their small party.

Byrnes was one of the most colorful characters in California. He had been a scalp hunter in Mexico, was a veteran of the Mexican War, and was a member of Harry Love's Rangers who had tracked down Joaquin Murrieta. He had also participated in the El Dorado County War of 1851, although a companion later recalled that Byrnes was "not cautious enough to be a good Indian fighter."

Despite his reputation, Byrnes quickly petered out while walking across the blistering, lava-capped foothills. By the time the volunteers made camp that night, Byrnes had had enough. The following morning, he returned to the Kibbe command.

After electing Breakenridge captain of the group, the men pushed up

Mill Creek into the unbelievably rough and forested country. They found abundant sign, but no Indians, and were convinced the Indians were luring them on. Traveling cautiously, and following the sign that was leading them south, the men killed and scalped an Indian scout just after discovering a rancheria beyond Chico Creek Canyon. That night the whites made their plans and crept into position. Daybreak found them surrounding the Indian camp. A Spaniard, or Mexican, was up and about early and was shot by Good as he approached Anderson's position.

"The camp was roused," Anderson wrote, "in a twinkling, up the Indians sprang, men, women and children and as if with one impulse they swarmed up the slope directly toward where I lay. In a moment I was enveloped in the wild stampede. I shot and then clubbed my rifle and struggled against the rush. Good and Jack came to my assistance and we turned them back...."

When the whites yelled that they would let the women and children pass out of the ambush area, the warriors managed to sneak out also, and the whites soon found themselves in possession of an empty camp.

Although newspaper accounts of the time stated that about ten Indians had been killed, Anderson recalled seeing about forty victims lying about. The whites had little time to congratulate themselves, however, as a rattling of gunfire from the Indians sent them scrambling for cover. A charge again scattered the natives, after which Breakenridge and his men plundered the camp, then retraced their steps to their pack train.

For various reasons, the whites felt sure the Indians were in league with rascally "squaw men" who lived on Butte Creek. These traders were thought to either fence stolen property, sell guns to the Indians, or both. The posse was certain they would find the fleeing natives at Butte Creek.

Keeping on the trail, the whites engaged in several more scrapes with the hostiles while tracing them to a mining camp at the forks of Butte Creek. Stalking into the rough village, the volunteers very nearly had a shoot-out with several of the local "squaw men" who were shielding fugitive Indians. Anderson found a wounded Indian hiding in the back of a store. After some harsh words were exchanged, Breakenridge and his men left and again returned to their pack train.

Writing from the forks of Butte Creek on July 29, a sympathetic inhabitant, or perhaps a man with an Indian wife, gave another version of the fight described by Anderson:

> The most brutal and atrocious wholesale slaughter of Indians that has occurred in Butte County for many a day was perpetrated at the Indian

rancheria yesterday. The rancheria, was attacked about daybreak, when an indiscriminate slaughter commenced. Nine Indians were killed—viz., five bucks, two squaws, and two children—and four others were wounded, two perhaps fatally.

These Indians have been here ever since the whites have and are known to have been peaceable. However, there were two or three bad ones among them, one in particular called 'Malo Jo.' ...It is believed that he and some of his companions have done mischief either in the valley or lumbering regions of Deer or Mill Creek, thus bringing a terrible vengeance upon himself and tribe.

When Breakenridge and his party learned that Anderson's house had been burned as well as the cabins of several others, they again began their relentless search for Indians.

To the north, the wagon road through the Pit River country had been fairly peaceful, although some travelers reported brushes with the natives over stolen stock. Dragoons from Fort Crook were able to escort most of the emigrants, and this too tended to keep the natives quiet. The Achomawi, however, were bitter—and hungry. Some of the natives huddled around Fort Crook, but there was never enough food to go around.

The officers at the fort issued rations to the Indians, but the practice became an increasing burden. Reports to their superiors complained that the fort was having to feed Indians for whom the Indian department should rightfully provide. Once again, the settlers' stock was eating the native food, while game was either being driven off or killed by the whites. Sam Lockhart wrote to the Shasta *Republican* that John Longley had killed five hundred deer over the winter. Still, no one really expected any trouble.

Several teamsters driving into Hat Creek station in mid-August were shocked to find the charred remains of the building, with the proprietor sprawled in the doorway. He had four bullets and an arrow in his body. The cook was found nearby, also shot full of arrows. The teamsters reported the tragedy at Fort Crook, and a detachment of soldiers was sent to bury the bodies.

Twenty men from A Company, under Lieutenant Brewer, were soon on the Indians' trail. They determined from sign that the hostiles were Atsugewi under a chief called "Shavehead." On the 23rd, they met a white man near Pit River who was looking for two missing friends. The soldiers joined in the search and soon found a wagon that had been pushed into Hat Creek. Its owner, David Wells, had also been shot full of arrows, weighted with rocks and thrown in the creek.

Moving on, the troops came to a toll bridge recently established by a man named Napoleon McElroy. Here again, a deathly silence told them something was wrong. The owner was found after a brief search, dead and half-submerged in the waters of Pit River. McElroy had reportedly killed several Indians the previous winter in a squabble over a stolen deer.

General Kibbe had meanwhile completed the formation of his "Kibbe Guards" and had begun ranging the creeks to the east of the Sacramento River. He had ninety men divided into three detachments under Bill Byrnes, and lieutenants Bailey and Shull. He had barely gotten under way when news of the Callahan and McElroy murders reached him. In his official report Kibbe claimed to have cleared the Tehama County area of Indians, but it is doubtful he even saw a hostile. Reacting to the news, he sent Lieutenant Bailey's company to scout the Pit River country and report on conditions there. Maybe the Achomawi would be easier to find than these phantom Yahi, anyway.

Frank McElroy, a brother of the murdered man, showed up in the valley in late August. He had brought several others with him and had no trouble enlisting some twenty local settlers and frontiersmen to join a volunteer group to hunt Indians. They called themselves the "Pit River Rangers." One of the locals referred to the group as being "of the roughest character…men whose white skins covered hearts as black, and natures as savage, as the red men whom they sought to destroy…."

The rangers lolled about for several weeks, eating up free provisions and waiting for a favorable opportunity to strike. Since some of his men were poorly armed, McElroy appealed to the commanding officer at Fort Crook for arms to use in their campaign. Only after the ranger leader promised not to molest

■ Report from Captain D. S. Simpson complaining about army food being issued to Indians at Fort Crook because the Indian Department was ignoring the problem.
National Archives.

the friendly valley Indians and operate in conjunction with a detachment of cavalry was he loaned any weapons. It was a bad mistake.

The rangers had a late supper on the evening of September 2, 1859, and then set out for a nearby Indian camp. C. H. Manning cooked the evening meal and watched the men disappear into the night.

"As they filed past the spot where I was standing," he later was to write, "many of them reeling drunk, armed with rifles, shotguns, revolvers, tomahawks and scalping knives, I could but feel that it would make little difference into whose hands an enemy would fall—the savage Indians, or that company of men who only differed from them by the color of their skins."

Joe Rolf, a local "squaw man" who lived on Beaver Creek, was harvesting hay with the help of a nearby group of friendly Indians. Rolf had a contract to sell 200 tons of hay to the army post and was glad to get all the Indian help he could get. The Indians had a summer camp nearby and it was here, about midnight, that the rangers took up their positions. There was plenty of tall grass for hiding. As the sky began brightening in the east, rifles were cocked in the clear morning air. Soon the first natives were up and stirring about. Manning later reported what he heard of the encounter:

> After the first fire, McElroy, who was in the lead, threw down his gun and drawing his revolver started for the wickiups crying out, 'Now boys, for revenge!' He had advanced but a few steps when he received a heavy charge of buckshot in his back, fired from the gun of one of his own men and which killed him instantly....
>
> The white men poured a deadly fire into their midst, killing indiscriminately men, women and children, until not a live Indian was to be seen, after which they set fire to the wickiups, burning everything they contained, even to the bodies of the occupants, many of whom were still alive, though too badly wounded to make an escape.
>
> A few who were only slightly wounded...were afterwards hunted down and shot wherever they were found. It was claimed that 60 Indians were killed in this fight, but only about fourteen of that number were men...the others being squaws and children....

McElroy was the only white casualty of the massacre. A newspaper report noted that the rangers "throughout the greater part of the day searched among the 'haycocks' with the hatchet and split the children's heads open." Afterwards, the men seemed to have resumed their Indian hunting, although details of their movements are lacking.

The commanding officer at Fort Crook was furious when he heard the news of the massacre and immediately reported the incident to his superiors. A detachment of troops was sent to investigate, but as usual, the soldiers were at odds with the settlers and nothing was accomplished.

Early in September, shortly after these events, Kibbe and his troops marched into the valley. After seven or eight days of scouting, they managed to capture two Indians who arranged a meeting with a principal chief of the area. The chief was told that he and all his people must come in and be taken to a reservation, and that failure to do so would mean immediate war. The chief replied that he would bring his people in the following day. When they did not show up at the appointed time, Kibbe made plans to launch an attack.

Two nights later, the Indian stronghold was attacked by forty of Kibbe's men. Several Achomawi were killed and others captured, and the balance who had fled were pursued for the next several weeks. At times, the Indians would make a stand, then they would flee again through the rugged canyons.

Kibbe noted that on one occasion some fifteen or twenty Indians took up a position in a rocky defile and dared the volunteers to fight them. "The challenge was at once accepted," wrote the officer, "[and] continued for upwards of an hour, in which time all of the enemy were killed, except one who effected his escape."

Since his orders from the governor were not to kill any Indians except those who would not surrender, Kibbe maintained later that during all the skirmishing an interpreter was constantly calling on the hostiles to surrender. After about five weeks of harassing the fleeing Achomawi, the chief sent emissaries who reported the natives ready to surrender and go to the reservation. This time the chief and some four hundred fifty of his people came in and the campaign was over.

The troops herded their captives along the wagon road to the nearest town where they were allowed to rest for a time. At Red Bluff, General Kibbe sent his report to the governor and announced the great success of his expedition. Writing on November 29, 1859, Kibbe modestly declared:

"I have the honor to report that I have succeeded in capturing all of the Indians with the exception of two or three who are implicated in committing depredations upon the lives and property of our citizens between Butte Creek and the head of Pit River...."

Boarding river boats, the captives were taken downstream and finally herded onto a vacant lot at the foot of Powell Street, in San Francisco. General Kibbe must have delighted in the public display of his prisoners. His bombastic reports indicate that a sense of modesty was not one of his personal attributes.

Squatting in the sand of North Beach, the prisoners were visited by nearly everyone in the city. A daguerreotypist captured the scene in his camera, and some of the chiefs were even allowed to make a short tour of the city. A ten-year-old white girl, a resident of the city, collected armsfuls of used clothes from her neighborhood to give to the destitute and ragged natives. Potatoes and beef were issued to the prisoners for their trip.

"This afternoon," noted an article in the *Bulletin*, "the whole company re-embarks for the Mendocino Reservation. It would be a good deal like affectation, considering their dirt, squalor, poverty and homelessness, even to add the Christian hope—'Joy go with them.'"

A new governor, John G. Downey, had taken office and in his January message to the Assembly noted that General Kibbe had presented the state with a bill amounting to nearly $70,000. "While I admit the necessity which led to this expedition," reported Downey, "...a few such will bankrupt the state treasury."

Late in February of 1860 the governor was concerned that yet another Indian war was in the making. Despite Kibbe's proclaimed successful campaign in Humboldt County the previous year, the newspapers were repeatedly chronicling troubles in the ranching districts surrounding Humboldt Bay. That same month, Governor Downey received a request from one Seaman Wright for arms and ammunition to supply his volunteer force. Long petitions of blue-lined foolscap pasted end-to-end were received, recounting depredations and asking for relief. Downey made the usual reports and requests to the military, hoping that things would meanwhile quiet down. When two whites were reported killed in Mattole Valley and word was received that the Redwood Indians were leaving the reservation and returning to their old homes, he knew matters were not going to get any better.

GENERAL KIBBE'S LATE EXPEDITION.—A long editorial appears in the Red Bluff *Beacon*, setting forth the result of the efforts of this officer in his late campaign against the Indians. The article of the *Beacon* is altogether too long for our columns at this time, or we would comply with its request to publish it. We compile from it the following statements:

That portion of the State east of the Sacramento and north of Butte creek has suffered much lately from Indian depredations. Among the killed by the Indians are the following: Bowles and three men; James Freman and four men; McIlroy and one man; Callaghan and two men; William Patrick and one man; Birney; McMacken and one man; Peter Lasson, Clapper, and two others; two men on Payne's creek—all known citizens of this county and vicinity. The destruction of property in Tehama county alone is estimated to exceed $100,000 since the year 1856. The Indians had driven off the stages on the only wagon road through from the Sacramento valley to Yreka, *via* the Pitt river country. Assistance from the Federal Government was solicited, but not obtained. Representations were made to the State Government, and complied with, and General Kibbe ordered to the field Aug. 15th. He organized a volunteer company, consisting of eighty men, and commenced operations. The campaign has closed; some lives have been taken, it is alleged, but in no case unless resistance was offered. The Indians have been subdued, and many taken prisoners. Hundreds of them have been sent to the Reservations, including a notorious chief and desperate warrior known as "Shavehead." It is said that not more than twenty-five have been left in the Pitt river country, and consequently the whites can dwell now in perfect security.

■ Sacramento *Daily Union*, December 12, 1859.

The Eureka *Humboldt Times*, edited by Austin Wiley, chronicled a steady series of Indian troubles, from the Bald Hills south to Hydesville near the mouth of the Eel River. Two small volunteer groups were reported operating in the Bald Hills, and troops from Fort Humboldt were sent out on several occasions. All three groups were ineffective. In the same Bald Hills area, Indians reportedly came right into a small settlement and drove off over one hundred cattle. "It is a shame and disgrace," railed Wiley, "…that some of the best sections of our county must be placed beyond the reach of the hardy frontiersmen by a few bands of miserable diggers." In another column, Wiley parroted the simplistic view of white-Indian relations held by so many frontier residents: "There is only one way to 'domesticate' the Indians in this county and that is to either send them so far away that they will never find their way back, or kill them."

Besides the usual reasons of being driven from their homes by settlers usurping their lands, a unique cause of Indian troubles was cited by a Humboldt County resident in the columns of the San Francisco *Bulletin*:

—Sometime in February last, a man named L, who has a stock ranch on Van Duzen River, had an Indian boy, whose family lived within half a mile of his place. L's boy would occasionally run off to visit his relations. This incensed L so much, that he went down one morning and slaughtered the whole family of about six persons—boy and all. He then made a rude raft of logs, put the victims on it, marked it to W. H. Mills who was known to be opposed to indiscriminate slaughter of the Indians—and started the bodies down the river."

The writer cited several other like incidents which pointed out the collision course toward which the area residents were moving. Many ranchers who had never abused the Indians were being robbed and were consequently siding now with the more radical elements. Many of the stockmen, both radical and moderate, were becoming frustrated beyond endurance.

At Fort Humboldt, Major Rains was again trying to maintain a low profile. The post was undermanned with green troops and he knew that most of the Indian raiding was a simple matter of hunger. In any case, aside from escort duty, there was little he could do in such a large area.

On Humboldt Bay, at the town of Union just north of Eureka, a young man named Francis Harte was a reporter for the local newspaper—the *Northern Californian*. Just twenty years old at the time, Harte had knocked about at odd jobs for a few years, but seemed to enjoy writing more than anything else. Colonel S. G. Whipple, the editor, frequently left Harte in charge while he was away and seemed to trust him, though others might view him as rather inept and eccentric.

Like all the whites in the county, young Harte was well aware of the native inhabitants of the area. The Wiyots combined with the neighboring Yurok to form a far western branch of the Algonquin Indian family. Locally, they ranged from the Mattole area up through Humboldt Bay to Trinidad Head—an area of only about thirty-five miles in length. Their territory stretched inland perhaps fifteen miles and consisted of vast redwood forests and prairies, while along the coast were sand dunes and tidal marshes. The center of their lands—of their world before the white man came—was Humboldt Bay.

Living was hard for the Indians in the late 1850s. Inland, they had been driven from their lands by the settlers and they had learned to steal or go hungry. Their lives were no longer the same as those of their fathers. The Great Spirit seemed to no longer watch over them. On the coast, however, they could still fish and gather mussels and clams for food.

Every year in February, the Wiyots gathered at the native village of Dulawat on Indian Island, in the bay opposite Eureka. Here a grand feast was held, along with religious ceremonies and dancing. The festivities lasted for a week and involved several hundred Indians from the area between the Mad and Eel rivers. It had been an annual event for as far back as anyone could remember. On the low, brushy sand dunes were two huge mounds of clam shells dating back into antiquity. Robert Gunther, an early white owner of the island, wrote that the mounds were as deep as twenty-two feet, and Indian bones, shells and relics could be found all the way down.

■ Fort Gaston was established in 1858 and helped keep the peace in Hupa Indian territory. Hupa women are shown waiting for food distribution in the 1870s. *Arizona State Museum.*

On the night of February 25, 1860, the week-long Indian celebration was drawing to a close. The native revelers danced and chanted and revelled far into the night. The fires burned brightly within and without the many low huts and shelters of the rancheria, until one by one they were allowed to die out and exhausted celebrants found a corner in which to sleep. A fierce wind was blowing from the northwest. This was the last day of the celebration—a Saturday—and many of the southern Indians had already returned home.

Early the next morning, a few hours before dawn, an Indian woman sat near the shore of the island. Suddenly, out of nowhere, she saw two boats manned by six or seven white men gliding silently toward her. She watched them curiously for several moments.

The woman knew how exasperated the whites were about the recent Indian troubles, and she felt a chill. Even the Indians had heard the stories that the coast Wiyot had been exchanging stolen beef with the mountain tribes for ammunition. Surely the whites knew that the Indian Island natives did not even eat beef, much less get along with the fierce mountain tribes.

Still, she watched silently as the boats were beached and the white men moved silently up the bank toward the village. As the silhouetted figures filed past her, she suddenly saw for the first time the hatchets and knives in their hands. With a gasp, she jumped up and ran screaming for the village.

Bob Gunther sat up in bed and listened. Had he been dreaming or had a noise awakened him? He roomed in the Picayune Mill office, and he got up and stepped outside to listen. "When I came out," he later recalled, "everything was still for an instant and then I heard two heavy blows or shots, in the direction of Indian Island and then all was still again. Shortly after a scream went up from many voices and I could plainly hear it was on Indian Island, for it was perfectly still and dark. Hearing no more I went to bed again." Gunther continued:

■ Francis Bret Harte, later a world-famous writer, did his apprentice newspaper work in Humboldt County. *Author's collection.*

Early in the morning Captain Moore came down and asked me to lend him my boat as he wanted to go to Indian Island. He had heard that some Indians had been killed by white men. I told him I had heard the trouble before daylight and I would go with him. When we came to the island we found Hatteway's squaw, who lived on the peninsula, sitting on the bank crying. She knew both of us and seemed to be glad to see

327

us. But what a sight presented itself to our eyes. Corpses lying all around, and all women and children, but two. Most of them had their skulls split. One old Indian who looked to be a hundred years old, had his skull split and still he sat there shivering.

...[T]he squaw told us that 40 in all were killed, but that many belonged to Mad River and that the Mad River Indians took their dead along as they went home. There were twenty-four dead lying on the ground, so 16 must have belonged to Mad River. The old man I spoke of, and a little child, died later. The child was about two years old and was dressed. We could see no injury, but it cried when we moved it. We asked permission to take the child to a doctor and the squaws were willing.

By that time some more people had come over from Eureka and we left. On the way home we planned to bring the parties to justice. Captain Moore was the Justice of the Peace. We soon found that we had better keep our mouths shut. We took the child to Dr. Manley. He examined it and found the spine out. He said it could not live and we had better carry it back and we did.

Eureka was buzzing with excitement, everyone anxious to know just what had taken place. Soon word was passed around that not only had the island Indians been massacred, but other villages had been attacked, also. A number of Wiyot had been slaughtered on South Beach, near the entrance to the bay, and others had been killed near the mouth of the Eel River. Many of the townspeople could not comprehend the enormity of the crime until some of the bodies were brought ashore. Young Harte was there and commented in the columns of the *Northern Californian*:

When the bodies were landed at Union a more shocking and revolting spectacle never was exhibited to the eyes of a Christian and civilized people. Old women, wrinkled and decrepit, lay weltering in blood, their brains dashed out and dabbled with their long, grey hair. Infants scarce a span long, with their faces cloven with hatchets and their bodies ghastly with wounds. ...No resistance was made, it was said, to the butchers who did the work, but as they ran or huddled together for protection like sheep, they were struck down with hatchets. Very little shooting was done, most of the bodies having wounds about the head. The bucks were mostly absent, which accounts for the predominance of female victims.

Major Rains was notified that morning and quickly rode over from Fort Humboldt. After a tour of the island and a conference with the local authorities, he returned to the post and sent a report to the adjutant general:

I have just been to Indian Island, the home of a band of friendly Indians between Eureka and Uniontown, where I beheld a scene of atrocity and horror unparalleled not only in our own country, but even in history, for it was done by men, self-acting and without necessity, color of law, or authority...perpetrated by men who act in defiance of and probably in revenge upon the Governor for the State not sending them arms and having

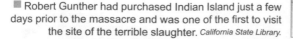

The shattering climax to California's 1850s Indian wars took place on Indian Island, shown just beyond the coastline wharves of Eureka. This view dates from some years after the event. *Peter Palmquist.*

them mustered as a volunteer company for the murder of Indians by wholesale…. At any rate such is the opinion of the better class of community as related to me this Sunday morning, I was informed that these men, volunteers, calling themselves such, from Eel River, had employed the earlier part of the day in murdering all the women and children of the above island and I repaired to the place, but the villains—some five in number had gone— and midst the bitter grief of parents and fathers, many of whom had returned, I beheld a spectacle of horror of unexampled description…and this done without cause, other wise, as far as I can learn, as I have not heard of any of them losing life or cattle by the Indians. Certainly not these Indians, for they lived on an island and nobody accuses them.

In a later report, Rains estimated the deaths at about one hundred eighty-eight Indians, mostly women and children: "55 at Indian Island, 58 at South Beach, 40 on South Fork Eel River and 35 at Eagle Prairie."

Young Harte was appalled at the tragedy and lashed out at the perpetrators in the *Northern Californian*:

> Our Indian troubles have reached a crisis. Today we record acts of Indian aggression and white retaliation. It is a humiliating fact that the parties who may be supposed to represent white civilization have committed the greater barbarity….

Robert Gunther had purchased Indian Island just a few days prior to the massacre and was one of the first to visit the site of the terrible slaughter. *California State Library.*

The friendly Indians about the bay have been charged with conveying arms and ammunition to the mountain tribes, and receiving slaughtered beef as a reward. A class of hard-working men who derive their subsistence by cattle raising have been the greatest sufferers, and if in the blind fury of retaliation they spare neither age or sex, though they cannot be excused, a part of the blame should fall upon that government which places the responsibility of self-defense on the injured party. If the deed was committed by responsible parties, we will give place to any argument that may be offered in justification.

"But we cannot conceive of no wrong that a babe's blood can atone for. Perhaps we do not rightly understand the doctrine of 'extermination.' What amount of suffering it takes to make a man a babe-killer, is a question for future moralists. How a human being, who could remember how he had been taught to respect age and decrepitude, who had ever looked upon a helpless infant with a father's eye—could with cruel unpitying hand carry out the 'extermination' that his brain had conceived who could smite the mother and child wantonly and cruelly, few men can understand."

Harte had gone too far. The smoldering undercurrent of hatred, noted by Gunther, quickly surfaced when the acting editor's comments appeared on February 29. Tradition says a mob collected and was preparing to wreck the newspaper office and lynch him when a cavalry troop arrived from the fort. This is not likely, but Harte was obviously as shaken by the events as his editor was displeased. The aspiring writer left Humboldt Bay on March 28, aboard the steamer *Columbia*, bound for San Francisco. This may have been due as much to the death of a girl friend as to his editorial, however. In any case, he resumed his literary career in that other bay city and as Bret Harte he was destined to became a far-famed fiction chronicler of early California.

Even Wiley of the *Humboldt Times* was hard put to justify the events on Indian Island: "If in defense of your property and your all, it becomes necessary to break up these hiding places of your mountain enemies, so be it; but for heavens sake, in doing this, do not forget to what race you belong."

Strangely enough, the only hint of some rational explanation for the cruel slaughter came from an Indian source. Jerry James, son of "Captain Jim" the chief of the Indian Island Wiyots, shed some light on the massacre many years later:

The white people began to hate the Athapascans [mountain Indians], and those at Eureka warned Captain Jim never to invite the mountain Indians down to his dances.

In 1860 he held a big dance and invited all the people around the bay, and those from Mad and Eel river. There was a man from Blue Lake who could speak the Athapascan language, and in the course of the dance he jokingly used that language and was overheard by the white men who were looking on. These were spies for the house. Before daylight the village was attacked by white men…most of the women and children were killed, and the houses burned. I was one year old. My mother was killed, and when I was picked up by a friendly settler I was covered with my mother's blood. That same night a village at Eel river and another at Mad river were treated in the same way.

In our struggle to comprehend the climate in which such horrendous events could take place, Jerry James' story is something we can touch and hold on to. It was a terrible mistake then, a cruel misunderstanding leading to emotions running amok among a class of Indian-hating settlers.

But still the ugly questions remain. Why did this story take so long to surface? Why was this story not offered in justification at the time—and there was indeed much attempted justification in the press at the time. But in the end, there is no way such a hideous slaughter of helpless women and children can be justified in any way.

To avoid further slaughter, immediately after the massacres Major Rains had taken custody of all the local Indians and sheltered them at the fort. The local whites would only be satisfied with nothing less than removal of any Indian survivors and, after petitioning the Indian office, the agent in charge of the Klamath Reserve showed up at the gates of Fort Humboldt. He had already removed what Mad River Indians he could find and he now asked Major Rains to provide an escort to help move the local Indians north.

Rains was disgusted at the whole business. These Indians had had friends and family butchered and now were to be uprooted from their homes as well. The officer finally agreed to ask the natives if they wished to go to

the reserve. "Ask Major Rains to provide an escort to help move the local Indian prisoners north?" rejoined the agent. It was "immaterial whether the Indians wished to go or not." When Rains refused to release them, Wiley and the local citizenry raised a fuss. In the end the Indians had to go, but only after a vigorous protest by Rains.

Saying goodbye to his prisoners, Rains could only wish them well at their new home. He gave the chief a note which might help him in his relations with the whites in the Klamath area:

■ Jerry James. *Smithsonian Institution.*

Notum Sit Omnibus—That the bearer of this, Ki-wal-lat-hah (Coonskin), is the acknowledged Chief of the Indians on Humboldt Bay. He had saved the lives of white men and, when hungry, fed them and taken care of them in sickness and want. Now, having been forced from his own land and domicile without recompense by men thirsting for the blood of his people, and by the express wish of eighty-four (84) citizens of Eureka—he now emigrates with such of his people as were saved from the murderers of 26 Feby. last and the friendship of all good people is solicited in his behalf.

Fort Humboldt, April 20, 1860

G. J. Rains, Major, U.S.A., Cmdg.

It seemed to be common knowledge that stock raisers from the Eel River country had made up the band of killers at Indian Island, but apparently little effort was made to apprehend them. These cattlemen were voters, as were the merchants who

◼ *Humboldt Times*, March 3, 1860.

supplied them. Sheriff Van Ness, to assure everyone just where he stood on the matter, published several newspaper articles which, although giving a brief paragraph to condemning the slaughter, devoted mo‹ space to a thinly veiled justification for what had been done. The sheriff and Major Rains engaged in a spirited newspaper controversy, both blaming the other for inaction in the troubles. But Major Rains, too, had antagonized the settlers for too long. The following July he was transferred to Washington Territory.

As for the Indians, many still tried to avoid conflict, but the ranks of the hostiles must have gained some converts. "An intelligent Indian," wrote a correspondent of the San Francisco *Bulletin*, "told the people of Eureka that the white men had killed his wife and children and he had nothing more to live for—and he was going to the mountains with what few of his tribe were left, to fight against the whites." This was possibly a Mad River Indian known as "Bill" who had always been friendly with the settlers, but whose wife, mother, sister, two brothers, and two small children were all killed that brutal Sunday morning.

In the north, the seeds of destruction had been sown well. With the exception of some limited warfare in Owens Valley and against the Yahi, Humboldt County was to bear the brunt of savage Indian fighting through

1865. No longer were the natives content to run off cattle, but now were burning, looting, and killing at every opportunity.

It no longer mattered what might have been. Both the whites and the Indians seethed with a hatred that only blood could resolve. No one cared any longer, or perhaps even knew, just how the trouble had all begun.

* * * * *

EPILOG

The Indian wars of the 1860s were the death throes of the California natives. Only the more remote tribes could briefly resist the white man. The rest huddled on the reservations or merely, tried to keep out of the way. Always, they were at the mercy of the invaders who grew numerically stronger every year. It is a chilling fact that throughout the latter part of the nineteenth century, a white man could kill an Indian with little fear of being convicted for the crime. At best, the California natives could make themselves useful and gain some kind of grudging acceptance based on white economic need.

The tragic fate of the California Indians was made inevitable by the failure of a federal Indian policy. In 1850 the government had been dealing with Indian affairs for some fifty years, yet its groping and indecisive efforts seemed more the trial-and-error fumblings of complete novices. But by 1850, factors other than inept politicians contributed increasingly to the problem. Congress was weary of the Indian treaty system and was anxious to abort it. A new concept gained recognition which would conveniently cancel the system—and with a clear conscience. This was the idea that Indians really had no valid claims to the land they inhabited. The principle caught on swiftly and was an important and primary reason for the rejection of the California treaties in 1852. In time, the government would manage to acquire the Indian lands, anyway, for a pittance of cost.

Nothing epitomized the floundering efforts of the Indian Affairs Office so much as the federal financial appropriations. Well over one million dollars was spent between 1850 and 1860, yet the government still had no idea how much money was necessary to do justice to the job of finding a place for the Indian in a white society. How much money was really needed? Was it the $400,000 appropriated in 1854-55, or the $84,000 ladled out in 1859-60? No one knew. Representatives, not knowing just how much was needed, let the federal budget be their guide in the allotment of California

Indian funds. When the budget was tight, the Indian appropriation would shrink accordingly.

With no Indian policy to guide them, senators now quarreled as to too much or too little being done for the Indians. Some advocated supporting them, at least in part, as restitution for taking their lands. Others argued that spending too much would make Indians dependent on government and they would never learn to take care of themselves. Whatever course was taken, there never really seemed to be a lack of funds. It was poor administration and fraud that so critically damaged the California natives.

The greedy politicizing of the reservation system was a tragedy from which the California Indian never really recovered. Whether things might have been different if Beale had originally been retained as superintendent is problematical. J. Ross Browne had been impressed with Beale's efforts, but Browne had been Beale's personal friend. Beale's appointment of special agents such as Walter Harvey, and a host of other out-of-work Democrats, and particularly the patronage age that he lived in, made it highly unlikely that a successful reservation system was possible at that time.

But neither Beale nor anyone else could implement a concept which dictated that the Indians were to be taken out of contact with the whites so as to teach them to be self-sufficient in a white society. Perhaps a start had to be made somewhere, but certainly this idea was a study in contradictions if ever there was one.

The damage caused by Henley's tenure as superintendent was monumental, and it is surprising that the reservation system even survived. At one point, the commissioner of Indian affairs actually did recommend that the system be abolished, but after all something had to be done. Finally, it

■ Old Fort Humboldt in its twilight years as depicted in an early county history. *Author's collection.*

was decided that anything was better than nothing. A new, less expensive system was later adopted, but it proved no more effective than the earlier effort. Nevertheless, with all its shortcomings, the California plan of plac-

■ The choice was now clear for the California Indian. It was assimilation or extermination. They must follow in the path of the white man. They could only try to salvage what remained of their culture.
Humboldt County Historical Society.

ing native Americans on small reservations was adopted and rapidly extended throughout the country. But it was an empty solution—an unfulfilled commitment.

In California, an opportunity had been lost, an opportunity that vanished in politics and greed and never came again. An innovative idea that might have been the starting place for a peaceful transition of the native population into the mainstream of American life was fumbled and corrupted and finally buried in the dust of the half-remembered names of the Tejon, Nome Lackee, Mendocino, and Klamath reserves.

But the time was not right, and perhaps no system would have succeeded. Venal politicians, prejudice, and government failures combined with white volunteers to "solve" the Indian problem in quite a different way. And the grim and heartbreaking solution will haunt us all, forever.

But even without the disastrous "wars" which decimated the native population, the Indians would have been hard-pressed to survive the white invasion. Various factors combined to destroy the native family unit and inhibit population growth. Thousands of white men took up with Indian women, either forced or otherwise. This broke up existing families or separated a native woman from her tribe and a prospective Indian husband. Abortion further reduced the native population, as many Indians refused to bring up children in a white man's world of hunger and abuse.

The white usurpation of Indian lands and food supplies ushered in a twilight existence of frequent starvation and malnutrition. Hunger became a constant companion to all but the more remote tribes.

The primary effect of the diet deficiencies among the Indians was a resulting weakness and increased susceptibility to the flood of new diseases brought among them by the invaders. Prostitution was accepted at an early date by the native women, mostly for economic reasons. This, coupled with rape and other white contact made the spread of venereal disease so rapid and widespread that none but the most isolated native groups escaped. Venereal disease, smallpox, diptheria and tuberculosis swept like wildfire through villages of people already weakened by malnutrition and hunger. Children and the aged were the first victims, but the effects of such catastrophes were to be felt genetically for many generations in the future.

It is estimated that disease alone accounted for some 60 percent of the Indian population decline in California. Epidemics and military operations had reduced one thousand Costanoan natives in 1848 to three hundred in 1880; fourteen thousand Yokuts had been reduced to six hundred; eight thousand Wintun had been chopped down to fifteen hundred, while nineteen hundred Yana had diminished to a remnant of twenty. Of fifteen hundred Wailaki, only one hundred fifty remained. Other tribal units—the Apiachi, the Yahi, the Esselen, the Chimariko, the Chunute and the Telumne were gone, exterminated, extinct.

A culture, a whole way of life, disappeared to live only in the memories of a few aged storytellers around flickering campfires. Gone the way of the grizzly bear and the thundering herds of tule elk. Gone the rustling wings of numberless waterfowl as they blacken the sky over pristine tule swamps and lakes. Now only in history books and legends do Indians in tule boats glide soundlessly over lakes once teeming with glittering fish, or play the native games on vast and grassy plains. No more do calls summon wild birds and rabbits to Indian snares along the streams of the hot and shimmering Sierra foothills. The freedom and plenty of a primitive native world is no more.

The Great Spirit has died and left them alone.

CHAPTER 18 / SOURCES

UNPUBLISHED MATERIAL

National Archives, Records of the Office of Indian Affairs, California Superintendency, Record Group 75, M234:

Moses J. Conklin to J. W. Denver, February 15, 1859.

D. E. Buel to Major G. J. Rains, April 11, 1860.

Document: Recommendation given to the Indian chief "Coonskin" by Major G. J. Rains, April 20, 1860.

Major G. J. Rains to Thomas J. Hendricks, April 30, 1860.

Office of the Secretary of State, California State Archives, Indian War Files, Sacramento:

Humboldt County petition to Governor John B. Weller, August 14, 1858.

John B. Weller to William C. Kibbe, September 5, 28, 1858; July 4, 1859.

John B. Weller to General Dosh, September 5, 1858.

Forty-eight settlers of Antelope and Deer Creeks area to Governor John B. Weller (petition), May 9, 1859.

Tehama County petition to Governor John B. Weller, May 11, 1859.

Citizens of Red Bluff (petition) to Governor John B. Weller, May 15, 1859.

Tehama County Petition to Governor John B. Weller, May 29, 1859.

Major W. W. Mackall to Governor John B. Weller, May 19 1859.

Governor John B. Weller to citizens of Tehama County, June 2, 1859.

General William C. Kibbe to Captain F. F. Flint, July 11, 1859 (two letters).

Captain F. F. Flint to General William C. Kibbe, July 12, 1859.

General William C. Kibbe to Governor John B., Weller, July 30, September 30, November 29, 1859.

Captain John Adams to Major W. W. Mackall, September 3, 1859.

Seaman Wright to Governor John G. Downey, February 6, 1860.

Petition signed by over one hundred Humboldt County residents and sent to Governor John G. Downey, February 23, 1860.

Beard, Estle, to the author, May 6, 1971.

Crockett, Bob. "The Indian Troubles in Tehama County (1857-1871), unpublished paper on file in the Tehama County Library, Red Bluff, California.

Potter, Elijah R. "Reminiscences of Early History of Northern California and of the Indian Troubles," unpublished manuscript in the Bancroft Library, Berkeley, California.

Opsahl, Gail. "Lo, The Poor Indian! An account of the attitudes and incidents of the 1850's which led to the massacre at Indian Island, Humboldt Co., Calif., February 26, 1860," unpublished paper in Special Collections, Humboldt State University Library, 1976.

NEWSPAPERS

San Francisco *Daily Alta California*, March 6, 1853; October 5, 1859.

San Francisco *Bulletin*, November 9, 1857; May 9, 1859; May 11, June 1, 1860.

Sacramento *Daily Union*, November 8, 1858; April 9, November 8,1859; May 26, 1860.

Humboldt Times, February 4, 11, March 3, 17, April 14, 1860.

Marysville Weekly Express, August 21, 1858.

The *Northern Californian*, February 29, March 28, April 18, 1860.

The *Sonoma County Journal*, June 25, December 10, 1858; April 15, May 6, 1859; March 16, 1860.

Tulare County Record and Examiner, August 20, 1859.

The *Weekly Butte Record*, September 25, October 2, 9, 1858.

PRINCIPAL PUBLISHED WORKS

Anderson, Robert A. *Fighting the Mill Creeks*. Chico, CA: The Chico Record Press, 1909.

Bledsoe, A. J. *Indian Wars of the Northwest*. Oakland: Biobooks, 1956.

Bleyhl, Norris A., compiler. *Some Newspaper References Concerning Indians and White Relationships in Northeastern California Chiefly Between 1850 and 1920*. Chico, CA: California State University, Chico, 1979.

Browne, Lina Fergusson. *J. Rose Browne: His Letters, Journals & Writings*. Albuquerque: University of New Mexico Press, 1969.

Cook, Sherburne F. *The Conflict Between the California Indian and White Civilization*. Berkeley: University of California Press, 1976.

Coy, Owen C. *The Humboldt Bay Region, 1850-1875*. Los Angeles: California State Historical Association, 1929.

Genzoli, Andrew M., and Martin, Wallace E. *Redwood Cavalcade*. Eureka, CA: Schooner Features, 1968.

Heizer, Robert F., editor. *The Destruction of California Indians*. Santa Barbara: Peregrine Smith, Inc., 1974.

_____, editor. *Handbook of North American Indians, Volume 8. California*. Washington, D.C.: Smithsonian Institution, 1978.

_____. *They Were Only Diggers*. Ramona, CA: Ballena Press, 1974.

_____, and Almquist, Alan. *The Other Californians*. Berkeley: University of California Press, 1971.

Hoopes, Chad L. *Lure of the Humboldt Bay Region*. Dubuque, IA: Wm. C. Brown Book Company, 1966.

Kroeber, A. L. *Handbook of the Indians of California*. New York: Dover Publications, Inc., 1953.

Neasham, Ernest R. *Fall River Valley, An Examination of Historical Sources*. Sacramento: The Citadel Press, Inc., 1957.

Wells, Harry L., and Chambers, W. L. *The History of Butte County*. San Francisco: H. L. Wells, 1882.

OTHER SOURCES

Appendix to the Journal of the House of Assembly of California at the Eleventh Session of the Legislature, Sacramento, 1860.

Carranco, Lynwood. "Bret Harte in Union, 1857-1860," *California Historical Society Quarterly*, June, 1966.

Holland, Annette Bouchey, "Love and Loss in Union: Bret Harte and Lizzie Bull," *The Humboldt Historian*, Winter, 1998.

Journal of the Assembly of California at the Eleventh Session of the Legislature, Sacramento, 1860.

Kelsey, Harry. "The California Indian Treaty Myth," *Southern California Quarterly*, Historical Society of Southern California, Fall 1973.

Sievers. Michael A. "Funding the California Indian Superintendency, A Case Study of Congressional Appropriations," *Southern California Quarterly*, Historical Society of Southern California, Spring 1977.

Webster, Debra. "Indian Island Massacre," *The Humboldt Historian*, May-June 1993.

INDEX

341

B orn in Fresno, California, in March of 1930, William B. Secrest grew up in the great San Joaquin Valley. After high school he joined the Marine Corps where he served in a guard detachment and in a rifle company in the early years of the Korean War. Returning to college, he obtained a BA in education, but for many years he served as an art director for a Fresno advertising firm.

Secrest has been interested in history since his youth and early began comparing Western films to what really happened in the West. A hobby at first, this avocation quickly developed into correspondence with noted writers and more serious research. Not satisfied in a collaboration with friend and Western writer Ray Thorp, Secrest began researching and writing his own articles in the early 1960s.

Although at first he wrote on many general Western subjects, some years ago Secrest realized how his home state has consistently been neglected in the Western genre and concentrated almost exclusively on early California subjects. He has produced hundreds of articles for such publications as *Westways*, *Montana*, *True West*, and the *American West*, while publishing seven monographs on early California themes. His book *I Buried Hickok* (Early West Publishing Co.) appeared in 1980, followed by *Lawmen & Desperadoes* (The Arthur H. Clark Co.) in 1994 and *Dangerous Trails* (Barbed Wire Press) in 1995. A biography of noted San Francisco police detective Isaiah Lees has been accepted for publication. A current project is a biography of Harry Love, the leader of the rangers who tracked down Joaquin Murrieta.